Triumph and Erosion in the American Media and Entertainment Industries

Triumph and Erosion in the American Media and Entertainment Industries

Dan Steinbock

Q

QUORUM BOOKS
Westport, Connecticut • London

Library of Congress Cataloging-in-Publication Data

Steinbock, Dan.
    Triumph and erosion in the American media and entertainment
industries / Dan Steinbock.
        p.   cm.
    Includes bibliographical references and index.
    ISBN 0–89930–914–3 (alk. paper)
    1. Mass media—Economic aspects—United States. I. Title.
P96.E252U67   1995
384'.0973—dc20   94–24600

British Library Cataloguing in Publication Data is available.

Library of Congress Catalog Card Number: 94–24600
ISBN: 0–89930–914–3

First published in 1995

Quorum Books, 88 Post Road West, Westport, CT 06881
An imprint of Greenwood Publishing Group, Inc.

Printed in the United States of America

The paper used in this book complies with the
Permanent Paper Standard issued by the National
Information Standards Organization (Z39.48–1984).

10 9 8 7 6 5 4 3 2 1

Contents

Tables and Figures

TABLES

FIGURES

Preface

Triumph and Erosion derives from a multifaceted research project on "American Media and Entertainment" that began in September 1986, when I first arrived in New York City as a visiting Fulbright scholar. After a brief affiliation with the Cinema Studies Department of New York University (1986–89), some studies at the New School for Social Research (Department of Photography), as well as linking with the Freedom Center of Media Studies (Columbia University), I focused my research on the competitiveness of the U.S. media and entertainment (M&E) industry. In 1987–90 I wrote several papers on the subject as a senior researcher of Finland's Academy of Sciences.

I was fascinated by the Janus face of American media and entertainment: triumphant products, eroding control. And I wanted to devise a comprehensive source on American M&E businesses that could serve general readers and be used as a text for graduate and advanced undergraduate students in a multitude of disciplines: film, television and communications studies, applied economics, industrial organization, competitive strategy, and corporate finance. The book should also prove a handy reference for M&E professionals, executives, financial analysts, investors, as well as journalists.

Since the focus of this work is on *major* American media and entertainment companies, I have left out issues involving TV producers, independent cinema, and public broadcasting. Focusing on *domestic* competition in

U.S. media and entertainment, I have also left out three significant subjects: foreign market segments and problems of globalization, organizational transformation in major M&E corporations, as well as dramatic shifts in American marketing and advertising industries. I will explore these subjects in a companion to the work at hand.

In the course of my research, several discussions added in various ways to the work itself. I'd like to single out interviews with Michael E. Porter (competitive strategy), Benjamin M. Friedman (American economic policy), Theodore Levitt (marketing issues), Graef S. Crystal (executive compensation), and even the controversial Pat Choate (foreign invasion). Also, I had highly illuminating interviews with audience research executives Michael Eisenberg (CBS) and Lawrence J. Giannino (ABC), and Arnold Becker, the legendary veteran of CBS's program testing department.

Still another contributing factor stemmed from the opportunities to meet and interview top talent in U.S. media and entertainment, including producer-directors (from Martin Scorsese to Spike Lee), actors (from Paul Newman and Dennis Hopper to Robert De Niro and Donald Sutherland), authors (E. L. Doctorow, Jay McInerney), poets (Joseph Brodsky), jazz musicians (Dave Brubeck, Branford Marsalis), and commercial producers (Joe Pytka). I also followed closely the efforts of my compatriots to break into Hollywood (Renny Harlin) and independent cinema (the Kaurismäki brothers).

I am especially grateful to Eric Valentine, publisher of Quorum Books, for his interest and confidence in the project, as well as to Katie Chase, Quorum copy editor, for her insightful corrections. Thanks to Herbert Rubin for guidance into accounting, and to Veli-Antti Savolainen for encouragement and support. Thanks, too, to Annabelle Minier, who was brave enough to struggle with my English and provided valuable suggestions, as well as to her husband, Heikki Sarmanto, the famed Finnish jazz musician whose artistic experiences in the United States (including a recording with Sonny Rollins), contributed to my first impressions of the American music business.

I am further indebted to several people who earlier pushed me toward my current interests, including Ilkka Heiskanen (professor of political science, University of Helsinki), Ritva Mitchell (Directorate of Education, Culture and Sports, Council of Europe), Ismo Silvo (executive director, Observatoire Européen de L'Audiovisuel), Erik Allardt (formerly director of Finland's Academy of Sciences), Risto Volanen (formerly vice-CEO of the Finnish Broadcasting Company), William R. Copeland (formerly director of Finland's Fulbright Commission), Eero Tarasti (professor of musicology, University of Helsinki), Pertti Ahonen (professor of political science, University of Tampere), J.-P. Roos (professor of sociology, University of Helsinki), and Jarmo Laine (Finland's Academy of Sciences).

My thanks to those who took time from their busy schedules to advise on the design of my project, including Hal Himmelstein (assistant professor, mass communications, Brooklyn College of City University), Everette Dennis (director of the Freedom Center for Media Studies), Sherry Turkle (assistant professor, sociology, MIT), Neil Postman (professor, media ecology, New York University), Ben Fernandez (formerly director of photography, New School for Social Research), William Simon (professor, cinema studies, New York University), and George Gerbner (The Annenberg School of Communications, University of Pennsylvania).

I'd also like to single out the criticism of Harold L. Vogel, the noted entertainment industry analyst whose *Entertainment Industry Economics* remains the classic in the field; and the personal encouragement of Elie Wiesel which, initially, led me to launch the project.

My thanks to Latin clubs and dance studios for the *salsa y sabor* that gave me the strength to complete the project.

I dedicate *Triumph and Erosion* to my family, my parents Rafael and Rea, and my brother Mika—all of whom I see too seldom and miss daily.

Dan Steinbock
June 1994

Triumph and Erosion in the American Media and Entertainment Industries

American Economy: U.S. Media and Entertainment

America is to entertainment what South Africa is to gold and Saudi
Arabia is to oil. . . . Look closer and it is less American.

The Economist[1]

America's economic competitiveness—defined as our ability to produce goods and services that meet the test of international markets
while our citizens earn a standard of living that is both rising and
sustainable over the long run—is eroding slowly but steadily.

Building a Competitive America[2]

Instead of building U.S. competitiveness through strategic government
intervention, the Reagan-Bush administrations put their faith in "free
market forces." Yet the new fiscal and monetary policies failed to resolve
the structural problems of the economy.

In the 1980s America lost its global financial hegemony to Japan. Moreover, a $4 trillion twin deficit posed a massive burden to U.S. companies.
Without regulatory constraints (and with new antitrust policies), the great
bull market of the booming 1980s boosted the fourth national wave of
mergers and acquisitions, which led to a foreign invasion of the U.S. private sector (including media and entertainment). After the demise of junk
bonds and high leverage, U.S. companies also turned to foreign banks for
low-cost capital.

Even prior to the early 1990s, the declining competitiveness was affecting the nation's internationally most successful industries—that is, aerospace and entertainment. The two were not insulated from the instability of the U.S. economy, capital markets, and corporate governance—even if the end of Cold War seemed to curse one and bless the other.

I will use the term "media and entertainment" (M&E) for a multitude of industries, such as broadcast and cable (basic and pay TV, pay-per-view, home shopping), motion pictures, theatrical exhibition, home video, syndication, theme parks, toys and video games and licensed merchandise, record and music industry, publishing (newspapers, magazines, books), as well as video games and other high-tech products (from CD-ROM to virtual reality). The focus is on those strategic groups that dominate these industries and, therefore, drive evolution in media and entertainment. Prior to the late 1980s, these groups included Hollywood studios, broadcast networks, and a cluster of cable companies and publishing concerns. In the early 1990s three additional groups surfaced, representing telecommunications, computers, as well as integrated electronics (especially consumer electronics).

Since the 1970s the failure of the American capital investment system has increasingly threatened the competitiveness of American companies and the long-term growth of the U.S. economy.[3] Difficulties were largely ignored as long as the nation lived in a growth economy; but, by the early '90s, certain fundamental patterns had a critical impact on the U.S. private sector in general and U.S. media and entertainment in particular:

- emergence of the twin deficit;
- booming stock market;
- troubled banking industry;
- transition to new antitrust rules and deregulations;
- fourth national mergers and acquisitions (M&A) wave (and the ensuing "foreign invasion").

FROM SUPPLY-SIDE REVOLUTION TO TWIN DEFICIT

In 1981 President Reagan introduced a new economic policy, which represented the most dramatic discontinuity since the 1930s. Seeking to break stagflation (slow economic growth, high unemployment, rising prices), the supply-side revolution proposed four kinds of changes: government spending cuts to transfer resources to the private sector and, along with faster growth, to help shrink the budget deficit; moderate monetary expansion to bring down inflation; tax cuts to provide incentives for greater economic activity; and removal of unnecessary federal regulations to cut business costs and make the economy more competitive.[1]

Although the Reagan administration could not coordinate the four fronts as planned, the new economic policy translated into drastic changes in public policy, monetary policy, tax policy—not to speak of the dramatic growth of the twin deficit.

Twin Deficit

The Reagan administration borrowed on a scale unprecedented in U.S. peacetime history. As a new fiscal policy evolved on mounting debt and asset sales, huge budget deficits and high interest rates strengthened the exchange rate of the dollar to the point where the ability of U.S. industries to compete with foreign rivals collapsed in both domestic and global markets.[2]

Despite the famous 1988 campaign promise—"Read my lips, no new taxes!"—the Bush administration both taxed and borrowed. Prior to the Reagan era, gross federal debt accounted for 33–34% of gross domestic product (GDP). In the end of Bush's term in 1992, the deficit amounted to $300 billion and debt to $4 trillion—nearly 70% of GDP. Federal spending did not manifest any signs of slowing until 1992–93.[3]

When Reagan became president, the United States was the world's leading lender; when Bush assumed office, the nation had become the world's largest debtor. America retained its rate of investment by becoming a massive net importer of capital.

New Tax Policies

Geared to accelerate American competitiveness, tax cuts proceeded in three stages, causing extraordinary volatility. The Economic Recovery Tax Act (ERTA, 1981) legislated the largest tax decrease in American history; the Tax Equity and Fiscal Responsibility Act (TEFRA, 1982) resulted in the largest peacetime revenue in U.S. postwar history; the net effect of the Tax Reform Act (TRA, 1986) was to raise corporate tax, and to eliminate or scale back many selective tax incentives.[4]

These changes had a direct impact on American corporations:

- although the Reagan tax cuts decreased nominal tax rates, they actually increased effective tax rates;

- since dividend payments were subject to double taxation (corporate level, shareholder distribution), the tax system favored retained earnings at the expense of paid dividends;

- new tax policies boosted debt financing—that is, interest payments to lenders were excluded from taxable income.[5]

From 1981 to 1986 the U.S. offered generous depreciation allowances that reduced effective corporate tax rates and made U.S. companies "more valuable" to American owners than potential Japanese acquirers. When the TRA reduced the nominal rate of corporate taxation (34% was less than many foreign tax rates) but increased the effective rate, the change contributed to the shift of foreign (especially Japanese) investment from passive portfolio investments toward direct acquisitions of U.S. firms. Although America became a tax haven for foreign investors, U.S. subsidiaries of foreign companies (including Sony and Matsushita) paid little or no U.S. income tax during the 1980s.[6]

Conversely, through their subsidiaries, American companies could keep foreign earnings out of reach of the U.S. tax system. Such "Cayman deals" offered significant, and often crucial, benefits to small and less diversified entertainment earners.[7] For example, Carolco, the '80s thriving ministudio that inflated Hollywood's production costs, exploited a 28-year-old clause in the U.S. tax code that allowed American companies operating overseas to engage in tax-sheltering strategies. When, in the late '80s, Hollywood studios' effective tax rates exceeded 40%, Carolco's rate varied around 1–6%.[8] Skillful use of international differences in taxation ensured many foreign companies a competitive advantage.

NEW STOCK MARKET

Since the 1970s the internal management and capital allocation process in major diversified U.S. corporations evolved to mimic America's external capital markets. As Michael Porter put it,

The external market with its transient ownership of companies, rapid reallocation of capital, limited information gathering, financial proxy-driven valuation, and minimal owner involvement, is reflected in a management process that has gravitated toward buying and selling businesses, financially based control and capital budgeting models, and diminished information creation and exchange in making management decisions.[1]

During the mid-1960s and early 1980s, the Dow Jones Industrial Average (DJIA) was locked in a trading range of 580–1,050 points. When interest rates almost collapsed, the stock market exploded with an institutional buying frenzy, and Wall Street witnessed the most stunning bear market reversal since 1932. Between August 1982 and October 1987, the bull market expanded from 777 points to 2,722 points. Neither two stock crashes (1987, 1989) nor the Persian Gulf War could contain the volatile bull market. Even if new kinds of trading in stock indexes, futures, options, and new markets continued to undermine the New York Stock Exchange's market share, the '80s saw an extraordinary expansion of financial volume.[2]

The bull markets, institutional investors, as well as junk bond financing accelerated dramatic changes in U.S. media and entertainment—well into the '90s.

Junk Bond Financing

In their search for low-cost capital, U.S. companies turned to foreign banks for loans, while the bond market came to represent an alternative mode of financing. With Michael Milken of Drexel Burnham Lambert, the new "high-yield market" enabled raiders to mount assaults on huge companies without putting up their own cash or borrowing it from banks.[3]

As early as 1978, Milken had moved his high-yield operation to Beverly Hills, California, which strengthened his ties with Hollywood. In 1979 Milken used junk bonds to finance casinos; three years later, Drexel was issuing high-yield debt for cable companies (TCI, Cablevision). By 1988, combined media and leisure segments issued 21% of junk bonds outstanding.[4] Virtually all significant M&E businesses developed a connection to Drexel.[5]

After the insider trading scandal, Milken's resignation prompted a frantic restructuring of the $200 billion junk bond market. In 1989 Drexel filed for bankruptcy-court protection and Milken became a scapegoat for the "decade of greed."

By 1993 the junk bond market had its greatest year ever: $68 billion plus, equal to the total raised in the period 1982–86.[6] The resurrected market was driven by companies refinancing to take advantage of low interest rates.

Widening access to capital markets, junk bond financing stimulated competition in U.S. media and entertainment. Still, the legacy of Milken and Drexel remains far from settled.[7]

The Rise of Institutional Investors

By the late 1980s there were two "separate and unequal" securities markets. One consisted of individual investors, whose absolute numbers continued to grow but whose relative control of the market had declined. (In the early 1990s, however, individuals returned in a big way, via mutual funds.)[8]

A far more expansive market was dominated by a tiny group of professional money managers; they ran trillions of dollars for institutional investors, focusing on quarterly results. From 1950 to 1989, the pool of total institutional assets grew from $107 billion to more than $5.7 trillion, with more than half of outstanding equities under their control.[9]

As the dominant force in the U.S. capital markets, institutional investors (especially giant private pension funds and life insurance companies) became a critical element in the capital formation process, expanding their economic power and exerting a substantial influence on U.S. corporate governance.[10]

As major M&E companies were taken over by large diversified conglomerates, institutional investors acquired significant positions in M&E businesses. By 1989 institutional holdings accounted for 51% of General Electric, 42% of Walt Disney, and 88% of Capital Cities/ABC. By 1990 institutional holdings in the top 1,000 U.S. corporations amounted to 51%, with conglomerates at 54%, leisure 52%, publishing/TV 40%, and telecommunications less than 40%. Money managers from the nation's 60 largest mutual funds invested over $8 billion in television, radio, and motion picture stocks, as well as $1.6 billion in leisure-time companies.[11]

While, in the United States, paper wealth went hand in hand with a shrinking industrial base, Japanese capital replaced the hegemony of the U.S. dollar in global finance and Hollywood—until Japan's speculative boom, fueled on cheap and easy credit, went bust.

After the M&A wave, the market returned from new methods of valuation (cash flow, breakup asset values) and aggressive debt financing to classic methods of valuation (earnings per share, price/equity) and conservative equity financing. Most M&E stocks and financings did not rebound from the crashes of 1987 and 1989.[12]

In April 1991 Wall Street cracked the 3,000 mark, fueled by the Federal Reserve Bank's (the Fed) policy of lower interest rates to boost the economy.[13] The inclusion of the Walt Disney Company in the DJIA was a tribute to the M&E business, the nation's second-highest export asset.

In January 1994 the three-year-old bull market, a growing economy, low interest rates, low inflation, and massive restructurings caused the DJIA to climb to close to 4,000. By March the bond market was clobbered by bullish economic data, while the Fed raised short-term rates. The happy days ended in the "minicrash of '94"—a volatile correction, as the observers put it.[14]

TROUBLED BANKING INDUSTRY

After motion pictures established their supremacy as popular entertainment, Wall Street lent money and placed officers on the boards of Hollywood studios. As with the Great Depression, the industry shakeout enhanced financial power in Hollywood.[1]

In 1933 the Banking Act (the Glass-Steagall Act) effectively separated commercial and investment banking. Banks were prohibited from operating nationwide, and entry into the industry was sharply curtailed. While the stable post–World War II environment favored "relationship banking" (transactions as part of an ongoing business relationship), the late 1970s saw a shift to "price banking" (transactions as independent, price-driven events). With deregulation and increasing competition, the U.S. financial system grew highly complex and differentiated.[2]

With deregulation, modern technologies, and the globalization of capital markets, the restrictions of the Glass-Steagall Act contributed to the shrinking business of U.S. banks. By the mid-1980s, however, market forces were shortcutting regulatory policies.[3]

Investment Banking

The booming 1980s saw a dramatic shift in the revenue sources of securities firms (which cut into the lucrative M&A market). Yet increasing expenses shrank revenue margins. While Wall Street's "Masters of the Universe" led a royal life, a "profitability drought" led to cutbacks at major investment firms. The shift to "fee-based" businesses incited conflicts over vested interests. In the past, investment banks had "assisted" in the M&A deals; now they were actively creating, promoting, and encouraging the business.[4]

Prompted by a decade of increasing competition and industry globalization, consolidation left the securities industry with fewer, but much bigger, firms. In the mid-1970s some 33% ($1.3 billion) of the industry's equity capital was concentrated in the top 10 firms, whereas by 1989 the top 10 firms controlled 61% ($23.9 billion) of the capital.[5]

In media and entertainment banking, financial transition coincided with professional specialization. Until the early '80s many investment bankers regarded themselves as generalists, whose contributions were applicable to a wide range of situations and industries. By the mid-'80s generalists were replaced by M&E groups, which served as gatekeepers between M&E companies and financial markets. (Harold L. Vogel's classic *Entertainment Industry Economics* appeared amid Wall Street's M&E boom.) While major investment banks structured in-house M&E practices, the work in the M&E industry became dominated by half a dozen Wall Street giants. The '80s also saw an expansion of smaller boutiques (Allen & Co.), which specialized in capital and M&A services.[6]

From 1982 to mid-1989 the tiny M&E arms of the colossal investment banks injected some $8 billion into a wide array of film, distribution, video, and TV program ventures. Almost half of that amount was infused in the peak year of 1986. Overall, debt (64%) was far more popular than stock (36%). Of the recipients, TV (37%) and major studios (31%) obtained the most significant portion of the capital (see Table 1-1).

The rise and decline of financial capital coincided with the fourth national M&A wave.

By the early 1990s the disillusionment of bigger players over the dra-

Table 1-1
Hollywood Capital Raised on Wall Street (1982–89) ($mil.)

Type of Issue	Straight Debt	Convertible Debt	Preferred Stock	Common Stock	Total ($)	(%)
1989*	$110	$25	-	$2	$137	1.7%
1988	878	-	-	30	908	11.4
1987	755	196	-	109	1,060	13.4
1986	1,215	310	$1,653	511	3,689	46.5
1985	410	65	4	214	693	8.7
1984	152	180	60	58	450	5.7
1983	750	-	-	125	875	11.0
1982	30	19	-	72	121	1.5
Total	$4,300	$795	$1,717	$1,121	$7,933	100.0%
%	54.2%	10.0%	21.6%	14.1%	100.0%	

-- Motion Pictures --

Type of Recipients	Major	Mini- Major	Indie	TV	Home Video	Theatres	Others	Total ($)	(%)
1989	-	-	$25	-	$110	-	$2	$137	1.7%
1988	$53	$200	25	$505	-	$125	-	908	11.4
1987	-	-	49	647	76	276	12	1,060	13.4
1986	1,375	267	408	1,376	105	95	63	3,689	46.5
1985	305	-	96	121	77	90	3	693	8.7
1984	-	210	11	188	-	32	9	450	5.7
1983	750	66	-	17	4	16	23	875	11.0
1982	-	-	3	64	54	-	-	121	1.5
Tot.	$2,483	$743	$617	$2,918	$426	$634	$112	$7,933	100.0%
%	31.3%	9.4%	7.8%	36.8%	5.4%	8.0%	1.4%	100.0%	

* 1989 figures through July 10 only, not full year.

SOURCE: The Hollywood Reporter Entertainment Finance Special Report 1989 (Joel H. Reader, Oppenheimer & Co., Inc., Los Angeles); amended by the author.

matic slowdown in dealmaking benefited smaller firms with greater commitment and specialized niche expertise in the M&E industry. Major players included firms like Lazard Frères, Allen & Co., Salomon Bros. and Goldman, Sachs (whose 1993 pretax profit of $2.7 billion ranked it as one of the most profitable companies in the world). Many banks that in the '80s boosted inflated prices were hired to correct their old mistakes. In 1992 *Variety* reported that "investment bankers specializing in workouts and restructurings are among the busiest people on Wall Street these days. And no area is commanding more of the workout artists' attention than the entertainment business."[7]

By 1994 the deluge of fees from underwriting new stocks and bonds was likely to continue to bring big profits to Wall Street investment banks.

Commercial Banking

At the end of the 1980s three strategic groups dominated U.S. commercial banking: money center banks (e.g., Citicorp, Chase Manhattan,

Table 1-2

A Sampler of Media and Entertainment Lenders (1989)

Bank	TV/Radio (mil.)	Cable (bil.)	Entertainment (mil.)	Total (bil.)
1st National of Chicago	$1,200	$1.78	$310	$3.29
Bank of New York	662	1.62	696	2.98
Bank of Boston	606	1.04	956	2.60
Manufacturers Hanover	445	0.90	600	1.95
Mellon Bank	450	1.32	-	1.77ᵃ
Bank of Nova Scotia	162	1.13	471	1.76
Chase Manhattan Bank	300	1.15	265	1.71
Citibank	1,600	-	-	1.60ᵃᵇ*
Chemical Bank	660	0.91	-	1.57ᵃ*
Philadelphia National Bank	150	1.20	200	1.55
Bank of New England	745	0.73	-	1.48
Security Pacific	400	0.25	800	1.45
NCNB, Texas	245	1.16	-	1.40ᵃ
NCNB, N.C.	110	0.93	195	1.24
National Westminster	296	0.89	-	1.19
Bank of California	99	0.39	-	0.48*
($mil)	$8,130	$15.40	$4,493	$28.02
(%)	29%	55%	16%	100%

Numbers are derived from funded and/or unfunded (money set aside for a specific company) commitments.   a. Estimate.   b. Includes cable. * Indicates company that may do entertainment lending but did not provide Broadcasting with figures.

SOURCE: Compiled from Broadcasting, Nov. 13, 1989, p. 76.

J. P. Morgan, Chemical), superregional banks (e.g., BankAmerica, Security Pacific, First Interstate, NCNB), and regional banks (e.g., Wells Fargo, C&S Sovran, Suntrust Banks, Republic New York).

By 1989 15 major commercial banks each lent in excess of $1 billion to TV/radio, cable, or entertainment. Altogether, these lenders were among the top commercial banks in the United States and accounted for more than $28 billion in loans to M&E businesses. The hierarchy of the recipients was determined by the perceived growth prospects of the industry: cable received 55% of the loans, TV/radio 29%, and entertainment 16%. In cable, every second major lender had more than $1 billion in loans (see Table 1-2).

In October 1989 the definition of the "highly leveraged transaction" (HLT) was implemented as a tool for banks to gauge risky loans. Virtually all M&E transactions qualified as HLTs, and were therefore hurt by the definition. Since foreign banks were not constrained by similar HLT restrictions, they seized the opportunity to enter the U.S. market. Despite its effect on pricing and availability of credit, the HLT definition was not eliminated until mid-1992.[8]

Between the early 1970s and early 1990s, commercial banks' share of U.S. financial assets declined to less than 25% from almost 40%.[9] By early 1991 banks were suffering more from losses on bad loans than at any time in the past 50 years, due to credit problems and regulatory concern with HLTs, the collapse of the junk bond market, the shift from earnings to asset values as loan criteria, and the rise of international competition.

Following tough new banking standards, banks and borrowers replaced hyperlending with hypercaution. Profits soared to record levels, the total level of bank capital, the cushion against losses, was at its highest since 1966. Yet loans were shrinking.

As the remains of the Glass-Steagall Act were collapsing, commercial banks entered the M&A market, underwriting, and equity participation. But things changed slowly and Congress rejected the Bush administration's proposal to modernize the American banking system. As a result, regional banks resorted to mergers, which in 1991 amounted to a record $21 billion. Promoted as a way to gain efficiency, boost profitability, and rebuild capital, consolidation was dictated by an eat-or-be-eaten environment.

Despite the recession, the crisis in the banking industry and Hollywood's realignment, classic M&E lenders continued to serve the major studios, even if lending strategies differed widely among other players (especially mini-majors and independent movie companies [indies]).[10]

Consolidation strengthened the bigger well-capitalized banks and restricted access to capital for smaller, less-established banks. It erected higher barriers of entry for the M&E industry.

Shifts in International Lending

The decline of American banking began in the mid-'70s. A decade later, growing problem loans and global concern about the stability of the U.S. banking system forced many U.S. banks to retreat from international operations. After European banks' brief interim leadership, Japanese banks began a spectacular ascendancy in the hierarchy.[11]

By 1989 Japanese-owned banks controlled 25% of the California banking market, the core production state in the M&E business.[12] During the boom years, Japanese investors poured an estimated $13–$15 billion into Hollywood. (In the early '90s, in their domestic market, the Japanese banks were hit by the worst economic bust since World War II.)

In the 1983–91 period, total lending to the U.S. commercial and industrial market by U.S. banks rose from $381 billion to $428 billion, whereas foreign-owned bank lending soared from $86 billion to $348 billion over the same period. America's largest corporations were relying more on foreign banks for credit and other services than on American banks, even when the banking services supported solely U.S. operations. Every second U.S. corporation had become dependent on foreign financing.[13]

Although foreign banks insulated themselves from losses better than the U.S. banks, there was a fallout, especially in indie financing. The Hollywood adventures of the French-Dutch Crédit Lyonnais illustrated the risks and rewards.

Independents and Crédit Lyonnais

In the 1980s almost $3 billion of Crédit Lyonnais's (CL) assets ended in Hollywood's indies. By the early 1990s the state-owned CL, a global top 10 bank, had become the most aggressive player in the U.S. media and entertainment industry. The bank's client list included the best known indies and mini-majors.[14]

In the early 1980s, CL's Nederland branch put Frans Afman in charge of the entertainment loan division. Following executive-level illegalities, CL cleaned up the operation and changed the branch's name to Crédit Lyonnais Bank Nederland (CLBN) N.V. Concurrently, project-by-project financing was replaced by generous credit lines, starting with Cannon and struggling indies. By 1986 CLBN's loans had soared to $300 billion. As large lines of credit went hand in hand with sloppy accounting, Afman left the bank. From 1981 to 1991 he was associated with a turnover of $2.5 billion in loans for indies.

Fearing that the European Community (EC) would make marginal players out of all but the biggest banks, Jean-Yves Haberer, CL's new president who was connected with the Socialists, announced an aggressive growth plan. The more CLBN lent to M&E companies, the longer it took for the bank to acknowledge its losses.

In 1990 Crédit Lyonnais's Dutch subsidiary allowed Italian financier Giancarlo Parretti to take over MGM/UA Communications, at the cost of $1–$1.5 billion in loans. Following a settlement with its creditors, CLBN pressured Parretti to leave the holding company. By mid-1992 CL had lent $2.5 billion, about 18% of its equity, to Hollywood, mainly through CLBN. When CL began pulling back its M&E lending, the indie niche was left to European, Japanese, and local banks.

By 1993 CL was struggling with a web of lawsuits over its financial dealings with the film industry. Allegedly, the bank's Dutch branch had worked with Parretti and Florio Fiorini, another notorious Italian financier, to launder money from dubious sources.[15]

In 1993, Jean-Yves Haberer was replaced by Jean Peyrelevade with the mandate to clean up CL's reputation and finances in preparation for its eventual privatization. The new approach required withdrawal from beleaguered companies like MGM.[16]

NEW ANTITRUST AND DEREGULATION

Classic Antitrust Policy

In the late 1970s the rise of new antitrust policies and deregulation was accompanied by the dismantling of the classic antitrust policy.

Antitrust Genesis (1890–1914)

With the U.S. industrial revolution, chains of small firms were transformed into complex oligopolies and monopolies. As a result, the first decisions of the Supreme Court dealt with classic trusts (the Sherman Antitrust Act, 1890; the Clayton Act, 1914), giving rise to regulatory agencies and antitrust policy.[1]

Antitrust Demise (1914–36)

During the "Roaring Twenties," antitrust activities were scaled back, despite the second national merger wave. While cartels were considered antitrust violations, close-knit consolidation was not. The 1914–36 period witnessed the first antitrust cases in the nascent motion picture industry.

Although the study of industrial organization (IO) began with the trustification of the first merger wave, modern notions at the center of the field had been discussed extensively by the mid-1920s. The "neo-classical" approach focused on the theory of perfect competition, stressed the efficiency of the competitive system and relied on highly abstract analysis. Ultimately, it justified oligopolies as competitive systems. The 1930s brought to the fore the "realistic" approach, which had a crucial impact on antitrust until the late 1950s. The focus shifted from theory, individual firm, and monopoly to empirical research, industry, and concentration.[2]

Antitrust Revival (1936–50)

As market forces fell into disrepute, Congress passed the National Recovery Act under the leadership of Franklin D. Roosevelt, whereas the law of monopolization evolved through several landmark cases. From 1937 to 1945 *U.S. v. Aluminum Co. of America* shaped the modern law of monopolization by incorporating "market definition" into IO economics. This period saw NBC's divestiture (1943), following monopoly investigations, as well as Paramount's consent decrees (1948), which resulted in the divestiture of the Hollywood majors' theatre chains.

The neoclassical tradition was augmented with a new paradigm, "structural consensus": industry structure influenced a firm's conduct, which determined a firm's performance. If a defendant had a high share in a market where there were barriers to entry, that indicated a higher likelihood of monopoly power. Armed with IO economics, structural consensus required active antitrust.

Antitrust Reformation (1950–75)

From the early 1950s to the late 1960s, antitrust activities slowed down, except for allegations of monopolization in several big-company cases (IBM, AT&T, Xerox). In media and entertainment, this period witnessed the Federal Communication Commission's (FCC) inquiry into networks' monopoly over program production and distribution, as well as *U.S. v. Loews* on block-booking movies to broadcast stations. The 1970s began with the enactment of financial interest and syndication (fin-syn) rules, and the Senate's ban of cigarette commercials from radio and television. By the end of the Carter era, however, "social regulation" and activist government would be associated with poor economic performance.[3]

New Antitrust Policy

Prior to the 1980s the government had initiated antitrust cases against various segments of the industry (e.g., *U.S. v. Western Electric, U.S. v. IBM*); in the Reagan era, times got tougher, and American companies turned against one another. Legal theory, too, shifted. Relying upon economic analysis, the courts focused increasingly on "market impact" in monopoly cases.

In addition to the erosion of the bipartisan consensus on classic antitrust and economic-legal criticism, the transition to new antitrust and deregulation was prompted by global competition. The transition got increasingly politicized during the Reagan-Bush era (especially when Vice President Dan Quayle adopted a high-profile deregulatory agenda).

In U.S. media and entertainment, the transition prompted four major developments: the home video boom (following the majors' failure to vertically integrate into pay cable), new merger guidelines, vertical reintegration of theater circuits, and the struggle over the fin-syn rules. Meanwhile, a series of FCC initiatives reflected the spirit of deregulation: extension of station ownership, cable deregulation, and the entry of telecommunications companies (telcos) into the television industry.

The Reagan Administration: Free Market Policies

As the dismal performance of the U.S. economy gave rise to laissez-faire policies, economists and legal theorists developed a free-market theory of industrial organization that was adopted by the Reagan administration.

New Industrial Organization Economics

The "new IO" theory adapted features from two other schools of research: the "contestability" school and the Chicago school. If the first held that internal industry structure was secondary in importance to entry from outside, the Chicago school reversed the direction of causation in the structural consensus paradigm. As relative efficiency was perceived as the real determinant of a firm's position, monopoly came to be seen as a sign of efficiency. Market dominance, argued theorists like Robert H. Bork and George Stigler, had minimal harmful effects. Criticizing the merger cases of the Warren Supreme Court era, the free market school charged classic antitrust for the problems of American business.[4]

New Merger Guidelines (1982–84)

The third merger wave had led to the issuance of the first set of *Merger Guidelines* in 1968, as well as two presidential task force reports on antitrust policy. Such consensus declined rapidly toward the late '70s and early '80s, when traditional merger rules were relaxed and, finally, rewritten. In June 1982 the Federal Trade Commission (FTC) issued its "Statement Concerning Horizontal Mergers," while the Justice Department issued the more comprehensive new *Merger Guidelines*, amended two years later. Prior to the 80s, antitrust policies tended to be strict on horizontal mergers, liberal toward vertical mergers, and neutral toward conglomerate mergers. The new *Guidelines* focused on horizontal mergers, whereas vertical mergers would be challenged only under narrowly prescribed conditions.

The Reagan Justice Department's weak antitrust enforcement policy contributed to the fourth national M&A wave. The power of the Reagan-Bush judges was enhanced by their dominance of the federal appeals courts.[5]

The FCC and Deregulation

Starting in 1981, the Reagan administration reversed the direction of regulatory activity in America. Loyal troops were brought to key federal agencies, including the Federal Communications Commission, the Federal Trade Commission, and the Securities and Exchange Commission (SEC). Meanwhile, the administration cut severely the budgets for the Justice Department's antitrust division and the FTC.[6]

The polarization between the Republican administration (new antitrust, deregulation) and the Democratic Congress (classic antitrust, regulation) spelled the demise of traditional bipartisan consensus over classic antitrust.

The FCC was first headed by Mark S. Fowler (1981–87), and later by Dennis R. Patrick (1987–89). "I'm not a closet Reagan supporter," said Fowler, who called the FCC "a New Deal Dinosaur." In the name of the free marketplace, Fowler changed many ground rules in cable and telecommunications. When he stepped down in 1987, Patrick's deregulatory zeal contributed to the erosion of the bipartisan consensus.

The Bush Administration: Conservative Pragmatism

Seeking to avoid ideological excesses, the Bush administration engaged in a pragmatic middle-of-the-road enforcement of new antitrust and deregulation. In 1989, after three decades as an antitrust litigator, James F.

Rill was appointed chief of the Justice Department's antitrust division, with a philosophical ally in Janet Steiger, the FTC's new chairman.

Seeking to promote an economic policy for telecommunications that emphasized competition, not regulation, the Bush administration charted an increasingly aggressive course. It opposed cable reregulation, allowed the telephone industry to compete with cable, and advocated auctions for the new spectrum.

In 1989 Alfred C. Sikes, head of the Commerce Department's National Telecommunications and Information Administration (NITA), became the FCC's new chairman. Sikes's free-market policies meant continued deregulation with moderate ideological zeal; to the critics, such pragmatism was equivalent to Bush's "vision thing"—lack of vision as vision.

Toward the end of Bush's first term, the administration was awakened by global competition. The first impulse was defensive. It considered an extension of antitrust laws to strike at American subsidiaries of foreign companies that were found to engage in various anticompetitive practices in *their* home markets.[7]

The Clinton Administration: Liberal Pragmatism

Philosophically, the Clinton administration's approach to competition and antitrust differed drastically from that of his Republican predecessors; in practice, the policy results were less different.[8]

Unlike previous Democratic administrations, the advent of the Clinton White House showed little inclination for a trustbusting crusade. Focusing on U.S. competitiveness, it welcomed cooperative activity among businesses, just as it seemed to favor "bigness" as a means of survival in the global economy. Also, the promise of an information superhighway entailed significant antitrust and deregulatory implications.

Like the Carter administration, the Clinton team revived the regulatory distinction between "economic" areas (e.g., telecommunications), where it pressed for deregulation, and "social" areas (e.g., consumer protection), where regulatory moves were more pronounced. Deregulation also applied to new technologies.

Demise of Fin-Syn Rules

In November 1993 the long-standing financial interest and syndication rules were finally lifted. As a result, the Big Three networks (ABC, CBS, and NBC) were expected to step up production and ownership of their prime-time TV shows, as well as explore mergers with studios.[9]

The FCC: The Hundt Commission

In December, Vice President Al Gore swore in Reed Hundt, a veteran antitrust litigator, as chairman of the FCC. As a "New Democrat," Hundt advocated both economic growth and social equity. Just as he believed the FCC should strive to unleash the power of private capital and encourage innovation (digital technology), he argued there need be no conflict between antitrust policy and expansion of the communications sector (the entry of telcos). After the FCC's renewed cable rate regulations, the M&E companies considered Hundt a "liberal Democrat and a bona fide consumer advocate."[10]

Antitrust as Trade Weapon

By early 1994 the Clinton Justice Department was prepared to bring cases against foreign companies that limited U.S. entry into their home markets. Despite legal obstacles and possible retaliation, the antitrust laws were seen as a potentially useful means of protecting national interest where private cartels sought to close foreign markets.[11] In 1994 the Justice Department reached a settlement with a British glass company whose patents and licenses had prevented American glass businesses from operating overseas. The case was perceived as a precedent to antitrust cases against Japanese companies.[12]

"It would be hard to find a President more enthusiastic about promoting technology than Bill Clinton," argued the *New York Times* in April 1994. "Yet in a striking number of cases, the Administration seems to be picking fights with the very companies that want to build its cherished information superhighway." As signs of the internal conflict, the *Times* cited Vice President Al Gore's high-profile trips to Silicon Valley *and* the Justice Department's antitrust investigation of the Microsoft Corporation; the broad vision of high-speed computer networks *and* the FCC's new rate cuts; law enforcement officials' right to wiretap telephone and computer networks *and* the Commerce and State Departments' relaxation of export restrictions on computer and satellite technology.[13]

These seemingly contradictory examples reflected a fundamental ambiguity in the Clinton administration's antitrust policies. In principle, new antitrust laws were supposed to maintain, or promote, economic growth *and* contain the economic and political power of big business. In classic antitrust, such objectives were considered mutually exclusive.

THE FOURTH M&A WAVE: FOREIGN INVASION

"Around the globe, folks just can't get enough of America," reported *Fortune* magazine in December 1990. "They may not want our *hardware* anymore—our cars, steel, or television sets. But when they want a jolt of popular culture—and they want more all the time—they increasingly turn to American *software*: our movies, music, TV programming, and home video, which together now account for an annual trade surplus of some $8 billion."[1]

In the 1980s, what conventional wisdom perceived as triumph was often a facade for erosion. Though American TV shows and Hollywood films continued to enchant audiences all over the globe, the ownership and, occasionally, management of U.S.-based media and entertainment companies was shifting to foreign hands.

With the kind of complacency, arrogance, and risk-averse mentality that accompanied the near-devastation of Detroit's auto manufacturers, American M&E dinosaurs took erosion for triumph—until they were taken over, digested, absorbed, and dismembered.

In the twentieth century, the U.S. economy has experienced four national merger and acquisition waves. Each boom was conditioned by rising stock markets, resulted in consolidation, and enjoyed easy access to credit.[2]

The first U.S. merger wave, known as "merging for monopoly," occurred in two stages (1890–93, 1895–1904). "Trustification" consisted largely of horizontal combinations to obtain market dominance. Aimed at "merging for oligopoly," the second merger wave (1925–30) increased vertical integration.

The third wave occurred in the "go-go" years of the late 1960s and included the greatest number of transactions. Without horizontal or vertical integration, the "conglomerate wave" (mergers between companies in unrelated businesses) had little effect on market concentration.[3] As antitrust policy confined mergers to conglomerates, synergy served as a rationalization for extensive diversification. Often, the true objective was stock promotion in the raging bull market. In corporate strategy, conglomeratization went hand in hand with decentralization, which led to portfolio management (which tended to ignore the value of linkages between business units).[4]

In gross sums, the fourth M&A wave dwarfed all previous waves. In 1980–89, the dollar value climbed from $33 billion to $254 billion. Transactions included a significant portion of M&E deals. In dollar value, broadcasting/cable was the third most active M&A industry in the '80s (over 2,000 transactions, $89 billion), while entertainment ranked 21st (441 transactions, $24 billion). Among the top 100 deals of the decade, entertainment firms changed hands in 11 transactions.[5]

Much of the "financial engineering" stemmed from an attempt to restructure poorly performing companies that had been combined for purely financial reasons in the '60s and early '70s. Often, M&As required the breakup of prosperous companies acquired with borrowings that could be repaid only through a partial dismantling of the purchase. Hence, the rapid growth of divestitures (see Table 1–3).

At one end, restructuring was carried out by corporate builders, at the other by financial raiders. If the former dismantled to build, the latter capitalized on dismemberment. After the 1987 crash, raiders fell victim to

Table 1-3
Mergers and Acquisitions (1980–90)

| | ------ # --------- | | | ---- $bil ----- | | | ---- % ------- | | |
	AA	DIV	LBO	AA	DIV	LBO	AA	DIV	LBO
1990	4168	1406	254	$172	$60	$16	100%	35%	9%
1989	4167	1333	382	254	67	67	100	26	26
1988	4233	1336	383	240	84	47	100	35	20
1987	4024	1221	279	178	58	36	100	24	29
1986	4463	1419	337	206	72	45	100	35	22
1985	3489	1041	255	146	44	20	100	30	14
1984	3176	794	254	126	31	19	100	25	15
1983	2395	661	231	53	13	5	100	25	9
1982	2298	562	164	49	8	4	100	13	7
1981	2329	476	100	70	10	4	100	14	6
1980	1558	104	11	33	5	0	100	15	0

Covers transactions valued at $1 million or more. Values based on transactions for which price data revealed.
All activity [AA] includes mergers, acquisitions, acquisitions of interest, acquisitions of controlling interest, divestitures, and leveraged transactions that result in a change in ownership.
Divestiture [DIV]: sale of a business, division, or subsidiary by corporate owner to another party. Leveraged buyout [LBO]: acquisition of a business in which buyers use mostly borrowed money to finance purchase price and incorporate debt into capital structure of business after change in ownership.

SOURCE: Based on the U.S. Bureau of the Census, Statistical Abstract of the United States: 1993 (113th ed.) Washington, D.C. 1993, Table No. 869.

a rising stock market, changes in tax policies, takeover laws, and disclosure rules. Major U.S. companies became catalysts in the M&A market.[6]

While U.S. companies in the 1980s may have been underleveraged by international standards, the U.S. capital investment system made debt highly risky. As American M&E companies' debt doubled from 1980 to 1986, these firms became susceptible to economic downturns.[7]

The change came in 1992, when corporate America underwent its largest balance-sheet cleanup ever, deleveraging a record $750 billion through stock and bond offerings. The proceeds were used to pay off high-cost debt piled up in the '80s, slash interest rates, and raise credit ratings.[8]

Foreign Invasion

The fourth M&A wave differed from all previous ones. It made possible foreign invasion of critical sectors of the U.S. economy, including M&E businesses. From 1975 to 1980, foreign assets in the U.S. grew from $221 billion to $501 billion; from 1980 to 1990, these assets more than quadrupled to almost $2.2 trillion. As foreigners bought controlling interests in major U.S. companies, the portion of foreign direct investment in the U.S. (FDIUS) in total foreign assets increased from 17% to 21%.[9]

Instead of building new assets, foreign investors were buying up existing productive assets. As FDIUS analysts put it, "One should think of Mat-

Table 1-4
Foreign Invasion: U.S. Media and Entertainment (1985–91)

Acquirer/Investor	Target	Deal	Price
1991			
Swiss insurer	20th Century Fox	Investment	$80 million
Nissho Iwai	Universal & Mount	Movie financing	$150 million
MICO (NHK)	Viacom	Financing of TV programming	Not reported
MICO (NHK)	Venture fund	Co-financing; co-production	$70 million
Canal Plus et al.	Carolco Pictures	Equity investment	23%+ of equity (1990-91)
1990			
Matsushita	MCA/Universal	Acquisition	$6.59 billion
Pathé Comm.	MGM/UA Comm.	Acquisition	$1.36 billion
Yamaichi Securities	Walt Disney	Investment in Disney movies	$600 million
Nomura Babcock & Brown	Interscope	Investment in Interscope/Disney films	$100+ million
Matsushita	MCA/Geffen	Part of MCA deal	$550 million
NBC/Jap. media firms	Unnamed Hollywood studio	Acquisition talks	–
Jap. investors	20th Century Fox	Investment talks	$500 million
1989			
Jap. investors	Pressman Film	Investments	Equity investment
Jap. investors	Continental Cable	Investments	$100 mil. in debt
Jap. markets	TCI	Investments	$200 million
Nomura Babcock & Brown	Morgan Creek	Joint financing of films	up to $100 million
Sony	Columbia Pictures	Acquisition	$3.4 billion
Polygram/Philips	A&M	Acquisition	$460 million
JVC/Matsushita	Largo Entert.	Movie financing	$100 million
TVS	MTM	Acquisition	$320 million
1988			
Parretti/Fiorini	Pathé/Cannon	Acquisition	$200 million
Carlton	Technicolor	Acquisition	$780 million
1987			
Sony	CBS Records	Acquisition	$2 billion
1986			
BMG/Bertelsmann	RCA	75% of RCA's (GE) record business	$300 million
1985			
Metromedia	News Corp.	Buy of 7 TV stat's	$2.05 billion
20th Century Fox	News Corp.	Acquisition	$575 million

sushita's purchase of MCA, not Honda's opening of its Marysville, Ohio, plant, as the characteristic way in which FDI has grown in the United States during the 1980s."[10]

The pattern of foreign invasion (from funding to acquisitions) in the U.S. M&E business imitated the general pattern of FDIUS (Table 1–4). If FDIUS in the M&E industry began in 1985 with the Australian-based News Corporation's acquisitions of Twentieth Century Fox and Metromedia stations, it peaked when Japanese firms like Sony and Matsushita joined the buying spree in 1987. At the height of FDIUS (1985–90), Japanese U.S.

investments were highest and most capital-intensive in entertainment (over $12.3 billion), whereas finance came in second (almost $9 billion).[11]

Broadcast Networks

Due to regulatory restrictions, foreign players could not purchase U.S. TV networks. When, for example, Rupert Murdoch purchased Metromedia stations in 1985 at $2.1 billion, he obtained American citizenship to form the fourth network (Fox Broadcasting Company). The purchase of studios or production companies, which operated in the syndication business, was another way to enter American television (as evidenced by the purchases of Columbia, MTM, and MGM/UA). Anticipating the collapse of the fin-syn rules, even U.S. networks explored strategic alliances in program production with Japanese and European investors in 1989–90.[12]

Record Companies

In 1986 the German publishing giant Bertelsmann paid $300 million for 75% of RCA's record business (owned by General Electric). In 1988–90, the U.S. recording industry was swept by "merger-mania" as most major labels and many independents were bought, merged, or otherwise altered.

Major Studios

Major foreign acquisitions in Hollywood took place from 1985 to 1990, including the purchase of Fox by News Corp.; the majority equity investment in Pathé Communications and Cannon Group by Italian investors; the $3.4 billion acquisition of Columbia by Sony; Matsushita's $6.6 billion acquisition of MCA; and the $1.4 billion acquisition of MGM/UA by Pathé. Among the mini-majors, the highly leveraged Carolco Pictures survived by losing its autonomy in equity sales to foreign companies.

Cable Television

By the turn of the '90s, a number of M&E companies (including cable) resorted to financing from foreign (mainly Japanese) commercial banks exempt from many U.S. regulations. The cable giant Tele-Communications, Inc. raised $200 million in the Japanese money markets (1989), Continental Cablevision followed TCI's lead, raising $100 million.

Independents: Movie and TV Companies

Indie acquisitions peaked in 1989, when MTM was purchased by TVS Entertainment, a British broadcaster, for $320 million. That year Japanese JVC Company and Matsushita jointly invested $100 million in Largo Entertainment, which heralded the "Japanese invasion of Hollywood." Meanwhile, Nomura Babock & Brown joint-financed Morgan Creek Productions' feature films up to $100 million. These years saw a rapid prolif-eration of joint ventures between U.S. TV producers and their foreign partners.[13]

The Issue of Foreign Ownership

Although foreign acquisitions began in the mid-1980s, a public debate emerged only toward the end of the decade, not least because of the high-profile coverage of the $5 billion Sony/Columbia deal.

In October 1989 former President Reagan made a visit to Tokyo, as the guest of the conservative Fujisankei Communications Group, a TV net-work/newspaper combine. "If America looks like a good investment, why, we should be pleased and proud of it," said Reagan who welcomed Jap-anese investment in the United States.[14] Reportedly, Fujisankei paid Rea-gan a $6 million fee for this visit.

The following month, the House Telecommunications Subcommittee held a hearing, which focused on weaknesses in America's ability to com-pete in the global media market. In October 1991 Rep. Leon Panetta (D-Calif.), then-chairman of the House Budget Committee, introduced legislation that intended to limit foreign ownership (a cap at 50%) of Hollywood studios and other American "cultural" industries.[15]

By the early 1990s major U.S. M&E businesses had fallen in foreign hands. In addition to ownership and investment capital, foreign control was based on new lending practices (U.S. companies got half of their loans from foreign banks). While large European and Japanese companies ac-quired American companies, U.S.-based companies faced barriers to own-ership in many overseas markets. Leaving foreign direct investment in the United States at the mercy of the "free market forces" was an argument nurtured by intellectual naiveté and financial cynicism. Takeover struggles and foreign investments were deficient safety valves. The real problem was the U.S. capital investment system. It had failed.[16]

In 1990 a sharp decline in British acquisitions and a single megatake-over propelled Japanese acquirers into first place among foreign buyers of U.S. companies. In 1992, however, foreign investors were taking out $4 billion more than they were putting into the U.S. economy.[17]

With the bursting of the Japanese "bubble economy" (and a critical change in Japanese tax policies), investment capital shrank and the lucra-tive incursion into Hollywood ended. Instead of the past megadeals, Jap-anese investors favored a more conservative approach (joint ventures, piece-of-the-action deals). Still, Toshiba and C. Itoh paid $500 million each for a 12.5% stake in Time Warner's M&E businesses.[18] America's failing capital investment system was not changing for the better. Rather, rival economies were less able to exploit it.

Old System, New Administration

With the Reagan administration, America was swept by optimism and promises of prosperity, coupled with a fatal attraction to debt. The prevailing economic and political ethos was not reversed until the early 1990s, when the realities of decline, downward mobility, and ever-increasing deficits became national obsessions. The end of the Cold War and the Persian Gulf crisis only intensified the focus on domestic problems. The U.S. economy had entered an "age of diminished expectations."[19]

When Bill Clinton began implementing his mandate for change in 1993, what was at stake was not just the hangover of "the Booming Eighties" but, far more importantly, the entire political and economic system that had been instituted following the Great Depression.

Toward the end of the '80s, technological advances (fiber optics, digital electronics, compression) prompted new strategic groups to enter U.S. media and entertainment. As new high-tech markets inspired strategic alliances between M&E companies and computer companies (from CD-ROM to virtual reality), telephone companies entered U.S. M&E distribution and program production.

In the fall of 1993 Viacom announced it would take over Paramount, while Bell Atlantic would acquire Tele-Communications. Wall Street was swept by a new takeover fever as investors and lenders returned to the M&A fray. The new M&A boom was funded largely with stock whose value had been swollen by a three-year bull market.[20]

Even if the collapse of the proposed $33 billion Bell Atlantic merger slowed significantly the transition to electronic superhighways, new opportunities were enhanced by the Clinton administration's technology initiative and its plan for a national information infrastructure. (In 1993 alone, almost 50% of all merger and acquisition activity entailed communications companies.)

America would pioneer the convergence of television, personal computing, and telecommunications. U.S. media and entertainment entered a revolutionary era.

PART I

INDUSTRY EVOLUTION

Broadcasting:
Decline and Rejuvenation

NETWORK BROADCASTING: EROSION AND UNCERTAINTY

Network Television

Since the late nineteenth century, the American marketplace has proceeded through three basic phases: fragmented markets (prior to the 1880s), mass markets (prior to the 1960s) and segmented markets (after the 1960s). If American advertising was born with mass marketing, the 1980s witnessed the splintering of the mass market. The segments had to be sufficiently large for the achievement of scale economies, while pricing went hand in hand with the value that the segment, not production costs, placed on the product. Deregulation provided a powerful boost to market segmentation.[1]

Until the late '70s the Big Three networks dominated 90% of the prime-time audience; in the '80s their combined share declined drastically. Such developments shifted network programming strategies from the ratings race to profit struggle. By 1990, for example, CBS won the Nielsen ratings, but ABC captured the "demographic cream" of the audience.

Remote Control: Transition to Viewer Control

In the '80s the use of remote control was greatly intensified by time-shifting (VCRs) and a rising number of channels (cable). By the turn of the '90s the penetration of remote control exceeded 80%. As Brandon Tartikoff, NBC's legendary programming chief, put it in the mid-'80s,

when you've got a Zap Box in your house, and the average number of channels in the typical household is somewhere in the twenty-five to thirty range, you've got much more control and many more choices. . . . Lucille Ball said that television changed with the invention of the remote control device. As soon as a guy doesn't have to get up from his chair to switch the channel, television becomes a new ball game. Viewer inertia, which supported many an uninspired show, has given way to viewer impatience.[2]

With remote control and cable, bargaining power in American television shifted from network dominance to viewer control, while the value and meaning of ratings was put into question. Despite the troublesome surveys and studies of the late '80s, the problem of zapping was largely ignored in the industry, just like the controversy about people meters.[3]

The People Meters Debate

The rise of segmentation in audience research resulted in an era of increasing competition, speeding up the development of research technology. In the late 1980s, regular measurements of ratings and shares were offered by A. C. Nielsen Co. and American Research Bureau (Arbitron) in more than 200 American TV markets, while Audits of Great Britain (AGB) and ScanAmerica (a joint venture of Arbitron and Time Inc.) tried to break into the research market.

Ratings measured by electronic people meters proved far lower than expected. In the 1987–88 season, the decline cost the Big Three $50 million in lost advertising revenue; in 1990, $200 million. As advertisers began to experiment with new distribution channels that were less costly and more efficient, new research efforts proliferated (from passive people meter and TV commercial tracking systems to single-source data and passive people meter).

After a bitter fight for market share in 1993, Nielsen captured the monopoly in the delivery of all TV ratings, and the TV networks decided to take ratings into their own hands. In February 1994 the Big Three announced that they would fund a three-year, $30 million project—managed by Statistical Research Inc. (SRI), which had had a bigger profile in radio ratings—to create the next-generation television ratings system.[4]

Redistribution of Television Advertising

In 1950, when the U.S. gross national product was $288 billion, total ad volume was 1.98% of GNP, while TV ad volume formed 3% of total ad

Table 2-1
Broadcast and Cable Television Advertising (1950–93)

Year	Grand Total	Broadcast TV					Cable TV		
		Total	Network TV	Nat'l spot	Nat'l synd.	Local spot	Total	Nat'l Cable	Local Cable
($mil)									
1993	30,584	28,020	9,369	7,800	2,416	8,435	2,564	1,970	594
1992	29,409	27,249	9,549	7,551	2,070	8,079	2,160	1,685	475
1991	27,402	25,521	8,993	7,110	1,853	7,565	1,941	1,521	420
1990	28,405	26,616	9,383	7,788	1,589	7,856	1,789	1,393	396
1989	26,891	25,364	9,110	7,354	1,288	7,612	1,527	1,197	330
1988	25,686	24,490	9,172	7,147	901	7,270	1,196	942	254
1987	23,904	22,941	8,500	6,846	762	6,833	963	760	203
1986	22,881	22,026	8,342	6,570	600	6,514	855	676	179
1985	21,022	20,298	8,060	6,004	520	5,714	724	594	130
1984	19,848	19,310	8,318	5,488	420	5,084	538	458	80
1983	16,759	16,427	6,955	4,827	300	4,345	332	282	50
1982	14,636	14,423	6,144	4,364	150	3,765	213	181	32
1981	12,846	12,729	5,540	3,746	75	3,368	117	100	17
1980	11,469	11,416	5,130	3,269	50	2,967	53	45	8
1970	3,596	3,596	1,658	1,234	–	704	–	–	–
1960	1,627	1,627	820	527	–	280	–	–	–
1950	171	171	85	31	–	55	–	–	–
(%)									
1993	100	92	31	26	8	28	8	6	2
1990	100	94	33	27	6	28	6	5	1
1970	100	100	46	34	–	20	–	–	–
1960	100	100	50	32	–	17	–	–	–
1950	100	100	50	18	–	32	–	–	–

SOURCE: Compiled from Television Bureau of Advertising research trend reports (McCann-Erickson).

volume. By 1987 the GNP had increased to $4,540 billion and total ad volume to 2.42% of GNP—but both total ad volume and TV ad volume were about to begin a slow decline (see Table 2–1).

Prior to the rise of cable, TV advertising had been synonymous with *broadcast* TV advertising. Prior to the mid-'80s, what the networks lost in audiences, they regained in pricing; in the long run, the strategy turned the advertising business against the Big Three and prompted a search for alternative outlets.[5] In the years 1982–86, the portion of TV ad volume peaked in total advertising (22% or more), but the action was in cable and syndication.

After the mid-'80s, audience erosion prevented the Big Three from covering ad losses with higher pricing. While annual growth in broadcast advertising hardly exceeded inflation between 1985 and 1990, cable advertising nearly doubled. From 1980 to 1993, the portion of broadcast TV in total TV advertising fell from 99.5% to 91.6%, whereas that of cable TV increased from 0.5% to 8.4%. Still, cable and national syndication failed to compete with network advertising, which continued to dominate mass markets.

Changes in Distribution

Until the 1980s, American television was near-synonymous with broadcast TV distribution that consisted of three basic players: the network owned-and-operated stations (O&Os) and affiliates (mostly VHF stations); group owners (mainly VHF stations, many UHF stations); and independents (mainly UHF stations). The distribution system of the Big Three dominated in more than 200 television markets.

Networks. Until the '80s, the largest first movers (the Big Three and a few group station owners) were the main beneficiaries of the FCC's station allocation policies. In addition to the O&Os, network affiliates were vital for new entrants hoping to secure distribution for their programming.

In the past, many of the nation's 600+ network affiliates had been virtual money machines, but when the networks began to lose ground, so did their affiliates. Network audiences migrated to cable, while affiliates were threatened by independent TV stations, syndicators, and cable operators. Collectively, the Big Three lost money on networks in 1991, for the first time ever.

In the past, affiliate stations were the networks' distribution system. With the proliferation of indie stations and the rapid expansion of the Fox Broadcasting Company (FBC) from 1980 to 1990, the number of total stations soared from 734 to 1,088. Meanwhile, the number of affiliates increased only from 615 to 648. Thus, the network proportion of broadcast TV stations plunged from 84% to 60%. In the new environment, they formed the core distribution system (broadcast affiliates), which was being supplemented by various auxiliary delivery systems (cable systems, pay-per-view).

Group Owners. In addition to the Big Three and FBC, group owners in the early 1990s included major players such as Tribune, Group W, Cox, Gannett, and Chris-Craft. With cable expansion and ownership changes, group owners began to shop UHF stations. From 1984 to 1990 the number of UHF stations controlled by group owners almost doubled (even if market expansion eroded group owners' dominance). By 1990 the number of group owners had increased to 207 and 77% of the top 100 markets were group owned. While only 9 group owners reached 5–10% of the nation's TV households, 118 garnered less than 1%.[6]

Independent Stations. Prior to 1980 less than a third of U.S. TV households had more than three VHF assignments. Program suppliers could reach a national audience only through the Big Three. In the '80s the absolute growth of broadcast TV stations, and the increased efficiency of the UHF stations as distributors, prompted a dramatic increase of independent stations—that is, stations not affiliated with or owned by a network. Following changes in ownership requirements, the growing indie marketplace was attracting bigger players, especially those building a "fourth network" (FBC), or eager to raise stakes in the syndication business (Paramount, Disney). The boom period came to an end in the mid-'80s. The bust of the indie marketplace was followed by a slow revival in the late '80s and early '90s.[7]

With the maturing of the cable business, the Big Three in 1992 regained a slice of the audience they had lost—for the first time since the rapid growth of the cable industry. While, in 1992–93, the combined share of the Big Three shrank to 60% (with Fox, to 69%), the defection went to tiny cable channels. Still, advertisers regarded network television as the most effective way to reach mass audiences.[8]

From Network Takeovers to Profit Squeeze

With the shift of consensus on antitrust and regulatory objectives, the 1980s saw increasing efforts toward vertical integration and the Big Three were eager to join the bandwagon. The FCC's new interpretation of the Communications Act of 1934 presumed that free market competition would be more effective than government regulation, while public interest was identified with the marketplace.

Deregulation, the M&A Wave, and Ownership Limits. The old 7-7-7 Rule (7 AM, 7 FM, 7 TV stations per single owner) survived from the early 1950s to 1984, when the FCC raised the station ownership limits to 12 AM, 12 FM, and 12 TV stations. The broadcast business was swept by the M&A wave. The increase in station transactions went hand in hand with the financial boom climaxing at $7.5 billion in 1987 (see Table 2–2).

By the early '90s the peak was followed by a rapid decline and a recession. While the prices and pace of broadcast acquisitions declined, cable deal-making continued. With the influx of new equity money and the relaxation of ownership rules in 1993, TV and radio station sales totaled $3.3 billion. While television boomed, the shakeout continued in radio; loosening the duopoly restrictions, the FCC allowed owners to "double up" in markets where they already owned property.

Network Takeovers. From the late 1940s to the early 1980s, commercial broadcast television had been dominated by the oligopoly of the Big Three—the first movers in the business:

- In 1926, Radio Corporation of America's (RCA) radio group, headed by David Sarnoff, created the *National Broadcasting Company* (NBC)—the first U.S. company organized to operate a broadcasting network.
- In 1928, United Independent Broadcasters (UIB) was acquired by William S. Paley, who developed the purchase into *Columbia Broadcasting System* (CBS). Until the mid-'70s, American television was dominated by the duopoly of NBC and CBS.

Table 2-2

Station Transactions: Dollar Volume of Transactions, Number of Stations (1954–93)*

| Year | ------ $ mil. -------- | | | Total | ------ # ------- | | |
	Radio	Groups**	TV		Radio	Groups**	TV
1993	$815.5	$756.7	$1,728.7	$3,301	633	na	101
1992	603.2	318.2	124.0	1,045	667	24	41
1991	534.7	207.0	273.4	1,015	793	61	38
1990	868.6	411.0	697.0	1,977	1,045	60	75
1989	1,148.5	533.6	1,541.1	3,235	663	40	84
1988	1,841.6	1,326.3	1,780.0	4,948	845	106	70
1987	1,236.4	4,611.0	1,661.8	7,509	775	132	59
1986	1,490.1	1,993.0	2,709.5	6,193	959	192	128
1985	1,414.8	962.5	3,291.0	5,668	1,558	218	99
1984	977.0	234.5	1,252.0	2,118	782	2	82
1983	621.1	332.0	1,902.7	2,855	669	10	61
1982	470.7	0	527.7	998	597	0	30
1981	447.8	78.4	228.0	754	625	6	24
1980	339.6	27.0	534.2	876	424	3	35
1970	86.3	1.0	87.5	175	268	3	19
1960	51.8	24.6	22.9	99	345	10	21

* Transactions approved by the FCC.
** Figures represent group deals involving combinations of radio and TV stations, multiple TV stations or multiple radio stations. Starting in 1993, the Radio column includes only standalone AM and FM deals and the Groups column contains AM-FM combos and all other multiple station deals. In previous year, the AM-FM combos were included under Radio.

SOURCE: Compiled from Broadcasting (various issues).

• NBC had been organized as two semiautonomous networks. The third major commercial network came about in 1943, when NBC, following the FCC's chain broadcasting investigation, was forced to divest its weaker network (the Blue Network). The *American Broadcasting Company* (ABC) remained behind NBC and CBS into the mid-'70s, due to its less comprehensive distribution system.

After the ownership changes in the mid-'80s, the Big Three were taken over by major U.S. corporations, in just nine months. As one observer put it, "Each of the acquirers pledged to run these huge television machines in a more businesslike fashion than before, with fewer frills and executive prerequisites, less staff, greater cost control and strict attention to bottom line."[9]

Capital Cities/ABC. In March 1985, for the first time in 30 years, a TV network was sold. In the then-largest U.S. merger, Capital Cities Communications, a $1+ billion media conglomerate, purchased ABC in a $3.5 billion transaction. The new owners brought a cost-conscious and decentralizing management philosophy into the freewheeling ABC.

Loew's Corp./CBS. In October 1985 Laurence A. Tisch of Loews Corporation increased his firm's share of CBS stock from 12% to 25%. As CBS, a $5 billion company, spent nearly $1 billion to fend off a takeover attempt by Ted Turner, it ousted its chairman and installed Tisch, a nonbroadcaster, as acting CEO, titularly under chairman William Paley.

General Electric/RCA-NBC. In June 1986, in a $6.5 billion deal, NBC parent RCA merged with General Electric (GE), a $28 billion conglomerate. GE soon named Robert Wright, a GE insider, as CEO.

As network takeovers transformed the broadcast TV business, deregulation intensified the competitive environment. Cable TV corroded broadcast TV's share of its prime-time audience, the number of indie stations exploded, syndication grew dramatically in stature, and Rupert Murdoch built the "fourth network" (FBC).

Fox Broadcasting Network (FBC). Fox Broadcasting Company was established in 1986 to provide first-run original entertainment programming to indie TV stations. By 1994 Fox's coverage of TV homes stood at 96%. Prior to the emergence of FBC, a unit of News Corp., all major attempts to launch a permanent fourth TV network (from the Dumont Network of the '50s to the United Network of the '60s) had failed, due to deficiencies in distribution and regulatory barriers. Prior to mergers, broadcasting had been a mature industry characterized by high levels of free cash flow, falling or low earnings but little debt. Network takeovers heralded a new era of restructuring and divestitures.[10]

Profit Squeeze

Network revenues reflect shifts in prime time ratings, ad volumes, and the consumer price index. Networks' revenue growth declined almost consistently from 22% to near zero from 1976 to 1986 (pretax income manifested negative growth by the mid-'80s). Despite the erosion, the annual growth of expenses amounted to 17–21% until the mid-'80s. By late 1991, CBS and NBC were put on the block. Only ABC remained profitable, while the Big Three collectively posted losses (See Table 2–3).

Diversification. Prior to network takeovers, CBS and ABC were essentially broadcast companies, whereas NBC constituted a segment at RCA. In the posttakeover environment, all networks became subsidiaries of major (diversified) U.S. corporations:

- Through the '80s, CapCities/ABC's broadcast group brought in about 65–74% of total revenues for the company. In the early '90s, the portion rose to 82%.

- CBS's asset divestitures led to a dramatic consolidation, with the proportion of broadcast revenues growing from 35% to 100% between 1980 and 1987. The shift rendered the company vulnerable to changes in business cycles.

- With GE as its parent, NBC's broadcast revenues declined from the premerger 24% to the postmerger 6–7%. In the early '90s, the portion declined to 5%.

- In News Corp., FBC's revenue strength increased gradually from 7% in 1983 to

Table 2-3
Network Finances (1980–93)

Year	Radio Nets	Radio Stats	TV Net	O&O	Cab	Total	Radio Nets	Radio Stats	TV Net	O&O	Cab	Total
	-------- Revenues ($mil) --------						------ Profits ($mil) ----------					
ABC												
1993	152	193	2730	807	781	4663	38	46	184	418	139	825
1992	142	175	2510	767	672	4266	25	39	92	385	127	6ь7
1991	149	169	2630	765	617	4330	39	35	120	399	124	716
1990	134	176	2606	822	546	4284	32	44	240	413	102	831
1989	127	174	2415	781	385	3856	31	48	226	405	121	839
1988	125	178	2382	770	340	3795	24	48	178	417	100	767
CBS												
1993	60	212	2732	506	–	3510	2	32	238	180	–	451
1992	57	207	2736	503	–	3503	(5)	27	5	175	–	202
1991	62	184	2388	401	–	3035	0.5	29	(439)	140	–	271
1990	60	190	2576	436	–	3261	2	35	(253)	166	–	(50)
1989	57	172	2320	414	–	2965	4	31	na	158	–	na
1988	57	153	2185	382	–	2777	8	29	43	152	–	232
NBC												
1993	–	–	2421	587	94	3102	–	–	45	243	31	319
1992	–	–	2698	585	80	3363	–	–	51	245	(37)	259
1991	–	–	2531	555	35	3121	–	–	(50)	219	(15)	154
1990	–	–	2638	598	–	3236	–	–	249	257	(29)	477
1989	–	–	2510	604	–	3405	–	–	365	270	–	605
1988	–	–	2185	590	–	3608	–	–	280	257	–	537

Year	NBC	CBS	ABC	Tot.	NBC	CBS	ABC	Tot.	NBC	CBS	ABC	Tot
	-- Revenues --				-- Expenses --				-- Pretax Income --			
86	2400	2237	2080	6717	2160	2161	2030	6351	240	76	50*	366
85	2150	2288	2165	6603	1963	2057	2010	6030	187	231	155	573
84	1930	2240	2640	6810	1830	1960	2380	6170	100	280	260	640
83	1700	1952	2073	5725	1645	1762	1838	5245	55	190	235	480
82	1500	1770	1861	5131	1475	1600	1651	4726	25	170	210	405
81	1242	1432	1563	4237	1282	1272	1348	3902	(40)	160	215	335
80	950	1390	1560	3900	945	1260	1369	3574	5	130	191	326

Cab = NBC's cable operations, ABC's video enterprises. O&O = owned-and-operated stations. Radio Nets = Radio networks. Radio Stats = Radio stations. Total = Total broadcast group. TV Net = TV network.

* Due to accounting (CapCities' acquisition of ABC), the network shows a gain rather than a loss.

SOURCE: Broadcasting (various issues); company reports.

13% in 1990 (including News Corp.'s European TV operations). In the early '90s, the portion rose to 15%.

After network takeovers, the Big Three cultivated harvest and divest strategies. The pattern and pace, however, differed. CBS resorted to rapid divestitures; although NBC used a harvest strategy to divest radio units and to invest in cable, the network's profitability declined drastically in the early '90s; ABC sought increasing profitability through demographics rather than ratings per se; and, after startup difficulties, FBC focused on cost leadership in youth-oriented markets.

With the continuing recession suppressing advertising revenues and entertainment program costs out of control, even Hollywood studios had little interest in buying the Big Three. Due to regulatory obstacles (fin-syn rules) they would have had to divest current businesses (syndication, cable) that were more profitable than network business.

By 1992 a combined TV network profit for the Big Three amounted to only $146 million, on revenue of almost $8 billion. Hence, the networks' increasing interest in strategic alliances with cable companies.[11]

Hybrid Affiliates and More Networks

The FCC had barred broadcast TV networks from owning cable systems as early as 1970, when the Big Three still had 90% of the prime-time audience. By the early '90s the competitive environment had drastically changed, as had the FCC. Broadcasters joined cable in joint ventures and revenue-sharing schemes.

By mid-1992 the FCC voted to allow broadcast TV networks to buy local cable TV systems, a move that could hasten a realignment of the television industry. It could also alter the historic relationship between the networks and local affiliates, which feared that the networks would favor pay-per-view systems with their most expensive shows and leave them with less popular low-cost shows.[12]

Around 1992–93, a number of powerful M&E players began to explore how to meld TV station groups by making program production companies and cable systems into hybrid networks. The idea was to build a fifth network to achieve a competitive edge prior to the coming of electronic superhighways, as well as to erode the viewer shares of Fox and the Big Three. The first candidates included Paramount (which planned to join forces with Chris-Craft Industries), as well as Warner Bros. (WB) (with Tribune), TCI, and QVC Networks. By April 1994 Paramount had signed 36 affiliates, against WB's 24; a month later, the team that launched the Fox network was reunited for the launch of the WB network.[13]

In the early '90s the decline of network business rendered it volatile and susceptible to price warfare. Typically, the networks sought growth by adding stakes in foreign television.[14]

In May 1994, in a sweeping realignment of the TV industry, Fox announced it would form a new alliance with a broadcast station group (New World Communications Group Inc., controlled by financier Ronald O. Perelman) that would result in the defection of eight CBS stations to Fox. In exchange, Murdoch agreed to invest $500 million for a minority stake in New World, which was trying to become a TV programming powerhouse as well as a station owner. In the "new" rivalry, ABC had 227 affiliates, NBC 213, CBS 206, and Fox 184 (of which 34 were partial affiliates).

The realignment prompted the Big Three to add pressure on the FCC to relax TV ownership rules that prevented them from owning more than 12 stations or covering over 25% of the country. In other words, Fox's move resulted in increasing consolidation.[15]

Murdoch's "raid" forced CBS into a scramble for affiliates in several crucial markets, which could spark a chain reaction of network-hopping. Even more importantly, Fox's strategic move reflected the unraveling of the network-affiliate relationship and the emerging distribution struggle among the major U.S. M&E companies.

By 1994 TV networks were no longer considered "dinosaurs." Instead, they had proved they could hold onto both a mass audience and a $9 billion share of the $25 billion annual TV advertising pie. In fact, the Big Three were about to post their highest collective operating profits in five years.[16]

The change anticipated the collapse of the financial interest and syndication rules no later than November 1995 when the networks could finally sell TV programs they owned (reruns *and* new syndicated series) throughout the United States. As investment banks were lining up to combine the Big Three with major studios (or even the telcos), capital flew back into the marketplace.

After years of a depressed economy, increased cable competition, and a proposed information highway that seemed to bypass broadcasters, station values, revenues, and audiences all were on the rise. No longer dinosaurs, TV networks dreamed of a return to happier days.[17] In fact, they were being circled by Hollywood studios, eager to ensure an extensive distribution pipeline for their product in the coming electronic superhighways.

Network Radio

In the years 1960–90, the number of commercial radio stations in the United States more than doubled from 4,144 to 9,379. The most important shift was the increasing popularization of the higher quality FM radio with the ensuing decline of the AM radio in the '70s. In 1960, AM stations dominated commercial radio, representing more than 80% of total stations; by 1990 the portions of AM and FM stations were near-equal, but FM radio stations collectively had three-quarters of the U.S. radio audience.[1]

Format Specialization: Audience Segmentation

As the first medium to gain widespread popularity, AM radio served as the vehicle of mass marketing in the 1920s. From the beginning, AM radio programming was characterized by format specialization.

With a shift to album-oriented pop music radio (the Beatles, the counterculture) and its high-fidelity stereo-signal capability, FM radio became the medium of choice of the rapidly expanding population of teens and young adults. Starting in the late 1960s, the proliferation of FM radio boosted format fragmentation. By the '80s, segmentation solidified popular formats, such as "Country," "Adult Contemporary," "News/Talk," "Top 40," "Album-Oriented Rock," and "Urban Contemporary."[2]

A Polarized Industry

In absolute terms, radio advertising doubled in the '80s, increasing to more than $8.7 billion in 1990; in relative terms, it represented about 7% of total ad volume in the United States (as it had since 1968). Since the late '70s, some 75% of radio advertising had been local; spot advertising accounted for almost 19%; networks garnered the remaining 6% (a steady rise from the record low of 3.8% in 1974).[3]

Starting in the early '80s, the growth of cable TV, telephone marketing, as well as other new forms of targeted advertising spurred intense competition for ad dollars. Following the FCC's mid-'80s deregulation, radio operators went on an acquisition binge. When ad revenue dried up, many stations got into trouble and a crushing debt burden caused one station after another to go off the air. Financially, radio became a sick industry.

While most stations were losing money, the business became polarized into two groups: big broadcasters thrived, small stations disappeared. In the '80s the FCC licensed 2,000 new stations, which brought the total to 10,800. The top 50 stations (less than 0.5% of the total) generated 11% of the industry revenues and half of its profits.[4] By 1992 the FCC hoped to stem the decline of commercial radio by easing ownership regulations. Consolidation would increase industry efficiency and strengthen big broadcasting companies.[5]

Radio Networks

In the post-World War II era, four major radio networks (NBC, CBS, Mutual, and ABC) owned more than 95% of all network stations. The peak phase was followed by a rapid decline to a record low of 23% in 1966. By 1980 the portion of the four networks grew to 40%. With network takeovers and the sale of the NBC Radio Networks in 1987, continuity in the business was finally broken.

Despite consolidations among networks, the (revenue-based) top hierarchy of major radio companies changed very little between the mid-'80s and early '90s. The major players were diversified broadcast TV and print corporations, with most garnering less than 10% of their media revenues from the radio industry. Having bought NBC Radio Networks and Mutual Broadcasting System, Westwood One was the only radio network that generated all of its revenues from the radio business.

Although they dodged much of the recession of the late '80s and early

'90s, radio networks in 1992 suffered from an advertising slump that caused their first down year since 1982. Still, the radio networks seemed well positioned for the future. Unlike broadcast TV networks, they had not lost listeners to rival media. In 1993 the industry continued to account for 6.7% of total ad volume in the United States; some 78% of radio advertising remained local. The business was also attracting new investors, such as Kohlberg, Kravis, Roberts and Company (KKR) which began buying radio stations in 1991.

By late 1993 consolidation was rapidly changing the landscape of American radio, with new powerhouses like Shamrock Broadcasting, the Disney family's radio group which had 21 stations and $110 million in annual billings, making it radio's fifth largest. Concurrently, Infinity Broadcasting, already the nation's biggest owner and operator of radio stations, announced a three-way deal that would give it control of both Westwood One and the Unistar Radio Networks. Running a star-studded network that rivaled ABC Radio in size and revenue, the Westwood-Unistar-Infinity umbrella employed shock jocks Howard Stern and Don Imus; talk hosts Larry King, Bruce Williams, Pat Buchanan, and G. Gordon Liddy; and countdown king Casey Kassem.[6]

In 1993 CBS maintained its first-place spot among the top radio groups, with 21 stations and 14.7 million listeners. It was followed by Infinity (25 stations, 13.4 million listeners), CapCities/ABC (18 stations, 11.8 million listeners), as well as Group W, Shamrock, Viacom, and Cox. The radio industry was dominated by major U.S. M&E companies.[7]

Radio's new ownership limits led to consolidation in many medium-size markets, pushed up station trading and values, and caused radio revenues to rebound. Combining station functions and cutting operating costs, consolidation also reduced total employment in commercial radio by 12% from 1989 to 1992. Concurrently, nationally syndicated talk radio programs, an inexpensive way to fill airtime with "quality programming," were booming, driven by the successful duo of Rush Limbaugh and Howard Stern; under the wings of Judith Regan, Simon & Schuster's editor and former reporter for the *National Enquirer*, both shock jocks were also leading the bestseller lists (*Private Parts* and *See, I Told You So*, respectively). The new ownership rules were transforming but not drastically changing the industry.

THE BIG THREE NETWORKS

CAPITAL CITIES/ABC: FROM HUNTER TO HUNTED?

If the American Broadcasting Company (renamed ABC in 1965) was a product of classic antitrust policy, it was nearly devastated by the very same policy. ABC was created in 1943, by Edward J. Noble, the maker of Life

Savers candy, when he purchased radio's Blue Network, which RCA-owned NBC was forced to shed, following the Federal Communication Commission's monopoly investigation. ABC's survival was sustained by the Paramount decrees (1948), another antitrust battle that made possible the merger of the nascent network and United Paramount Theaters, whose president, Leonard Goldenson, became president of the new entity, AB-PT. Indeed, it was Goldenson who steered ABC from a third position to competitive equality in the late '70s, and to the merger with Capital Cities in the mid-'80s.[1]

The Third Network: Years of Struggle

As the infant "third network," ABC was forced to innovate in order to survive. Hence, its demographic approach in product development, a decade before CBS and NBC. From *The Fugitive* and *Maverick* to *Ben Casey* and *77 Sunset Strip*, ABC's entire slate had a more youthful look.

The 1960s saw an expansion of ABC's programming. While Goldenson boosted ABC News to enhance the network image, Roone Arledge and ABC Sports played a crucial role in the network's growth into a competitive third network. With *Peyton Place*, the first prime-time soap opera, ABC increased its ratings, if only temporarily. Meanwhile, ABC Radio achieved a near-revolution in network radio broadcasting with four different, non-competing services. By the end of the '70s the number of its affiliates had soared to 1,600. Its AM and FM broadcast operations were the most successful in the business.

In December 1965, ABC and ITT agreed on the "largest merger in the history of communications," but, after more than two years of procedural delays, ITT backed out. Suffering from increasing financial problems, ABC still lacked color broadcasting. Until the mid-'70s its competitiveness depended on theatrical movie nights and made-for-TV movies.

Without a powerful parent company, ABC resorted to aggressive risk taking. With its "business portfolio approach," it launched a different business plan for each daypart, engaging in both cost-cutting and investment. In 1972, ABC's reorganization made it the least bureaucratic of the Big Three. Under Elton Rule, new president and chief operating officer (COO), division presidents dealt directly with the top. Soon rivals emulated ABC's new organizational structure.

From 1974 to 1980, ABC added or switched some 70 TV stations, reaching distribution parity with its rivals. Fred Silverman intensified ABC's rise to network leadership with able programming talent. Moreover, the new "family viewing hour" policy contributed to ABC's first audience leadership in 1976–77, with sitcoms like *Happy Days* and fantasy adventure like *The Six Million Dollar Man*. Billings jumped from $700 million to over $3 billion. Besides sitcoms and drama, ABC's success was riven by the rise of miniseries (*QB VII*, *Rich Man, Poor Man*, *Roots*, and *The Winds of War*); an exclusive deal with Aaron Spelling Productions (from *Charlie's Angels* to *Dynasty*); Roone Arledge's ABC News (costly talent raids turned broadcast journalists into Hollywood stars); and new franchises that Arledge created by building programs around ABC's news talent (Barbara Walters in *20/ 20*, *World News Tonight* with Peter Jennings, *This Week with David Brinkley*, Ted Koppel's *Nightline*, Sam Donaldson in *Primetime Live*). By the late '70s ABC dominated the prime-time market. Revenues amounted to over $2 million and net income to $159 million.

Merger Turmoil

In the past, ABC had supplemented its broadcasting revenues with those of nonbroadcasting operations in publishing, theatres, records, scenic attractions and theme parks, as well as real estate. Like CBS, it aimed to achieve 50% of total revenues and profits from nonbroadcasting revenues. Through diversification, the two networks also sought to protect themselves against the Nixon administration, special interest groups, and technological developments.

In 1979 ABC had an opportunity to expand its publishing holdings, but the billion-dollar unit decided against the acquisition of Macmillan, presumably for cost reasons. By the mid-'80s nonbroadcasting operations had been divested. With few exceptions, ABC reemerged as a "pure" broadcasting company.

By the early '80s ABC operated in four major business segments: broadcasting, publishing, new media technology, and other operations. These segments entailed six separate operations and more than 20 subsidiaries. Though a divisionalized company, ABC got 90% of its revenues from broadcasting. The remaining 10% helped to fund start-up costs of strategic new projects.

Rejecting the hardware side of the business (where it lacked expertise), ABC poured funds into ABC Video Enterprises (Hearst/ABC Video, Telefirst, ESPN), which provided programming for new technologies, like video cassettes, video discs, and cable networks (including Arts & Entertainment [A&E], Lifetime). ABC's greatest success in cable came through its involvement with ESPN.

After his first heart attack in 1971, Leonard Goldenson had distanced himself from ABC's daily operations. At the turn of the '80s, high interest rates, cable TV's coming growth, and the ensuing plunge of ABC stock forced him to return to the network. In 1981 Goldenson signed another four-year contract as ABC chairman and chief executive officer (CEO). A year later, *Forbes* published a cover story on "ABC's Leonard Goldenson: A Shrewd Strategy for Staying on Top."[2] In reality, ABC had begun a steady decline. Except for Spelling's popular shows (*Three's Company, The*

Love Boat, Dynasty, and *Hotel*), ABC had few hits in the early '80s. Innovation flourished elsewhere (news, daytime, children's programming, miniseries, and made-for-TV movies). Despite record revenues and profits from the Los Angeles Olympics, a weak prime time schedule pushed ABC back to third position.

The decline of ABC stock attracted corporate raiders and market speculators around the network, most notably Loews Corporation's Laurence Tisch (who had been a go-between in the failed ITT-ABC merger). Following Goldenson's request, Tisch sold most of his stock. By 1983, most of ABC's outstanding common stock was held by large institutional investors, with less than 2% owned by ABC management. Lew Wasserman wanted to merge MCA with the network, but Goldenson rejected the offer.

When the FCC unveiled its proposal to deregulate TV station ownership in August 1984, ABC was "in play." In December, Thomas Murphy, Capital Cities chairman, met Goldenson and suggested a merger.

Capital Cities Communications

In 1954 Frank Smith and some 20 other investors purchased a near-bankrupt UHF broadcast TV station in Albany, New York. Smith's acquisition spree of valuable but undermanaged assets boosted the rise of Capital Cities Communications (CCC). In 1960, when Thomas Murphy moved to CCC's headquarters in New York, he was succeeded by Daniel Burke in Albany. The two began a successful partnership.[3]

Even after Smith's death in 1965, Murphy continued his strategy of growth-by-acquisition. Three years later, CCC branched into publishing with Fairchild Publications, a fairly large company that owned *Women's Wear Daily* and seven other titles. In 1970 the $100 million purchase of Triangle Broadcasting turned CCC into a major force in U.S. broadcasting.

As ABC's largest single affiliate group, CCC enjoyed the benefits of the Silverman era without any of the costs. Instead of paying dividends to their public shareholders, Murphy and Burke reinvested the profits from television into newspapers and other media properties. In 1980–81, CCC got into the cable industry, acquiring almost 50 cable franchises. While Murphy was credited with the acquisition spree, Burke played an important role in the purchase process. Both relied on the advice of Warren Buffett, the investor wizard who had a major interest in CCC.

Broadcasters considered CCC a public-spirited enterprise, whereas, in the newspaper industry where profit margins remained lower and acquisitions were more recent, it was regarded as a union-busting cost-cutter. On Wall Street, CCC had a reputation of a tightly run, broad-based, billion-dollar company. CCC's clout was enhanced by Murphy and business associates Buffett, Tisch, Katharine Graham (of the *Washington Post*), and the like.

The Merger

Despite the fluctuation of its fortunes after the Silverman years, ABC's revenues soared from $1.1 billion to $3.7 billion in the years 1975 to 1984. Some 89% of profits came from broadcasting and 9% from publishing, whereas video enterprises, scenic attractions, and other businesses accounted for just 2% of revenues. In the process, ABC's debt ratio decreased from 37% to less than 9% (which attracted an increasing number of raiders).

Following the 1985 Super Bowl, Robert Bass made a major purchase of ABC stock. The Bass brothers had diversified out of oil and real estate and expanded rapidly in M&E businesses (a major stake in Disney). Since the fin-syn rules might not permit one owner to control both a motion picture studio and a TV network, Goldenson managed to deflect the attack. Other candidates followed, including Gulf + Western, Gannett, Coca-Cola, and Pepsico. After his 79th birthday in December 1984, Goldenson himself approached IBM (which rejected the offer to buy the network).

In February 1985 Murphy called Goldenson again to talk about a merger. He also called Buffett. He needed a long-term equity investor who would not sell, just like the Sulzberger family protected the *New York Times*. Buffett committed $517 million of his Berkshire Hathaway, Inc. money, his largest investment ever, to purchase 17% of the merged CCC/ABC.[4]

By March 1985 Murphy and Goldenson agreed on $118 per share ($530 million over the initial $3 billion bid). In numbers, CapCities, a mouse, was swallowing ABC, a cat. The takeover took place in a controlled manner that enabled Goldenson to keep his company relatively intact. With Murphy and Burke, he also solved the succession problem.

Four years after the merger, CCC/ABC was a money machine. An initial share of Capital Cities stock, issued in 1957 at $5.75, was worth more than $4,000 in 1990. But the network misfired.

An Era of Uncertainty

By 1990 CCC/ABC had fared better than its two rival networks. The results stemmed from restructuring in ABC and a compromise with CCC's management philosophy.

From Decentralization to Restructuring

A few weeks after the deal, advertising sales throughout the industry collapsed. Initially, too, CCC's decentralization contributed to problems. ABC proceeded with program production, while being aware of the coming losses (e.g., the costly miniseries *War and Remembrance*, $30 million; the Communist-invasion flop *Amerika*, $20 million; the 1988 Winter Olympics, $75 million). The new management took a hands-on role. Burke concentrated on broad, postmerger problems and Murphy on the network. Focus shifted from the ratings struggle, which ABC had fought with little regard to costs, to building profits. Next, they started pruning perks, payrolls, and expenses. The reductions cut ABC's projected loss of $150 million to $70 million in 1986, but resulted in a "culture clash."

Prior to 1985, CCC's revenues exceeded $1 billion. The merger with ABC raised revenues to over $4.1 billion in 1986, and to nearly $5.4 billion in 1990.

Diversification: Business Segments

Before the merger with ABC, publishing accounted for 63% of CCC's net revenues. Yet the company got 52% of its net income from broadcasting and only 48% from publishing. CCC saw its future in broadcasting rather than publishing. In its first merger year, CCC/ABC earned 77% of its net revenues from broadcasting, and only 23% from publishing. The relative proportion of broadcasting grew steadily to 82% in the early '90s, while publishing declined to 18% (See Table 2–4).

Broadcasting. By 1994 CCC/ABC's broadcasting operations consisted of the ABC Television Network Group, the Broadcast Group, the Cable (ESPN, A&E, Lifetime) and International Broadcast Group (joint ventures in foreign-based TV operations), and the Multimedia Group. The broadcast group comprised eight TV stations (and 230 primary affiliated stations); 18 radio stations (which continued as industry leaders and served about 3,400 affiliates nationwide). At the turn of the '90s, the profitability of the TV network was severely strained by a decline in national advertising revenues, higher programming costs, and substantial sports losses. Increasing revenues of ABC's video group and cuts in network compensation prompted conflicts with the affiliates.

Publishing. CCC/ABC's publishing operations comprised two groups: Newspapers and Shopping Guides (8 daily newspapers, almost 80 weekly newspapers, over 60 shopping guides and real estate magazines), and Specialized Publications (diversified publications, Fairchild fashion and merchandising group, financial services, and medical group). The effect of the 1991 ad recession was more severe on print than on other media.

In 1994 CCC/ABC created a Multimedia Group to explore using video and print material to create new programming and to explore investment opportunities in emerging multimedia and interactive technologies (equity stake in Yes! Entertainment, minority stake in Alpha Software). The division included a video publishing unit, which acquired rights to and produced programming for the home video market.

Table 2-4
Capital Cities/ABC: Business Segments (1983–93)

	--- Broadcasting ----		----- Publishing ----		----- Total --------	
	Net revenues	Income from operations	Net revenues	Income from operations	Net revenues	Income from operations*
($mil)						
1993	4,663	778	1,010	126	5,674	904
1992	4,266	619	1,079	136	5,344	756
1991	4,330	670	1,052	123	5,382	793
1990	4,284	830	1,102	132	5,386	963
1989	3,890	836	1,057	130	4,957	967
1988	3,750	722	1,024	130	4,773	852
1987	3,434	633	1,007	147	4,440	780
1986	3,154	475	971	159	4,124	634
1985	378	151	643	139	1,021	289
1984	348	144	592	133	940	277
1983	303	125	460	104	762	229
(%)						
1993	82	86	18	14	100	100
1992	80	82	20	18	100	100
1991	80	84	20	16	100	100
1990	80	87	20	13	100	100
1989	79	87	21	13	100	100
1988	79	85	21	15	100	100
1987	77	81	23	19	100	100
1986	77	75	23	25	100	100
1985	37	52	63	48	100	100
1984	37	52	63	48	100	100
1983	40	55	60	45	100	100

* Excluding general corporate expense.

SOURCE: Capital Cities/ABC, Inc.

Problem of Programming Costs

Although Capital Cities was able to turn ABC around organizationally, rising production costs remained a problem until Murphy and Burke reshaped the budget and cut back expensive one-time (sports) events that tended to be money-losers. As a result, Roone Arledge lost his sports presidency. In the 1985–86 season, ABC had popular new shows (*Who's the Boss?*, *Growing Pains*, *Moonlighting*), but it lacked the kind of locomotive comedies that were necessary to build an entire evening schedule. When Brandon Stoddard took over as president of ABC Entertainment in 1985, the network's prime-time fortunes plummeted, but Stoddard turned the schedule around with new shows, such as *Thirtysomething*, *China Beach*, and *The Wonder Years*. Like *Moonlighting*, most new product introductions were geared at a specific demographic section of the TV audience. ABC lifted itself out of third place with *Roseanne*, which captured prime-time leadership in the 1989–90 season.

In March 1989 Robert Iger became the new president of ABC Entertainment. To attract proven producers, Iger gambled with unlikely new series, such as *Twin Peaks*, a subversive melodrama thriller, and *CopRock*, the (short-lived) cop show done as a musical. While *Home Videos* generated high profits with low costs, the high-cost *Twin Peaks* enhanced ABC's high profile. Meanwhile, CCC/ABC poured over $1 billion into TV programming, attracting critical acclaim and significant audiences.[5]

With the demise of the fin-syn rules, CCC/ABC sought to increase its ownership rights of TV programs (hence CCC/ABC's joint venture with Brillstein-Grey Entertainment, one of Hollywood's leading talent firms, in 1994), while focusing on innovative research and development. Adapting to segmented marketing, ABC in 1990–91 rejected the overall household ratings as an outmoded measure for competition; the standard of success was the demographic breakdown favored by advertisers. "It's not worth being No. 1 in the household ratings if you're No. 3 in profits," said Iger.[6]

By the early '90s Roone Arledge's ABC News had a slate of prestigious and profitable news magazines (*Nightline, 20/20, Primetime Live*), as well as the highest-rated evening newscast. The success of *World News*, however, depended on the strength of ABC's O&O stations, which carried *The Oprah Winfrey Show* (the syndicated daytime talk show often led into the news blocks).

Burke's Era: Fluctuating Fortunes

In May 1990 Thomas Murphy turned 65 and stepped down as CEO (he remained chairman). Dan Burke was his successor. With $5.4 billion in revenue, CCC/ABC was thriving. The stock hit a high of $633, but, when Burke took over, it fell 23%. The Gulf War and recession kept advertisers cautious, which compelled the network to slash ad prices. Though losses were small compared with the other two networks, they raised questions on Burke's management abilities.

Through his 42% ownership in Berkshire Hathaway, Inc., Warren Buffett had an 18% stake in CCC/ABC. Despite his criticism of Wall Street's takeover mentality, Buffett joined the buccaneers. From 1977 to 1991, Berkshire Hathaway grew from a pool of $180 million to over $11 billion in risk capital. After the mid-'80s, some of his long-term investments plateaued or declined in value. While Buffett insisted that stock fluctuations had little bearing on these companies' intrinsic value, many holdings had peaked—including CCC/ABC.

From Strategic Scenarios to Murphy's Return

In fiscal 1991 CCC/ABC's earnings fell 28%, marking the first profit decrease since new management took over the network in 1986. When Murphy and Burke purchased the wasteful and overstaffed ABC in 1986, they assumed that prudence and problem-solving (which had worked at

Capital Cities) would do the job at ABC. In the short term, cost-cutting enhanced CCC/ABC's profitability; in the long term, it was not enough.

By December 1990 CCC/ABC's registration to float up to $500 million in debt raised the specter of speculation once again. The company was positioning itself for a possible acquisition of a studio, if the fin-syn rules were repealed.

Meanwhile, entertainment programming became CCC/ABC's fixation. Burke hoped to bring more creative, cost-effective approaches to negotiating sports rights fees and entertainment program productions, as well as managing ABC's entertainment, sports, and news operations.[7]

The pace of strategic activity increased around 1992–93, when CCC/ABC concluded that flat ad revenues indicated a continuing trend rather than a cyclical downturn. The future of the business depended on controlling costs and finding new revenue sources, domestically and internationally. While program production constituted the key to both, regulatory barriers (fin-syn rules) obstructed major investments in wholesale production.

Repositioning

In December 1992 CCC/ABC announced it was interested in buying a major Hollywood studio. With current assets and potential loans, it had a capacity to make an $8 billion deal. The announcement was perceived as an overture to solicit interest from Hollywood (i.e., Paramount). By February 1993 CCC/ABC and Turner Broadcasting were bidding jointly for the 1996 Summer Olympics in Atlanta and the network was among Turner's possible merger partners.

In 1993 ABC News announced a news-gathering partnership with BBC, and developed a new incentive plan for live clearances of *Nightline*, whose format evolved in a more investigative direction. In the fall season, Steven Bochco's new and racy series, *NYPD Blue*, generated considerable controversy and a wave of affiliate defections, although strong ratings brought advertisers back. Most importantly, ESPN, ABC's 80%-owned cable sports network, launched a major expansion. As if 4,500 hours of programming covering 65 sports was not enough, ESPN decided to introduce the youth-oriented ESPN2, or "The Deuce." Unlike ESPN, which took six years to stop losing money, ABC hoped to bring profitability faster to ESPN2.

As CCC/ABC announced a repurchase of 12% of its shares through a "Dutch auction," it was repositioning itself in the new merger environment. Of the 2 million shares the company wanted back, it got only 1.1 million (and 1 million of those belonged to majority holder Warren Buffett). After Murphy and Buffett found M&A targets like Paramount and Turner too expensive, debt repayment and self-investment became viable alternatives and the company itself turned into a potential acquisition candidate.

Meanwhile, succession problems deepened. Bob Iger, president of the ABC Television Network Group and CCC's executive VP, would not be the anointed heir. Instead, Murphy returned to CCC/ABC. In other words, the company needed time to plan for the transition.

In 1993 CCC/ABC doubled its internal prime-time production from the previous year to about 200 hours. While the activity reduced its cash reserves from about $1.7 billion to some $300 million, the company's $600 million in cash flow and $4 billion in borrowing power still meant substantial dealmaking capability, including a potential alliance with Disney, Turner, or even King World.[8]

GENERAL ELECTRIC/NBC: FROM BOOM TO BUST?

In the late 1920s, Radio Corporation of America, a former subsidiary of General Electric, was the most powerful vertically integrated M&E corporation in the United States. In the late 1950s RCA operated in manufacturing, broadcasting, and communications. The decline of the company began with the retirement in 1969 of David Sarnoff, who had steered RCA for half a century.[1]

Ultimately, Sarnoff himself contributed to the demise of the legendary company. A fervent believer in monopoly order, he became the victim of his own ideology. Not only did he fail to prepare RCA for competition; through foreign licensing, he also contributed to the coming industry leadership of Japanese consumer-electronics firms.

During the conglomerate era, the new management fought foreign competition and market maturity by diversifying into nonrelated business areas. Sarnoff's "old" RCA differed dramatically from the "new" RCA. The first one had long-term goals, diversified in related businesses, and sought growth through innovation. The new RCA focused on short-term goals, diversified in unrelated businesses, and associated growth with acquisition activity.

NBC Television Network

The National Broadcasting Company was forced to divest one of its networks (the core of the future ABC) following the FCC's monopoly investigations in the early '40s. Having experimented with television since 1925, RCA also got involved in every phase of the TV business, including broadcasting. NBC served as a marketing extension of the vertically integrated corporation. RCA's efforts to build and develop the network peaked and declined in the '50s—that is, with the first-generation TV sets.

Between 1968 and 1971, NBC achieved a tie with CBS in three consequent seasons; the shift from home ratings to demographics prompted NBC to renew product development and focus on younger and ethnic audiences (*The Flip Wilson Show, Sanford and Son, Rowan & Martin's Laugh-In, Julia*). The '70s, however, were dismal at NBC, which saw a rapid succession of top executives. As new president (1978–81), even Fred Silverman failed to replicate the success he had achieved at CBS and ABC.

The Merger: General Electric and RCA

Executive turmoil added to RCA's problems. In the mid-'70s the board replaced Robert Sarnoff, David Sarnoff's son, as chairman and CEO, with Anthony L. Conrad, whose brief reign was followed by that of another career employee. After Edgar H. Griffith offered to take early retirement in mid-1981, the board chose as his successor Thornton F. Bradshaw, an outside director of RCA, who accepted writeoffs in troubled business segments, sold noncore businesses, divested unrelated entities, and refocused RCA on electronics, communications, and entertainment. Bradshaw appointed Grant Tinker, the former head of MTM Productions, as NBC's chairman and CEO.

By late 1984 the network was a strong second in prime-time ratings; the next year it attracted the largest audience, for the first time since Paley's talent raids in 1948. By 1985 Grant Tinker and Brandon Tartikoff steered NBC to prime-time leadership. With hit shows like *The A-Team* and *Miami Vice*, profits increased sevenfold, from $48 million to $333 million. With sales exceeding $10 billion, and operating income at a record $1,231 million, Bradshaw had reversed the fortunes of RCA, which would soon become a unit of its former parent, General Electric.

General Electric: The Welch Era

By the late '60s, GE was a widely diversified decentralized conglomerate. If diversification and decentralization reflected the strategic and organizational thrust of GE's post–World War II CEOs (Ralph Cordiner, Fred Borch), the move toward strategic planning typified the era of Reg Jones. Starting in 1972, Jones, GE's new chairman and CEO, reduced 190 departments to 43 "strategic business units" (4 groups, 21 divisions, 18 departments), while a total of 73 product lines were discontinued. To defeat a balkanization of the highly diversified company, Jones began to emphasize "a single General Electric identity." By 1980 GE's sales had grown to $25 billion.[2]

In April 1981 Jack Welch took office as the new chairman and CEO of GE. As an engineer he was comfortable with technology (high-tech businesses were GE's promising growth area), had an excellent record of financial performance, had proved a master at managing change, and was something of an entrepreneurial maverick.[3]

Welch's changes derived from GE's focus on three "strategic circles": core manufacturing units (33% of profits in the early '80s), high-technology businesses (30%), and services (29%). Each business had to rank first or second in its global market. Only those businesses that dominated their markets were placed in one circle or another, whereas those outside these circles had to come up with a strategy to get in a circle or they would be divested. The contractions drove the new CEO's restructuring of GE's organization. Between 1980 and 1984 the total workforce was reduced from 402,000 to 330,000. Almost 40% of the "destaffing" was attributed to cutbacks in businesses with lower sales volume. The efforts earned the new CEO a notorious nickname, "Neutron Jack."

By the mid-'80s GE's revenues amounted to more than $28 billion, while its net income hovered around $2.3 billion. Welch embarked on building a revitalized "human engine" to animate GE's formidable "business engine."

The GE/RCA Merger

In 1985 RCA's Bradshaw announced he was stepping aside as CEO (but staying as chairman), while Robert Frederick, RCA's president and a GE veteran, assumed the position of CEO. As the transition took place, RCA became a takeover target in the M&A market. Defeating the takeover efforts by Bendix Corporation and Irwin Jacobs, RCA rejected a leveraged buyout proposal by Kohlberg, Kravis, Roberts & Company, and a merger with MCA. Instead, top executives explored various solutions to long-term survival in an era of increasing global competition.

Meanwhile, after a study of 3,000 companies, GE decided that RCA possessed complementary strengths that would propel GE to global leadership. While most U.S. companies saw merger as a means to join global competition, GE thought RCA would strengthen its domestic businesses and presence in the service sector.

In late 1985 Felix Rohatyn of Lazard Frères brought together GE's Welch and RCA's Bradshaw. At $6.28 billion, the nation's largest nonoil merger made GE America's seventh largest industrial enterprise. NBC was one of the new entity's service businesses, along with financing and communications.

In 1986 the network was still first in prime-time ratings, late-night programming, and Saturday morning children's programming. It was also the industry leader in satellite distribution and network news-gathering. With RCA, GE got a cash-flow bonanza from NBC, enabling it to evolve into the world's second-largest defense electronics producer after General Motors' Hughes Electronics. Welch hoped that profits from insulated domestic operations would provide the financial sinews to fight low-cost foreign competitors.

In the '80s Welch bought companies worth $16 billion, and sold operations worth $9 billion. Welch's financial performance was excellent, with (inflation-adjusted) earnings per share rising an average of 7.6% a year, compared to 4.9% under Jones, and 1.6% under Borch. Concurrently, GE had increased its stock market value from $12 billion to *$58 billion*—more than any other U.S. company. While financial indicators made shareholders smile (even if acquisitions raised GE's leverage from 5% to over 44%), 100,000 eliminated jobs left labor uncertain of its future. Yet the "new" GE sought to strengthen its diversity with more acquisitions, preferably No. 1 or No. 2 companies in high-profit, growth industries.

By the early '90s GE's 350 product lines and business units had been squeezed into 13 big businesses: aerospace, aircraft engines, appliances, financial services, industrial and power systems, lighting, medical systems, NBC, plastics, communications and services, electrical distribution and control, motors, and transportation systems. To avoid "bureaucratic laxness," Welch continued to instill an entrepreneurial competitiveness in the world's tenth largest company. The profit orientation contributed to GE's high-profile corporate scandals well to the early '90s.[4]

Prior to the merger, RCA's broadcasting segment had been the cash cow of the corporation; by the early '90s, however, NBC was contributing to GE's slow stock appreciation and reputation as a portfolio-managed conglomerate.

NBC as GE's Subsidiary: Rise and Decline

From 1986 to 1992 NBC's payroll was reduced to 4,500 people from 7,500. During the first postmerger years, NBC cut an average of $50 million annually (8% of jobs) from its overall spending. With restructuring, Robert Wright sought new (nonnetwork) revenue sources. In the process, he spent $10 million to acquire a 38% stake in Visnews Ltd., the Reuters-owned international news-gathering and distribution network; NBC's *Today* show went through highly publicized turmoil; and Michael Gartner, NBC News's president, began to reposition *NBC Nightly News with Tom Brokaw*.[5]

NBC's ownership of seven stations ended in early 1990, when the network sold a 50% ownership stake in its Cleveland TV station. By late 1992 only 14% of NBC stations carried the shows live as the network fed them and it was running a distant third to CBS and ABC in the overall daytime ratings. NBC's affiliates were increasingly concerned over their role in distribution, especially as NBC began to use its affiliate stations to promote the pay-per-view (PPV) segments of its 1992 Olympics coverage, and toying with the idea of a daytime shopping show.

In the late '80s GE considered Brandon Tartikoff, NBC's president of entertainment, as the key to NBC's $500 million annual profits. Amid its prime-time leadership for the fifth consecutive year, the network's winning margin was narrowing and its demographics were "graying." By early 1991 Tartikoff was under rising crossfire at NBC, where production costs rose rapidly for the most potent programming vehicles (*Cheers, The Cosby Show, A Different World,* and *Golden Girls*).[6]

After a historic 68-week winning streak, NBC lost its prime-time leadership, while, following a car crash, Tartikoff left for Paramount. Warren Littlefield, Tartikoff's protégé and follower, launched a programming shift "from complacency to risk-taking" (*Law & Order, Fresh Prince of Bel Air*). Initially, NBC continued to pay for the costly old hits (*The Cosby Show, Golden Girls, Cheers*). Soon, however, it let several hit shows drift to other networks, while most new shows proved demographic and critical disappointments. Meanwhile, high-profile turmoil intensified with the firing of the producer of Jay Leno's *The Tonight Show,* and the growing irritation among NBC's program suppliers. NBC had failed to adjust to the new competitive environment.

In the early '90s GE's broadcasting consisted mainly of NBC, whose principal businesses were the furnishing of network TV services to 211 affiliated TV stations; the production of live and recorded TV programs; and the operation, under licenses from the FCC, of six owned-and-operated VHF TV broadcasting stations. NBC's operations also included investment and programming in cable television, principally through investments in the Consumer News and Business Channel (CNBC); various regional Sportschannels (starting in 1989); and the 1991 acquisition of Financial News Network (FNN), which was subsequently merged with CNBC.

GE's interests in M&E businesses included revolving credit and inventory financing in the TV and movie industries via General Electric Financial Services, Inc. (later General Electric Capital Services, Inc. [GECS]), a wholly owned consolidated affiliate; and GE Americom, a leading domestic satellite carrier.

Even in its peak years, broadcasting played a minor role in GE's overall portfolio. The portion of NBC's revenues increased from 4.5% in 1986 to 7.3% in 1988, declining to 5.2% in 1991. A year later, GE's restated segments raised NBC's contribution to 5.9% in consolidated revenues and 3.3% in operating profits. The decline stemmed from NBC's poor performance, as well as a combination of higher program costs, lower prime-time ratings, Gulf War costs, the worst advertising market in 20 years, and the necessity to write down future sports rights commitments. While 1993 revenues were down from 1992, earnings were up (See Table 2–5).

Search for New Revenue Sources

In 1988 NBC's nonnetwork revenues accounted for 1% of its $3.5 billion in total revenues. To benefit from this Golden Age in pay TV, Wright eagerly sought new revenues in cable and pay-per-view.

Cablevision, Bravo and AMC, Sports Channels. In the late '80s, NBC moved heavily into cable, investing $137.5 million for a half-interest share in Ca-

Table 2-5

General Electric: Industry Segments (1986–93) [$mil.]

	1993	1992	1991	1990	1989	1988	1987	1986
Revenues								
GE								
Aerospace	–	–	5,326	5,614	5,282	5,343	5,262	4,318
Aircraft Eng.	6,580	7,368	7,899	7,558	6,863	6,481	6,773	5,977
Appliances	5,555	5,330	5,451	5,706	5,620	5,289	4,721	4,352
Broadcasting	3,102	3,363	3,121	3,236	3,392	3,638	3,241	1,888
Industrial	7,379	6,907	6,928	7,040	7,059	7,061	6,662	6,770
Materials	5,042	4,853	4,722	5,167	4,929	3,539	2,751	2,331
Power Systems	6,692	6,371	6,185	5,804	5,129	4,805	4,995	5,262
Technical	4,174	4,674	5,224	4,783	4,545	4,431	3,670	3,021
Total GE[1]	40,359	40,254	45,227	44,879	42,650	40,292	40,516	36,725
GECS								
Financing	12,399	10,544	10,069	9,000	7,333	5,827	3,507	2,594
Insurance	4,862	3,863	2,989	2,853	2,710	2,478	2,217	2,026
Securities	4,861	4,022	3,346	2,923	2,897	2,316	2,491	1,176
Total GECS[2]	22,137	18,440	16,399	14,774	12,945	10,655	8,225	5,814
Consolidated revenues[3]	60,562	57,073	60,236	58,414	54,574	50,089	48,158	42,013
Operating Profit								
GE								
Aerospace	–	–	655	648	646	640	603	608
Aircraft Eng.	798	1,274	1,415	1,263	1,050	1,000	940	869
Appliances	372	386	435	467	399	61	490	462
Broadcasting	264	204	209	477	603	540	500	240
Industrial	782	888	837	884	847	798	302	575
Materials	834	740	803	1,017	1,057	733	507	424
Power Systems	1,143	1,037	932	739	507	503	199	354
Technical	706	912	746	595	589	484	275	112
Total GE[4]	6,935	7,158	7,545	7,385	6,801	5,715	4,440	4,310
GECS								
Financing	1,727	1,366	1,327	1,267	1,152	899	636	(99)
Insurance	770	641	501	457	361	334	183	132
Securities	439	300	119	(54)	(53)	64	(23)	83
Total GECS[4]	2,648	2,035	1,657	1,395	1,138	1,027	572	(61)
Consolidated Operating Profit	7,789	7,708	7,943	7,707	7,036	5,940	4,450	3,736

1. Includes "All Other" category as well as corporate items and eliminations.
2. Includes "All Other" category.
3. Includes eliminations.
4. Includes "All Other" category.

SOURCE: General Electric Co.

blevision systems, the nation's eighth largest cable operator. As part of its ventures with Cablevision, NBC co-owned the Bravo movie channel, seven regional cable sports channels, and a stake in the American Movie Classics (AMC) channel.

PPV: The 1992 Barcelona Olympics. NBC paid over $400 million to acquire the TV rights for the 1992 Summer Olympics, which were to introduce PPV to American viewers. In the end, NBC hobbled away with a loss of at least $50 million.

ACTV and HDTV. An Advanced Compatible Television system (ACTV) was being developed by a consortium involving NBC. In 1990 NBC joined forces with two rival consumer electronics manufacturers, Philips Consumer Electronics Co. and Thomson Consumer Electronics, Inc., forming a consortium to develop a system for high-definition TV (HDTV).

Direct Broadcasting Satellite. In 1990 NBC also got into a joint venture—with Cablevision, News Corp., and GM's Hughes Communications—to launch a direct broadcast satellite (DBS) service.

Through aggressive diversification, Wright's goal was to give GE an "entertainment conglomerate" with stakes in broadcasting, cable, and production. He also invested in multimedia (joint venture with IBM) and international entertainment/information (a broad alliance with Mexico's TV Azteca, a privately owned broadcaster attempting to take on the country's long-dominant Grupo Televisa SA). Diversification coincided with the dramatic growth of *GE*'s interest in global partnerships (broadcasting and cable) through General Electric Capital Services, Inc.[7]

GE Capital Services: M&E Investing

With $91 billion in assets in 1990, the finance subsidiary could have qualified as the fourth largest U.S. bank. GECS's major segments encompassed financing, insurance, and a securities broker-dealer (Kidder Peabody). Through GECS, GE also sought interests in cable and motion pictures. By late 1990 some 38% of GE Capital's risky highly leveraged transaction portfolio stemmed from investments in cable, media, and broadcasting. GE Capital established itself as a major financial force in the M&E businesses, providing more than $2.7 billion for 19 deals in cable, broadcast TV, radio, and publishing.[8]

NBC: For Sale, Not For Sale, For Sale . . .

In 1990 GE's strength lay in strong earnings from GECS and long-cycle businesses (aircraft engines, power systems, medical systems). Its weakness was in short-cycle business (plastics, NBC). Unlike GE's other businesses, its broadcasting segment did not hold up well in the recession. And since hanging to an also-ran was not consistent with Welch's style, analysts anticipated the sale of NBC, which was valued at $4.0–$6.5 billion.

In spring 1991 Kidder Peabody was studying ways to dispose of the network with Paramount as prospective buyer. The problem with the studio alliance scenario was that any studio that acquired NBC might have to give up a large portion of its lucrative syndication rights.

By January 1992 Welch conceded GE was seeking a "strategic solution" with NBC to offset major declines in advertising revenues. Later, Barry Diller, FBC's former chairman, denied rumors he was seeking to buy a 20% equity interest in NBC (with the balance being spun off to GE shareholders), whereas Bill Cosby, NBC's megastar through the '80s, launched a high-profile quest trying to rally partners to join him in a bid. Although Paramount came close to buying NBC from GE, the deal fell through at the last minute.

Since GE had paid $6.4 billion for NBC in 1986, it was expected to wait until NBC's fortunes improved. As if the network did not have enough problems, NBC's *Dateline* in February 1993 featured a framed story about exploding General Motors trucks, which forced NBC to issue a humiliating on-air apology to the automaker, leading to the resignation of Michael Gartner, president of NBC News.

In April 1993 Robert Cornell, a research analyst, anticipated a write-down of NBC by GE.[9] To respond to mounting sales rumors, GE chairman Jack Welch reassured the network's news employees that "NBC is not for sale." Welch may also have been motivated by a recent fin-syn ruling that opened new revenue sources, thereby enhancing NBC's potential. Still, few analysts took Welch's statement seriously. NBC's revenues had slid since 1988, while operating profit was at a third of its 1989 peak. From 1987 to 1992, program costs had soared to $1.2 billion from $800 million, even though the shows delivered less than in the past. NBC had fallen to third in the prime-time game and had just one show in the top 10. David Letterman had defected to CBS. The *Dateline* debacle had humiliated NBC News. And the network expected the viewing audience of the Big Three to plummet to 42% by the turn of the century. With Goldman, Sachs, Bill Cosby began a second run at buying NBC.

In 1993 NBC entered a period of rapid diversification. "We are a pro-gramming company that is creating new channels of distribution," said Tom Rogers, executive VP of NBC, Inc. and president of NBC Cable & Business Development. New diversification included ownership/major stakes in cable TV (from CNBC to A&E, AMC, Bravo, Court TV, Prime Sport Channel America, eight regional sports networks, several cable news channels); place-based media (NBC On-Site); interactive media technol-ogies (NBC Desktop News, NBC Direct, a joint venture with IBM, as well as Interactive Network). GE also signed a deal with Rupert Murdoch's Star TV to launch an Asian clone of its business and news CNBC channel.[10]

That year, *Business Week* published two cover stories on General Electric. While "GE's Money Machine" described the success of GE's huge finance arm, "GE's Brave New World" was an account of the aggressive push of America's third most profitable company into India, China, and Mexico, with Southeast Asia close behind. Obsession with growth was rapidly trans-forming GE into a global company, whose overseas revenues accounted for 40% of total sales. If the strategy was "wrong, it's a billion dollars, a couple of billion dollars," said Welch. "If it's right, it's the future of the next century for this company."[11] Even with its diversified operations, NBC would have a marginal if any role in GE's brave new world.

LOEWS CORP./CBS: END OF THE TIFFANY NETWORK?

It was William Paley (1901–90) who created "the Tiffany Network" and ran CBS from the late 1920s until 1977.[1] In the late 1940s Paley raided NBC's most popular stars, ensuring the competitive edge in the programming struggle. Focusing on the color TV system, CBS diversified into set production. When the FCC reversed its standards policy in 1953, CBS, unlike its rivals, owned hardly any broadcast TV stations; building a full complement of TV stations in the "right" cities, the network could not draw upon revenues from TV manufacturing to underwrite network expenses.

Three Transitions

In 1951 CBS was restructured into six autonomous divisions: CBS Radio, CBS Television, CBS Laboratories, Columbia Records, Hytron Radio and Electronics, and CBS Columbia. Each operated like a separate company with its own president and staff. "I just looked up Alfred Sloan's old memorandum on how to organize General Motors into decentralized parts, and the course was clear," recalled Frank Stanton, president of CBS.[2] The postwar reorganization brought a long period of management continuity, leading to CBS's 24-year reign as America's most popular network.

In 1962 Harbridge House's management consultants urged CBS to derive no more than half of its income from broadcasting and related businesses. Instead of buying into the media business, as Stanton proposed, CBS bought the New York Yankees, as Paley demanded. It was a misguided diversification.

By 1966 CBS had 10 large divisions reporting directly to Stanton and Paley. With the assistance of management consulting firms, CBS was divided into two groups: broadcasting and nonbroadcasting activities (CBS/Broadcast Group and CBS/Columbia). Paley's opposition kept CBS away from feature film production well into the late '60s, and changes in regulation forced CBS to divest its cable properties in Canada.

While CBS revenues were resurging, Wall Street expected CBS to invest its cash to avoid taxes and use acquisitions to propel the company's growth and enhance its stock price. By the '70s nonbroadcasting activities were too burdensome for one group president. Thus evolved the third major form of the CBS organization, with 16 divisions reporting to four group presidents in broadcasting (TV network, entertainment, sports, TV stations, news, radio), records (domestic, international), publishing (educational, consumer, professional, international), and Columbia (Columbia House, musical instruments, retail stores, toys divisions), as well as motion pictures, cable, and electronic video recording. The diversification drive lasted until the early '80s.

Programming Leadership

CBS acquired audience leadership in radio news during World War II, introducing the first generation of news journalists (from Edward R. Murrow to William L. Shirer). In 1948 the network began *CBS-TV News* with Douglas Edwards, the first regularly scheduled TV network news program. From the early '50s, TV news operations were augmented by newsmagazines (from *See It Now* to *CBS Reports*). Concurrently, Paley's talent raids contributed to the growth of CBS leadership in audience ratings, providing a model for "packaged programs"—that is, shows developed, owned, and scheduled by the network itself. *I Love Lucy* set the pattern for sitcoms to come, building and expanding CBS's prime-time leadership.[3]

As the launch of the "Early Bird" satellite made CBS first in the regularly scheduled use of satellite television news, Walter Cronkite began his two-decade career as the anchorman of the *CBS Evening News* and the nation's premier newscaster. The new network president, James T. Aubrey, propelled the company into ratings success and financial prosperity (*The Dick Van Dyke Show, The Beverly Hillbillies, My Favorite Martian*).

At the turn of the '70s the shift from home ratings to demographics led to CBS's new programming, which replaced old, rural audiences with the young, urban "Now Generation." The shift ensured leadership, with male-oriented action series (*Hawaii Five-O, Kojak*) and female-led sitcoms (*The Mary Tyler Moore Show*) that spun off other popular shows (*Rhoda, Phyllis*). Indeed, *All in the Family* and *M*A*S*H* exemplified an entire era of programming.

By 1978 CBS took in $3 billion. More than half of sales came from nonbroadcasting activities. Despite many acquisitions, CBS failed in achieving linkages among various businesses. Paley opposed all the right moves, including the expansion of movie production, a studio alliance, a cable news channel, expansion into video, and a merger effort with a large financial parent. By 1980 CBS was a declining $4 billion conglomerate.

After half a century of CEO power, Paley could neither accept Stanton as his successor nor leave the company. Like King Lear, he could find no son to fill his seat. Hence, the departures of Charles T. Ireland, Arthur P. Taylor, and John D. Backe in the 1970s. A costly executive shuffle turned Wall Street critical of the 80-year-old Paley and CBS directors. By April 1983 Paley was forced to relinquish the chairmanship to Tom Wyman. Prior to network takeovers, the "Tiffany network's" revenues amounted to over $4.8 billion (debt ratio remained at 18%). Thereafter, it was downhill.

From Takeover Attacks to Loews Control

In January 1985 an archconservative group led by Jesse Helms, Republican senator from North Carolina, declared a drive to purchase enough stock in CBS to exert an influence on the "liberal" company. When Helms's attack put CBS "in play," Paley tried a leveraged buyout (LBO) to get even with Wyman. The poorly conceived effort was doomed from the start. In April, just three days after CBS had stopped Helms, the master arbitrageur Ivan Boesky disclosed he had gathered 8.7% of CBS stock. Although CBS deflected the intervention, its stock climbed.

After mid-April, Ted Turner offered to purchase 67% of CBS stock using Turner Broadcasting's stock and high-yield, high-risk junk bonds with a total value of $5.41 billion. Instead, Wyman sought a $9 billion merger with Time and Gannett, unsuccessfully. When Capital Cities, one-fourth the size of its target, bought ABC for over $3.5 billion, CBS caved in. The board offered to buy back 21% of CBS's stock (a total purchase of $955 million), while its debt rose from $370 million to $1 billion (Wyman sold $300 million in assets and cut staff).

July 1985 heralded a new struggle for strategic control as Laurence Tisch, chairman of Loews Corporation, a $17.5 billion holding company with several interests, bought 5% of CBS stock.

Loews Corp.: Contrarian Diversification

In the mid-'80s Loews comprised a theater circuit with 102 screens, 13 hotels worldwide, Lorillard (cigarettes), CNA (insurance), real estate holdings, and a $3.5 billion investment portfolio. By early 1987 Loews— led by two founding brothers, Laurence (Larry) and Preston (Bob) Tisch—had grown into a highly diversified $5.5 billion concern. While Larry excelled in finance, Bob took care of the operational side. (In 1986 the brothers embarked on separate careers; and by the early '90s the personal fortune of each was estimated at $1.7 billion.)[4]

The run at CBS was Larry Tisch's effort. In summer 1985 he announced his readiness should CBS be searching for a "white knight." In October he raised his interest to 12%, which made him the largest shareholder. Claiming to remain a "passive investor," he would not buy more than 25%.

Problems in diversified units were accumulating rapidly, while debt ratio jumped from 18% to 54%. When Wyman invited Tisch on the CBS board, hoping to neutralize him from the inside, Paley and Tisch began a series of meetings. When GE announced it would buy RCA/NBC, Marvin Davis met Wyman to buy CBS for $160 a share. Although Wyman successfully deflected the bid, it led Bob Tisch to declare his family's intention to "control and operate" CBS. By late summer 1986 the Tisch stake had increased to 24.9%.

To deflect the Tisch threat, Wyman sought a merger with Philip Morris, Gulf + Western, Westinghouse, Coca-Cola, and Disney, but lost the power struggle (he got a $3.8 million settlement, and an annual $400,000 for life). Paley and Larry Tisch were named acting chairman and CEO, respectively, to bolster the impression that the solution was temporary. The

facade suited Paley, who thought he could use the chairmanship to rees-
tablish control, while Tisch would use Paley's name to legitimize his rule.
It was neither a hostile takeover nor a friendly merger. Tisch had achieved
control of CBS, Inc., just as he acquired Loews/MGM in 1958–60—without heavy costs.[5]

As Paley's health deteriorated, Tisch acquired operating power in CBS.
Slashing costs, he intended to downsize CBS into a lean, low-cost operation. That meant a drastic transformation of its corporate culture. In 1987
Tisch sold CBS Magazines for $650 million to a purchasing group made
up of senior officers of the division; and in 1988 Sony acquired CBS Records for $2 billion. With stars like Bruce Springsteen, Michael Jackson,
and Barbra Streisand, the unit had accounted for nearly 40% of CBS's
total operating profit and over 30% of its revenue. It was the world's
largest producer, manufacturer, and marketer of recorded music.

Renewed Programming Leadership

In the early '80s the high spending of national advertisers in CBS shows
(*60 Minutes, M*A*S*H, Magnum, P.I., Dallas*) had spared network news
from more severe cost-cutting. In 1985–86, however, NBC captured CBS's
leadership in the prime-time ratings. Thus began CBS's cost-cutting
drives.[6]

By summer 1987 the ratings slide of *CBS Evening News* left Dan Rather
in third place. He was rescued only by the new people meter that improved his ratings consistently. Volatile changes were accompanied by executive turmoil.

By the 1987–88 season, CBS was no longer even second in the ratings
game. With only two durable top shows, *60 Minutes* and *Murder, She Wrote*
(the first was introduced in 1968, the second in 1984), it hit the bottom,
for the first time in network history. Donald (Bud) Grant had served as
president of CBS Entertainment during the years 1980–87. He was replaced with Earle H. (Kim) LeMasters and Barbara Corday (who would
leave only two years later). As Steven Bochco and Marcy Carsey proved
too expensive, Tisch in December 1989 hired Jeff Sagansky, the president
of Tri-Star Pictures, as president of CBS Entertainment. As Tartikoff's protégé at NBC, Sagansky had overseen the development of shows like *Cheers,
The A-Team,* and *Miami Vice.*[7]

Since Grant's era, researchers had called CBS the "gray" network. It
failed to attract viewers aged 18–34, even when leading in overall household ratings. David Poltrack, CBS's research chief, argued that older viewers' discretionary income was high and would continue to rise with the
aging of the baby boom generation.

In 1989–90 CBS was the only network that improved its prime-time ratings, while NBC and ABC were both declining. Yet its "major sports events
strategy" set off a costly spending spiral ($1.1 billion for a 1990–93 con-

tract). In 1991 CBS finished $86 million in the red because of the contraction, new competition, and, most importantly, because it had overpaid for sports events, especially major league baseball.

The highly rated *Lonesome Dove*, the eight-hour network version of the Pulitzer Prize-winning Western saga, anticipated better days. By mid-April 1992 CBS finished in a strong first place, dominating household ratings and defeating competition in the category of 18–49 year-old women. For the first time, a broadcast TV network went from worst to first. CBS was powered by *Murphy Brown, Northern Exposure,* the long-lasting *60 Minutes,* a potent collection of TV films and specials, as well as the World Series, the Super Bowl, and the Winter Olympics. It also was about to obtain new shows from proven winners (Bob Newhart, Diane English, Linda Bloodworth-Thomason, and David E. Kelly). Concurrently, CBS's renewed dealmaking with advertisers, suppliers, and in licensing reflected efforts to exploit shifts in the bargaining power.

Still, CBS's ratings strength was confined to Sundays and Mondays. New programs did not work. Rivals and many advertisers considered younger audiences and the profits they brought more important than total ratings. The early '90s witnessed the network rise from third to first in prime time and in late night. Yet it was Kim LeMasters, Sagansky's predecessor, who was responsible for many of CBS's hits. (When Sagansky left the network in the fall of 1994, he was replaced by Peter Tortorici, executive VP of CBS Entertainment.)

The New CBS

In less than half a decade, the huge diversified media conglomerate had been reduced to a skeleton of broadcast operations. In the early '70s CBS had employed nearly 40,000 people; in 1990 it had less than 7,000. CBS's financial results continued to decline. In the mid-'80s CBS brought in $4.8 billion in revenues and over $500 million in operating income; in 1990 revenues declined to $3.3 billion, while operating income showed a $22 million deficit (the loss was CBS's first since 1986). Continued cost-cutting advocated by consultants from McKinsey & Company was becoming a curse at CBS. When the 89-year-old William Paley died in late October 1990, few cared. CBS was no longer a stock to be chased.

By the early '90s, broadcast operations consisted of the CBS Television Network (affiliate relations were in turmoil until 1993), the 7 CBS-owned TV stations, 206 affiliated stations, the CBS Radio Networks, and 21 CBS-owned radio stations. CBS Enterprises sold internally produced programming worldwide.

In the old CBS, broadcasting revenues accounted for about 60% of total revenues. While the records business brought in about 10% of total revenues, magazines accounted for slightly less than 10%. Tisch's divestitures

Table 2-6
CBS Inc.: Business Segments (1982–93)

	Broadcast Group	Records Group	Magazines Group	Other
Revenues ($mil)				
1993	3,510	–	–	–
1992	3,503	–	–	–
1991	3,035	–	–	–
1990	3,261	–	–	24
1989	2,961	–	–	10
1988	2,778	–	–	34
1987	2,762	–	–	22
1986	2,817	1,489	407	42
1985	2,785	1,230	407	33
1984	2,721	1,265	331	38
1983	2,389	1,159	316	30
1982	2,165	1,067	281	30
Operating Income ($mil)				
1993	411	–	–	–
1992	180	–	–	–
1991	(271)	–	–	–
1990	(50)	–	–	24
1989	274	–	–	10
1988	236	–	–	34
1987	225	–	–	22
1986	229	192	14	(5)
1985	374	90	5	8
1984	409	124	19	6
1983	292	109	18	(17)
1982	271	22	6	(5)

SOURCE: CBS Inc. (various years) Annual Reports. Used by permission.

had been dictated by operating profits. Through most of the early '80s, the broadcast business accounted for 70–80% of total operating profits, although it brought in only 60% of the revenues. The profit performances of CBS's records and magazines businesses were much less consistent, and much more erratic. Finally, profits of other businesses that brought in about 1% of revenues lacked consistency and often showed deficits (see Table 2–6).

By the early '90s CBS remained the only network that had ignored buying into cable, or joint ventures, even though it was reconsidering its cable policy and a joint venture with CNN.

Loews Corp.: The Boom Years

With their 24% ownership, the Tisch brothers continued to run Loews Corp. as if it was their own, rather than a public company. In the '80s it became one of the top U.S. companies in profitability, earnings growth, and stock market appreciation.

During the years 1986–91, Loews Corp.'s revenues increased from $8,607 million to $13,620 million, while net income rose from $546 million to $904 million. In the next two years, revenue growth slowed down and net income declined.

By the early '90s Lorillard was the Tisches' cash cow; cigarettes brought in almost $2.2 billion in revenues and $525 million in net income. The second-ranked revenue source was life insurance. Other units—hotels, watches/timing devices, shipping, drilling—played minor roles in the total revenues. When tobacco stocks rose from the ashes in 1993, Loews hardly budged. Yet money managers remained interested in the stock, which was considered "dirt cheap."[8]

After the mid-'80s the brothers began to invest in "prestige ventures" (Larry's interest in CBS, Bob's major stake in the New York Giants). Despite their high profile, these ventures were mere niches in the overall Loews portfolio.

Amid abundant channels and viewer choices, noted Tisch in the 1992 *Annual Report,* network television's competing strengths were twofold: viewers got programming for free, and advertisers enjoyed the world's most efficient mass-marketing medium. Whatever Tisch's agenda, his handling of CBS's divestitures was questionable; asset dispositions indicated an investor inclination to treat CBS as a money market fund. Tisch had acquired CBS purely for financial gain—or had come to think that way.

In February and March 1990, merger rumors were pushing the CBS stock up to $189 a share, well above the $130 that Tisch had paid but below the $221 peak in 1989. Since its turnaround in the mid-'80s, Disney had sought to expand into broadcasting; by early 1990 it was courting CBS.

In December 1990 Larry Tisch was named CBS's chairman (he also continued as president and CEO). Under Tisch's full control, CBS offered to buy back 10.5 million shares (about 44%) of its common stock for $190 a share (about $23 billion). Tisch denied the network was for sale, but the decision to halve the current market capitalization of roughly $4 billion made it easier for another company to come in and acquire CBS.[9]

Toward the end of 1992 the worst was over for CBS. It enjoyed a newfound ratings leadership; having swallowed $600 million in pretax losses on sports contracts, it had a cleaner balance sheet; against $900 million in debt, it had $1 billion in cash and securities. Tisch had enough wealth, but, as the owner of CBS, he had profile.

Programming Investments

Prior to summer 1993, CBS became the first of the Big Three to enter the domestic syndication market with the formation of a new, nonnetwork programming unit: CBS Productions had the most in-house shows in development of any network (six sitcoms, two dramas). Like other networks, it was seeking a piece of the $5 billion worldwide market for syndicated programming.

To "change the dynamic" of the all-male network evening newscasts, network executives made Connie Chung Dan Rather's co-anchor. By the end of 1993, CBS's $50 million investment in *The Late Show with David Letterman* seemed to be paying off. While *Letterman* garnered 5.3% of the nation's 94.2 million TV homes, NBC's long-dominant *Tonight Show* and Paramount's syndicated *The Arsenio Hall Show* were slipping and FBC's *The Chevy Chase Show* flopped. CBS got entry into a new part of the broadcasting day. Meanwhile, it developed new hit shows (*Dr. Quinn, Medicine Woman*).

Although CBS had been synonymous with the National Football League (NFL) for 38 years, FBC's $1.56 billion bid beat out CBS in December 1993. When losses seemed inevitable, tradition was no longer an argument. In effect, when CBS, in January 1994, won the rights to televise the 1998 Winter Olympics in Nagano, Japan, for $375 million, it was criticized for paying too much.

"An Impressive Turnabout"

After summer 1993, CBS planned an all-news cable network. Costing $100 million to start up and $30 million a year to run, the CBS Public Affairs Channel prompted resistance from TCI and Time Warner, whose subscribers CBS needed but who were major shareholders in CNN. Ultimately, the network managed to reach agreement with only one major cable company (Comcast) to carry the proposed cable channel.[10]

In September 1993 CBS conceded defeat in its bitter struggle to win payment from the cable systems that carried the signals of the broadcast stations it owned. The acknowledgement came after CBS had failed to win acceptance for three channel concepts—a news channel, a sports news channel, and an entertainment channel (repeats of old CBS shows). CBS was the only network that failed to create a new cable channel and receive payment for it from the cable systems in lieu of retransmission fees. Hence, its drive into more in-house production and syndication. Despite the nasty cable debacle, Tisch was triumphant in the CBS *Annual Report* (February 1993): "CBS staged an impressive turnabout in 1992."

While other major players were frantically repositioning into new M&E businesses, Laurence Tisch saw little sense in buying businesses long on potential but short on cash flow. But as the cable debacle indicated, conservative caution had a price.

The true significance of CBS in the Loews portfolio was reflected by its equity in income of CBS, Inc. Net income rose to $11 million in 1990 (1.4% of total), showed a deficit of $23 million in 1991, and increased to $25 million in 1992 and $53 million the following year. Whether asset divestitures benefited CBS or not, the network's contribution grew in the Loews portfolio.

In 1993 Loews' stock dropped 23%. The cigarette price war savaged the tobacco unit, while claims for Hurricane Andrew and asbestos-related litigation hit the insurance holding. Other operating units were performing poorly as well. The luxury hotels, for example, suffered from the postcontraction economy, while sales of clocks stagnated. Even if Tisch was just biding his time before selling off one or more of the businesses, Loews was no longer a treasure.[11]

As the demise of financial interest and syndication rules and the telco/cable mania in 1993 also drove up CBS's value, the sale of CBS was no longer a matter of principle—it was a matter of time. In May 1994 CBS faced a shock. New World Communication Group, Inc., controlled by financier Ronald O. Perelman, dumped all 12 of its network affiliations, eight of them with *CBS*—and signed on with Rupert Murdoch's Fox (FBC). Even if CBS executives struggled to find a silver lining, the raid forced the network into a scramble for affiliates in critical markets. More importantly, it vaulted Fox into the same league as the Big Three—at the expense of whatever was left of the once invulnerable Tiffany network.[12]

As CBS ran after new affiliates, it also, reportedly, resumed talks with Disney and other Hollywood players.

Cable: Growth and Consolidation

THE RISE OF CABLE

Cable growth remained modest until the end of the 1950s, when operators began to use microwaves to transmit signals from faraway broadcast stations and offer these and local stations on their systems. In the early 1960s the FCC began to make cable decisions on a case-by-case basis, and to regulate microwave systems serving cable. Attempts to create cable regulations were subject to excessive political interference.[1]

By the mid-'60s the importation of distant broadcast signals began to concern local TV stations. While the FCC required cable systems to carry all local TV stations, it imposed a "freeze" from 1968 to 1972 on the development of cable in the top 100 TV markets. Cable television was changing from a broadcast retransmission service into a full-fledged industry. Concurrently, a new technology (direct broadcast satellite) and a new programming concept (HBO) revolutionized cable evolution.

Domestic Communications Satellite

When the first domestic geostationary satellite was launched in 1974, the new technology offered cable programmers a potentially cost-effective method of national distribution. Programmers could relay transmissions from earth to the satellite, which would then retransmit the signals back to cable system satellite dishes.

HBO and Superstations

By late 1975 Home Box Office (HBO) became the first programmer to distribute its signals via satellite (RCA's SATCOM I), serving about 400,000 cable households. While the concept of pay-TV for cable systems originated with Charles Dolan, it was developed by Gerald Levin (who, in 1992, succeeded Steve Ross at Time Warner). Bouncing his signal off the satellite to reach a nationwide audience, Ted Turner's independent WTBS became the first "superstation." By the mid-'80s satellite distribution was used by the Public Broadcasting System (PBS), major cable program services, syndicators, and NBC.

A complex mixture of federal, state, and municipal regulations had emerged to govern the cable business, creating a confusing dual regulatory structure. Even when the FCC deleted cable rules, local governments franchised systems (which prompted antitrust problems). So cable operators called for a federal cable policy.

Basic and Pay Cable

Based on a compromise by the National Cable Television Association, the National League of Cities, and the U.S. Conference of Mayors, the Cable Communications Policy Act (1984) gave the cable industry a statutory renewal expectancy, freeing cablers from municipal oversight, allowing them to raise subscriber rates—and giving rise to their growth and monopolistic tendencies.[1]

The erosion of the networks' prime-time audience *preceded* cable deregulation. From 1983 to 1992, basic cable networks' viewing shares increased from 9% to 24%, while the shares for broadcast network affiliates declined from 69% to 54%. The change was more pronounced in cable households.[2]

In the early years of the industry, the number of cable TV households grew slowly. Prior to the '70s, cable represented less than 7% of all TV households; by 1992, over 60% (more than 55 million households) (see Table 3-1).

Between 1976 and 1984, revenues for basic cable increased from $887 million to more than $3.6 billion, whereas revenues for pay cable soared from just $66 million to over $3.4 billion. With deregulation (1984–89), basic revenues increased to more than $8.7 billion, whereas pay revenues grew to "only" $4.8 billion. As subscriber growth decreased in basic cable, high revenue growth was maintained through rate increases. By 1993, for the first time, cable operators changed their marketing habits. Switching dollars from basic cable toward premium and pay cable, they spent less than 50% of their marketing dollars promoting basic cable.[3]

Table 3-1
Growth of Basic Cable and Pay Cable (1952–94)

Cable Households[1]

Year	Cable HHs (mil)	% of TV HHs	Pay Cable HHs (mil)	% of TV HHs
1994	58.75	62.4%	26.07	27.7%
1993	57.20	61.4	25.85	27.8
1992*	55.49	60.2	25.99	28.2
1991	54.86	58.9	27.04	29.0
1990	51.90	56.4	27.12	29.4
1985	36.34	42.8	21.84	25.7
1980	15.20	19.9	5.20	6.8
1975	8.60	12.6	0.14	0.2
1970	3.90	6.7	-	-
1965	1.30	2.3	-	-
1960	0.65	1.4	-	-
1955	0.15	0.5	-	-
1952	0.01	0.1	-	-

Basic/Pay Cable Subscribers and Revenues[2]

| | ----- Basic Cable ------- | | | | ----- Pay Cable --------- | | | |
| | Subscribers | | Revenue | | Subscribers | | Revenue | |
Year	(mil)	(%)	($mil)	(%)	(mil)	(%)	($mil)	(%)
1991	55.8	1.6%	$11,357	11.7%	41.9	1.0%	$5,141	0.7%
1990	54.9	4.4	10,169	17.3	41.5	1.0	5,105	4.4
1989	52.6	8.1	8,670	18.1	41.1	5.9	4,890	8.9
1988	48.6	8.0	7,343	22.1	38.8	11.5	4,491	9.4
1987	45.0	6.6	6,014	23.0	34.8	8.4	4,106	5.4
1986	42.2	5.8	4,891	18.0	32.1	4.9	3,895	4.5
1985	39.9	7.0	4,145	16.9	30.6	2.0	3,727	10.6
1984	37.3	9.4	3,545	16.3	30.0	13.6	3,370	22.7
1983	34.1	16.4	3,048	20.5	26.4	26.9	2,747	36.0
1982	29.3	26.3	2,530	22.8	20.8	34.2	2,020	53.4
1981	23.2	31.1	2,061	27.6	15.5	70.3	1,317	72.2
1980	17.7	19.6	1,615	21.2	9.1	59.6	765	79.2
1979	14.8	10.4	1,332	16.1	5.7	72.7	427	77.9
1978	13.4	6.6	1,147	14.2	3.3	106.3	240	95.1
1977	12.2	13.0	1,004	18.0	1.6	60.0	123	89.2
1976	10.8	na	851	na	1.0	na	65	-

* Reflects adjustments to conform to the 1990 census.
1. Cable-A.C. Nielsen (NTI), Jan. 1 each year; TvB estimates for pay cable prior to 1982.
2. Cable Television Developments, NCTA, October 1992 (A.C. Nielsen Co.; Paul Kagan Associates, Inc.).

Basic Cable Networks

Unlike the pay networks, which had a single revenue flow (subscriber fees), basic networks enjoyed a dual revenue stream (subscriber fees plus advertising). In 1983 only one cable TV programming service had been profitable (Ted Turner's superstation WTBS); five years later, 12–15 of the biggest advertiser-supported basic cable networks made money. If pay cable networks introduced cable in the late '70s and early '80s, the growth of basic cable networks took off after the Cable Act. The first movers dominated the rivalry (see Table 3-2).

Table 3-2
Top 15 Satellite-Fed Advertiser-Supported Cable Networks (1984–93)
[subscribers in millions]

	Programming service	(Companies, start-up year)	1993	1992	1990	1988	1986	1984
1	ESPN	(CapCit/ABC, RJR Nabisco 1979)	62	59	60	51	42	36
2	CNN	(TBS+17 other MSOs 1980)	61	58	54	50	39	30
3	USA	(Paramount+MCA 1980)	60	58	55	47	36	26
4	TBS	(TBS+major MSOs 1976)	60	57	54	46	36	31
5	A&E	(Hearst, CC/ABC, NBC 1984)	60	50	47	36	22	19
6	Nickelodeon	(Viacom 1979)	59	58	54	43	30	21
7	Discovery Ch.	(TCI+3 other MSOs 1985)	59	56	51	32	–	–
8	MTV	(Viacom 1981)	58	55	54	45	32	23
9	TNT	(Turner+major MSOs, 1988)	58	55	45	–	–	–
10	FAM	(Christian Brcst 1977)	57	55	52	44	35	25
11	TNN	(Oklahoma Publ. 1983)	57	54	53	43	29	16
12	Lifetime	(CC/ABC+Hearst+Viacom 1984)	56	53	51	41	28	–
13	The Weather Channel	(TWC 1982)	53	50	46	37	23	13
14	CNN Headline	(TBS+17 other MSOs 1980)	51	48	44	34	21	–
15	CNBC	(NBC 1989)	48	47	–	–	–	–

SOURCE: Cablevision Advertising Bureau's Cable TV Facts (various issues).

By the early '90s the big cable networks were seeking ways to hold on to existing audiences. Since most areas had been wired for cable, cable networks no longer grew with new subscribers. With cable systems adding more channels, competition for audiences and programs became intense. Entrenched cable networks consolidated to prevent newcomers from gaining footholds, and bought up programs that new channels needed. In 1983 cable networks spent only $153 million of their $255 million programming budgets on original programs—by 1990, $1.3 billion (more than half on original shows).[4]

Despite economic contraction, the big ad-supported cable networks increased their circulation in the early '90s, but the introduction of new cable services had become very difficult. Cable channels were jammed to capacity. Due to increasing capital requirements and major distributors' high bargaining power, upstarts had little chance to survive without financial and distribution support. With declining domestic growth, cable networks geared up for international expansion. Major multiple system operators (MSOs) acquired new and promising niches, including comedy (HBO and MTV Networks), sci-fi (USA Network), and court channel (Time Warner). Since MSOs had substantial interests in cable programming services and networks, the new niches were subject to a vertical price squeeze.

By spring 1994 several newcomer cable networks had a strong head start in distribution, including America's Talking, FX, Television Food Network, ESPN2, and Home & Garden Television. And other would-be channels kept popping up, including the Popcorn Channel, the Cupid

Network, the Automotive Television Network, American Political Channel, Parenting Satellite Television Network, and Hobby Craft Network.[5]

American companies already dominated the sale of individual shows to local broadcasters in Europe, but rapid changes in technology (cable systems, direct broadcast satellite) led many U.S. cable programmers to explore the export of entire networks. Following Turner's CNN and Viacom's MTV, cablers like Nickelodeon (Viacom), Sci-Fi Channel (USA Network), and Discovery Channel were being aired or launched in Europe, Asia, and the Middle East.[6]

Pay Cable Networks

Pay cable networks offered program services supported by optional extra subscriber fees. Subscribers paid an additional monthly fee ("premium") for the basic cable to receive pay cable networks. From the late '70s to early '90s, Home Box Office almost monopolized the pay market.

In 1978 ATC, a major cable operator, became part of Time Inc., the parent of HBO. If one offered programming, the other provided a distribution system. By the early '80s, HBO's bargaining power grew rapidly: it used volume discounts to entice cable operators to affiliate with it; it had some exclusive programming, which it usually refused to license to other pay-TV companies; as a producer, it distributed films to cable operators and other outlets; and with its buying power, it was able to bargain for low prices in dealing with the movie companies.

In April 1980 four major studios—Columbia, Twentieth Century-Fox, Universal (MCA), and Paramount—along with Getty Oil, created a joint venture, Premiere, to set up a satellite-fed pay-TV service. The venture prompted an antitrust suit by the Carter Justice Department in *U.S. v. Columbia Pictures Industries* (1980). The court concluded that the pricing agreement and group boycott were anticompetitive. Ironically, the Premiere case became a critical factor in the growth of a rival ancillary industry. By boosting home video, studios retaliated, hurting HBO and causing a long-lasting stagnation for pay cable.[7]

From 1984 to 1987, cable operators deemphasized pay channels, focusing on discounted packages that blurred the difference between pay and basic channels. Competition resulted in HBO's entrenchment and diversification, while subscriber growth flattened out in the mid-'80s. After the mid-'80s the pay industry went through a period of consolidation that reduced the number of rivals from more than ten companies to just three—Time Warner (HBO and Cinemax), Viacom and TCI (Showtime, The Movie Channel), and Disney (Disney Channel) (See Table 3-3).

As pay cable matured, HBO's bargaining power lessened and it adopted a more reconciliatory tone with Hollywood. To maintain its pay-market leadership, HBO struggled for differentiation (movies, family entertain-

Table 3-3
Top 4 Pay-Cable Networks (1980–93)

Pay Cable Network	------------------ Subscribers (mil.) -----------								
	1993	1992	1991	1990	1989	1988	1987	1986	1985	1980
HBO (TW 1972)	17.4	17.4	17.3	17.6	17.3	17.0	15.9	15.0	14.5	8.1
Showtime (V+TCI 1980)	7.3	7.6	7.3	7.4	7.4	6.7	5.9	5.3	5.4	1.2
Disney Ch. (WD 1983)	7.1	7.1	6.2	5.6	5.0	4.3	3.8	3.2	2.1	–
Cinemax (TW 1980)	6.3	6.2	6.2	6.3	6.4	6.0	5.1	4.2	3.3	–

TCI = Tele-Communications, Inc.   TW = Time Warner.   V = Viacom.   WD = Walt Disney.

SOURCE: Company reports, industry analysts.

ment, boxing, and comedy). By the late '80s, movies comprised 70% of HBO's programming.

Most pay services lost customers during the 1990–91 economic contraction. Since 1989 the industry also had been divided, due to the $2.4 billion antitrust lawsuit filed against it by Viacom, the parent of Showtime, which charged that HBO waged a systematic and aggressive campaign to put Showtime out of business (a settlement followed in 1992).

From 1988 to 1993 Disney's subscribers grew from 4.3 million to 7.1 million, whereas HBO's amounted to 17.4 million and Showtime's hovered around 7.3 million. While the Disney Channel's growth was most dramatic, industry leaders HBO and Showtime were also showing gains after years of modest declines and losses.[8] In 1993 HBO won 17 Emmys (*Stalin, Barbarians at the Gate*) and made $215 million on revenues of $1.4 billion, more than the Big Three networks combined. Getting ready for hundreds of cable channels, HBO and Showtime were focusing on "multiplexing," whereby cable systems simultaneously ran several separately programmed feeds.

In October 1993 Liberty Media's upstart Encore pay-TV network announced the largest film package deal in Hollywood history, agreeing to buy movies from Disney's Touchstone, Miramax, and Hollywood units. The $1 billion deal followed a year-long buying spree in Hollywood by Encore, which had 4 million subscribers for one pay cable network and planned to launch seven other specialized channels over the next year. The deal heightened stakes in the Paramount takeover battle, which was being waged by Viacom, Showtime's parent, and QVC Network, partly owned by Liberty Media, Encore's parent.[9]

By the early '90s the pay-TV market enjoyed a rebound with new marketing, programming, and pricing strategies.

Multiple System Operators and Consolidation

Cable began maturing in the late 1980s, well before reregulation. By 1991–92 the growth of cable households slowed down, whereas the number of pay-cable households and pay-cable penetration has declined since 1990.

From Basic Cable to Tiering. Until the late '80s, cable systems typically included the programming of basic cable networks (30 or more "basic" services) in the regular monthly subscription price, whereas pay subscribers paid an additional monthly fee to receive pay-cable networks (half a dozen "premium" services). By 1990 the line between the two had become blurry. Faced with surging programming costs and rate reregulation, some cable operators unbundled their basic offerings, charging subscribers higher rates.[10]

In the long run, economic and regulatory barriers prevented operators from raising their basic service rates ad infinitum. So they "returned" to tiering (a mixture of cable networks sold at a package price), which had been widely used by systems prior to deregulation. By the early '90s tiering had spread to nearly 60% of all cable subscribers, promulgating consolidation and integration of entrenched players, and jeopardizing channels that were not intrinsically linked to a program theme (ESPN and sports) or a specialized audience (MTV and teenagers).[11]

Major cable companies considered cable TV a "natural monopoly." As the number of new basic subscribers got smaller, rates increased rapidly; the basic rate grew from less than $7 to more than $15 from 1976 to 1989. Hardly surprisingly, rate-based revenues remained the most significant portion (almost 90%) of total revenues.[12]

Consolidation of Distributors. The absence of regulatory barriers boosted concentration in cable. With increasing economies of scale, greater access to capital, and more experienced management, companies that purchased systems in many cities turned into colossal multiple system operators. In 1977 the biggest MSO, Tele Prompter, had 1.1 million subscribers (9% of the total), whereas by 1993 TCI's subscribers amounted to 10 million (16%). Concurrently, the top 4 ratio had increased from 24% to more than 35%, whereas the top 8 ratio rose from over 35% to almost 46%. Even prior to the '90s, only 10% of all systems had 76% of all subscribers (see Table 3-4).

By 1992 complaints were reverberating about cable companies as "unregulated monopolies." Fewer than 1% of the U.S. cable markets were served by two or more providers. Rates had risen an average of 61% for the most popular service. Despite the rhetoric of competition, megaoperators sought to lock out or cripple would-be competitors, engaged in disabling price wars, filed lawsuits, and lobbied local and state governments to keep their territories exclusive. Sponsoring a bill calling for sweeping cable reregulation, then-Senator Albert Gore, Jr. called some large MSOs "godfathers" and labeled the industry the "cable Cosa Nostra" for its policies of extracting "tribute" from new channels.[13]

In March 1992 the broadcast TV networks actually regained a slice of

Table 3-4

Top 10 Cable Companies: Basic Cable Subscribers and Shares (1977–93)

Rank	Company	1977	Company	1987	Company	1993
Subscribers (mil)						
1	Tele Prompter	1.073	TCI	5.200	TCI	9.988
2	ATC	0.625	ATC	3.695	Time Warner	6.792
3	TCI	0.561	Continental	2.169	Continental	2.898
4	Warner Comm.	0.560	Storer	1.453	Comcast	2.852
5	Cox Cable	0.466	Cox Cable	1.438	Cablevision Syst.	2.122
6	Viacom	0.330	Warner Comm.	1.406	Cox Cable	1.774
7	Sammons Comm.	0.300	Comcast	1.343	Jones/Spacelink	1.561
8	Communication	0.290	United	1.179	Newhouse	1.417
9	UA-Columbia	0.222	Newhouse	1.061	Cablevision Ind.	1.295
10	United Cable	0.197	Viacom	1.068	Adelphia	1.225
Share (%)						
1	Tele Prompter	9.0%	TCI	12.7%	TCI	15.6%
2	ATC	5.3	ATC	9.0	Time Warner	10.6
3	TCI	4.7	Continental	5.3	Continental	4.5
4	Warner Comm.	4.7	Storer	3.5	Comcast	4.4
5	Cox Cable	3.9	Cox Cable	3.5	Cablevision Syst.	3.3
6	Viacom	2.8	Warner Comm.	3.4	Cox Cable	2.8
7	Sammons Comm.	2.5	Comcast	3.3	Jones/Spacelink	2.4
8	Communication	2.5	United	2.9	Newhouse	2.2
9	UA-Columbia	1.9	Newhouse	2.6	Cablevision Ind.	2.0
10	United Cable	1.7	Viacom	2.6	Adelphia	1.9
Basic Cable Subs.		11.9 mil.		41.0 mil.		64.1 mil.
Top-4 Ratio (%)		23.7%		30.5%		35.1%
Top-8 Ratio (%)		35.4%		43.6%		45.8%

SOURCE: For 1977 and 1987 totals, see Television and Cable Factbook (various issues); for 1992 companies and totals, see Cable Television Developments, NCTA (various issues).

audience lost to cable. A decade of explosive cable growth ended in October 1992, with the Cable Television Consumer Protection and Competition Act. It was the first veto override of the Bush administration. Before the new law took effect, major MSOs raced to impose a new round of increases, surcharges, and pricing packages.[14]

Retransmission Consent. The Cable Act of 1992 let broadcast stations, for the first time, demand payment from the local cable systems that carried their signals. Yet the major MSOs threatened to drop broadcast stations from their lineups rather than negotiate new retransmission fees. While CBS led efforts to get retransmission legislation passed, its position was undermined in summer 1993 by rival networks that created new cable channels (instead of demanding cash payments from cable operators). By the spring of 1994 the deals that ABC, NBC, and Fox made with cable systems were about to give the networks' new channels (ABC's ESPN2, Fox's FX Channel, and NBC's "America's Talking" channel) much wider distribution much faster than the many other cable channels introduced in recent years.[15]

The Cable Pact. In June 1993 seven of the nation's biggest MSOs settled a five-year antitrust investigation and agreed to make programming more available to aspiring rivals. Allegedly, cable companies had smothered competition by blocking access to popular channels, such as HBO or 24-hour sports networks. The cable pact hoped to spur competition and reduce prices. Both the struggle over retransmission consent and the long-running antitrust investigation reflected shifts of bargaining power, caused by the increasingly powerful MSOs.

New Rate Cuts. In February 1994, conceding that the cable TV regulations it had adopted a year before were inadequate, the FCC ordered cable rates cut again, by an average of 7%. While the FCC believed the additional cuts would force 90% of all cable systems to reduce at least some of their prices (saving cable subscribers $3 billion), the industry complained that the rules would curtail investments in new interactive technology. Typically, when the Bell Atlantic-TCI deal collapsed a few days later, both parties blamed the rate cuts, instead of the price disagreements and differing corporate cultures.[16]

Pay-Per-View

In the early '90s the leading MSOs set their hopes on home shopping and pay-per-view. While both represented potential growth markets, each had been around for about a decade. The attractiveness of PPV—cable programming (rock concerts, professional wrestling, prize fights, movie premieres, Broadway shows) for which subscribers paid on a one-time basis—increased with the new fiber-optic technology.[1] By the mid-'90s PPV's growth depended on technological innovation, rapidly expanding PPV consumer universe, and high-profile, big-name PPV events.

From Emergence to Growth

Pay-per-view emerged in 1977, when Warner Cable's QUBE in Columbus, Ohio, introduced eight PPV channels as part of its interactive cable system. In 1982 Warner offered the Larry Holmes-Gerry Cooney heavyweight title fight on QUBE systems. Three years later, professional wrestling entered the nascent PPV marketplace, and "Wrestlemania I" became the World Wrestling Federation's first PPV event. Although buy rates remained below 10% in the most popular PPV events of the decade, top event prices climbed rapidly from $15 to $40, and total revenue to $25.6 million.[2]

Although the number of PPV events doubled in 1989, competition, too, had intensified. By 1990, PPV networks offered three main groups of programming: movies, concerts, and sporting events (which delivered larger audiences). "New Kids on the Block Live! In Your House" became the most successful PPV concert, whereas "Wrestlemania VI" generated $24.7

Table 3-5
Dominant Pay-Per-View Networks (1986–92) [addressable subscribers in millions]

PPV Networks* (owner/launch year)	-- addressable subs (mil) ---						
	1992	1991	1990	1989	1988	1987	1986
Viewer's Choice (S+V 1985)	10.2	9.8	9.3	5.5	3.5	2.2	1.2
Request Television (RME 1985)	9.5	8.7	6.8	5.2	3.7	2.5	1.4
Spice (G PPV 1989)	4.5	5.0	3.0	-	-	-	-
Cable Video Store (G PPV 1986)	2.0	1.8	1.0	1.0	0.2	0.0	-

* Viewer's Choice 2 had 3.8 million, Request II 5.1 million and
   Action Pay Per View 4.0 million addressable subscribers.

G PPV = Graff Pay-Per-View. RME = Reiss Media Ent. S = Showtime.
V= Viacom.

SOURCE: Company reports, industry analysts.

million in gross PPV revenue. In 1991 the Holyfield-Foreman fight brought in $55 million in gross PPV revenue.[3]

In the '80s some 90% of top 20 PPV events involved professional sports, but boxing and wrestling were not enough to have a mature business. Events made the headlines, but movies were the staple for the business. By 1992, ABC and NBC took an active role in the emerging industry. While ABC started slowly, trying to build up a number of small events, NBC pushed everything else aside to focus on its PPV Olympics Triplecast. Despite a record $401 million for TV rights to the 1992 Summer Olympics, it was expected to hobble away with a loss of at least $50 million.

To pay networks, PPV served as a weapon against home video, whose earlier access to films put an end to pay cable's growth. They hoped to developed PPV into a significant pretheatrical revenue source.

Top Industry Players

Deregulation shifted the MSOs' focus from basic cable to pay cable. In 1985 Viewer's Choice and Request Television were both launched as national services (Request 2 was launched in 1988), followed by Graff Pay-Per-View's Cable Video Store and Viewer's Choice 2. At the same time, the maturing of the basic market and the flattening of the pay market reshifted focus onto PPV networks. By the early '90s the PPV business was booming with new programmers, producers, and distributors. The marketplace was dominated by two or three major players (see Table 3-5).

Viewer's Choice (I-II). Launched by Viacom, Viewer's Choice was owned by Pay Per View Network, Inc., whose partners included the major MSOs. Two PPV channels offered top Hollywood films, sports, and entertainment. By 1992 Viewer's Choice was serving 9.8 million addressable subscribers in 18.5 million cable homes.

Request Television (I-II). Request's two PPV channels were owned by Reiss

Media Enterprises and Group W Satellite Communications, which offered box-office hits and special events. By 1992 TCI and Twentieth Century Fox bought Request, which was serving 8.7 million addressable subscribers in 14.7 million cable homes.

Graff Pay-Per-View (Spice, Cable Video Store). Mark Graff owned and operated two PPV channels. While Cable Video Store offered new movie titles and special-interest programs, Spice provided "cable version" adult films on pay-per-view or pay-per-night. By 1992 the former had 1.8 million subscribers, the latter 5 million.

By the early '90s, PPV growth depended on the expansion of the addressable units. Studios perceived PPV and home video as substitutes rather than complements. Many cable operators, so used to getting a monthly fee regardless of hours watched, did little to promote PPV. Beyond basic marketing and promotional strategies, information on PPV viewers remained scarce. Finally, there was the strategic issue of whether PPV was, would be, or should be event- or movie-driven.

By 1993 gross pay-per-view revenue amounted to an estimated $377 million, up from $326 million the previous year. With more PPV events (62) than ever before, revenue was driven by movies (adult and action categories). To breathe new life into PPV heavyweight boxing, which had suffered from sluggish revenue amid a scarcity of big-name bouts and the absence of Mike Tyson, Time Warner's HBO and its PPV unit signed a six-fight deal with Riddick Bowe. Film premieres on cable TV were in the works as TCI considered investing $90 million in Carolco Pictures, in exchange for the right to show the mini-major's movies on a PPV basis simultaneously with the theatrical release.[4]

As a precursor of video-on-demand services, pay-per-view provided a preview of the information superhighway. For example, *The Miss Howard Stern New Year's Eve Pageant* (December '93) garnered roughly $16 million in revenue, far outpacing all other nonsports PPV events to date, including *New Kids on the Block* ($5.5 million in March '90) and *The Judds* ($5.5 million in December '91). By the mid-'90s pay-per-view was the fastest-growing segment of theatrical revenues. However, it represented less than 1% of total distribution revenues (compare Table 4-1).

Home Shopping

Home shopping revenues took off in 1986, with 14 major home shopping networks (and another three being founded), and 60 retailers plying their products on the airwaves. Except for one (Tempo TV), *all* had been founded in the mid-'80s. Most were single-service players. The one major exception was Cable Value Network, whose owners included MSO heavyweights like TCI, Warner Communications, United Cable (as well as McCaw Communications). The services offered a variety of items (jewelry,

Table 3-6
Major Home Shopping Networks (1986–92) [subscribers in millions]

Name (Launch Date)	1992	1990	1987	1986
QVC Network (Nov 1986)	42.8	35.0	10.5	5.1
Home Shopping Network (Jul 1985)	21.0	21.0*	15.0*	13.0
Home Shopping Network II (Sept 1986)	13.0	21.0*	15.0*	2.3
J.C. Penney Shopping Network (1987)	–	10.0	–	–
QVC Fashion Channel (Oct 1991)	7.2	–	–	–
Home Shopping Network Entert. (Sep 1991)	2.6	–	–	–
Video Shopping Mall (Jun 1986)	–	–	20.0	7.0
Consumer Discount Network (Sep 1986)	–	–	20.0	na
Cable Value Network (May 1986)	–	–	19.5	na
Telshop (Aug 1986)	–	–	10.0	10.0
The Travel Channel (Feb 1987)	–	–	7.0	–
The Fashion Channel (Oct 1987)	–	–	6.5	–
The Shop Television Network (Oct 1986)	–	–	1.0	12.0
Sky Merchant (Sep 1986)	–	–	1.0	0.6
American Shopping Channel (Oct 1986)	–	–	–	15.0
Tempo TV (Jan 1979)	–	–	–	12.5
Texas Shopping Club (Aug 1986)	–	–	–	0.8
Crazy Eddie (Nov 1986)	–	–	–	na
Cable Shopper's Network (late 1986)	–	–	–	na
Total	86.6	87.0	110.5	78.3

* HSN and HSN II combined.

SOURCES: Company reports, industry analysts.

electronics, appliances, sporting equipment, hardware, toys), whereas smaller ones specialized in niches (upscale, trendy merchandise, children's items, outdoor products) (see Table 3-6).[1]

Home Shopping Network

The initial growth of the business was due to "800" numbers and the persistence of Home Shopping Network (HSN). When the MSOs, led by TCI, opted for their own home shopping services instead of offering HSN on their systems, the Florida-based shop-by-TV channel acquired 14 UHF stations in the top 20 markets.[2]

There had been regional shopping networks before HSN went national, but HSN and HSN II brought in a record $107 million in sales during the first nine months of 1986. In a few months HSN's stock soared from the $18 initial public offering to $282 in January 1987. When stockholders sued, alleging HSN had filed false and misleading data, the stock plunged to just $16. Including major retailers like J.C. Penney, Sears Roebuck, and K-Mart, competitors seized the opportunity and moved in while shop-by-TV was being offered by cable, broadcast, and even, briefly, syndication. Concurrently, criticism mounted over HSN's merchandise, which came to represent everything that had gone wrong with HSN and the shopping craze.

The proliferation of channels went hand in hand with consolidation at the top. By 1987 there were only half a dozen major national shopping networks. While first movers like HSN and QVC Network continued to grow, the MSOs boosted the expansion of Cable Value Network, whose subscribers increased from near zero to almost 20 million.

The great shakeout followed in 1988, when TV merchandising settled in with about $1 billion in annual sales, shared by the parents of a half-dozen leading networks (QVC, CVN, and HSN). In the post-shakeout environment, the industry set its hope in the coming interactive services. The new trend was illustrated by experimental niche services. As telcos and computer firms entered into the industry, the coming age of interactivity prompted intensified consolidation.

QVC Network

In 1986 Joseph Segel, the marketing phenomenon who had founded almost 20 companies, launched QVC—for Quality, Value, Convenience (he sold his stake in 1992). In 1986–87 QVC's subscriber count doubled from 5 million to over 10 million; in the period 1987–92 it quadrupled to 43 million. If HSN still struggled with misguided aggressiveness in business and image problems, QVC's difficulties stemmed from the merger-caused debt.[3]

By the early '90s, QVC was 80% owned by major MSOs like TCI and Comcast. Amid the contraction, it acquired the J.C. Penney TV Shopping Channel, but retired over $160 million in debt and improved gross margin by a gradual shift in product mix to favor higher-margin merchandise.[4]

From Duopoly to Monopoly

After the 1990–91 contraction, two events shook the shopping industry: merger talks between QVC and HSN, and Barry Diller's equity stake in QVC. Both were prompted by the convergence of home shopping and interactive technologies. In February 1992 QVC and HSN were exploring a "possible business combination." Together, the two reached almost 90 million subscribers, accounting for the bulk of sales in the $2 billion industry. While HSN was known for advanced telecommunications and technology, QVC's strength was its more polished retailing style and inventory. QVC focused on a more upper-middle-class audience, HSN had a lower-end appeal.[5]

Just months after merger talks between HSN and QVC failed, TCI's spin-off, Liberty Media, moved to gain control of the two TV shopping networks, agreeing to pay $150 million in cash and stock for a controlling interest in HSN. Two weeks after the reported merger talks, Barry Diller left Fox, cashed out his profit participation, and sold his stock to buy into QVC. As Liberty Media and Comcast sold QVC shares to Diller, the three became equal partners. Diller quickly lured Saks Fifth Avenue to pitch wares on QVC and announced plans to launch Q2, a new lifestyle channel.

The network expanded abroad through separate ventures with News Corp.'s satellite operation and with Mexican media giant Grupo Televisa. Diller had decided that digital-compression technology was about to revolutionize the cable-driven M&E business. He hoped "someday to control either the wire highway to each home or the switching mechanism that would someday direct video traffic or the computer data bases that would serve as a library or the technology that converted pictures and programming to digital signals and back again."[6]

HSN: Toward Another Scandal

Toward the end of 1992, Liberty Media had hoped to close a $160 million cash-to-stock transaction to buy an 80% stake in HSN. The bid hit an antitrust snag. By mid-'93 Roy Speer, who had pioneered both Home Shopping Channel and the nascent industry, steered HSN to a swirl of allegations that the company's executives took commercial bribes, held secret investments in suppliers, engaged in hush-money payments, fired would-be whistle-blowers, and had ties with the mob. While a federal grand jury in Tampa was issuing subpoenas, the SEC was investigating HSN, which was also being audited by the Internal Revenue Service.[7]

In July Diller announced that QVC would acquire HSN in a $1.1 billion stock swap. In the fall, QVC launched a hostile takeover of Paramount Communications, with a bid of $10.4 billion, which exceeded Viacom's $9.6 billion offer. The delay of the proposed merger of QVC and HSN provided an opportunity to Diller to back out of the merger talks and proceed with the bid.[8] After QVC lost the takeover struggle for Paramount, it also lost its luster on Wall Street. (See Chapter 6 for a detailed account of the Paramount takeover.) In May 1994 QVC's stock hovered at $30—roughly where it was when Diller arrived.

Though just a tiny niche in the near $1 trillion retailing market, the $2 billion home shopping industry was growing fast, about 20% a year (4–5 times faster than the beleaguered retail trade). Department store chains, specialty outlets, catalog retailers, and mass merchants were reexamining home shopping. Some were selling their wares on the existing channels, planning to launch their own shopping channels. In June 1993 R.H. Macy announced it would launch a 24-hour "TV Macy's," whereas other big retailers (Saks, Bloomingdale's) were testing the new vehicle.[9]

In September 1993 TCI teamed up with the German Bertelsmann to launch a hybrid music video home shopping cable channel that could provide the first national competitor to Viacom's MTV and VH-1 channels. Spiegel, the catalogue company, announced it was teaming up with Time Warner (TW) to create two home shopping cable channels; the first one, Catalogue 1, would start operating in early 1994, while the other would debut soon on TW's interactive cable network in Orlando, Florida.

Still other competitors were laying plans for high-tech interactive services, or investing on infomercials (program-length ads), an $800 million market. While, for example, Marshall Field's was on GE's CNBC, cataloguer Fingerhut was developing infomercials tailored to CapCities/ABC's cable channels. By October 1993 mass telemarketer CUC International teamed up with Time Warner and Viacom (with AT&T as partner) to create an interactive home shopping service for trial cable systems of the future. Three months later, HSN announced it would launch Television Shopping Mall to sell merchandise from name-brand retailers, cataloguers, and consumer product companies.

In 1989 J.C. Penney, the giant Dallas-based retailer, had launched its own home shopping network, but the channel folded after only 18 months. Now U.S. retailing viewed home shopping television as a low-cost distribution system, which slashed high expenses in rent, sales help, and advertising. Few expected home TV shopping to "cannibalize" store sales; instead, it was viewed as a vehicle to expand retailers' reach and accelerate their sales. In spring 1994 Ted Turner explored the use of HSN's 12 UHF affiliate stations as a launching pad for a fifth network. By May 1994 Norstrom and J.C. Penney, two of the nation's largest retailers, teamed up with US West, a regional telephone company, to launch an interactive home-shopping channel.

From 1988 to 1993 product sales generated by infomercials grew from $350 million to $900 million, whereas total revenues of home shopping channels soared from $1.05 billion to $2.95 billion. Industry analysts expected the next generation of home shopping to be even more profitable.[10]

Toward Electronic Superhighways

By mid-1992 the FCC allowed telcos to transmit television programming to homes over their telephone lines, launching a formidable competition for cable TV companies. In December TCI's President and CEO John Malone gave cable TV's channel-expansion dreams a $200 million shot in the arm by committing to purchase the technology to launch 50–60 digital TV services. In January 1993 HBO was launching four digital satellite signals (three HBO, one Cinemax) via Galaxy I. The key to both commitments was the digital video compression technology. In the short term, compression would provide the biggest opportunity for PPV. In the long term, digitized TV was expected to speed up the shift to micromarketing, via "personalized communications choices."

By the early '90s most major cable companies were diversified operations. There were essentially three kinds of major cable companies: distributors with extensive system operations, programmers with popular network services, and wholesalers with integrated hybrid operations.

The first kind is illustrated by Tele-Communications, Inc. (TCI), the second by Turner Broadcasting Systems (TBS) and the third by Viacom.

TELE-COMMUNICATIONS, INC.: THE DEAL MACHINE

In 1952 Bob Magness, a former Oklahoma cottonseed salesman and part-time rancher, sold his cattle and mortgaged his house to buy a cable franchise in Texas. He also collected systems in Montana, Nevada, Colorado, and Utah. Magness had a simple basic principle: "Pay Interest, Not Taxes." The most effective way to accumulate assets was to borrow heavily, while reporting low profits. By the mid-'60s, 17 systems served nearly 37,000 subscribers. In 1970 he took TCI public. Three years later, the company was flirting with bankruptcy and Magness hired 32-year-old business wizard John Malone as president of TCI.[1]

Vertical Integration

In the late '70s TCI was reliant on institutional investors, but continued to be run in an entrepreneurial manner—aggressively, even arrogantly. Not only was Malone an early junk-bond customer of Milken's Drexel Burnham Lambert; he also foresaw the coming explosion of the cable industry. As satellites boosted a generation of cable networks, cable programmers needed operators to receive the signal. The bigger the operators, the greater the market; the larger the size, the lower the costs.

Unlike most major cablers, TCI often purchased pieces of cable properties rather than entire systems. Acquiring companies "in little bites rather than great big swallows," the company gained in subscriber counts, without added managerial duties. Malone saw TCI as an "investment vehicle," in which companies were "run autonomously by their own entrepreneurial managers."[2] The complex structure involved wholly owned subsidiaries and partnerships with other companies and individuals, as well as exotic financing structures.

Despite decentralization, TCI's decision making was dictated by a pyramid-like hierarchy extending from the executive committee to consolidated and unconsolidated subsidiaries. All policy decisions were made by a three-man executive committee (Malone, Magness, and an outside director). In 1979 Malone and Magness had been concerned about losing control. Through a series of complex transactions, the two ended up controlling about 60% of TCI's votes while owning only 11% of its shares.

TCI's M&A-Driven Growth

By mid-1989, Malone had made 482 deals. Although the majority of these acquisitions involved MSOs, they included home shopping services, program producers, microwave common carriers, and others. He positioned TCI for a breakup—to prepare for monopoly-busting legislation.

TCI minimized whatever it paid in taxes, paid little attention to reported earnings, and employed high leverage, which was necessary to purchase new cable systems. Cash flow enabled the company to cover its interest payments and buy more systems. It was Malone who persuaded Wall Street to focus on cable's prodigious cash flow and rising asset value rather than its heavy debt and nonexistent earnings. The key to TCI's success lay in Magness's business philosophy, in asset appreciation.

The ceaseless M&A activity boosted cash flow and asset valuations. From 1974 to 1989 the value of a TCI share soared more than 91,000%, from $1 to $913. TCI continued to pursue acquisitions and deemphasize net income, while its cable-system assets threw off impressive operating cash flow. Instead of paying in taxes from operating income, the company paid interest costs from acquisitions. Ultimately, TCI's bites became huge swallows as at least three deals (Heritage Communications, United Artists Communications, and Storer Communications) exceeded over $1 billion each. By 1990 the fourth M&A wave was over, and TCI had a virtual moratorium on cable system purchases.

Leverage had made possible frantic deal-making. Without acquisitions, however, cash flow did little for the stock, and investors took another look at earnings; when they saw a deficit of $287 million instead of an operating income of $1.3 billion, TCI's shares began to decline. Through the '80s TCI had pushed debt away from the holding company. By 1990 direct investments and (off-balance-sheet) private partnerships bled red ink on a consolidated basis. Long-term debt had risen from $174 million to $9.3 billion, causing the debt ratio to soar to 83%. So TCI began implementing a "new financial strategy" to broaden its debt sources to strengthen its capital base.

By 1990 TCI was almost three times as large as its rival, American Television & Communications (owned by Time). It had 6.5 million subscribers in its consolidated operations and another 5 million in companies where it owned minority stakes; it had equity stakes in basic cable networks and a majority interest in regional cable sports networks; it owned United Artists Entertainment's (UAE) cable systems and theatre division (the largest American theatre circuit), and it was among the largest distributors of direct broadcast satellite services.

TCI's penchant for bailing out ailing programmers (including a 25% interest in Turner Broadcasting) improved its reputation as a benevolent force in the cable business; when the MSOs came under scrutiny for skyrocketing basic rates and access for programming, services like The Discovery Channel, along with C-SPAN and CNN, served as excellent public-relations vehicles. Indeed, TCI's control of distribution and production could make or break a new channel.

Table 3-7
TCI Operations (1986–93)

| | ------ Revenue ------ | | | --- Operating ------- Income | | |
	Cable	Theatre	Total	Cable	Theatre	Total
($mil)						
1993	$4,153	–	$4,153	$916	–	$916
1992*	3,574	–	3,574	864	–	864
1991*	3,214	–	3,214	674	–	674
1990*	2,940	–	2,940	546	–	546
1990	2,942	$683	3,625	628	$26	654
1989	2,362	664	3,026	516	53	569
1988	1,710	572	2,282	435	56	491
1987	1,225	484	1,709	310	48	358
1986	646	–	646	154	–	154
(%)						
1993	100%	–	100%	100%	–	100%
1992*	100	–	100	100	–	100
1991*	100	–	100	100	–	100
1990*	100	–	100	100	–	100
1990	81	19%	100	96	4%	100
1989	78	22	100	91	9	100
1988	75	25	100	89	11	100
1987	72	28	100	87	13	100
1986	100	–	100	–	–	100

* Restated and reclassified.

SOURCE: Tele-Communications, Inc.

From 1987 to 1990 TCI's cable revenues more than doubled (81% of total), far outweighing theatre revenues (19%): cable's operating income doubled (*96%* of total), whereas that of theatre shrank (*4%*). The diversification had been a mistake (see Table 3-7).

Spinoff of Liberty Media

Increased vertical integration prompted TCI to restructure prior to reregulation. The idea was not new to Malone, who, armed with his degrees and financial expertise at AT&T's Bell Labs in the 1960s, had written a 300-page treatise on maximizing profits in a regulated company.

In January 1991 TCI outlined plans to spin off significant cable TV assets. It would transfer $298 million worth of cable systems and $307 million of mainly minority interests in programming services into the new Liberty Media subsidiary. With cable revenues at $12 million, the programming entity generated over $94 million in programming revenues. Starting in December 1992 Liberty went on a buying binge, trying to acquire Home Shopping Network (it already owned a substantial stake in the rival QVC); it also planned to combine Prime Network, a loose affiliation of regional sports stations, with SportsChannel to create a nation-wide network that would rival ESPN.[3]

The spin-off was a "cosmetic" move designed to refine the edges of a decentralized structure that remained tightly controlled by Malone and Magness. Initially, Wall Street had discouraged the investment. By late 1991 Liberty looked more attractive.

Tales of the Dark Side: TCI and BCCI

In the late '80s Malone's efforts to expand TCI's customer service program went hand in hand with rising regulatory pressures. With the revelation of TCI's links with the Bank of Credit and Commerce International (BCCI), the public relations (PR) struggle was doomed.[4] Bob Magness, chairman of TCI, and Larry Romrell, senior VP, were the founding shareholders of Capcom Financial Services Ltd., which was connected with BCCI, which had been seized by regulators in the previous July on charges of laundering drug profits, brokering illegal arms sales, and harboring money for terrorists. As BCCI's investment company, Capcom had been indicted in 1988 in a $32 million money-laundering and cocaine-trafficking case. By 1992 British and American investigations indicated that TCI executives served as strategic conduits in BCCI's campaign to enter American real estate and communications industries.[5]

New Strategic Direction

TCI generated an annual cash flow of $1.7 billion—more than ABC, CBS, NBC, and FBC combined. Together, TCI and Liberty owned stakes in a dozen top cable channels. TCI's vertical integration had become an argument for cable reregulation (see Figure 3-1).

In January 1992, the *Wall Street Journal* published a critical article on TCI's self-dealing and hardball tactics. By then, one out of every five American cable users was wired into TCI, and about 20% of the industry's revenues flowed to the giant MSO, which then-Senator Al Gore, Jr. had called the "ringleader" in the "cable Cosa Nostra." The *Journal's* investigation appeared on the eve of the cable reregulation vote in the U.S. Senate. It showed that Bob Magness and John C. Malone built and dominated the company in part through internal self-dealing.[6] Despite controversies, TCI continued to enjoy Wall Street's support. When the Senate passed the reregulatory package in February 1992, TCI opted for a new strategic direction.

Toward the Digital Era

As cable boom days were over, TCI poured funds into new technologies that it hoped would become growth engines. Concurrently, it began efforts to cut into the Baby Bells' marketplace.

Figure 3-1
TCI's Corporate Structure (1992)*

```
                              TCI INC.
        ┌────────────────────────┴──────────────────────────────────┐
       CABLE                                            PROGRAMMING & OTHER
        │                                               ─────────────────────
  ┌─────┴───────────────────────┐                       Discovery Channel (49%)
Managed Cable      Unconsolidated Investments           Turner Broadcasting (25%)
TV Affiliates      & Non-Managed Affiliates             United Artists Theatres
──────────────     ─────────────────────────              2,600 screen theater chain
TCI Northeast      Bresnan Comm. (80%)                  Cable Adnet Partners
TCI North Central  Halcyon (75%)                          advertising time marketer
TCI Great Lakes    Caguas/Humacao (50%)                 Netlink USA (80%)
TCI East           Heritage Partnerships (30%)            home satellite-dish
TCI West           Intermedia Partners (32%)              programming
TCI Central        Storer Comm. (35%)                   Cable TV joint venture
TCI Southeast      UAE Partnerships (11%)                  (New Zealand)
Washington, DC                                          Cable TV partnership
  (75%)                                                   (England)
WestMarc Comm.                                          Liberty Media (5%) owns:
Heritage Comm.                                            Black Entertainment TV
  (80%)                                                     (17%)
United Cable                                             Courtroom TV (33%)
                                                          QVC Network Inc. (49%)
                                                          Family Channel (16%)
                                                          American Movie Classics
                                                            (50%)
```

* Unless noted in parentheses ownership is 100%.

SOURCE: Reprinted by permission of *Wall Street Journal*, copyright 1992
       Dow Jones & Company, Inc. All Rights Reserved Worldwide.

Entry into Telco Businesses. In February 1992 TCI bought a 49.9% stake in Teleport Communications Group, Merrill Lynch's fiber-optic subsidiary. A day after the Teleport deal, TCI sold its UAE theater chain for $680 million. Two months later it expanded involvement in telcos by entering a joint venture with a US West subsidiary to explore cable and telephone opportunities in Europe. The two companies were already in a partnership to jointly operate telephone and cable in the United Kingdom.

Diversified Revenue Sources. By the end of 1992 TCI received 65% of its revenues from basic cable, 18% from pay cable, and 17% from "ancillary" sources. The latter stemmed from cable advertising, pay-per-view, home shopping, program guides, satellite and microwave services, and other activities, which were changing the face of the company's revenue.

TCI's repositioning was dictated by reregulation in cable and Malone's vision of cable evolution (put forward in the 1990 *Annual Report*): (1) The industry was born in the '50s with the introduction of coaxial cable and broadband amplifiers. (2) It went through a technological revolution in the '70s with the deployment of space satellites, which changed the economics of mass distribution of information, drastically and irreversibly. (3) At the turn of the '90s the industry was on the threshold of still another revolution. While optical fiber offered a cost-effective way to improve the reliability and quality of video signals, digital compression condensed and processed video signals, further improving quality. (Hence TCI's investments in Faroudja Research Enterprises, Inc., Cable Labs, and Eidak Corp.)

The $18 billion cable TV industry was about to cut into the $11 billion home video business. By December 1992 TCI announced it planned to introduce digital-compression technology that could let it provide 500 or more channels to cable subscribers by 1994. "Television will never be the same," predicted Malone. The next April he unveiled TCI's $2 billion fiber upgrade, which was to replace coaxial cable in four years to accommodate hundreds of channels, as well as enhance PPV and other new technologies.[7]

Acquisition of TV Shopping Networks. While TCI's spinoff, Liberty Media, announced it would pay $150 million for a controlling interest in Home Shopping Network, the board of QVC Network, HSN's main rival, was weighing a proposal from Liberty and Comcast to cede board control to the two companies, which together owned 53% in QVC.

Following reregulation, the reticent Malone started a hyperactive PR campaign to position TCI in the new environment. The company bought a 25% interest in Carolco Pictures, which enabled TCI to create a PPV special event by playing a high-profile theatrical motion picture from Carolco simultaneously with its run in theatres. The $90 million plunge into PPV marked TCI's first foray into the film business. Through a deal with Sega Enterprises and Time Warner, TCI tapped the children's market to create the Sega Channel. Both TCI and Time Warner continued to own a significant stake in Turner Broadcasting. In September 1993 TCI announced a new music-television cable network in partnership with Bertelsmann AG; it was designed to take on MTV, the subsidiary of Viacom (which was accusing TCI of monopolizing the cable business).

Although the FCC's new rate regulations were not expected to seriously harm TCI's annual revenues (the company tended to have lower rates than the industry as a whole), the cable giant's arrogance created new image problems in November 1993 when the *Washington Post* published an internal TCI memo that urged local managers to raise cable rates and blame increases on the reregulation act.

When Malone testified at the 1989 Senate hearings on media concentration, he argued that the entire media business was driven by the fact that the creation of software was expensive, whereas the marginal cost of the end product was very low. Therefore media companies were driven by external growth. Despite its investments, TCI's portfolio lacked a significant programming source. So Malone helped finance the $9.9 billion offer by QVC Network and its chairman, Barry Diller, to acquire Paramount.

In early 1991 TCI had spun off Liberty to deflect congressional criticism over its control of cable programming; by October 1993 TCI moved to reacquire Liberty Media through a $4 billion stock swap, to boost Liberty's

QVC Network in its bid for Paramount, and to position TCI in the electronic superhighway (half a year later, the Justice Department cleared the way for the reacquisition).

While AT&T had been testing movies on demand with TCI and US West, McCaw Cellular had run a trial of cellular phone service using TCI's coaxial network. In mid-October 1993 Bell Atlantic and TCI agreed to pursue a $33 billion merger. Amid the industry turmoil, TCI sought to link up with still another studio and approached the parent companies of Universal Studios, Twentieth Century Fox, and Columbia Pictures for either a large stake in a studio or a joint venture.[8] At the end of October, Encore, Liberty Media's upstart pay-TV network, announced a $1 billion film package deal.

Malone saw a revolution taking place in telecommunications. Video, computer, and telephone technologies are converging into one. TCI was laying a claim to a share of a pie of more than a half-trillion dollars.

TURNER BROADCASTING SYSTEMS: THE MAVERICK AND HIS SHADOW PARTNERS

In 1965 Ted Turner's father committed suicide. Although the father had begun the sellout of the family's billboard company in Atlanta, Georgia, his 25-year-old son halted the transactions. By the end of the '60s Ted Turner had turned the ailing billboard business into a multimillion-dollar conglomerate.[1]

From Superstation WTBS to News Empire CNN

In 1970 Turner merged his outdoor advertising company with a broadcasting company and purchased a weak UHF indie station in Atlanta, and another one in Charlotte, North Carolina. He also began to build a movie library of some 5,000 titles, along with a growing roster of old TV shows. From 1970 to 1975 revenues nearly doubled, from $6.8 million to $12.6 million.

Superstation WTBS

When the FCC ruled that indies could send their signals to more distant markets, WTBS in 1976 became the first U.S. superstation, with programming distributed 24 hours a day via satellite to cable systems across the country. In addition to the growing WTBS film and TV library, Turner needed sports franchises to support the programming of his superstation; in the long run, gains in ad sales would be accompanied by the rise of the costs of TV rights. Hence the purchases of baseball and basketball teams—the Atlanta Braves and the Atlanta Hawks.

During the period 1975–80 TBS's revenues more than quadrupled to

$55 million; from 1980 to 1985 revenues grew nearly sevenfold to $352 million and advertisers were flocking to WTBS.

Cable News Network (CNN)

As the Big Three ignored worldwide newsgathering and Time's HBO was not investing in the emerging market, Turner in 1978 thought about a 24-hour, all-news cable network. At first, he saw Cable News Network (CNN) as "a half hour of news, like *Time* magazine. Then a half hour of sports, like *Sports Illustrated.* Then another half hour of features, like *People* magazine. And a half hour of business news, like *Fortune.* We're gonna repeat it every two hours, twenty-four hours a day. . . . We're gonna do this half-hour format and freshen it up every two hours."[2]

In 1979 Turner put his Charlotte station up for sale to fund the world's first 24-hour news network, which the Big Three ridiculed as "Chicken Noodle News." Financially, this period was a difficult one at TBS.

In 1980–81 ABC and Westinghouse combined their forces in Satellite NewsChannels (SNC), a joint venture designed to produce *two* 24-hour channels of advertiser-supported cable news. ABC's and Westinghouse's combined revenues amounted to $11.8 billion, whereas TBS generated about $1 million. In numbers and resources, it was the fly against the giants. Yet Turner opted for a preemptive first strike against SNC by beginning *another* 24-hour, all-news service, Cable News Network II. It went on the air in just four months. Turner got advertisers behind him (although SNC was offered free), and severely restricted SNC's subscriber potential. The two CNN services were augmented by CNN Radio.

By 1985 CNN was in the black and, unlike the Big Three, it distinguished itself with a more critical focus on the Reagan administration's policies.[3]

The track record was not spotless. When Turner diversified into businesses that required skills that neither WTBS nor CNN provided, efforts failed. In 1984, for example, Turner launched the Cable Music Channel (CMC), a music-video service. It provided little competition to Viacom's MTV and closed down in a month.

After futile merger talks with CBS, Turner sought a partner among the Hollywood studios, Metromedia, Time, Gannett, and MGM. He wanted the controlling interest. In late 1984 he rejected friendly merger plans and decided to take over a network. When Turner told his bankers to prepare a bid for ABC, Capital Cities Communications was already merging with ABC. In April 1985 Turner offered a complicated package of $5.4 billion for CBS. Though financed by junk bonds, the merger concept was economically viable, even though rejected by CBS.

As trading of the company's common stock began on the American Stock Exchange in 1985, CNN started the first live 24-hour news service distributed to European audiences. Turner defeated NBC's takeover attempt, but he was growing hungry and impatient.

The MGM Deal

After three years of informal talks with Kirk Kerkorian, the financier behind MGM/UA, Turner moved to acquire the studio. In July 1985 he accepted Kerkorian's price—much too hastily—as long as the financier would sweeten the initial 3,000 MGM classics with some 1,450 additional old movies from the RKO and pre-1950 Warner libraries, from *The Wizard of Oz* to *Gone with the Wind*, for use on his superstation WTBS. Although it almost broke his back, buying the library was an ingenious strategic move that ensured the future of TBS's cable properties.

In the summer of 1986 TBS cosponsored and telecasted the first Goodwill Games held in Moscow. Unable to compete with the Big Three for the TV rights to the Olympics, Turner sought to strike back at the networks, but, instead, suffered a $26 million loss. That same year TBS launched the Color Classic Network to begin the colorization of 100 classic black and white films in Turner's library, which would serve as a pivotal asset for Turner Network Television (TNT, founded in 1988).

Debt Crisis and Struggle for Control

Soon CNN expanded its reach to every continent and major capitals. By 1987 CNN and superstation TBS were the second and third largest cable services, respectively (in number of cable TV homes served). In June *Larry King Live*, a one-hour interview program, debuted on CNN. As CNN's portable satellite up-links changed the face of TV journalism, Headline News went on the air in July 1987 from the new headquarters in the CNN Center.

Yet the mid-'80s were financially painful to Turner, who was going through a $40 million divorce and had overpaid some $300 million for MGM/UA. In 1987 Turner was forced to auction off many of Kerkorian's assets, as well as 36% of Turner Broadcasting. Since TCI's John Malone wanted to keep CNN out of the reach of *his* rivals (Time, NBC, News Corp.), he outlined a bailout plan in which a consortium of 26 MSOs bought $565 million worth of TBS stock, reduced Turner's ownership from 81% to 51%, got seats on a new Turner board, and could veto new initiatives. Initially Time hoped Turner would sell part of CNN, but in May 1987 it joined in and formed a directorate-within-a-directorate with TCI. Time sought control of CNN, while TCI needed program sources. Viacom, however, left the consortium in protest.

To Turner the bailout plan was preferable to Kerkorian, who would have divested TBS's assets. For the same reason, TCI and Time did not want noncable interests to control TBS. Though Time and TCI appointed seven directors to join Turner's eight board members, Turner still retained majority control and intended to take advantage of the animosity between TCI and Time.

By 1989 *Business Week* valued a disassembled Turner Broadcasting at $5 billion: superstation TBS (1.5 bil); CNN and Headline News (1.5 bil); Turner Entertainment Co. (1.5 bil); Turner Network Television ($615 mil); real estate ($165 mil); sports franchises ($150 mil). A year later Hank Whittemore, the historian of TBS, valued the same properties at $6.6 billion.

Ted Turner had become respectable. Just as his many female companions had been replaced with Jane Fonda, his holdings were no longer sexy one-night stands but pillars of envy. In the absence of new and risky ventures, the old businesses grew, expanded, and matured. That was a little boring to Turner, who turned his attention to social issues (which enhanced TBS's clout).

Diversification

In the early '90s TBS was operating in five separate business segments: entertainment, news, syndication/licensing, sports, and real estate (see Table 3-8).

Entertainment. Entertainment encompassed superstation TBS and TNT, as well as TNT Latin America, Cartoon Network, H-B Production Co. (an animation entertainment production studio), as well as Turner Publishing, Inc. From 1986 to 1992, the portion of entertainment rose from 37% to 48% in revenues.

News. The news segment included CNN, Headline News, CNN International, as well as Turner Private Networks, Inc. In the years 1985–90 the segment's revenue portion declined from 35% to 30%. Until 1988 revenues from news exceeded those from entertainment at TBS. By 1992, however, entertainment revenues constituted 48% of the total, as against 30% from news. In operating profit, entertainment results exceeded those of news in 1992.

Syndication/Licensing. This segment encompassed Turner Entertainment Co. (the TEC film library), Turner Program Services, Turner International, Turner Home Entertainment, World Championship Wrestling, and Hanna-Barbera Entertainment. Despite strong growth in the late '80s, the segment's revenue portion declined to 15% in 1992.

Sports. The segment entailed the Atlanta Braves, the Atlanta Hawks, and SportSouth Network. During 1985–90 this was the only segment that remained in the red. Losses were recorded as "program costs." The early '90s, however, witnessed a strong rebound. The real estate segment encompassed CNN Center in Atlanta, as well as Omni Coliseum adjacent to the Center.

Table 3-8
Turner Broadcasting System Inc.: Business Segments (1985–93)

	Entertainment	News	Syndication/ Licensing	Sports	Real Estate	Other	Total[1]
Total revenue ($mil)[2]							
1993r[4]	$1,162.2	$599.4	–	–	–	$182.3	$1,921.6
1992r	1,078.6	531.2	–	–	–	180.7	1,769.9
1991r	869.0	478.3	–	–	–	144.0	1,480.2
1992	$847.0	$535.5	$258.9	$83.3	$41.1		$1,769.9
1991	711.3	479.4	192.3	53.2	39.9		1,480.2
1990	662.9	405.2	248.6	31.3	42.6		1,393.5
1989	386.5	349.6	253.3	27.1	42.1		1,065.1
1988	266.1	267.1	204.3	23.6	43.3		806.6
1987	222.3	208.6	159.0	22.8	38.0		652.4
1986	204.4	167.2	134.9	23.9	23.5		556.9
1985	186.2	122.9	10.1	21.8	8.0		351.9
Operating Profit ($mil)[3]							
1993	$142.2	$212.2	–	–	–	$(33.3)	$302.1
1992	151.8	178.4	–	–	–	(36.8)	289.4
1991	146.5	165.3	–	–	–	(14.8)	297.1
1992	$176.3	$154.9	$(15.8)	$11.2	$0.5		$289.3
1991	159.5	167.6	(5.5)	2.3	0.5		297.1
1990	75.5	134.4	28.8	(17.2)	3.4		201.3
1989	104.2	135.9	47.3	(3.9)	0.7		266.1
1988	53.4	85.5	1.6	(5.3)	2.2		119.7
1987	61.8	55.3	(10.0)	(6.7)	1.6		84.3
1986	12.5	38.6	(6.7)	(13.8)	(1.2)		18.0
1985	60.2	12.5	1.9	(9.2)	(0.1)		57.7

1. Includes "other" category (revenue, income).
2. Less intersegment revenue
3. Equity in income (loss) of unconsolidated entitities.
4. In fiscal 1993, TBS presented three rather than six segments restating figures for 1991-93.

SOURCE: Turner Broadcasting System Inc.

Real Estate. In real estate, revenues climbed rapidly until 1987. Through the rest of the decade, they remained almost flat.

From 1980 to 1992 TBS's revenues grew from $54 million to almost $1.8 billion, its total assets increased from $54 million to over $2.5 billion, and stock price soared. Yet TBS's net income showed deficits in the late '80s and earnings remained in the red, while TBS's debt/capital ratio hovered around 102–108%. In one of its last underwritings, Drexel helped TBS to restructure $1.6 billion in high-cost debt. The recapitalization took some pressure off CNN and other TBS operating units, giving the company seven years to boost cash flow without the banks' increasing pressure. The bailout reduced Turner's autonomy and increased the MSOs' control within the organization. He served increasingly as a figurehead for TCI and Time Warner.

The Launch of Turner Network Television (TNT)

TNT, a sports-and-entertainment cable network, was designed to attract new viewers to cable, while making more productive use of the existing programming assets. In three months, TNT's circulation exceeded the target of 30 million subscribers in 1989, debuting 15 original movies. The purpose of NBA games and original movies was to raise the cable-service prime-time ratings.

Global News Village: Identity Crisis

By 1990 several revenue streams (broadcasters, hotels, institutions, cable subscriptions, and advertising) had saved CNN from dependence on advertisers, which, in turn, enhanced its global influence and diplomatic role, not least because of the turmoil in China, the Soviet Union, Eastern Europe, and the Persian Gulf. When Turner planted a UN flag outside the old mansion where CNN began its operations, he envisioned the cable service as a global network. In 1980 CNN reached less than 2 million households in the United States; in 1990, about 54 million. The news service was also viewed in 89 countries and some 6 million households (of which 4–5 million in Europe).

When something happened, the ratings boomed; when things were quiet, ratings plummeted. CNN's fate was dictated by international misfortunes. Advertisers called it the "Cable Crisis Network." CNN began to reposition itself and developed news program franchises, hoping that these would grow into hits like the hour-long *Larry King Live*.[4]

Avoiding tinkering with proven concepts (existing newscasts), CNN sought new audiences with news program franchises (the launch of *CNN World Report* in 1987, *World Today* and the investigative Special Assignment Unit in 1989), and efforts at low-cost production through strategic alliances (talks with CBS and NBC, the programming pact between TBS and Tribune in 1990).

By 1992 CNN had a staff of more than 1,700, its global reach exceeded 75 million homes, and its budget was growing while the Big Three were cutting back. The network had established its credibility and was making money. Yet international expansion was a necessity since the appeal of CNN had inspired imitators. In 1988 TBS founded Noticiero Telemundo-CNN, transmitting CNN news in Spanish to the U.S. Hispanic audience and to Latin American countries. By 1993 some 10 M&E giants were rushing to launch their own satellite news programs, in direct competition with CNN. The list included TCI, the Big Three networks, *Wall Street Journal* publisher Dow Jones, as well as four British firms (Reuters Holdings Plc., *Financial Times* publisher Pearson Plc., Murdoch's Sky Television, and the BBC).[5]

In the aftermath of the bailout, TBS had entered an era of executive turmoil. Similarly, CNN was a factionalized organization, where management style nurtured infighting. To boost the morale, Turner chose as new president of CNN a newspaperman, vice-chairman of the *Los Angeles Times* Tom Johnson.[6]

The Launch of The Cartoon Network

Just as Turner had bought the MGM library to launch TNT, in late 1991 he acquired Hanna-Barbera's 3,000 animated half-hours and 350 series and films, to launch The Cartoon Network, a 24-hour basic cable animation channel. Turner used the industry slump and economic contraction to his advantage. Both lowered the new channel's startup costs.

In January 1992 *Time* chose Ted Turner as its "Man of the Year." Stabilized by psychiatric counseling and the companionship of Jane Fonda, Turner celebrated his 53rd birthday, surprised to reach the age at which his father had committed suicide. If CNN had acquired enormous clout as a result of its coverage of recent crises (the Persian Gulf War, the Russian Coup), Turner, too, had mellowed.[7]

In March-April 1993 Time Warner and TCI were discussing a plan to divide the primary assets of Turner Broadcasting System, a move that was expected to break up Turner's $6 billion news and entertainment empire. Previously, Turner himself had discussed a merger or combination with several M&E companies, including Capital Cities/ABC and Paramount Communications. The efforts had been frustrated by his inability to make any deal without the approval of Time Warner and TCI.[8] Turner, who still owned a 51% voting stake in his empire, would not give in to his "shadow partners." He began positioning TBS for the information superhighway.

In August 1993 Turner spent an estimated $30 million by picking up exclusive rights to 300 titles from Paramount. He bought New Line Cinema Corporation and Castle Rock Entertainment for $600 million in cash and stock and assumed $200 million in debt. He was exploring agreements with two major studios to add 1,500 films to the growing library. The idea was to secure more products for cable networks, such as Turner Classic Movies (the latest Turner network set to debut in April 1994), and possibly the American Movie Classics network (half-owned by Liberty Media), which he was interested in acquiring.[9] Turner's objective was to become one of the largest and most profitable providers of quality TV programming in the world.

With two Hollywood studios in the bag, Turner was on the prowl again in 1994. He had talks with NBC and ABC, as well as Columbia. Seeking a network, he was prepared to give up his 51% voting control.[10] By mid-March Turner got interested in using Home Shopping Network's 12 UHF affiliate stations as a launching pad for a fifth network.[11] Half a year later, he resumed talks with the existing TV networks.

In April 1994, while the Center for Communication was honoring Ted Turner as its guest of honor in New York City, Turner started his new cable channel, Turner Classic Movies (TCM), at Times Square's giant Jumbotron screen above Broadway. As the cable industry struggled amid an enormous turmoil, triggered by the new rate cuts, Turner was "Singin' in the Rain."

VIACOM: SEARCH FOR GROWTH

Viacom International Inc. was organized in Delaware in August 1970 as CBS's wholly owned subsidiary. A year later, due to regulatory barriers, CBS spun off its cable-TV and program syndication divisions into a new company. Viacom, short for "via communications," was reincorporated in April 1975.[1]

When the syndication operation, Viacom Enterprises, expanded into program production (networks and syndication market), it grew into the sixth largest MSO. In 1976 Viacom also entered the pay-TV business with Showtime, HBO's primary rival. In the following years, Viacom went through intensive expansion and takeovers. In 1983 Warner-Amex sold The Movie Channel (TMC) to Showtime; through its ownership of Showtime and TMC, Viacom hoped to compete against HBO's near-monopoly in pay cable.

From National Amusements to Viacom

By 1986 the 63-year-old Sumner Redstone's family business, National Amusement, had grown from a string of over 50 drive-in theatres into a modernized theatre circuit with some 350 screens. Redstone considered cable TV's growth as the flip side of the maturing theatre business and invested in major M&E companies. In 1981 Redstone made some $20 million selling a 5% interest in Twentieth Century Fox to Marvin Davis; a year later, he earned about $25 million from selling Columbia Pictures stock to Coca-Cola; in 1985 he sold back his share in MGM/UA Home Entertainment to financier Kirk Kerkorian, making another $15 million.

After surviving a 1979 hotel fire, business routines had few challenges for the billionaire, who in all his life had owned just one modest home. Then Redstone "fell in love" with Viacom, which was thriving with its 5 TV stations, 16 cable systems, 1.1 million subscribers, 7 cable networks, syndication rights to *The Cosby Show* and other hits, as well as network series like *Frank's Place*, *Matlock*, and *Jake and the Fatman*.

Viacom International Inc.

When Viacom's management attempted to acquire the company in a leveraged buyout, Redstone began positioning for Viacom. Although he had never borrowed more than $25 million at National Amusements, Redstone learned quickly how publicly traded companies changed hands.

In November Redstone organized Arsenal Holdings, Inc., to acquire Viacom (which he won in a bitterly contested LBO). As he took Viacom public with the debt used to acquire it, Viacom International became an indirect wholly owned subsidiary of Viacom, Inc., which became an 83% owned subsidiary of Redstone's National Amusements. Although Viacom's stock amounted to nearly $3.4 billion, the LBO left the company $2.7 billion in debt.

By 1992 National Amusements owned 750 screens and had $250 million in revenues. Real estate formed the basis of Redstone's personal fortune, which was estimated at over $3.3 billion.[2]

Posttakeover Viacom: Vertical Integration

Instead of selling off pieces of the company, Redstone and his new president/CEO Frank Biondi, formerly a rising star at HBO, managed the posttakover phase with skill that boosted further expansion. In January 1986, after a failed LBO by MTV executives, Viacom took over MTV Networks. With strong cash flow, the company avoided asset dispositions. The LBO did little to constrain Redstone's eagerness for new acquisitions, including his 1988 bid for the beleaguered Orion Pictures.

From 1985 to 1990 Viacom's annual revenues more than tripled to $1.6 billion, while operating income more than doubled to $224 million. Concurrently, long-term debt increased to over $2.5 billion and debt ratio exceeded 87%. Yet the company was able to up its line of credit to $1.7 billion. By the early '90s Viacom was a diversified M&E company with operations in four major segments: networks, cable television, entertainment, and broadcasting (see Table 3-9).

Viacom Networks. The networks segment operated three advertiser-supported basic cable TV program services: MTV Music Television (including MTV Europe), VH-1, Nickelodeon/Nick at Nite, and three premium subscription TV program services: Showtime, The Movie Channel, and Flix. Directly and through Viacom Networks, the company participated in three additional basic-cable program services: Lifetime, Comedy Central, and the All News Channel. The company also distributed special events and feature films on a PPV basis through its Set Pay Per View and provided for the sale of satellite-delivered program services to home satellite dishes through its Showtime Satellite Networks.

From the mid-'80s to the early '90s, networks generated 50–57% of Viacom's revenues and about 60% of its operating income. In the long run, the company's growth was based on acquisitions and well-managed operations, especially MTV Networks (and its spinoff, Video Hits One, VH-1) which had been launched in 1981.

Viacom Cable Television. This segment owned and operated cable TV

Table 3-9
Viacom: Business Segments (1985–93)

	Cable TV	Broadcasting	Networks	Entertainment	Total[1]
Revenues ($mil)					
1993	$416.0	$181.8	$1,221.2	$209.1	$2,004.9
1992	411.1	168.8	1,058.8	248.3	1,864.7
1991	375.0	159.2	922.2	273.5	1,711,6
1990	330.5	164.0	843.0	282.2	1,599.6
1989	300.6	146.1	752.0	254.5	1,436.2
1988	330.0	141.2	642.6	161.1	1,258.5
1987[2]	282.7	132.1	523.6	81.6	1,010.8
1986	232.8	111.3	510.4	77.3	919.2
1985	206.1	83.7	86.5	66.5	444.1
Operating Income ($mil)					
1993	$110.2	$42.3	$272.1	$32.5	$385.0
1992	122.0	32.0	205.6	59.7	348.0
1991	104.0	27.7	172.3	73.2	312.2
1990	76.5	38.3	90.2	76.4	223.8
1989	60.9	35.2	77.0	71.9	144.7
1988	58.1	35.5	46.1	61.3	159.7
1987	46.3	40.4	40.9	25.2	134.0
1986	46.4	37.2	37.0	21.7	121.2
1985	33.0	25.1	20.3	25.5	92.7

1. In revenues, total revenues include "other" and "intercompany
   eliminations"; in operating income, total revenues include "other
   [income]" and "corporate expenses." Pre-1987 earnings from operations
   prior to corporate expenses.
2. In Viacom's financial statements, the year 1987 comprises two parts
   divided by a merger transaction, i.e., Jan. 1 through June 8 and June
   9 through December 31. These parts have been combined in the above
   presentation.

SOURCE: Viacom Inc.: 10-K's.

systems in California, the Pacific Northwest, and the Midwest regions. In
December 1992 Viacom's cable operation was the twelfth largest MSO in
the United States. While it offered PPV events as an affiliate of the Viewer's Choice network, it withdrew from the DBS operation. Cable was Viacom's second largest revenue source, generating about 20% of total (down
from a peak of 28% in 1987), as well as some 35% of total operating
income.

Viacom Entertainment. This segment distributed and produced filmed entertainment for domestic and international TV markets, through Viacom
Enterprises, Viacom Productions, Viacom New Media, and Viacom MGS
Services. Entertainment's revenue portion had risen steadily in the late
'80s (peaking at almost 18%), declining to 13% in 1992. Operating income remained somewhat higher.

Viacom Broadcasting. The segment owned and operated 5 network-
affiliated TV stations and 13 radio stations. In 1992 segment revenues and
operating income were below 10% of total.

Viacom's business segments in distribution and production provided significant synergic possibilities, attracting some of Hollywood's greatest talent in the '80s, including Carsey-Warner Company (*The Cosby Show, A Different World, Roseanne*). But Viacom lacked a studio arm. Without such a pipeline, it remained dependent on outside product for distribution.

Globalized Viacom

By the early '90s Redstone's Viacom was driven by financial deleveraging and corporate globalization. The two objectives were interrelated. Financial stability made possible investments in flourishing businesses. Through shrewd financial engineering, Redstone and George S. Smith, Jr., Viacom's chief financial officer (CFO), cleaned up the company's balance sheet. While total debt in 1992 still hovered around $2.5 billion, it was considered manageable, with cash flow covering interest payments 2.3 times over.[3]

Viacom produced virtually all of its programming by its own employees with low-cost in-house talent. Like Paramount in the '70s and Disney in the '80s, Viacom preferred a high-concept approach to talent shmoozing; its networks were built as brands (just as "Disney" connoted children, "MTV" came to signify teens and young adults, and "Nickelodeon" children); finally, Viacom employed segmented marketing.

In 1989 Viacom filed a $2.4 billion antitrust lawsuit against HBO for a systematic and aggressive campaign to put Showtime out of business. The suit was settled in August 1992 on highly favorable terms.

Viacom's increasing earnings stemmed from its cable networks, which accounted for half of the company's revenues and profits. As Nickelodeon followed MTV's globalization, that growth was expected to accelerate.

Transformation of MTV

After MTV's early profitability, fortunes reversed in 1987. The network replaced Robert Pittman with MTV marketer Thomas E. Freston, who began implementing a new strategy in 1990, forging partnerships with advertisers to promote events. MTV also shifted to an almost all-show format using genre-based narrowcasting to segment its audiences. The shift became all the more important as rivals (Video Jukebox Network [VJN]) cut into MTV's territory.

In the early '90s MTV was shaken by a management shuffle, another lineup introduction, as well as a channel split plan, with which it hoped to increase audience segmentation (neutralize the threat of VJN) while retaining its national focus. At the same time, the rapid expansion of MTV Europe, a subsidiary of Viacom, signaled the music network's growing globalization. By May 1992 the value of Viacom's music-video network was put at an estimated $2.6–$4 billion.[4]

Opting for rapid globalization, Viacom tried to replicate the music channel's success among teens and young adults with Nickelodeon among children.

Nickelodeon's Growth

In 1979 Nickelodeon was a commercial-free channel. The change came in 1985, when Warner-Amex (Viacom acquired control that year) decided the channel would take advertising. Geraldine Laybourne, Nickelodeon's president, was credited with Nickelodeon's success. The next year she created Nick at Nite, a prime-time block of oldies, such as *The Dick Van Dyke Show* and *Get Smart*. She also gave the go-ahead to creative-risks like the game show *Double Dare* and the *Ren & Stimpy* cartoon hit. Laybourne transformed a throwaway channel into a $200 million-plus headquarters for children's entertainment.[5]

By 1993 Nickelodeon entered 58.5 million homes, and children ages 2 to 11 watched more of it than the four major broadcast networks combined. Just like MTV, Nickelodeon represented a branded channel with its overall look, style, and rhythm; and just like youth marketers had "discovered" MTV in the 1980s, kid marketers (toys, fast food, cereals) found that the channel consistently delivered an elusive audience. It had only one major competitor, the commercial-free Disney Channel for which 6.3 million subscribers paid a monthly charge.

Globalization

Prior to the 1987 takeover battle, MTV had been considered a fading asset. Afterward, Viacom expanded MTV Networks into Europe, Australia, Latin America, Asia, and Japan. Indeed, MTV globalized faster than CNN: it was beamed into over 70 countries, reaching 210 million TV households; it obtained consistently targeted demographics (from teens to young adults), while its annual revenue gains exceeded those of CNN. While Redstone was planning to expand Nickelodeon into Europe on the heels of MTV, Viacom was linking with Japanese investors in coproduction and cofinancing.[6]

By the early '90s Redstone was eager to strengthen internal growth with external growth. He wanted control of any merged entity. With its debt pared, Viacom could pursue a strategic acquisition. It began merger talks with Paramount Communications and Matsushita's MCA subsidiary.[7] (On Viacom's takeover struggle for Paramount and merger effort with Blockbuster, see Chapter 6.)

Entertainment: Market Multiplication

ENTERTAINMENT CONGLOMERATES

By the early 1990s, Hollywood was the leading producer of jobs in the Los Angeles area, eclipsing the 1980s boom industries (real estate, aerospace, tourism), which were all in decline. In classic Hollywood, the expansion had been driven by domestic box office but new Hollywood was being boosted by international box office and emerging M&E technologies. Moreover, vertical integration was transforming American media and entertainment.[1]

Hollywood Studios

Following the peak years of classic Hollywood from 1946 to 1956, the average weekly theatre attendance declined from 90 million to just 40 million.[1] In the early years of broadcast television, most production was carried on by newly formed enterprises, such as Desilu Productions, Ziv-TV Programs, and Official Films. After the mid-'50s, major studios made their first big push into network television, forcing out and buying up smaller suppliers. Following Columbia, majors organized subsidiaries to enter TV production:

Parent Firm	*Subsidiary*
Allied Artists Pictures	Interstate Television
Columbia Pictures	Screen Gems
Republic Pictures	Hollywood TV Service
RKO Teleradio Pictures	RKO Television
Twentieth Century Fox	Twentieth Century Fox TV Prods.
Universal Pictures	Universal International Films
Walt Disney Pictures	Walt Disney Productions
Warner Bros.	Sunset Productions

With the demise of classic Hollywood, the majors cooperated with the new medium and sold rights to their film libraries.

Conglomerate Takeovers

In the 1960s, declining movie revenues left vulnerable the studios that owned valuable real estate, music publishing houses, theatres in foreign countries, and attractive film libraries. Hence the rapid surge of conglomerate takeovers. In 1962 Music Corporation of America (MCA) acquired Universal Pictures from Decca Records; four years later, Gulf + Western purchased Paramount and TransAmerica acquired United Artists; in 1968 Warner Bros. went to Seven Arts and a year later to Kinney National Services, which changed the parent's name to Warner Communications, Inc.

When, at the end of the '50s, the FCC decided to support the broadcast networks' greater control of TV programming, the indies' marketplace shrank. In the late '60s the rules changed again. As the networks demanded equity interests in the suppliers' shows, as well as syndication rights, the FCC issued the financial interest and syndication rules that restricted the networks' ability to own programming, barred the Big Three from sharing in profits from the syndication market, and restricted their in-house production. As a result, the '70s market belonged to innovative indies, such as Norman Lear (*All in the Family*) and Grant Tinker (*The Mary Tyler Moore Show*).

From 1969 to 1972, seven major studios suffered substantial losses, which contributed to the rise of independents. Concurrently, the Big Three networks failed to capture young audiences with a fading product (*Bonanza, Gunsmoke, The Red Skelton Show*), just as Hollywood majors failed to attract the "Now Generation" with biblical epics and clones of *The Sound of Music*. Growth in movie attendance began only with renewed products (*Bonnie and Clyde, The Graduate, Easy Rider, The Godfather*). Distributors continued to dominate the business, even if exhibition, distribution, and production remained unintegrated.

After the mid-'70s Hollywood witnessed the emergence of blockbuster movies and sequels. If the trend originated from the 1975 *Jaws*, it peaked with sci-fi fantasies, such as *Star Wars, Close Encounters of the Third Kind, Raiders of the Lost Ark, E.T. The Extra-Terrestrial,* and *Ghostbusters.* Toward the late '70s HBO, initially ignored by Hollywood, achieved a near-monopoly in pay cable and became the nation's biggest programmer. While majors turned out some 80–100 movies a year (less than 200 hours), HBO had to fill 8,760 hours of programming annually. Following the new distribution systems and increasing access to capital, demand for motion pictures and TV programs rose rapidly.

Industry Reintegration

In the '80s, Wall Street's financial boom and Washington's new antitrust policies prompted a wave of consolidation among the Hollywood majors. Moreover, the rise of ancillary and complementary markets, as well as the increase in foreign demand, served as the ethos for the merger craze.

Starting with domestic and international exhibition, industry consolidation proceeded through frantic dealmaking, including Disney's expansion of its theme parks, studio activities, and entry into TV programming; the merger of Lorimar and Warner Bros.; the LBO of Twentieth Century Fox by Marvin Davis and Marc Rich; the ensuing acquisition of Fox by Rupert Murdoch and the launch of the Fox broadcasting network; MGM/UA's reorganizations under Kirk Kerkorian and Giancarlo Parretti; the attempt at a "fifth network" by MCA and Paramount; the merger between Time and Warner; Sony's purchase of Columbia from Coca-Cola; as well as Matsushita's acquisition of MCA Universal.

Escalation of Production Costs. "Costs. They're like a fungus on the face of our industry, always itching, but never really going away," said Jack Valenti, president and chief executive of the Motion Picture Association of America, in March 1993. "Each year we apply some new ointment, and each year the fungus grows."[2]

Although stars have never come cheap, times have changed from the year 1917, when Chaplin signed the first $1 million, eight-film contract. Through the '80s, production volume in television and motion pictures increased dramatically, but costs grew even faster. In 1980 an average studio picture cost $13.7 million. Production costs accounted for $9.4 million, print and advertising (P&A) costs $4.3 million. By 1990 total costs had near-tripled to $38.4 million. Production costs accounted for $26.8 million, P&A costs $11.6 million. Both grew twice as fast as the consumer price index. By 1994 Hollywood's average movie cost $30 million to produce, while marketing costs had leaped to $14 million.[3]

Despite high revenues, the new production-line system failed to contain costs, not least because of highly priced talent contracts. Due to increasing back-end participations (as evidenced by the case of *Buchwald v. Paramount*), negative costs were hardly an accurate reflection of the true cost of production. Unlike most American industries which were retrenching prior to an impending contraction, Tinseltown intensified its spending spree. When Sony paid three-quarters of a billion dollars to have Peter Guber and Jon Peters run Columbia Pictures, Hollywood's salary structure crumbled overnight.[4]

In a controversial 1991 memo, Jeffrey Katzenberg, Disney Studios chairman, associated the "blockbuster mentality" with the spectacles of the late '50s and early '60s, which contributed to the decline of major studios and the rise of independent film production.[5] By turning its back to modestly budgeted mid-size pictures, Hollywood had boosted big grosses and cost overruns, instead of profitability and cost control. Due to cost factors, top-grossing films were seldom high-profit films.[6]

With the M&A wave, movie marketing, pioneered by Joseph E. Levine, went through a dramatic change, too. Until the '80s the movie industry had just two basic "market windows": theatrical exhibition and television. When these were augmented by new distribution systems, marketing increased in complexity, demanding greater professionalism. As studios began to recruit veteran ad executives, Madison Avenue arrived in Hollywood.[7]

Cost increases were credited to big-budget films and sequels like *Lethal Weapon 3*, *Batman Returns*, and *Dracula*—which, in 1993, were followed by offerings like *Jurassic Park*, *Cliffhanger*, and *Last Action Hero*. Production costs hurt the major studios, as well as the Big Three networks, which paid increasing attention to escalating costs in the posttakeover years. By the early '90s the bulk of programming money still went to Hollywood, even if it was targeted at less costly genres. Instead of a diverse slate of hour-long shows, the networks had reality shows in all dayparts. At the same time, U.S. program producers sought to offset high costs (and avoid import quotas) by filming in foreign locales.[8]

As the shift to deficit financing was coupled by a dramatic rise in production costs and contraction in syndication, indies were squeezed out of the marketplace. Most signed on with major studios or networks, or closed up shop. The M&A wave and cost increases prompted a consolidation of program producers. By the early '90s only Cannell and Viacom were operating at levels comparable to the late '80s; Lorimar-Telepictures had become a subsidiary of Warner Bros.; GTG had been disbanded; Witt/Thomas/Harris (*Golden Girls, Empty Nest, Beauty and the Beast*) joined Disney's Touchstone Television; the legendary MTM (*Hill Street Blues, St. Elsewhere, Newhart*) scaled back operations and was bought by the British TVS; focusing on international activities, New World sold most of its domestic production assets to Columbia; Orion filed for Chapter 11 protection; Republic had no first-run series on the networks or in syndication.[9]

Despite oft-heard cries for lower production costs, increasing consolidation and rising costs went hand in hand in Hollywood. By the end of 1992 the future prospects of MGM/UA, Orion, and Carolco seemed dubious, and chaos caught up with major studios. Executive turmoil swept through Hollywood.[10]

When Paramount's Frank Mancuso was ousted in 1991, he was replaced with Brandon Tartikoff, NBC's programming chief, who was soon followed by Stanley Jaffe. After a brief stay at Fox, Joe Roth left for Disney and Rupert Murdoch assumed his duties. In 1992 high acquisition costs forced Sony to subject both Columbia and Tri-Star to a drastic cost-cutting program.

Typically, the studios that led in domestic box office market shares and released the largest number of films had longer lasting regimes—Disney (8 years), Warner (12 years), and Universal (6 years). After stumbling with the $60 million *Dick Tracy*, Jeffrey Katzenberg cut the average production cost from $24 million to $16 million at Disney, Touchstone, and Hollywood Pictures. At Warner, the studio's president Bob Daly (movies) and its chairman Terry Semel (television) had been working partners since 1980. Universal's Tom Pollock, a former top entertainment lawyer, excelled in controversial long-term talent deals (with Imagine Entertainment, Largo Entertainment, Martin Scorsese, and Spike Lee). In the past, top executives had played, now they paid.

Talent Agencies

With the demise of classic Hollywood and the rise of broadcast television, agencies took over talent development, which controlled access to stars, and, thereby, increased their bargaining power. By the early '90s, increasing costs and a relatively static pool of superstars contributed to a shift of bargaining power in Hollywood. Project decisions were made by few handlers and gatekeepers of top stars and filmmakers—that is, talent agencies.[1]

After the oligopolization of major studios in the '20s, agencies had consolidated, too. William Morris, headed by Abe Lastfogel, set up its first Hollywood office in 1933. Four years later it was followed by the Music Corporation of America, led by Jules Stein. The two recruited most stars in the industry. Two decades later, under Lew Wasserman's leadership, MCA had a virtual monopoly in the agenting business. In 1962 the Justice Department deemed MCA's mix of TV production and agenting a conflict of interest; to expand and diversify its lucrative production business (Universal), MCA gave up its talent arm.[2]

In the early and mid-'70s an M&A wave augmented William Morris with two new agencies, International Creative Management (ICM) and Creative Artists Agency (CAA). These became the Big Three of the agency business. CAA thrived by raiding clients from other agencies. It transformed the business by focusing on team effort and the agency as a whole. Applying the concept of TV packaging in the movie industry, it contributed to the dramatic rise in production costs. Finally, it lured Harvard-trained MBAs away from studios and Wall Street, to add corporate clients.

By the late '80s CAA had a near-monopoly in the agency business. As junk bonds declined as a financing tool for acquisition, Michael Ovitz, CAA's president, emerged as the single most powerful figure in Hollywood. In late 1989 he advised Sony on its purchase of Columbia; a year later he brought together Matsushita and MCA.[3] After the M&A brokering, Ovitz represented Apple Computer, Paramount, and Coca-Cola. Just as MCA in the early '60s struggled under antitrust pressure, CAA's alignment with Coca-Cola in the early '90s prompted antitrust charges.[4]

In addition to CAA's hegemony, the '80s also witnessed the emergence of several mid-sized agencies that would play a critical role in the turmoil of the early '90s, including Triad Artists, InterTalent, and United Talent Agency.

With increasing revenues in the '70s and '80s, personal relations in M&E businesses had been replaced by contractual links and price-oriented instruments. After the contract replaced the handshake, the importance of the agents who negotiated contracts, and the number of lawyers who drafted them, grew as well. Indeed, a number of Hollywood lawyers had reached the industry elite, with some running studios (Universal's Tom Pollock, Columbia's Alan Levine, and Disney's Frank Wells).[5]

Despite their increased bargaining power, the agencies depended on the studios for the bulk of their revenue. As Hollywood majors began consolidating in the midst of an economic contraction, shrinking business and declining margins prompted a dramatic realignment in agenting. InterTalent's top agents joined ICM and, to lesser extent, United Talent Agency, while, following numerous defections, the vulnerable Morris decided to acquire Triad.[6]

Just as Hollywood has witnessed an expansion from movies and television to media and entertainment, Ovitz's push to catapult CAA beyond mere moviemaking reflected agencies' expanding industry scope and business mission. Hence CAA's deals in advertising (Coca-Cola account), sports (Nike, Magic Johnson's ventures), technology (Microsoft, AT&T, Apple), and investment banking (Sony/Columbia, Matsushita/MCA, Crédit Lyonnais/MGM, Seagram's stake in Time Warner, advisory work for Paramount). In January 1994 CAA announced still another coup: a joint venture with N. S. Bienstock, the leading agency representing TV news stars like Dan Rather, Diane Sawyer, and Mike Wallace.[7]

By April 1994 the cover story of the *New York Times* business section wondered whether the enigmatic Ovitz had provoked the top levels of both Time Warner and Sony, "leading to speculation that Mr. Ovitz . . . is seeking to take control of those companies in the United States."[8]

Two months later Robert Kavner, AT&T's former CFO who headed its expanding multimedia efforts, joined CAA. The information superhighway had become an integral part of Hollywood's future. Ovitz's lone shadow fell upon Tinseltown.

"With more and more money chasing a relatively static pool of superstars, there's been a subtle but pronounced shift in the balance of power in Tinseltown," noted *Variety* in late 1993. "The new 'power elite'—those who really decide what projects get made in Hollywood and at what price—increasingly consist of the handlers and gatekeepers of top actors and filmmakers."[9] The result? Spiraling salaries for top talent and soaring budgets for important films would continue to defy any cost-conscious studio efforts.

PRIMARY MARKET

Until the late 1940s, theatrical exhibition was the dominant mode of distribution for U.S. movies. From the 1950s to the end of the 1970s, exhibition revenues decreased in proportion to television; in the 1980s the composition of theatrical revenues shifted drastically as exhibition and television were augmented by new modes of distribution (see Table 4.1).

In 1980 the combined revenues of the new distribution channels totaled only $145 million (5.8% of all theatrical revenues); by 1994 they exceeded $11.4 billion (63.1%). In 1980 box-office rentals and television accounted for 76% and 17%, respectively, of total theatrical revenues; by 1994 exhibition and television accounted for just 26% and 11%, respectively. Meanwhile, both exhibition and TV became increasingly dependent on the foreign market (which I intend to explore in a future study).

By the late '80s the function of theatrical release was to generate interest from other windows down the line. It opened the way into syndication, network TV, foreign TV, pay TV, worldwide home video, pay-per-view, as well as foreign theatrical exhibition. Financially, the ancillary/secondary markets (back end) grew more significant than the primary marketplace (front end).[1]

Domestic Theatrical Exhibition

Until the mid-'80s the industry was dominated by six major distributors: Paramount Pictures, Warner Bros., Universal, Twentieth Century Fox, MGM, and United Artists. As MGM and UA encountered increasing problems, Disney's distributor arm (Buena Vista) captured market leadership in 1988. The M&A wave among Hollywood majors restructured the market-share breakdown.

Majors and Independents

By the early '90s the market was controlled by a handful of major distributors. Except for the slump of 1981, Hollywood majors (top 8 ratio)

Table 4-1
Distribution of Theatrical Revenues (1980–94) [$mil.]

	1980	1981	1982	1983	1984	1985	1986	1987	1988	1989
Box Office										
Rentals										
Domestic	1235	1335	1555	1700	1800	1635	1650	1830	1920	2165
Foreign	650	675	775	910	900	795	850	940	1100	1225
Total	1885	2010	2330	2610	2700	2430	2500	2770	3020	3390
Pay TV										
Domestic	120	225	350	550	600	625	600	575	630	670
Foreign	0	0	0	0	0	0	35	70	110	225
Total	120	225	350	550	600	625	635	645	740	895
Home Video										
Domestic	10	50	150	400	950	1335	1630	1915	2460	2760
Foreign	15	100	200	350	450	625	885	1135	1460	1690
Total	25	150	350	750	1400	1960	2515	3050	3920	4450
Television										
Domestic	350	370	390	410	410	450	450	425	425	525
Foreign	75	95	105	125	135	145	175	250	550	575
Total	425	465	495	535	545	595	625	675	975	1100
Video Disks										
Domestic	0	0	25	50	10	1	2	5	30	40
Foreign	0	0	0	0	0	0	0	5	40	50
Total	0	0	25	50	10	1	2	10	70	90
Other										
Domestic	30	35	45	50	50	55	60	60	60	65
Foreign	10	10	10	15	15	15	20	20	20	20
Total	40	45	55	65	65	70	80	80	80	85
Total										
Domestic	1745	2015	2515	3160	3820	4101	4392	4810	5525	6225
Foreign	750	880	1090	1400	1500	1580	1965	2420	3785	3785
Total	2495	2895	3605	4560	5320	5681	6357	7230	8805	10010

dominated 91–96% of the market from 1980 to 1984. Booming Wall Street and the rise of indies decreased the majors' dominance to 83–89% from 1985 to 1987. With the demise of indies and consolidation, six majors—Sony (Columbia), Warner Bros. (Time Warner), Disney, Paramount, Fox, Matsushita (MCA/Universal)–reinstituted their leadership, with 89–97% of the market from 1988 to 1993 (see Table 4-2).

Warner Bros. The purchase of Lorimar-Telepictures by Warner Bros. made the combination the world's largest distributor of TV programming. In the '80s WB captured industry leadership three times; in the early '90s its market share continued to hover around 13–18%, (the newly consolidated WB Television occupied nearly 15% of the four networks' schedules in 1993). By 1990 Time-Warner's cost-containment strategy forced WB's chairman Robert Daly and president Terry Semel to close a $600 million financing deal with three major European entities. As WB continued to release high-risk, high-budget action/adventure movies/sequels (*Batman, Lethal Weapon, Robin Hood*), these were supplemented by "serious drama" (from *Driving Miss Daisy, Presumed Innocent,* and *GoodFellas* to *JFK* and *Final Analysis*) and a shift toward wholesome family entertainment (*Dennis the*

Table 4-1 continued

	1990	1991	1992	1993	1994E	Shares (%) 1980	1994
Box Office							
Rentals							
Domestic	2260	2160	2100	2163	2190	49.5	13.9
Foreign	1380	1460	1575	1750	1850	26.1	11.8
Total	3640	3620	3675	3913	4040	75.6	25.7
Pay TV							
Domestic	725	750	770	790	800	4.8	5.1
Foreign	300	350	370	395	420	-	2.6
Total	1025	1100	1140	1185	1220	4.8	7.7
Home Video							
Domestic	3220	3760	4150	4360	5000	0.4	31.8
Foreign	1945	2120	2460	2605	2900	0.6	18.4
Total	5165	5880	6610	6965	7900	1.0	50.2
Television							
Domestic	600	650	675	700	725	14.0	4.6
Foreign	700	750	800	850	925	3.0	5.9
Total	1300	1400	1475	1550	1650	17.0	10.5
Video Disks							
Domestic	85	150	295	340	360	na	2.3
Foreign	90	150	225	275	300	na	1.9
Total	175	300	520	615	660	na	4.2
Pay-Per-View*							
Domestic	60	80	115	125	150	na	1.0
Foreign	0	0	0	5	7	na	0.0
Total	60	80	115	130	157	na	1.0
Other							
Domestic	65	70	75	80	85	1.2	0.5
Foreign	22	25	25	25	30	0.4	0.2
Total	87	95	100	105	115	1.6	0.7
Total							
Domestic	7015	7540	8180	8558	9310	69.9	59.1
Foreign	4437	4905	5455	5905	6432	30.1	39.9
Total	11452	12475	13635	14463	15742	100.0	100.0

* Prior to 1990 included in other.

SOURCE: From Richard P. Simon and Stephen G. Abraham, "Movie Industry Update - 1994," Goldman Sachs/Entertainment: U.S. Research, April 4, 1994, p. 3.

Menace, Free Willy). With the No. 1 spot at the national box office in 1993, WB's revenues were driven by the blockbuster *The Fugitive* and several modestly budgeted hits. In March 1994 the shared partnership of Daly and Semel was formalized. Rival studios considered WB the most formidable and powerful studio in Hollywood.

Sony Pictures Entertainment (Columbia, Tri-Star). From 1978 to 1989 Columbia Pictures Entertainment had four different chiefs. Frank Price (1978–83), had the best track record, with one blockbuster almost every year (*Kramer vs. Kramer, Tootsie, Ghostbuster*); Guy McElwaine's reign (1983–86) inflated costs and ended with flops (*Ishtar*); the brief rule of David Puttnam (1986–87), a British producer, was a costly disaster that prompted Coca-Cola to restructure the studio into Columbia Pictures Entertainment (Columbia, Tri-Star). Dawn Steel, a veteran of Paramount production wars and the first woman to take charge of a stu-

Table 4-2
North American Theatrical Film Rental Market Shares (1980–93)[1]

Year	COL[1]	DIS[2]	FOX[3]	M/U[4]	NL[5]	ORI[6]	PAR	TRI[1]	UNI[7]	WB[8]	C4	C8
1993	11	16	11	2	3	–	9	6	14	**19**	60	89
1992	10	**19**	12	2	3	–	13	8	14	18	64	97
1991	9	14	12	2	4	9	12	11	11	**14**	52	92
1990	5	**16**	14	3	4	6	15	8	14	13	59	91
1989	8	14	6	6	1	4	14	7	17	**19**	64	91
1988	3	**20**	11	10	2	7	16	6	10	11	58	91
1987	4	14	9	4	2	10	**20**	5	8	13	57	83
1986	9	10[b]	8	4	–	7	**22**	7	9	12	53	84
1985	10	3	11	9	–	5	10	10	16	**18**	54	89
1984	16	4	10	7	–	5	**21**	5	8	19	66	91
1983	14	3	**21**	10	–	4	14	–	13	17	66	96
1982	10	4	14	11	–	3	14	–	**30**	10	68	96
1981	13	3	13	9	–	1	15	–	14	**18**	60	86
1980	14	4	16	7	–	2	16	–	**20**	14	66	93

Annual market share leaders in bold.
C4 Top 4 companies (4-firm concentration ratio).
C8 Top 8 companies (8-firm concentration ratio).
a. Market shares = Percentage of annual film rentals to distributors
b. The first year a mini-major joined the top 4 market-share leaders.

(1) Tri-Star Pictures began operations in April 1984, absorbed Columbia Pictures late 1987; corporate name changed to Columbia Pictures Entertainment (CPE). Columbia and Tri-Star retained separate sales staffs, but certain administrative functions were performed by Triumph Releasing, an entity which had no operational significance. In 1989, CPE was acquired by Sony.
(2) Buena Vista released Walt Disney Co. pix from various production subsidiaries.
(3) Since 1987, owned by News Corp.
(4) The "old" MGM exited distribution in 1973. MGM/UA meant the present distribution company and the "old" UA, which took over domestic distribution of MGM product in 1973. Since 1990, MGM/UA had been under Pathè; in 1992, Credit Lyonnais acquired control.
(5) New Line.
(6) Included old American International Pictures (1970-79), and Filmways Pictures (1980-81). Name changed to Orion in 1982.
(7) In 1990, MCA/Universal was acquired by Matsushita Electric Industrial.
(8) Lorimar acquired assets in 1981. Lorimar began domestic distribution operations in August 1987. Warner Bros. acquired Lorimar in late 1988.

SOURCE: Reprinted with permission of <u>Variety</u> magazine © (various issues) by Cahners Publishing Company; concentration ratios supplemented by the author.

dio, contributed to a turnaround. In 1989 Sony bought Columbia (and Guber-Peters) intending to use its massive film and TV library to push new forms of hardware. Guber and Peters named Michael Medavoy, an Orion executive, chairman of Tri-Star, while Universal's Frank Price became chairman of Columbia. Sony invested heavily in studio operations, which enhanced its market share (*Total Recall, Misery, Terminator 2, City Slickers, Hook, Prince of Tides*). After three strong years, Sony had a rocky ride in 1993, when the much-anticipated *Last Action Hero* flopped and the studio ranked second after WB; disappointments were followed by an exodus of executives (Mike Medavoy, Jonathan Dolgen). By 1994

Sony executives realigned under CEO Peter Guber (but a $3.2 billion write-off loomed ahead).

Walt Disney. In the '80s the new management team transformed the old Disney. Despite an excellent track record (*Honey, I Shrunk the Kids, Turner and Hooch, Dead Poet's Society, Father of the Bride*), it was swept by the blockbuster fever. After *Dick Tracy,* Jeffrey Katzenberg distanced Disney from high-cost production. Starting in 1989, Disney's animation division was revived and animated characters were "updated" in hugely popular releases (*The Little Mermaid, Beauty and the Beast, Aladdin*). The studio sought multipicture deals with talented stars whose careers had stalled. Hoping to double its feature production to 30 films a year, Disney launched Hollywood Pictures to complement its Touchstone operations and partnerships like Interscope (*Outrageous, Cocktail, Three Men and a Baby*). While it recruited Fox's Joe Roth, it also purchased Miramax, a prolific and highly profitable indie. In 1993 the studio had 28 releases but few hits (*The Nightmare Before Christmas, Cool Runnings*). In April 1994 Disney put David Hoberman, Touchstone's president, in charge of all three motion picture arms; the appointment signaled consolidation and a shift toward risky, expensive action films as well as high-profile directors.

MCA/Universal. After the mid-'80s MCA/Universal continued to release hits, but none were as profitable as *E.T.* (including *Back to the Future* and *Out of Africa*). Seeking long-term relationships with strategic talent, Tom Pollock, Universal's new chairman, rebuilt the neglected inventory. While the approach led to several box-office hits (*Dragnet, The Secret of My Success, Batteries Not Included, Back to the Future II, Beethoven, Backdraft*), deal structures grew complex and controversial (*Twins*). Pollock also paid attention to prestige projects that had the potential to become critically acclaimed event movies (Martin Scorsese's *The Last Temptation of Christ* and *Cape Fear,* Spike Lee's *Do the Right Thing,* Oliver Stone's *Born on the Fourth of July*). In early 1990 Universal took another unusual step, bypassing pay TV and selling directly to CBS. With the exception of the $800 million-plus (worldwide) garnered from *Jurassic Park* in 1993, Universal mainly released films that grossed $30 million-plus (*Carlito's Way, Dragon: The Bruce Lee Story, Cop and a Half*). With *Schindler's List,* Spielberg became the director of the year.

Paramount. In 1984 Frank G. Mancuso, a Paramount veteran, replaced Barry Diller as studio chairman and CEO. In early 1985 Marvin Davis and Mancuso installed Mel Harris, another veteran, to head the TV group. With some of the industry's most bankable talent (Eddie Murphy, Don Simpson and Jerry Bruckheimer, Stanley Jaffe and Sherry Lansing, Gary David Goldberg), Paramount topped the feature competition in 1986–87. By summer 1990 industry volatility forced the studio to shake up its management, and to buy out top producers Simpson and Bruckheimer. Due to climbing costs, Paramount resorted to runaway products, nonunion labor, and co-ventures. Concurrently, the studio's profits grew with *The Hunt for Red October,* the modestly budgeted *Ghost,* and *Patriot Games,* as well as *Addams Family* and *Naked Gun 2½.* In 1993 Paramount was the only studio with two films garnering more than $100 million (*The Firm, Indecent Proposal*), and other hits (*Addams Family Values, Wayne's World 2*).

Fox. After the early '80s, Fox's market share declined and it competed with mini-majors like Orion and Tri-Star. By the late '80s new management and new product strategy led to several hits (*Broadcast News, Wall Street, Big, Young Guns II, Alien Nation, Working Girl*). Under Joe Roth, Fox's market share increased from 6% to 14% in 1989–90. Fox had a blockbuster (*Home Alone*), and some hits (*Die Hard 2, Edward Scissorhands, My Cousin Vinny, White Men Can't Jump, The Last of the Mohicans*). When a series of expensive projects proved financial disappointments, Roth left for Disney and Murdoch assumed leadership in the studio. The transition saw some hits, too (*Sleeping with the Enemy, Hot Shots*). In 1993 Fox named as president of its film unit Bill Mechanic, who had built and managed Disney's highly profitable home-video unit. Despite turmoil, *Home Alone 2* and *Mrs. Doubtfire,* both greenlighted by Roth, enabled Fox to attain the No. 5 spot in the box office.

Independent Cinema. Independents grew dramatically until the mid-'70s, when they declined equally dramatically. From the early '80s to early '90s, the studio oligopoly (top 8 ratio) left indies only 4–11% of the rental market. To save production costs, majors also relied increasingly on indies, and acquired the biggest of them, including Disney's Miramax and Caravan (Joe Roth), Turner's New Line, and Blockbuster's Republic and Spelling. Sony and Universal also had specialized divisions that ventured into traditional indie territory. By the early '90s indies like Gramercy, Savoy, and Goldwyn competed with one another, and with a new generation of entities that produced like them but had the support of the majors' financing and marketing prowess.

Theatrical Exhibition

During the period 1980–94, exhibition revenues grew from $1.9 billion to over $4.0 billion, but the significance of theatrical exhibition as the single most important market window declined dramatically. After the late '60s there were three distinct periods in domestic theatrical exhibition.[1]

Fiscal Depression (1969–74). As the "go-go" years of the '60s resulted in the fiscal depression of the early '70s, all majors posted large write-offs. The period had its share of hits, from *Butch Cassidy and the Sundance Kid* and *Love Story* to *The Godfather, The Exorcist,* and *The Sting.*

Restabilization (1975–80). In the late '70s major distributors began to experiment on a nationwide basis, with hits like *Close Encounters of the Third Kind, Grease,* and *Superman.* The period also saw the emergence of block-

Table 4-3
Domestic Theatrical Movie Industry (1980–93)

Year	Box Office ($bil)	Box Office (%chg)	Admissions ($bil)	Admissions (%chg)	Average ticket price ($)	Average ticket price (%chg)	Number of Screens (#)
1993	5.15	5.8	1.24	6.0	4.14	(0.2)	25,737
1992	4.87	1.4	1.17	2.9	4.15	(1.4)	25,105
1991	4.80	(4.4)	1.14	(4.0)	4.21	(0.3)	24,570
1990	5.02	(0.2)	1.19	(5.9)	4.23	6.0	23,689
1989	5.03	12.9	1.26	na	3.99	na	23,132
1988	4.46	4.8	1.09	(0.3)	4.11	5.2	23,234
1987	4.25	12.6	1.09	7.0	3.91	5.2	23,555
1986	3.78	0.8	1.02	(3.7)	3.71	4.6	22,765
1985	3.75	(7.0)	1.06	(11.9)	3.55	5.6	21,147
1984	4.03	7.0	1.20	0.2	3.36	6.8	20,200
1983	3.77	9.1	1.20	1.8	3.15	7.1	18,884
1982	3.45	16.4	1.18	10.2	2.94	5.7	18,020
1981	2.97	7.9	1.06	4.5	2.78	3.3	18,040
1980	2.75	(2.6)	1.02	(8.9)	2.69	6.9	17,590

SOURCE: Motion Picture Association of America.

busters. *Jaws* and *The Empire Strikes Back* drew $130–$140 million and *Star Wars* nearly $194 million in rentals.

Boom (1981–89). In 1980 domestic box-office rentals generated 71% of total theatrical revenues. Hence a growing demand for feature films. Just as anthology series sold the first-generation TV sets, blockbusters were now selling new distribution systems. With $230 million in rentals, *E.T.* was followed by *Raiders of the Lost Ark*, *Ghostbusters*, and *Batman*. Product polarization reduced the number of mid-sized pictures.

Peaking in 1989, box office receipts advanced to a record $5.03 billion (see Table 4-3). The explosion in ancillary markets did not subvert the "no growth" admissions environment. While frequent moviegoers were seeing fewer flicks and the younger market was shrinking, the older audience (40+) was growing. New demographics were influencing Hollywood's primary market.[2] In 1993 the record-high $5.24 billion, driven by Universal's *Jurassic Park*, marked a solid recovery from the recession.

Reintegration

American theatrical exhibition has evolved in conjunction with antitrust. Shifts in the distributor-exhibitor relationship evolved in four distinct phases: integration (1920s–1948), divestitures (1948–59), increasing consolidation (1959–86), and reintegration (1986–   ).[3]

The domination of vertically integrated Hollywood majors ended with the Paramount decrees in 1948. With divestitures, the number of theatre screens declined by 12% between 1948 and 1958; the slump of domestic exhibition from 1958 to 1963 resulted in an additional 23% decrease.

Figure 4-1
U.S. Theatrical Exhibition: Reintegration (1986–87)

     January 1986 Coca-Cola, parent of Columbia, spent $17 million to purchase New York's 12-screen Walter Reade chain.

     May 1986 MCA, the parent of Universal, used $159 million to acquire a half stake in Cineplex Odeon, which owned almost 1,200 screens. (When Matsushita in 1990 acquired MCA, it also obtained the Cineplex stake.)

     October 1986 Through its Tri-Star division, Columbia spent $320 million to purchase 230 screens owned by Loews Corp. (When Sony acquired Columbia in 1989, it also obtained the Loews circuit.) Also, Paramount (still known as Gulf + Western) acquired 360 Mann Theaters for $220 million, followed by a $65 million acquisition of the 91-screen Festival circuit and the 21-screen Trans-Lux Theaters.

     February 1987 Warner Communications Inc., parent of Warner Bros., purchased from Paramount a 50% interest in three circuits (Mann, Festival, Trans Lux), comprising 119 theatres with 469 screens. The theatres were acquired by Cinamerica Theatres, L.P., a newly created limited partnership in which Warner and Gulf + Western were co-equal partners. At the time, Cinamerica's screens constituted about 2% of the total 22,000 screens in the country. WCI's $150 million stake in Paramount's exhibition business startled the industry.

During the years 1970–80 the number of domestic screens increased from 13,750 to 17,590.

In the Reagan era, changing antitrust policy allowed the studios to return to a vertically integrated mode. During the 1986–87 buying spree, four major studios paid more than $770 million for substantial interests in 1,890 domestic screens (8% of total).[4] In a single year, Columbia (Sony), MCA (Matsushita), Paramount, and Warner Bros. (Time Warner) achieved an important presence in exhibition, which they had been forced to leave some 40 years earlier. In the '80s the four-firm concentration ratio peaked before and after the merger wave (66–69%, 1982–84; 57–64%, 1988–90). Yet numbers fell below the high ratios of the late '70s, which saw the demise of the independents (4-firm ratio at 64–67%, 8-firm ratio at 94–99%) (see Figure 4.1).

The ancillary markets transformed the function of theatrical exhibition. In absolute terms, the 1948 *Paramount* case entailed about 214 U.S. theatres, while the 1987 merger wave changed ownership rights of 1,890 U.S. screens. In relative terms, the *Paramount* case involved about 17% of all U.S. theatres, whereas the merger wave comprised only half of that. Prior to the *Paramount* case, the theatrical segment accounted for 100% of total revenues, whereas in 1987 (after reintegration), the portion was less than 39% and continued to decline.[5] Domestic theatrical exhibition had become a mature business.

Table 4-4
Theatre Circuits: Concentration (1977–92)

Circuit	Screen Total	(%)	Circuit	Screen Total	(%)	Circuit	Screen Total	(%)
1977			**1987**			**1992**		
General Cin.	739	4.5%	United Art.	2050	9.0%	United Art.	2398	9.8%
United Art.	661	4.0	Cineplex	1685	7.4	Cineplex	1700	6.9
Multi-Cinema	462	2.8	Multi-Cinema	1530	6.7	Multi-Cinema	1629	6.6
Plitt	412	2.5	General Cin	1360	6.0	General Cin.	1466	6.0
Commonwealth	347	2.1	Paramount	899	3.9	Carmike	1387	5.6
Mann	310	1.9	Carmike	670	2.9	Cinemark	939	3.8
Fuqua-Martin	283	1.7	Col/TriStar	627	2.7	Loews	890	3.6
Kerasotes	180	1.1	Commonwealth	435	1.9	National Amu.	725	3.0
Top-4	2274	13.8%		6625	29.1%		7193	29.3%
Top-8	3394	20.6%		9256	40.5%		11134	45.3%

Screen total (March 1992); number of all screens (1991).

SOURCE: Motion Picture Association, Inc.; company reports.

Dominant Theatre Circuits

Between 1977 and 1992 the top 8 theatre circuits more than doubled their market concentration, from 21% to 45% (the top 4 ratio grew from 14% to 29%). Huge debt, however, constrained M&A activity among the top 4 circuits (see Table 4-4). By the early '90s, consolidation continued among the leading theatre circuits, which dominated almost half of the business.[6]

United Artists. United Artists Entertainment, the nation's largest chain (2,766 screens), found little strategic advantage to owning 10% of the nation's screens if they were scattered over 39 states. By 1992 TCI sold UAE, which had proved a disappointment to the growth-focused cable MSO.

Cineplex Odeon. Driven by Garth Drabinsky's meteoric rise and fall, the frantic overexpansion of the Canadian-based Cineplex Odeon circuit resulted in a $610 million debt burden. Despite its 50% stake, MCA was unable to restrain the juggernaut (it could only vote a minority position under Canadian law). Deposed in 1989, Drabinsky was followed by Allen Karp, who began slashing costs.

American Multi-Cinema. In the '80s AMC was swept by the M&A wave, opening one new multiplex after another. Heavily indebted by the '90s, it started cutting back, suffering from losses.

General Cinema. By the early '90s General Cinema's core business (movie theatres) was doing poorly. Its Neiman Marcus was one of the largest national specialty chains, but it, too, was suffering. Hence General Cinema's bid of more than $1.5 billion for the beleaguered publisher Harcourt Brace Jovanovich.

In the early '90s a handful of second-tier major circuits (Carmike, Cinemark, National Amusements, Act III Theaters, TPI Enterprises) emerged as the new titans of exhibition. In the '80s these circuits had resisted the costly acquisition-building spree; in the early '90s they made bargain acquisitions from overextended competitors and excelled in rationalization.[7]

Overall, most studio-run circuits had not lived up to expectations. As growth markets emigrated overseas, maturity contributed to disillusionment. Reportedly, Universal (Cineplex Odeon), Paramount (Cinamerica) and Warner Bros. (Cinamerica) were considering exiting from the exhibition business.[8]

Megacircuits were paying little attention to potential alternatives in theatrical exhibition. Only smaller players, such as Imax, Iwerks Entertainment, and Showscan, were competing to create a future in which a giant screen played a role. Only the majors had done some exploration of technological innovation in exhibition—but even they confined exploration to microscale efforts at theme parks.[9]

ANCILLARY MARKETS

Home Video

Following the studios' failure in 1980 to set up a pay-TV service of their own, they retaliated by boosting home video, which hurt HBO and caused a long-lasting stagnation for pay cable (on the Premiere case, see the section on basic and pay cable in Chapter 3). In 1980 domestic and foreign videocassettes accounted for just 1% of total theatrical revenues, whereas by 1989 they garnered 50.2%. As a revenue source, home video had become far more important than box-office rentals (25.7%).

From 1980 to 1993 the VCR penetration soared from 2% to 77%, even though growth stagnated toward the end of the decade (see Table 4-5). In April 1994 the HD Digital Conference, representing 50 major electronics companies in Asia, Europe, and the United States, agreed on a proposed standard for digital VCRs. Paving the way for the next generation of VCRs, the new machines were expected on the market by 1995–96 (it will take a few years for cost to come down).[1]

From Rentals to Sell-Throughs

From 1980 to 1994 the portion of home video in theatrical revenues grew from $25 million to *$7.9 billion* (see Table 4-1). At first, the studios released their films on tape at high prices ($89.95) and retailers bought tapes that were rented out. The selling of movies to a mass market began in 1987, when Paramount released *Top Gun* for $26.95 (it sold 3.5 million copies). A year later, when *E.T.* was offered for sale, Universal sidestepped

Table 4-5
VCR Households and VCR Penetration (1980–93)

Year	TV HHs (mil)	VCR HHs (mil)	VCR HHs penetration (%)	VCR HHs change (%)
1993	93.1	71.7	77.0%	–
1992	93.1	70.3	75.6	1.9%
1991	92.0	67.5	73.3	4.3
1990	93.1	65.4	70.2	3.2
1989	92.1	62.3	67.6	5.0
1988	90.4	56.2	62.2	10.8
1987	88.6	45.8	51.7	22.7
1986	87.4	32.5	37.2	40.9
1985	86.1	23.5	27.3	38.3
1984	85.3	15.0	17.6	56.7
1983	84.2	8.3	9.9	80.0
1982	83.7	4.8	5.7	72.9
1981	81.9	2.5	3.1	92.0
1980	78.0	1.9	2.4	35.1

HH = Household.

SOURCE: Motion Picture Association of America, Inc.

the rental stage and put 14.5 million copies on the market at $24.95 each. As the rental market matured, the sell-through market soared. Mass marketing, lower pricing, and a blockbuster product went hand in hand. In 1989 *Batman* went on sale for $24.98. Indeed, rental and sell-through markets co-existed side by side, for different products.

Sell-Through Market	*Rental Market*
Blockbusters	Medium/niche pictures
Seasonal business	Seasonal variation
Targeting teens/children	Targeting adults
Focus on sales	Focus on volume
Mass audiences	Segmented audiences
Lower-priced purchases	Rental packages
High marketing costs	Increasing marketing costs
One-step process (sell-through)	Two-step process (sell-through and/or rental)

Despite the explosive growth of home video, research (as a vehicle of segmentation) joined the bandwagon only with the maturing of rental *and* sell-through markets.[2]

Disney's Push: Studios and Mass Merchants

Though it did not invent the sell-through market, Disney, with its impressive film library, pioneered many efforts in sell-through marketing.

The studio's releases accounted for five of ten all-time home video best-sellers. In October 1992, when *Beauty and the Beast* went on sale, Disney's home video division manufactured and shipped 17 million videocassettes to stores; bypassing local mom-and-pop video stores, it employed mass-merchandising giants (Toys 'R' Us, Wal-Mart, and Target). Operating with a low profile not to upset the industry, Disney eliminated the middlemen—that is, video distribution companies that shipped copies to the stores.[3]

Supplier Consolidation

While concentration in the home video marketplace remains lower than in theatrical exhibition, studios have consolidated their dominance since the mid-'80s. From 1986 to 1993 the combined share of the top 4 suppliers grew from 43% to 61% (68% in rental revenue, 57% in sell-through revenue) (see Table 4-6).

By the early '90s the studios' home video divisions were under increasing pressure to make up for lagging theatrical revenue. Though film production remained the glamorous side of business, the profits were increasingly made in the low-profile home video divisions, which thought like soap companies and whose bargaining power increased within the studio structure. Similar concerns motivated the players: globalization of operations, the sell-through market, product diversification, technological innovation. Many top independent companies had merged, assigned their distribution to others, or had run into difficulties.

By the early '90s home video was evolving toward a record-industry model of distribution, with a handful of powerful majors gaining control of distribution and independent companies making label deals with the few entrenched majors.

Retailer Consolidation

By the late '80s video distribution was dominated by three types of retailers, which controlled more than 95% of the business: video specialists (major retail chains) (62%), mass merchants (20%), supermarkets (13%)—as well as drug stores, convenience stores, and record stores. The explosion of the rental market boosted the growth of video specialty stores, which mushroomed from 2,500 to 30,000 in the '80s. The relative decline and consolidation of the rental market went hand in hand with the decrease of video specialty stores to about 27,000 in 1992. Blockbuster boasted a 13% share in the near-$11 billion industry (99 of its closest competitors together grossed less than it did).

In the early '90s the top 8 companies controlled 16–18% of the marketplace (of which Blockbuster single-handedly dominated 93%). While the portion of the top 100 video stores of total video retail revenue had

Table 4-6
Home Video: Leading Suppliers (1986–93)

Rank/Company	1986	1988	1990
1 Buena Vista	8.2%	11.4%	17.1%
2 RCA/CPHV	9.5	7.4	11.3
3 Paramount	11.0	10.7	10.2
4 Warner	8.5	9.8	10.1
5 MCA/Universal	7.1	11.1	9.5
6 LIVE	1.8	2.5	7.5
7 CBS/Fox	13.7	9.2	6.0
8 MGM/UA	8.0	4.5	5.5
9 Orion/Nelson[1]	-	5.2	4.7
10 HBO	7.0	4.4	3.1
Top-4	42.7%	43.0%	48.7%
Top-8	75.4	70.9	77.2

	Rental Revenue			Sell-Through Revenue			Total Revenue		
Rank/Company	1992 (mil)	1993 (mil)	1993 (%)	1992 (mil)	1993 (mil)	1993 (%)	1992 (mil)	1993 (mil)	1993 (mil)
Buena Vista	220	290	13.7%	785	960	31.1%	1005	1250	24.0%
HBO	nc	23	1.1	nc	57	1.8	nc	80	1.5
Cannon	nc	5	0.2	nc	2	0.1	nc	7	0.1
MGM/UAN/C	53	na	nc	46	na	nc	99	na	-
Warner Bros.	nc	307	14.5	nc	270	8.7	nc	577	11.1
Total Warner	380	388	18.3	310	375	12.2	690	763	14.7
Col/TriStar	nc	410	19.3	nc	75	2.4	nc	485	9.3
New Line	nc	114	5.4	nc	44	1.4	nc	158	3.0
Total Col/TriStar	395	524	24.7	155	119	3.9	550	643	12.3
Fox[2]	250	230	10.8	145	289	9.4	395	519	10.0
MCA	205	240	11.3	135	91	2.9	340	331	6.4
Paramount	260	225	10.6	139	90	2.9	399	315	6.0
LIVE	80	70	3.3	35	71	2.3	115	141	2.7
Orion	40	21	1.0	50	30	1.0	90	51	1.0
Republic	nc	35	1.6	nc	15	0.5	nc	50	1.0
Vidmark	nc	30	1.4	nc	10	0.3	nc	40	0.8
Total	1955	2122	100.0%	2619	3086	100.0%	4574	5208	100.0%
Top-4		68.0			56.6			61.0	
Top-8		93.7			65.7			77.1	

na = Not applicable. nc = No comparable data.
1. In 1987 Nelson's share was 3.7%, and in 1988 2.4%, whereas Orion's share was 2.8% in 1988. The shares of the two companies have been combined (actually combined in 1989).
2. CBS/Fox sales included in sell-through estimate.

SOURCE: Video Store Magazine (various issues).

increased from 17% to 24%, the video retail industry remained fragmented.

Blockbuster: The Home Video McDonald's. Starting in 1987, H. Wayne Huizenga turned Blockbuster into a powerful chain by buying other video chains (and absorbing smaller operators), such as Movies To Go (1987), Video Library (1988), Major Video and Video Superstore (1989), as well as Applause Video and Erol's (1990). Driven by a "superstore" concept, Blockbuster soared from 19 stores to nearly 1,300 nationally, in three years. As "America's Family Video Store," it positioned itself as the retailers' McDonald's ("McVideo" was the often-used term).[4] Indeed, Blockbuster had to continue expansion to enjoy strong revenue growth.[5]

Despite its success, Blockbuster's stock price stagnated by mid-1991. Despite short-term concerns (contraction, the Gulf War), other troubles loomed on the horizon. In 5–15 years, competing technologies (PPV movies, phone companies) would prove fatal to the home video business. Thus, the company went international (Western Europe, Japan, and Latin America).[6]

Preparing itself for the decline of the home video market, Blockbuster began diversifying. With Philips Electronics as a part owner, Blockbuster ex-plored various options. Overall, Huizenga bought all or part of sports businesses (15% of the Miami Dolphins, 50% of Joe Robbie Stadium, 80% of the Florida Marlins baseball team, 100% of the Florida Panthers hockey team), music store chains (100% of Super Club Retail, 100% of Sound Warehouse, 100% of Music Plus), as well as indie movie and TV companies (35% of Republic Pictures, 64% of Spelling Entertainment). The reorganized Blockbuster also joined with IBM to produce a machine that made music CDs on demand (without record companies' support the venture failed). Huizenga was planning a massive futuristic entertainment and sports complex in South Florida, as well as a Blockbuster cable TV channel.[7]

With revenues at $2.2 billion in 1993, the video portion still accounted for some 88% (58% rental, 30% video store product sales) of Blockbuster's total revenues. The number of video stores had increased to 3,593, while music stores had mushroomed to 531. As diversification could not wait, Huizenga joined in Viacom's bid for Paramount. (On Viacom's takeover struggle for Paramount and merger effort with Blockbuster, see Chapter 6.)

Syndication

Like theatrical exhibition, the market for syndication evolved with antitrust policy. Initially, the Big Three enjoyed a virtual monopoly in TV distribution and production. Popular shows were owned and/or controlled by the networks, which distributed the reruns to local stations and overseas for huge profits.

Financial Interest and Syndication Rules

Restricting the networks' ownership rights, the financial interest and syndication (fin-syn) rules boosted Hollywood majors' supplier power, while protecting bigger independent producers.[1]

From the enactment of the fin-syn rules to the Reagan era, the networks, studios, and the FCC negotiated ceaselessly over the fin-syn rules. When the FCC was expected to repeal the rules, the Reagan White House intervened at the studios' request. Congress asked the studios and the networks to work out a compromise. In 1985 the studios and CBS reached a settlement, but it collapsed when both ABC and NBC disagreed. Next year saw another possible settlement, but with network takeovers the new owners balked. In 1987 the talks began anew.[2]

Until the early '70s it was difficult for syndicated programs to achieve a national audience. Things changed with the fin-syn rules. By 1990 most top shows had a coverage of 90+%, including game shows (*Wheel of Fortune, Jeopardy*), talk shows (*Donahue, The Oprah Winfrey Show*), tabloids (*A Current Affair*), and entertainment magazines (*Entertainment Tonight*).

Traditionally, syndication had meant off-network programs, which were distributed through direct syndication. By the early '90s barter (ad time paid in lieu of cash for programming) was the dominant mode of distribution, while reruns were augmented by first-run syndicated shows that dominated more than half of the market (Paramount's new *The Untouchables* and *Deep Space Nine*).

In the past, syndicators had served primarily U.S. and foreign broadcast TV stations. By the late '80s syndication comprised three basic markets: domestic broadcast television (network affiliates, indies, hybrids, DBS), domestic cable television (MSOs, indies), and overseas sales (broadcast, cable TV, DBS).[3]

Hollywood studios had a competitive edge in developing and selling programs to independent TV stations and to network affiliates. Also, majors' syndicated programs stayed on the air longer, leaving fewer openings for new products. As the market tightened, small firms were the first to feel the pinch.

By the late '80s the M&A wave heralded a new era in the fin-syn talks. If Hollywood studios were allowed to vertically integrate (and be bought by Japanese giants), why couldn't the (American) networks enter the syndication market?[4]

Demise of the Fin-Syn Rules

By the early '90s only FBC—a foreign-based de facto network—could syndicate all of its series as long as it did not exceed 15 hours a week of prime-time programming. Hollywood studios provided 75% of the networks' prime-time series, while the Big Three produced less than 10%. The U.S. syndication market was a booming $4.3 billion business, of which barter and independent stations accounted for $1.3 billion each, cable $1 billion, and network affiliates $0.8 billion. In addition, TV movies and theatrical films to the rapidly growing overseas TV channels were expected to hit more than $2.6 billion.[5]

In April 1993 the FCC reversed itself, saying that networks should be allowed to own the rerun rights to the prime-time shows they carried. In November the fin-syn rules were lifted and the networks were allowed to

Figure 4-2
Struggle on Financial Interest and Syndication Rules (1959–93)

Year	Regulation and Antitrust Activities
I. Phase: The FCC Initiatives	
1959	FCC begins inquiry into whether the networks wield monopoly power over program production and distribution
1970	FCC passes financial interest and syndication rules (fin-syn), forces networks out of syndication, bars them from sharing in rerun sales, and prohibits them from ownership rights
1972	Nixon administration's Justice Department files antitrust suit against CBS, NBC, and ABC, alleging anticompetitive behavior
1977	FCC begins new study to toughen fin-syn rules
1978	NBC signs consent decree with Justice Department; incorporates fin-syn rules and adds new limits to how many 100%-owned shows the networks can put on the air; limit to expire November 1990
1980	CBS and ABC sign similar consent decrees
II. Phase: Negotiations	
1982	In study begun in 1977, FCC finds networks have not been anti-competitive; FCC starts new study of staff findings
1983	As FCC prepares to repeal fin-syn rules, Reagan White House intervenes at studios' request, FCC delays action, and Congress asks Hollywood studios and networks to work out a compromise
1985	Studios and CBS reach settlement, which collapses when ABC and NBC will not agree
1986	A new settlement is reached, but three networks' new owners balk
1987	Studios and networks begin new talks, but little progress is made
III. Phase: Wave of Vertical Integration	
1989	Networks resort to restructuring, while major studios are acquired by foreign interests, except for Disney and Time Warner
1990	Seeking relief from the fin-syn rules, Fox causes confusion among the studios and networks which fail to reach a compromise; FCC begins rewriting rules while Justice Department joins networks
1991	White House argues for fin-syn elimination; with chairman Alfred Sikes dissenting, FCC votes for majority plan, which means Hollywood's triumph over networks
1992	A record 77% of fall network schedule is handled by studios; fin-syn battlefront shifts to court
1993	FCC reverses itself and says the networks should not be restricted from owning a financial stake in programs they broadcast; U.S. District Court lifts the consent decrees

SOURCE: Reprinted by permission of Wall Street Journal, copyright 1989 Dow Jones & Company, Inc. All Rights Reserved Worldwide.; updated and amended by the author.

share in the syndication profits (see Figure 4-2). In the written decision, Judge Manuel Real said: "The logic of restricting markets to aid competition is flawed. It is eminently possible that even in 1970, the antitrust theory applicable to the fin-syn rules was flawed."[6]

In the 1993-94 season, syndication was producing more nonsports programming (i.e., 272 weekly hours on-air) than the Big Three combined (i.e., 235 weekly hours on-air).[7] Meanwhile, the struggle for available time slots heated up. *Thunder Alley*, a new comedy on ABC, was dismissed by most critics. The high ratings derived from the show's most-favored-program status, between two episodes of *Home Improvement*, the top-rated sitcom, at 8:30 P.M. on Wednesdays. As both co-owner and scheduler of *Thunder Alley*, ABC hoped to reap some of the profits. As a result, the studios were about to launch networks of their own.[8]

By the 1994–95 season, the Big Three TV networks were part of the top 10 prime-time TV development suppliers.[9] Even more interestingly, studios—which fought the networks so long and bitterly on the fin-syn rules—hedged bets by partnering with the Big Three on program projects.[10] Product development was *in*.

COMPLEMENTARY MARKETS

In addition to their primary market (theatrical exhibition) and ancillary markets (network TV, pay TV, home video, syndication, foreign markets), entertainment conglomerates had other sources of revenue. Operating along the traditional primary and ancillary markets, these businesses served as complements; promoting other products, they had substantial strategic significance.[1]

Financially, for example, Disney's theme parks generated greater revenues than its filmed entertainment; strategically, however, the former owed their life to the latter. Theatrical exhibition was the window that presented the beloved characters, who then found their way to ancillary markets, including theme parks. With complements (from theme parks to interactive multimedia), strategic priorities drove financial priorities, not vice versa.

Theme Parks

Amusement parks came to the United States in the late 1800s. As streetcar companies built picnic groves to attract weekend riders, major facilities sprang into national prominence. By the 1920s there were some 1,500 such parks in the United States. The industry declined after the Depression, the boom of classic Hollywood cinema, the rise of television, and the decay of the inner cities. When Walt Disney became obsessed with the idea of a theme park, there were few clean parks left, especially for family-oriented fun.[1]

In 1955 Disney opened its first theme park, Disneyland, in Anaheim, California. It incorporated major attractions of the Tivoli Gardens (Copenhagen), older European pleasure gardens, and Coney Island's amusement park. *The Mickey Mouse Club* TV show promoted the theme park, which, in turn, promoted Disney TV shows and motion pictures, with a variety of consumer products.

Despite Disneyland's success (theme parks kept Disney in the black when film production slumped), larger public companies began investing in the theme-park business only in the late '60s.

Two decades later, Disney reinforced synergic linkages between filmed entertainment and theme parks, designing more rides, attractions, and shows around blockbusters, such as *The Little Mermaid, Honey, I Shrunk the Kids, Who Framed Roger Rabbit?*, and *Indiana Jones*. By 1990 the company owned and operated two top-ranking U.S. theme parks (Disneyland and Walt Disney World in Orlando, Florida), with 43.3 million annual visitors—as against 29.4 million for the remaining top 10 parks. Eight of the top 10 theme parks were located in California and Florida. As the industry consolidated, rivalry intensified.

From Disney Monopoly to Studio Wars

In 1964 MCA's Universal Studios Hollywood tour drew only 39,000 guests; a quarter of a century later it had 5 million visitors annually. In June 1989 Disney opened a $300 million 135-acre Disney-MGM Studios park near Orlando, featuring attractions based on Hollywood and the movies; a year later followed MCA's Universal Studios Florida, a $630 million, 444-acre theme park, 10 miles down the road. Since MCA could not compete head-on with Disney World's family entertainment, it focused on teenagers.[2]

Through the booming '80s, baby boomers and an expansive economy boosted American tourism and theme parks. Although Disney increased its theme-park price nine times, attendance continued to grow and fuel the company's explosive growth. In 1990–91, however, contraction and the Gulf War resulted in a decline in theme-park attendance, forcing Disney to cut prices (it was the first temporary price cut in Disneyland's 35-year history). What once was a Disney monopoly was evolving into an oligopoly dominated by the Hollywood majors.

As Disney increased its capacity in Florida, it contemplated two new parks in Southern California, amid finishing Euro Disney near Paris, France. With the acquisition of MCA, Matsushita became the owner of Universal Studios, and, thereby, a major theme-park player in Southern California (Universal Studios Hollywood) and Florida (Universal Studios Florida). Warner acquired a significant stake in the Six Flags amusement parks. Through its newly acquired Columbia Pictures, Sony was planning a Sonyland theme park in Southern California. And just as Anheuser-Busch (Busch Gardens) acquired Sea World, the country-music-oriented Gaylord Entertainment also played the marketing game.

Except for Disney, the new entrants were not building theme parks, due to significant land, construction, and labor costs. Instead, Time Warner, Paramount (Kings Dominion), and Anheuser-Busch were buying parks that had been built during the '70s boom.

In the early '90s Disney World remained the most popular U.S. theme park, with more than 30 million annual guests. Disneyland's attendance volume hovered around 12 million, while MCA's Universal Studios and

Knott's Berry Farm attracted some 4–5 million guests. Attendance volumes for other major parks—Sea World of Florida, Sea World of California, Six Flags Magic Mountain, and Cedar Point—hovered around 3–4 million a year.

In 1992–93 an intense battle between Disney and Time Warner reflected the new competitive environment. When TW's national ad campaign presented the seven Six Flags amusement parks as cheaper, closer to home, and as much fun as Disney parks, Disney pulled its advertising from TW's magazines and refused to broadcast Six Flag's Magic Mountain park on its Los Angeles television station.[3]

As the saturated U.S. market entered a low-growth era, the contractionary business gave rise to innovation in technology, segmentation, regional theme parks, and foreign markets.

From Simulated Rides to Virtual Reality Theme Parks

As long as the booming economy fueled price increases in megaparks, huge M&E corporations continued massive investments in the business. Meanwhile, a high-tech spin was put on the old roller-coaster ride and "simulated" rides were touted as cost-efficient alternatives, from Las Vegas (Douglas Trumbull's entertainment complex) to San Francisco (Iwerks's Turbotour simulation ride). High-tech virtual reality attractions turned up at casinos and shopping centers. In 1993 Sega, a thriving video-game company, announced it would build dozens of smaller virtual reality theme parks, each at an estimated $10–$50 million. Following suit, other companies developed similar parks, including Namco, Edison Brothers, Paramount, and Sony.[4]

From Mass Marketing to Segmentation

In 1991 the top 4 theme parks had captured about 70% of the visitors in the top 10 U.S. theme parks, while attendance volumes for the remaining six operators were far smaller. Despite size differences, however, major theme parks offered similar family entertainment. When Universal Studios Florida focused on teenagers, segmentation arrived into theme parks.

From Destination Resorts to Regional Theme Parks

In the past, baby boomers had crowded destination resorts with their children; by the early '90s the aging boomers were catered to by substitutes like casinos and country-music parks, including Fiesta Texas, Opryland, and Branson, Missouri. Even a Las Vegas Casino, the MGM Grand, opened a theme park within its hotel. In November 1993 Disney joined the regional rivalry, announcing it would build a new $800 million theme park in Virginia, while the Denmark-based Lego Systems planned a $100 million Lego Land in Carlsbad, California (for kids too young for roller coasters). As value-minded baby boomers took shorter trips close to home, full-fledged destination resorts lost some of their attractiveness.

Foreign Growth

In January 1994 MCA announced it would develop and help operate a $1–$2 billion "Universal Studios Japan" theme park in Osaka, slated to open in 1999. MCA also continued to discuss future sites in Europe, while Disney was intent on building a new maritime theme park, DisneySea, at Tokyo Disneyland. In 1993 Euro Disney's first-year loss amounted to about $930 million; in March 1994, after months on the edge of bankruptcy, a $1 billion plan to save the troubled theme park was worked out with Disney and a steering committee representing creditor banks. American theme-park rivalry was being exported to foreign markets. Despite the problems of the $4 billion Euro Disney, the fastest industry growth came outside of the saturated U.S. market.[5]

Toys, Video Games, Licensed Merchandise, and Retail Chains

Toys

In the early '80s explosive growth in the toy business stemmed from blockbuster sales of a few key products, an expansionary business cycle, burgeoning child demographics, the resurgence of traditional toys, and a shift toward year-round sales. Retail growth stagnated only at the end of the decade. During Christmas 1991, U.S. toy industry and exports boomed again. America remained the largest market in the worldwide toy industry. From 1980 to 1992 U.S. retail sales in toys and video games grew from $6.7 billion to $17.0 billion (see Table 4-7).[1]

Despite growth, America's toy trade deficit doubled to $5.2 billion after the mid-'80s. Japan (video games) along with China, Taiwan, and Hong Kong became the leading suppliers of toys imported into the United States.[2]

Despite industry volatility, staple toys remained perennial bestsellers and played a critical role in M&E licensing and merchandising. By the early '90s, dolls, activity toys, vehicles, and infant/pre-school items dominated over half of the marketplace.

The late '80s also witnessed the rejuvenation of video games, a business thought to be dead. In the total industry (toys and video games), the share of video games soared from near-extinction to over 26% ($2.7 billion) in 1990. The introduction of a third generation of video game systems did not let toy companies rest easy.

Hollywood Majors and Toy Business. Hollywood majors entered the toys and video games market in the early '80s. Unlike its major rivals (Warner, MCA), Disney had been in the business ever since the licensing of Mickey

Table 4-7
Toys and Video Games: Annual Sales/Estimated Manufacturers' Shipments by Product Category (1984–92)[1]

ANNUAL SALES ($bil)[2]	1984	1986	1988	1990	1992
Manufacturers' Shipments	$8.27	$8.32	$8.69	$8.57	$11.39
Retail Sales	12.34	12.42	12.97	13.13	17.00

GAMES BY MAJOR CATEGORIES

Category	1984	1986	1988	1990	1992
Toys (%)					
Infant/Preschool	8.9%	9.8%	11.6%	11.6%	9.6%
Dolls	18.4	20.0	11.1	15.5	17.8
Plush	6.6	12.8	7.9	5.8	5.0
Male Action Toys	11.4	13.3	6.0	8.1	4.7
Vehicles	9.5	9.2	14.7	14.2	11.2
Ride-ons (excl bic.)	3.4	3.5	7.0	4.8	4.2
Games/puzzles	14.6	9.1	10.9	11.0	9.5
Activity toys	13.1	10.2	16.0	13.2	13.2
All other toys	14.1	12.1	14.8	15.8	24.8
Total Toy Industry ($mil)	$8,270	$8,323	$8,690	$8,575	$11,391
Video Games[3]					
TV Video Units	-	-	40.7%	27.2%	31.8%
8-Bit TV Video Software	-	-	55.6[4]	53.7[4]	13.8
16-Bit TV Video Software	-	-			30.0
8-Bit TV Video Accessories	-	-	3.7[5]	3.1[5]	1.8
16-Bit TV Video Accessories	-	-			4.8
Portable Video Hardware	-	-	-	8.9	7.7
Portable Video Software	-	-	-	7.0	8.9
Portable Video Accessories	-	-	-	0.0	1.1
Total Video Games ($mil)	-	-	$1,890	$3,064	$3,951
TOTAL INDUSTRY WITH VIDEO GAMES ($mil)	-	-	$10,580	$11,639	$15,342

1. Based on manufacturers' prices. 2. Figures do not include video games.
3. 1990 and 1988 figures based on limited sample. 4. All video software.
5. All video accessories.

SOURCE: Toy Manufacturers of America.

Mouse in the late '20s. In the '80s the record was mixed for other Hollywood majors.

Disney. While consumer products continued to be Disney's smallest segment, it had the highest growth potential. The segment consisted of the licensing and production of film, audio, and computer software in the children's market in the United States and internationally. Disney stores provided retail outlets for the merchandise.

Warner. In the early '80s Warner expanded its interests in the video-game business (Atari). In 1989 it also acquired a 17% interest in Hasbro.

MCA. In mid-1985 MCA acquired LJN Toys. After dramatic growth, LJN's losses accumulated. The unit launched an aggressive expansion, including video games based upon the company's popular motion pictures (*Who Framed Roger Rabbit?*, *Friday the 13th*, and *Back to the Future*). MCA discontinued LJN's operations in 1989.

Toward Consolidation

Consolidation in the toy business—historically a fragmented industry—increased toward the late '80s, due to sluggish sales by traditional toymakers, strong performances by video game makers, and the 1990–91 contraction.

Hasbro. After the death of Stephen Hassenfeld, his younger brother, Alan Hassenfeld turned Hasbro into a formidable player. With the Tonka acquisition, Hasbro picked up Tonka trucks, and added the Parker Brothers unit (Monopoly) to its Milton Bradley division (board games). By the early '90s Hasbro played it safe, scaling back product introductions by half and investing in classic toys.[3]

Mattel. With Barbie, Mattel survived its mid-'80s plunge to become one of the fastest-growing toy companies on Wall Street. Through M&E licensing deals and partnerships, it was taking increasing risks by unveiling a broad array of toys tied to hit movies and TV shows. In August 1993 Mattel and Fisher Price announced a merger in a $1 billion stock swap. By the spring of 1994 Mattel's miniature cars represented the company's latest push to lessen its dependency on Barbie, which accounted for 35% of its $2.7 billion in sales.[4]

In industry revenues, Hasbro's acquisition of Tonka boosted the consolidation of the top 4 companies from 58% to 70%, while the top 8 ratio soared from 77% to 88%. In addition to M&A activity in the toy business, Nintendo's near-monopoly in video games contributed crucially to (total industry) consolidation.

Video Games

It was Nolan Bushnell who introduced Pong, the first video game. He also tried to sell Atari to Disney until Warner acquired his company for $27 million in 1975. There have been two phases in the video game industry:

The First Video Game Craze (1976–84): Boom and Bust. Despite a meager $39 million in sales for fiscal 1976, Warner Communications, Inc. (WCI) infused millions into Atari to develop and manufacture Video Computer System (VCS), a home video game system that could play different game cartridges. As Atari evolved into WCI's profit center, the video craze overheated the marketplace. In 1979 the toy industry offered consumers about 100 different electronic products. In 1980 the market for hand-held electronic games collapsed. The rapidly growing industry attracted many new entrants, including Mattel's Intellivision and ColecoVision. By 1982 Atari accounted for most of the $2 billion in WCI's consumer electronics segment. As every major studio was seeking a piece of the action, even broadcast companies joined the licensing frenzy. In 1984 slowing retail sales and inventory glut resulted in a collapse of sales. WCI suffered a near-bankruptcy and sold Atari while retaining a 25% interest. Next year, Mattel and Coleco exited the business. Sales for the video game industry fell from $3 billion to $100 million (from 1983 to 1985.)

The Second Video Game Craze (1985–90): The Nintendo Monopoly. Founded in the late 1880s as a manufacturer of playing cards, Nintendo Ltd. was one of Japan's leading manufacturers of electronic toys. In the mid-'80s, when video games were largely written off, it began testing the U.S. market with a more sophisticated machine. With sales at $3 billion in 1990, Nintendo captured a near-monopoly. One out of every four families in the United States connected the Nintendo Entertainment System (NES) to the back of the TV. The company offered more than 200 titles on themes ranging from baseball to medieval warfare. As Super Mario Brothers, the all-time best-selling series of games (39 million copies), became an international cultural icon, Nintendo hoped Mario would establish interactive entertainment, just as Mickey Mouse helped pioneer animated pictures in the 1930s.

When Nintendo's rapidly growing sales led to the second video game craze, the weakened U.S.-dominated toy business began consolidating.[5] By 1990 Nintendo had an 87% share of the $4 billion video game market. Although in Europe Sega Enterprises Ltd. (a former subsidiary of Gulf + Western) beat Nintendo to market with both 8- and 16-bit machines, it lost the 8-bit battle in the United States. Peaking at $3.1 billion in 1990, video games accounted for more than a quarter of total industry (toys and video games). But Nintendo's "golden era" was over.

Maturing Video-Game Industry (1990–present). Due to its licensing rules, Nintendo became embroiled in the politics of U.S.-Japan trade, and sales slowed following an antitrust investigation.[6] To boost revenues, it introduced the new Super Nintendo Entertainment System—a risky (it made the existing Nintendo system obsolete) and expensive (it cost an estimated $190, plus $60 for each game, an almost 80% increase compared with the old system) strategic move. The contractionary environment did not bode well for Super Nintendo. The trend was toward classic staples. Also, as American computer software makers began to introduce games for Nintendo-type machines, the marketplace was getting crowded. The video game industry entered its third phase.[7]

In 1991 Nintendo's share of the video game market had shrunk to 70%, against 20% for Sega and 10% for others.[8]

Price War: Nintendo v. Sega. In spring 1992, 37% of American families owned a video-game system and slowing sales prompted a price war between the two dominant systems, Nintendo's Super NES and Sega's Genesis. With its first-generation system (an 8-bit computer chip), Nintendo had engaged in little or no price cutting. With the second-generation (16-bit) Super NES, price cuts (and shrinking profit margins) were inevitable.

With its lower price and the popularity of Sonic the Hedgehog, Sega's Genesis outsold Nintendo's Super NES during Christmas 1991. In summer 1992 Nintendo's price cuts and Street Fighter II beat Sega. By late 1992 Sega signed up software houses (Acclaim, Konami) that used to work solely for Nintendo. It was also about to unveil a $299 compact disk attachment that would play standard music CDs or live-action video software. Concurrently, a $40 million feature adaptation of the Nintendo game was released in the United States by Disney's Buena Vista.[9]

Blockbusters and Video Games. By the '80s Hollywood majors found a new licensing niche in video games based on blockbusters and complemented traditional movie merchandising (T-shirts, toys, posters). Hence the conversion of successful movies and TV programs into electronic game formats. *Star Wars* and *Raiders of the Lost Ark* brought new life to the action/adventure/fantasy genre of filmmaking, leading to the emergence of related games (*Star Trek, RoboCop, Batman*). The success of the Teenage Mutant Ninja Turtles and Acclaim's move to Hollywood illustrated the convergence of Hollywood and video game companies.[10]

As early as 1988–89, Warner Bros. had worked closely with its licensees from *Batman*'s concept stage through the development and distribution of the video game. By 1990 the pace of conversions from film to video games speeded up dramatically as the *Total Recall* game became available almost simultaneously with the picture. Such "development bonding" played an important role in the quality of film-inspired games.

As an ancillary revenue source, licensed video games added value to the studio product; as marketing vehicles, they increased product awareness. The blockbuster-driven motion picture industry and the title-driven video game industry went hand in hand. With Nintendo's and Sega's second generation of interactive computer games, the number of Hollywood-themed software packages was rising in the $4 billion-a-year industry. Recognizing the profit potential, Disney and Lucasfilm opened software games divisions. Concurrently, the California-based Sierra On-Line, Inc. became the first company devoted exclusively to games, while its subsidiary, the Sierra Network, a telephone-linked computer network, was planning to extend an all-video game network across the nation.[11]

Toward Oligopoly: Sega's Rise and New Competitors. In 1989 Nintendo had controlled some 80% of home video game sales. When Sega hit the market with its 16-bit Genesis player, Nintendo responded too late; Sega's $150 Genesis undersold the $200 Super Nintendo Entertainment System; and Sega beat Nintendo by getting a CD-ROM player to market. The industry was moving toward a Nintendo-Sega duopoly.

Though Nintendo continued to dominate U.S. homes with its video game machines and games, Sega's U.S. subsidiary, led by sales of Genesis players, edged ahead of Nintendo's U.S. subsidiary in the critical market for 16-bit machines. The $3.6 billion company received more than $1 billion from its virtual reality (VR) arcades and announced it would open more than 100 VR arcades worldwide, each costing $10–50 million. Through strategic alliances, it positioned itself in the new competitive environment. The Sega Channel was a joint venture between Time Warner, TCI, and the video game company; the Channel made a library of Sega titles available for download to Genesis through most basic cable systems, with a special tuner/decoder cartridge. With AT&T and PF Magic, Sega was working on The Edge 16, a Genesis peripheral that transmitted a gamer's joystick movements via phone lines to any similarly equipped Genesis machine. In January 1994 Microsoft announced it would supply portions of the basic software for controlling Sega's new video game machine.[12]

In spring 1993 Sega boosted its distribution and bolstered its image as the "hipper" alternative. While Nintendo defined its market too narrowly (8 to 14 year-old boys), Sega targeted the older crowd. Its sales were boosted by a more violent version of the best-selling Mortal Kombat game, developed by Acclaim. To deflect criticism, Sega initiated a self-imposed rating system, pushing the boundaries in sex and violence. Its version outsold Nintendo two to one. (In 1986 Nintendo had set strict limits on its programs, to avoid criticism and continue monopolistic expansion.)[13]

Following Mortal Kombat, Disney/MGM released the game version of *Aladdin*, Propaganda Films debuted *Voyeur*, an adult-oriented interactive movie, and 3DO, a start-up company founded by Trip Hawkins and backed by telco and M&E giants (AT&T, Time Warner, Matsushita), introduced its $699 Multiplayer designed to blast the market into three-dimensional levels of graphic reality.

Prior to Christmas 1993, Nintendo was pushing its Super Mario All-Stars; Sega featured NFL Football '94 Starring Joe Montana. Yet the new high-profile challengers, including 3DO's $700 32-bit player and Atari's $249 64-bit Jaguar, were getting the most attention, even if the software was too limited and prices too expensive to pose a threat to the Nintendo-Sega duopoly. Nintendo was projected to end the year with a 55% share of the U.S. market, compared with 43% for Sega; whereas in 1994 Sega was projected to take the lead with a 54% share to Nintendo's 44%. While Sega and Hitachi were developing a 32-bit CD-ROM-based Saturn, Nintendo was working with Silicon Graphics on a 64-bit player that it would introduce in 1995; with "Project Reality," it hoped to leapfrog the third-generation players and recapture the industry leadership.[14]

In February 1994 Sega and MCA announced they planned to build a new entertainment attraction as part of MCA's Universal Studios Hollywood complex in Southern California. Unlike Nintendo, which focused on video games, Sega was betting on a multimedia future.

In Hollywood, the studios viewed games as the precursors of interactive home entertainment. By Christmas 1994 Sony was set to enter the global video game market with PlayStation, a 32-bit player that offered a startling new generation of 3-D computer graphics, and capitalized on Sony's know-how in CD technology. As industry analysts speculated whether PC games, boosted by CD-ROM disk technology, would capture video games' customers, the $6.5 billion video game industry was about to explode with new gaming platform formats shaking up the marketplace.[15] The surest sign of a lucrative growth business? Agents began a contest for video game profits.[16]

Licensed Merchandise

As a complement, licensed merchandise—paying for the use of a name, an endorsement, a logo, a look, a product, or a concept—is the opposite of a substitute. The sale of one (*Star Wars*) promotes the sale of another (licensed merchandise based on *Star Wars* characters, robots, gadgets).

We call ourselves an industry, but in truth we are not an industry; rather, we are a business that crosses every other industry. A manufacturer of shirts may want to take license to use a property originating in the toy industry. A toy manufacturer may want the rights to an upcoming film animation. A retailer of fast foods may feel his brand name is perfect to extend into the sporting goods market. These are just a few examples, but that's what licensed merchandising is all about. And that is the essential makeup of this $60 billion "industry."[17]

From Teddy Bears to Blockbusters

Licensed merchandise began in 1913, when the Ideal Toy Company secured permission from President Teddy Roosevelt to manufacture and sell the "Teddy Bear." The first licensed product was followed by Raggedy Ann and Mickey Mouse. It was Disney that first grasped the principal realities of the business. First, licensing involved a character, or some other desirable characteristics. Second, licensing was geared toward children, which accounted for the close link with the toy industry. Though Disney's *Snow White and the Seven Dwarfs* was the first feature to license products for merchandising, the next major licensing boom from movies did not occur until 1964, when Disney released its *Mary Poppins*.[18]

In the past, buyers chose the stock in the stores and parents had considerable influence on purchase decisions. Network television reached children directly, with toy manufacturers bypassing both buyers (large-store buyers, wholesalers) and the parents. The new era began in 1955, when Mattel first sponsored Disney's *The Mickey Mouse Club* on ABC. The show served to promote Disneyland and precipitated the integration of the toy business, children's television, and licensed merchandise.

In the toy industry, licensing increased in importance through the '60s and '70s, with character licensing predominating. Until *Jaws*, movies did not have the staying power to sell merchandise, except for Disney releases. In 1977, however, the licensing business began a dramatic growth with the success of George Lucas's *Star Wars* series, followed by the *Indiana Jones* sequels, and climaxing with *E.T.* in 1982. By the end of the '80s the *Star Wars* trilogy had sold $2.6 billion worth of merchandise. It transformed licensed merchandising and the toy industry, while sequels extended the movies' staying power in the market.

In the '80s, studios continued to offer blockbusters with high licensing and merchandising potential (Warner's *Batman*, Disney's *Dick Tracy*, Columbia's *Ghostbusters*, Carolco's *Total Recall*, and New Line's *Nightmare on Elm Street*). Yet broadcast TV's licensing and merchandising potential tended to be more predictable (greater reach and frequency of exposure, long runs of children's shows). New children's characters were inspired by toy companies' products and translated into syndicated TV shows (Mattel's *He-Man and Masters of the Universe*, Hasbro's *G.I. Joe*), which served as half-hour commercials for existing brands. Since the cost and risk of building a new brand was higher than ever, consolidation proceeded rapidly among major companies, which made it nearly impossible for new products to unseat a market leader.

In 1976 licensed toys generated 20% of all toy sales; by the end of the '80s, nearly 60%. Following *Star Wars*, licensing evolved from a marketing tool to a marketing goal. Instead of product development, big toy companies relied increasingly on licenses taking their cues from popular TV shows and soon-to-be-released big-budget movies. While the business was fragmented into segmented property areas (licensing of character, sports, corporate, entertainment, brand extension, lifestyle, nostalgia), character-driven campaigns were the backbone of the industry.

In 1980 the total value of licensed merchandise at retail amounted to $13.7 billion. In 1992 apparel/accessories (32.2%), toys/games (12.2%), and home furnishing/housewares (11.4%) dominated licensed product retail sales, accounting for 56% of the $65 billion marketplace.[19]

Struggle for Effective Properties. After the boom years 1977–82 (*Jaws, Star Wars, E.T.*), movie merchandising declined drastically—until the triumph of *Batman*. In early 1989 Warner's Licensing Corporation of America (LCA) began to stimulate buyer interest as some movie-licensed goods entered the marketplace. By June there were more than 100 licenses for Batman products, while some 300 different items hit the stores. When *Batman Returns* hit the theatres in mid-1992, the late introduction of merchandise in retail went hand in hand with a meticulously crafted marketing plan. Overall, Batman merchandise rang up an estimated $500 million in sales ($250 million wholesale with Warner's royalty fees at 6–10% of total).[20]

After *Batman's* success, majors, mini-majors, and independents were exploiting films to the maximum. Disney's efforts to acquire Henson's Muppets exemplified the importance the company attached to licensed merchandise. Meanwhile, several properties aided the recovery of new juvenile licenses (Fox's *The Simpsons,* New Line's *Teenage Mutant Ninja Turtles,* Fox's *Beverly Hills 90210*). As merchandising of cartoon characters in stores and at theme parks proved as lucrative as a theatrical release, full-length features came to be seen as commercials for characters created with licensing and merchandising considerations. Inspired by the success of movies like *Who Framed Roger Rabbit?, Oliver and Company, The Little Mermaid,* and *An American Tail,* the studios were encouraged by the demographic data on childbearing baby boomers, and intent to reduce Disney's market monopoly.

The golden years of licensed merchandise were only beginning, due to the convergence of traditional M&E businesses and toy and video game industries, coupled by growing licensed merchandising and M&E giants' retail outlets, as well as globalization.

Licensed Merchandise and Sports Franchises. From 1985 to 1992 sales of all sports merchandise soared from $5.3 billion to $12.1 billion. In December 1992 Disney paid a $50 million fee for a National Hockey League franchise in Anaheim, California; though the San Jose Sharks' on-ice performance had been dismal, their $150 million merchandise sales were 27% of the league's total and the highest in the league. Even prior to Disney, other M&E companies had acquired sports franchises to use their teams for TV programming, including the Tribune's Chicago Cubs; Turner's Atlanta Braves and Hawks; Paramount's New York Knicks, New York Rangers, and Madison Square Garden.[21]

In October 1993 the new competitive environment was heralded by the combined earnings for Steven Spielberg's *Jurassic Park* from movie tickets and promotional tie-ins, which passed the $1 billion mark. Over the next few years, MCA's merchandising executives hoped the dinosaur thriller would generate close to $3 billion in related revenue, as well as become the single largest merchandising property in film history.[22]

In 1994 Universal's modern-stone-age epic, *The Flintstones,* illustrated the new wave of giveaways, tie-ins, and contests. Indeed, the expansion of licensing and merchandising went hand in hand with the ever-increasing role of consumer promotions in marketers' strategies. The shift stemmed from the 1990–91 downturn, when profit pressures and value-minded shoppers forced companies to focus on keeping cash registers ringing.[23]

Retail Chains

In 1987 Disney started selling licensed merchandise (from T-shirts, caps, jackets, to toys and videos) in its own retail stores. The trend derived from the memorabilia stores at Disney's theme parks where logo-emblazoned merchandise had been sold since the '50s, as well as the on-the-lot studio stores, which had been around since the early '70s. By 1993 all major M&E corporations saw retail circuits as sources for new revenue streams.[24]

Disney. With its 250 retail outlets, Disney was not only the first mover but the dominant player in the business. In October 1993 it became the first M&E conglomerate to launch a new retail store in a foreign location (Frankfurt, Germany).

Time Warner. Time Warner had 61 retail stores, including a thriving Warner Bros. flagship store, on 5th Avenue next to Tiffany's and Bergdorf-Goodman, in New York City.

Sony. In November 1993 Sony opened its first Sony Signatures store at the base of its mid-Manhattan headquarters, seeking to differentiate itself by a mix of sales of its high-tech video and audio hardware, in addition to the regular array of memorabilia.

Paramount. After converting licensing and merchandising divisions into a separate entity, Paramount planned to build its own retail chain.

Turner. Turner Entertainment's thriving Hanna-Barbera expected to jump in the business, starting with in-store boutiques in major chain stores based on the Cartoon Network.

Polygram. Replicating the success of the high-concept Hard Rock and Planet Hollywood restaurants, Polygram NV was planning Motown stores and restaurants.

In 1993 Disney's and Warner's combined store sales were expected to double to $700 million, driven not only by baby boomers (Disney's *Beauty and the Beast* and *Aladdin,* Warner Bros. *Tiny Toons Adventures*), but M&E conglomerates' positioning in the coming electronic superhighways.

Record and Music Industry

Until the 1940s, records had spun at 78 rpm. The emergence of two new formats—RCA's 7-inch record (45 rpm) and Columbia Records' 12-inch, long-playing record (33 rpm)—revolutionized the recording industry, historically a cyclical business. In 1977, at the height of their popularity, 344 million albums were sold in the United States. In 1979–80 disco's collapse translated to the flattening of the sales of the U.S. recording industry. After a dramatic growth in the early '80s, changes in technology, demographics, and business itself contributed to a new competitive environment—one that would ultimately cause the acquisition of CBS Records by Sony, prompting a merger mania, and industry globalization.[1]

CD-Led Growth

In the '80s the industry's dollar value grew from $3.9 billion to $7.5 billion. The growth numbers were highest after the introduction of compact discs (CDs) in 1983–84, and in the late decade. Price increases played

Table 4-8
Recording Industry: Formats and Dollar Values (1980–92)*

	CDs	Cassettes	Cassette Singles	Music Videos	Vinyl Singles	CD Singles	LPs/ EPs	Total Value
Dollar Value								
1992	5,327	3,116	299	157	66	45	14	9,024
1991	4,338	3,020	230	118	64	35	29	7,834
1990	3,452	3,472	258	172	94	6	87	7,541
1989	2,588	3,346	195	115	116	1	220	6,579
1988	2,090	3,385	57	na	180	10	532	6,255
1987	1,594	2,960	14***	na	203	na	793	5,568**
1986	930	2,500	na	na	228	na	983	4,651**
1985	390	2,412	na	na	281	na	1,281	4,379**
1984	103	2,384	na	na	299	na	1,549	4,370**
1983	17	1,811	na	na	269	na	1,689	3,814**
1982	na	1,385	na	na	283	na	1,925	3,642**
1981	na	2,063	na	na	256	na	2,342	3,970**
Percentage of Value by Format								
1992	59.0%	34.5%	3.3%	1.7%	0.7%	0.5%	0.1%	100%
1991	55.4	38.5	2.9	1.5	0.8	0.4	0.4	100
1990	45.8	46.0	3.4	2.3	1.2	na	1.1	100
1989	39.3	50.9	3.0	1.7	1.8	0.1	3.3	100
1988	33.4	54.1	0.9	na	2.9	0.0	8.5	100
1987	28.6	53.2	0.3*	na	3.6	0.2	14.2	100
1986	20.0	53.7	na	na	4.9	na	21.1	100
1985	8.9	55.0	na	na	6.4	na	29.2	100
1984	2.4	54.5	na	na	6.8	na	34.4	100
1983	0.4	47.5	na	na	7.1	na	44.3	100
1982	na	38.0	na	na	7.8	na	52.9	100
1981	na	26.8	na	na	6.4	na	59.0	100
1980	na	20.1	na	na	7.0	na	59.3	100

*   Computed from manufacturers' dollar value.
**   Reflects inclusions of discontinued configurations not itemized in the table.
***   Represents six months of sales for cassette singles (introduced in the second half of the year).

SOURCE: Recording Industry Association of America, Inc.

a critical role in revenue growth.[2] Concurrently, the proliferation of portable cassette players, Walkman-type stereos, and audio-cassette decks increased the popularity of cassettes, which became the predominant format for prerecorded music. By the early '90s, CDs and cassettes accounted for 94% of total value (almost $7.4 billion) in the business (see Table 4-8).

In the early '90s, CD unit shipments continued double-digit growth, whereas cassettes began a double-digit decline, due to the emergence of portable CD players. Record companies employed play-it-safe strategies by repackaging old material by established artists in boxed CD sets. Indeed, the industry's fundamental problem was the lack of genuine hits.[3]

The year 1992 witnessed the debut of Digital Compact Cassette (DCC) players, developed by Philips, and Sony's MiniDisc. Unlike the CD players, the new machines could both play and record. While each format had its

advantages, DCC had initially been better positioned for consumer acceptance. Unlike the MiniDiscs, DCC machines played older analog tapes.
On the other hand, MiniDiscs were more durable than tapes and initially
cost several hundred dollars less than the $600 DCC machines.[4]

MTV and Segmentation

In the '80s the distribution and exposure system of the U.S. recording
industry went through a dramatic transformation, starting with the launch
of MTV in August 1981. Based on demographic segmentation, MTV provided much-needed product relatively cheaply, subverting the rhythm,
pace, and aesthetics of traditional music performance.[5]

Warner and American Express gave John Lack, the "father of MTV,"
some $20 million to launch the new channel concept. In 1983 Lack was
succeeded by Robert Pittman, who developed nonnarrative programming
for audience segments (suburban, white) that he considered the mass
audience. The flawed programming concept left little room for black artists, heavy metal, or country. Though Michael Jackson's *Thriller* album
(1983) opened the screen for some "crossover" artists, MTV's overall
strategy did not change until 1988, when it began airing a rap show.

To respond to Ted Turner's rival Cable Music Network, Pittman, in
1985, started a more mellow music channel, Video Hits One (VH-1), for
the 24–49 age group. That year American Express got out of the cable
business. After the failure of a Pittman-led LBO by a group of MTV executives, Viacom International came through with a higher bid.

Viacom's MTV Networks. Viacom replaced Pittman with MTV marketer
Thomas E. Freston, who, at the end of the '80s, steered MTV toward an
all-show format by employing genre-based narrowcasting to segment audiences. In the process, certain shows (*Club MTV*) evolved into MTV franchises. In late 1989, for example, MTV's *House of Style*, hosted by Cindy
Crawford, enabled the unit to diversify into fashion, licensing, and merchandising.

By 1990 MTV drew an average 0.6%, or 300,000, of its 50.4 million U.S.
subscribers at any given time—a relatively weak showing, even by cable
standards. Though MTV had significant brand loyalty, it was no longer
the only shop around. When it rejected Madonna's steamy video *Justify
My Love*, the major beneficiary was the Miami-based Video Jukebox Network, Inc., which offered the video to 12 million subscribers.[6]

With the coming of compression technology and fiber optics in the
early '90s, MTV was preparing itself for 150-channel cable systems with
three specialized networks. Though each served a different genre, all targeted the same 12–34 age demographic.

In January 1992 MTV shook up its program lineup again by adding new
entertainment and sports-related series, including *MTV Sports* and *The Real
World*. It tried to develop lifestyle programs that complemented music

programming and added to the network's image. The shake-up was intensified by an ambitious campaign whose stated goal was to get young Americans to vote, but which also made it more difficult for MSOs to drop MTV from basic service.

Concurrently, the rapid expansion of MTV Europe, the launch of MTV in Asia, and MTV Latino in Latin America signaled the music network's growing globalization. By May 1992 the value of MTV was estimated at $2.6–$4 billion—almost as much as a Big Three broadcast network. Two years later, Time Warner and Sony, Thorn-EMI, and PolyGram were pushing global music video service that could be the first significant competitor to MTV Networks.[7]

Segmentation of Supply, Graying of Demand

In addition to drastic changes in the distribution pipeline, the industry also experienced shifts in supply and demand. If demographics indicated slight "adultification" of demand, shifts in types of music reflected increasing supply segmentation.

From the late '80s to early '90s, the 15–24 age segment remained the dominant consumer group, though its portion of sales declined from 45% to 34%; the 24–34 age segment increased from 23% to 29%; and the 35–44 age segment grew from 13% to more than 18%. The big six music conglomerates were all experimenting with new marketing strategies to woo the affluent "baby boomers with gold cards."[8]

Unlike the gradual graying of demand, supply redistribution took place in just a few years. "Two 13-year-old rappers [Kris Kross] who wear their clothes backwards," reported the *Wall Street Journal* in August 1992, "are currently selling more records than Bruce Springsteen, while an opera recording by three famous tenors has outsold the last two Rolling Stones albums combined."[9]

From the eclipse of the big band era, the U.S. recording business had been dominated by rock 'n' roll. Though popular rock bands, such as U2 and Guns 'n' Roses, still led in sales, the era of rock as the single unifying force was ending without replacement. In the mid-'80s rock controlled 47% of the dollar volume; by the early '90s its dominance had declined to 36%. The genre had never been besieged by so many convergent competitive forces. Rock's three-decade-long rebellion against itself had generated a variety of segmented subcategories; teenagers were increasingly buying rap; country was booming; CD sales delayed the decline of rock as baby boomers bought digitized reissues of their old hits. Meanwhile, the multiplication of distribution systems (from the '50s AM radio to FM and AM radio, network and cable TV, VCRs, and Walkmans) boosted further fragmentation of a single rock culture into a plurality of competing subcultures.[10]

Since the '50s the radio business had exploited the concept of Top 40 radio, playing and hyping only the 40 best-selling singles. Fragmentation of genres, however, prompted a rapid decline of the hit-radio format. From 1990 to 1993 the audience for Top 40 stations in the nation's 30 major markets declined by 40%, while the number of Top 40 stations roughly halved, to about 500.[11]

Computerized Tracking Methods. Segmentation went hand in hand with research sophistication. But just as the people meter confirmed the corrosion in networks' prime-time audience, *Billboard*'s new computerized tracking methods developed by Soundscan contributed to dethroning rock in 1991–92.[12]

Mergers, Majors, and Consolidation

If Elvis and rock 'n' roll transformed the record business in the '50s, the invasion of the Beatles in 1964 shook the industry again. Irrespective of the evolution of styles (from pop to disco) or technology (CD, Walkman), the next transformation entailed a corporate shift rather than an artistic earthquake. In the '80s foreign multinational corporations absorbed the dominant American record companies. In both the motion picture and record industries, consumer electronics giants complemented their "hardware" segments with proper "software." The trend began with Sony.

Sony's Acquisition of CBS Records. In 1987–88 CBS Records—the world's largest producer, manufacturer, and marketer of recorded music, home to recording stars like Bruce Springsteen, Michael Jackson, and Barbra Streisand—accounted for over 30% of CBS's revenue and nearly 40% of its total operating profit. In January 1988 Sony bought CBS Records for $2 billion. Engineered by Walter Yetnikoff, the unit's controversial president, the acquisition prompted a two-year merger mania in the industry.[13]

In a 1989 congressional hearing, Yetnikoff emphasized CBS Record's creative and business autonomy, testifying that there was "no threat to try and control technology and new formats through our software. The hardware does not and will not control the software." Asked whether Sony could use such an integrated strategy, Yetnikoff said such a plan was "unrealistic," adding that "I don't think Sony has even thought of it."[14] In reality, Sony's footholds in hardware and software were geared precisely to gain market dominance in one field to drive success in another. Since the Betamax failure, this had been Sony's *stated* corporate goal, driving its diversification into U.S. entertainment.[15]

In April 1988 Yetnikoff brought in his protégé, Thomas Mottola, to run CBS Records' domestic division. The next year CBS Records generated an estimated $2.8 billion in sales. In three years the unit's earnings dropped, Yetnikoff was fired and was succeeded by Mottola.

From Merger Mania to Indie Squeeze. In the 1988–90 period the U.S. recording industry was swept by a merger mania, during which most major labels and many independents were bought, merged, or otherwise altered:

- Sony's purchase of CBS Records (and Columbia);
- the Time Warner merger, and the ensuing combination of Warner/Elektra/Atlantic;
- the acquisition of PolyGram, as well as A&M for $500 million and Island (as well as Mercury) by the Dutch Philips;
- the purchase of Capitol and Virgin by the British Thorn-EMI (the purchase of Virgin alone cost $960 million);
- the purchase of RCA's record arm by Bertelsmann, Germany's publishing giant;
- the acquisition of Geffen by MCA for about $545 million, followed by the purchase of MCA by the Japanese Matsushita.

A new "business discipline" was imposed on an industry that used to make deals on an entrepreneurial basis and, occasionally, was condemned for its ties with organized crime.[16]

Indies had always played a minor role in the market, but, in the capital-intensive environment of the early '90s, their combined share shrank from 10% to about 4%. A flock of new record labels were lured by the CD boom and the rising prices paid for record companies by multinational giants, including Disney's Hollywood Records, Giant Records (Time Warner and Irving Azoff), Zoo Entertainment and Imago (Bertelsmann), Interscope and Morgan Creek, DGC (David Geffen), and SBK (Thorn-EMI).

The notion of an "independent" label was largely a myth. These companies (Chrysalis, A&M, Island, Virgin) depended on majors for distribution and, in many cases, manufacturing. With increasing consolidation, the industry evolved into a two-tiered system. If indies handled specialized styles and new performers, scouting and marketing the talent, the majors picked up the cream.[17]

The Big Six

After the end of the M&A wave, the industry was dominated by Sony, PolyGram, Bertelsmann, Thorn-EMI, Warner, and MCA, which controlled over 95% of the market. Being "fully vertically integrated," each operated in production, manufacturing, and distribution. Following the merger wave, foreign companies owned five of the six U.S. majors. A significant contributor to surplus in foreign trade had been lost.

Warner Music Group (Warner, Elektra, Atlantic). Since 1977 Henry Droz had steered the massive WEA distribution operation, turning it into the industry leader. Suffering from chart-share erosion (loss of Island, Geffen, Virgin), WEA still had 30% of the market. While maintaining its worldwide industry leadership, the group continued to bring new products under its control, through start-up labels and joint ventures (Pendulum, East/West America, Def American, Interscope).

Sony Music Entertainment (Columbia, Epic). From the mid-'80s to early '90s, Sony served as the industry trendsetter. It introduced the CD, shook the industry by acquiring CBS Records, and inflated deal prices by making a deal with Michael Jackson. After Yetnikoff's departure, Tommy Mottola, the head of Sony Music, continued to sign costly deals with top talent (Michael Jackson, Aerosmith) and negotiate on others (Billy Joel, Julio Iglesias), which contributed to Hollywood's profit crunch (due to another Sony subsidiary, Columbia Pictures). When it tried to sell 29% of its Japanese music subsidiary to the Japanese in November 1991, Sony's flagging performance prompted many investors to sell their holdings. By 1993 Sony Music's fortunes improved in the music charts, the profits rose, and Mottola was promoted to president of Sony's worldwide music operations.

MCA Music Entertainment (MCA, Geffen). With black music and country keeping MCA Records afloat, the subsidiary had problems developing an artist roster. Adopting an aggressive posture in the global market, MCA added Geffen to its fold in 1991, almost doubling its share (from Nirvana to Peter Gabriel, and Guns 'n' Roses). Although it lost Motown to PolyGram, MCA Records transformed black music into America's popular music, from new jack swing stars (Bobby Brown, Mary J. Blige) and singing groups (Bell Biv DeVoe, Jodeci) to crooners (Chante Moore); it stayed away from rap's excesses, focusing on its street feel and waxing romantic.

Thorn-EMI (Virgin, Chrysalis, SBK). After the Beatles broke up in 1970, EMI suffered. By 1979, having lost its knack for finding new talent, it was on the verge of bankruptcy and merged with electrical manufacturer Thorn Electrical Industries. From 1985 to 1989 Colin Southgate disposed of over 60 businesses, molding Thorn-EMI into a music company. Under Jim Fifield, president of EMI Music, the company embarked on an aggressive acquisition spree (Virgin, Chrysalis, SBK Records). With 15% of the global market in 1993, EMI was just slightly behind the record industry's big three (Time Warner, Sony, and PolyGram).

PolyGram (Island, A&M, Motown). Acquisition of Island and A&M provided the PolyGram distribution group with a potential talent pool. The unit, 75% owned by Philips, also benefited from Motown's defection from MCA. In the early '90s PolyGram's CEO Alain Lévy transformed the once-sleepy classical music company into an entertainment powerhouse in the United States.

Bertelsmann Music Group (RCA, Arista). Arista's Clive Davis continued to find mega-artists, from Barry Manilow to Whitney Houston, expanding into country, R&B, and soundtracks. Except for Arista, the Bertelsmann Music Group suffered from a weak talent roster and lack of an effective management team.

As the majors began to attract high-priced talent to fill their new and expanding distribution pipelines, industry consolidation translated to increasing organizational complexity and costly dealmaking.

Organizational Complexity

The major recording companies had grown mainly through acquisitions. What made the '80s so extraordinary was the frantic pace of external growth, as well as the huge size and high number of acquisitions.

Time Warner's Music Group. In the past, the affiliated labels of Warner, for example, had been independent companies. By the early '90s the company boasted a premier array of artists (from Metallica to Phil Collins and Madonna). It was vertically integrated, including powerful record labels, the world's leading music publisher, manufacturing and distribution networks throughout the world, quality printing and packaging capabilities, as well as half ownership of America's leading music and video club. Yet Warner Music Group was not only one of the leading music companies in the world; it was also a unit of the merged Time Warner corporation. The size of operations necessitated a multilayered structure, in which TW served as the parent company for five groups of subsidiaries. Each group comprised several subsidiaries, which, in turn, consisted of numerous companies (see Figure 4-3).

Mini-Maxi Deals

To control distribution, majors needed attractive talent. To lock up top talent, majors had always signed lucrative recording contracts with their stars, or allowed them to command their own labels (from Frank Sinatra's Reprive and the Beatles's Apple to Capitol's M.C. Hammer and Poly-Gram's Jon Bon Jovi). Starting in the '70s, however, the prices began a rapid escalation, almost doubling every five years.[18]

When, in 1970, Neil Diamond made his 10-album deal with Columbia Records for $4 million, it shocked the industry. Only a few years later, Elton John, Paul Simon, and Stevie Wonder were getting $10–14 million long-term guarantees. As bidding wars continued, the price of talent escalated even further. To pump products into the distribution pipeline, RCA signed Kenny Rogers for $21 million in 1982. A year later Walter Yetnikoff of Columbia Records used $28 million to enlist Mick Jagger and the Rolling Stones, for prestige reasons.

In 1991–92 majors began another costly bidding war for the top talent, including Janet Jackson's historical contract with Virgin for $35–$50 million; Michael Jackson's $60 million pact of multimedia projects with Sony Music including his own record label; Aerosmith's planned return to Columbia Records for $35 million; Motley Crue's reupped deal with Elektra Records worth $22.5 million; Madonna's $60 million arrangement for Warner and her own label; the Rolling Stones's new $35 million-plus deal with Virgin; the rock group ZZ Top's $35 million contract with RCA;

Figure 4-3
Time Warner Music Group (1993)

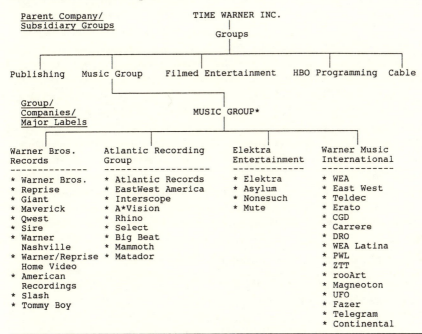

Parent Company/ Subsidiary Groups	TIME WARNER INC. | Groups

Publishing   Music Group   Filmed Entertainment   HBO Programming   Cable

Group/ Companies/ Major Labels	MUSIC GROUP*

Warner Bros. Records	Atlantic Recording Group	Elektra Entertainment	Warner Music International

* Warner Bros.
* Reprise
* Giant
* Maverick
* Qwest
* Sire
* Warner
  Nashville
* Warner/Reprise
  Home Video
* American
  Recordings
* Slash
* Tommy Boy
	* Atlantic Records
	* EastWest America
	* Interscope
	* A*Vision
	* Rhino
	* Select
	* Big Beat
	* Mammoth
	* Matador
		* Elektra
		* Asylum
		* Nonesuch
		* Mute
			* WEA
			* East West
			* Teldec
			* Erato
			* CGD
			* Carrere
			* DRO
			* WEA Latina
			* PWL
			* ZTT
			* rooArt
			* Magneoton
			* UFO
			* Fazer
			* Telegram
			* Continental

* These are not all subsidiaries of the Music Group, only the ones with
  affiliated labels. There were seven additional subsidiaries: Warner
  Music International, Warner/Chappel Music, WEA Corp, WEA Manufacturing,
  Ivy Hill Corp., Warner Special Products and Warner New Media.

SOURCE: Compiled from Time Warner 1993 Annual Report.

Prince's $100 million deal with Warner Bros. Records, including financing for his Paisley Park label and a position as a vice president at Warner; Garth Brooks's search for a $35 million deal (including TV and possible film options); and Barbra Streisand's negotiations with Sony on a $40–$50 million multimedia deal.

Instead of breaking new acts, majors were interested in retaining old and proven ones. Most of these "mini-maxi" deals were designed to protect the company (top talent did not gain as much as the widely publicized gross amounts suggested). Besides the merger mania, the 1991–92 bidding battle was prompted by contraction, the business slump, posturing among major players, and a push for global clout and synergies.

Since the early '80s and the introduction of the CD, the majors' bottom line had been eroded by overpriced talent contracts. By the early '90s a new and even costlier bidding war for the top talent squeezed shrinking margins.

The mini-maxi deals and superstar mentality of the record industry went hand in hand with megadeals and the blockbuster craze in motion pictures and the inflated author deals in publishing. In each industry the major M&E companies sought to ensure the access to top talent, in order to exploit the new distribution pipelines.

Although majors saw industry prospects as promising, there were legitimate doubts about the future. In November 1992 the British pop star George Michael filed a lawsuit against CBS Records, trying to break his contract with the Sony-owned major. Accusing the company on prioritizing "hardware" at the expense of the "creative process," the artist was questioning the entire hardware/software concept. Of the six majors, four—Sony, Matsushita, Philips, Thorn-EMI—were electronic giants that manufactured both software and hardware.

The issue was about corporate mission. Were they marketing software to sell hardware? Or were they marketing hardware to sell software? What kind of business were the majors in?

Publishing: Newspapers, Magazines, Books

American printing and publishing ranges from newspapers, periodicals, book publishing, book printing and commercial printing, to smaller industries (manifold business forms, greeting cards, bookbinding). In the '80s, newspapers, magazines, and book publishing were swept by the fourth national M&A craze, invaded by foreign investors, and transformed by consolidation. A handful of giant M&E companies took over American publishing industries. By 1994 newspapers (21%), periodicals (17%), and book publishing (12%) accounted for almost half of the $177 billion in printing and publishing revenues.[1]

Newspapers

In 1992 booming newspaper revenues masked structural changes in the industry. The number of daily newspapers declined, from 1,745 to 1,570, and circulation decreased from 62.2 million to 60.1 million. Newspaper employment grew to 475,000 in 1990, but declined to 453,000 by 1992. Although total newspaper advertising rose steadily until 1990 ($32.3 billion), its portion of total U.S. ad volume shrank from 27.6% to 23.2% in the 1980–93 period (see Table 4-9).

The extraordinary growth in classified advertising hid erosion in local advertising (newspapers were primarily local ad vehicles), especially in retail advertising. In other words, revenue growth stemmed from price increases. With the decline in newspaper penetration rate per household, newspapers became more expensive to advertisers. As divestitures reduced the number of ad customers, consolidations shifted their accounts to national advertising.[1]

Higher Concentration. Despite demographic growth, the number of daily

Table 4-9
U.S. Newspaper Industry (1950–93)

Year	Total Daily [Morning/Evening] Newspapers Number #	Circulation (mil)	Readers[2] (%)
1993	1,556[1]	59.8	61.7
1992	1,570	60.2	62.6
1991	1,586	60.7	62.1
1990	1,611	62.3	62.4
1985	1,676	62.8	64.0
1980	1,745	62.2	67.0
1970	1,748	62.1	78.0
1960	1,763	58.9	na
1950	1,772	53.8	na

Year	Newspaper Employment (000s)	Of Total Employment (%)	Newsprint Consumption (millions of metric tons)
1993	451.7	0.49%	11,643
1992	451.3	0.38	11,622
1991	458.9	0.39	11,380
1990	474.3	0.40	12,198
1985	450.1	0.42	11,571
1980	419.9	0.42	10,133
1970	373.0	0.47	8,271
1960	325.2	0.49	na
1950	na	–	na

U.S. Daily Newspaper Advertising Expenditures

Year	National ($mil)	Retail ($mil)	Classified ($mil)	Total Newspaper Advertising ($mil)	Of Total U.S. Ad Volume[3] (%)
1993	12.2%	52.8%	35.0%	$32,000	23.2%
1992	12.5	52.4	35.1	30,667	23.4
1991	12.9	52.2	34.9	30,348	24.1
1990	12.8	51.6	35.6	32,280	25.1
1985	13.3	53.4	33.3	25,170	26.6
1980	13.3	58.2	28.5	14,794	27.6
1970	15.6	57.7	26.7	5,704	27.8
1960	21.1	57.0	21.8	3,681	30.8
1950	25.0	56.8	18.2	2,070	36.3

1. There were 21 "all-day" newspapers in 1992. They are listed in both morning and evening columns but only once in the total. The number of newspapers is calculated through Feb. 1, 1994.   2. Weekday readers [% of total adult population], based on Simmons Market Research Bureau national survey estimates.   3. McCann-Eriksson.

SOURCE: Based on Facts About Newspapers 94.

newspapers has remained relatively constant since World War II, while the number of owners has declined. Instead of launching new ones, large and well-capitalized chains acquired existing small or mid-sized newspapers. The increase in chain ownership stemmed from sharp growth in costs of paper and labor, and increasing competition for ad dollars.

Concentration changed the industry structure. After World War II, 60 newspaper chains controlled more than 40% of total daily newspaper circulation. From 1945 to 1970 the number of cities with competing dailies shrank from 117 to 37; 98% of U.S. cities had no competing newspapers.

In 1970, 157 chains dominated 60% of total circulation; by 1988 over 140 chains owned about 1,250 dailies, representing 76% of all dailies and 83% of total circulation. Even in the booming '80s, group owners' profits stemmed largely from increases in ad rates and the disappearance of afternoon dailies. The profits hid erosion in readership. In the late '60s, 76% of American adults read a newspaper on a typical weekday; by 1990 only 62%—despite the growth of the adult population. As monopolies in their home markets, newspapers ignored the customer (especially the younger generation), whereas new initiatives were scorned by rivals. When Gannett launched the colorful *USA Today* in 1982, it was widely ridiculed as "McToday," a newspaper equivalent of MTV. Even if *USA Today* generated losses through most of the boom decade, its style left an impact on "serious" newspapers.[2]

The news marketplace was transformed. Prior to the '80s, local and national broadcast TV news reduced newspapers' informative function by cutting into the market. In the '80s the rise of segmented cable news services (from Turner's CNN to C-SPAN and GE's CNBC) reinforced competition. Although newspapers still perceived themselves as "purveyors of information," their function was no longer the same.

The M&A Wave. The fourth national M&A wave reinforced concentration and chain ownership in the newspaper business:

- From 1979 to 1984 Robert Erburu of Times Mirror went on a $1.2 billion buying spree, which resulted in the divestiture of 17 properties for $1.1 billion in 1985–87 (the company settled on running papers in cities where it held a monopoly);

- starting with 10 newspapers prior to the '80s, the *New York Times* had 35 by the end of the decade (it diversified into TV and radio broadcasting, adding daily and magazine properties);

- even though talks of a merger with Time Inc. failed, Gannett outbid others for several big-city newspapers in the mid-'80s (e.g., *Des Moines Register & Tribune, Detroit Evening News*);

- anticipating the rush to electronic services (and focusing on its big papers), Knight-Ridder sold TV stations and two newspapers in 1989, spending $355 million to buy Lockheed's Dialog Information Services.

The M&A wave was accompanied by foreign invasion in the U.S. publishing business. Prior to News Corp.'s debt crisis, Rupert Murdoch acquired papers in Chicago and New York, while the late Robert Maxwell bought the *New York Daily News* from Tribune. By 1990 an estimated 10% of U.S. papers were foreign-owned—mostly by two Canadian publishers (Hollinger and Thomson).

The hierarchy of the largest U.S. newspaper companies changed little from 1977 to 1992, but concentration increased from 21% to 26% among

Table 4-10
Newspaper Groups: Concentration (1977–92)

Rank	Company	1977	Company	1987	Company	1992
Daily Circulation (mil.)*						
1	Knight-Ridder	3.68	Gannett	6.03	Gannett	6.02
2	Newhouse	3.20	Knight-Ridder	3.84	Knight-Ridder	3.76
3	Tribune	3.10	Newhouse	3.02	Newhouse	3.06
4	Gannett	2.77	Tribune	2.71	Times Mirror	2.80
5	Scripps-Howard	1.90	Times-Mirror	2.57	Dow Jones	2.41
6	Times-Mirror	1.88	Dow Jones	2.54	Thomson	2.30
7	Dow Jones	1.78	New York Times	1.82	New York Times	2.13
8	Hearst Corp.	1.44	Thomson	1.73	Scripps-Howard	1.62
9	Cox	1.18	Scripps-Howard	1.60	Tribune	1.49
10	New York Times	0.98	Hearst	1.44	Cox	1.44
Total		61.4		62.8		60.7
National Share (%)**						
1	Knight-Ridder	6.0%	Gannett	9.6%	Gannett	9.9%
2	Newhouse	5.3	Knight-Ridder	6.1	Knight-Ridder	6.2
3	Tribune	5.1	Newhouse	4.8	Newhouse	5.0
4	Gannett	4.5	Tribune	4.3	Times Mirror	4.6
5	Scripps-Howard	3.1	Times-Mirror	4.1	Dow Jones	4.0
6	Times-Mirror	3.1	Dow Jones	4.0	Thomson	3.8
7	Dow Jones	2.9	New York Times	2.9	New York Times	3.5
8	Hearst Corp.	2.4	Thomson	2.7	Scripps-Howard	2.7
9	Cox	1.9	Scripps-Howard	2.5	Tribune	2.5
10	New York Times	1.6	Hearst	2.3	Cox	2.4
Top-4 Ratio		20.9		24.8%		25.7%
Top-8 Ratio		32.4		38.5		39.7

*   Average for six months ended March 31, 1992.
** National numbers understated true concentration figures since most
     newspapers were local in scope.

SOURCE: Facts About Newspapers (various issues).

the top 4 chains and from 32% to 40% among the top 8. While industry leaders defended acquisitions that added to scale economies (professional management, infusion of capital, national ad sales), the purchases boosted monopolization (see Table 4-10).

By the early '90s, half a dozen top players each generated $1–$2 billion annually; there have been few changes in the hierarchy. While most received over 50% of their revenues from newspapers, the parents operated mainly in broadcasting, cable TV, magazines, book publishing, and information services. By the early '90s Gannett, the industry leader, owned 80 dailies (including *USA Today*) and 50 nondailies, had interests in broadcasting (10 television stations, 15 radio stations) and was the nation's largest outdoor advertising company.

From Severe Recession to Slow Recovery. The 1990–91 contraction meant layoffs at newspapers, while the industry's employment shrank by 5%. Even profitable newspapers nationwide lost their reputations as cash cows. While expansion-oriented publications found it hard to adjust to harsh realities, cost-cutting spread to flagship papers, including the *New York Times*, the *Wall Street Journal*, the *Los Angeles Times*, the *Miami Herald*, the *San Francisco Chronicle*, the *Boston Globe*, the *Chicago Sun-Times*, and many others.

In the past, the growth of the U.S. economy and cyclical fluctuations went hand in hand with group owner's monopoly profits. "The press titans took their profits and built their fortunes when times were good," one observer noted. "When recessions came along, they were able to adjust by accepting little or no profit, if necessary. Because they relied on equipment that was decades old, the 1960s and '70s found many of these publishers debt free."[3]

A new era of diminished growth prospects changed things. Instead of growth stocks, the newspapers became "cyclicals." The 1990–91 contraction devastated critical supporting industries, adding to group owners' difficulties. The newspapers' best retail store clients (Macy's, Campeau) were in the worst condition, while other retailers (May Department Stores, Sears) moved toward low-price strategies, spending less on ads promoting special sales.[4] As the national economy began getting into gear in 1993, advertising lineage seemed to rebound. Yet the industry was going through more than a mere cyclical downturn—as evidenced by the struggle of the *New York Times* and the *Los Angeles Times*.[5]

The New York Times' Purchase of the Boston Globe. In June 1993 the *New York Times* announced it would purchase the *Boston Globe*, one of the few large American newspapers that remained under family control. Under a $1.1 billion merger agreement, the *Globe* would retain its management and editorial autonomy. Still, the acquisition added to consolidation. Although both Affiliated Publications (the *Globe*'s parent) and the *Times* spoke of the synergic business potential of the merged entity (ad packages, new electronic information services), the purchase's strategic value appeared questionable.[6]

The "New" Los Angeles Times. In 1993, mainly because of ad declines, revenue for the *Los Angeles Times* was $150 million less than its 1990 peak of $1.1 billion; it was the third consecutive year of revenue declines. Daily circulation was down by more than 120,000 from more than 1.2 million, and the staff of 8,500 had been cut by 2,000 since 1990. Like many other big-city dailies, the *Los Angeles Times*'s troubles derived from declining newspaper readership and increasing battles for advertisers. If the *L.A. Times*'s rapid growth paralleled the fast development of Southern California, its problems mirrored the region's severe recession.[7]

In 1990–91 the newspaper industry entered a difficult period of structural transformation, due to the demise of big retailers, plummeting advertising revenues, and the expansion of new ad vehicles (cable, direct mail). To find revenues, many publishers launched new ventures, including selling marketing information about readers and local residents to enhance demand for advertising. Concurrently, new antitrust and deregulation brought other changes into the maturing environment.

Toward Electronic Services.

In late 1991 the U.S. Court of Appeals upheld a decision to allow the Baby Bells to own and offer information services. To defend their classified ad base, newspapers supplemented automobile, employment, and real estate listings with telephone and fax services.[8] As newspapers became concerned over classified ad business, strategic alliances followed with potential rivals. Even before the telco decision, Gannett's *USA Today* entered in a joint venture with Prodigy to provide on-line information and entertainment to PC users. Newspapers' entry into electronic services was a defensive reaction. Bitter memories dictated caution.

The First Foray into Electronic Services. Newspapers first entered the market for electronic publishing in the '80s, but the forays were marred by overly ambitious expectations. While, for example, Knight-Ridder's Viewtron allowed subscribers to call up the day's paper, play video games, send electronic mail, bank and shop at home, its transmission speed was too slow, cost structure too high, subscriber base too limited, and terminals too expensive. After three years of "videotext" services and $50 million in losses, Viewtron was closed in 1986.

Between the mid-'80s and early '90s, technology progressed in leaps, costs declined, and subscriber potential multiplied. Starting in the '50s newspapers in Florida and California pioneered the use of color. In 1970 some 12% of U.S. newspapers printed some of their news pages in color. When *USA Today* started in 1982, the move accelerated. A decade later, over 97% of U.S. newspapers had adopted color.[9]

In May 1993, 17 major companies, including some of the nation's biggest newspapers, formed a research consortium with the MIT Media Laboratory to explore new ways to use computers and telecommunications in news delivery.[10] The new environment prompted the industry to shelve old rivalries. Hence, newspapers' alliances with broadcast TV and radio stations, and ventures into TV. With TV stations in major markets, parents of the *Chicago Tribune*, the *New York Times*, and the *Washington Post* found the combination helped them bridge the gap between electronic media and print.[11]

By late 1993 electronic news was arriving on PC screens as subscriber-supported on-line editions of major papers were launched across the country. As supplements to the newspaper, many offered a "read more about it" assortment of background readings. A major factor in the acceleration of on-line services was the sharp increase of PC households with telephone-line hookups, from 300,000 in 1982 to over 12 million in 1993.[12]

To retain control of information delivery, the newspaper industry

Table 4-11
Newspapers' On-Line Services (1982–94)

Newspaper	On-Line Service	Launch Date	User Cost
The Fort Worth Star-Telegram	StarText	1982	$9.95/mon
The Middlesex (Mass.) News	Fred the Computer	1987	Free
St. Louis Post-Dispatch	Post-Link	1992	$9.95/mon
The Chicago Tribune	Chicago Online via America Online	1992	$7.95/mon
The Atlanta Journal and Constitution	via Prodigy	1993	$6.95/mon
The Los Angeles Times	via Prodigy	1994	NA[1]
New York/Long Island Newsday	via Prodigy	1994	NA[1]
The New York Times	via America Online	1994	$9.95/mon[2]

1. Monthly fee to be determined.   2. Up to five hours.

SOURCES: Industry sources.

rushed into the electronic marketplace in 1992–94 (see Table 4-11). Seeking new ways to exploit information that was gathered at great costs but printed only once, group owners viewed electronic superhighways as *their* ancillary markets.

By spring 1994, 2,700 U.S. daily and weekly papers were offering voice or information services, compared with 42 papers in 1989. As *Editor & Publisher* put it in 1994, "Now newspapers have reached a key moment in their history—and the best newspaper executives, managers and editors know it. The old truck stop has got to change with the times or go the way of the general store. . . . The new model for the interactive newspaper takes advantage of every medium available to deliver news and advertising."[13]

In May 1994 Nynex and the Times Mirror Company announced a joint venture to offer electronic shopping services in New York City. After a decade of bitter fighting, the merging information highway brought telcos and newspaper companies together.

Magazines

The Golden Era of American magazines coincided with the peak of U.S. mass markets. Prior to the 1930s, magazines accounted for more than 40% of national advertising expenditures. That period also saw the evolution of basic magazine types, including the digest (the *Reader's Digest*); the news magazine (*Time* and its major imitators, *Newsweek* and *U.S. News*); and the pictorial magazine (*Life, Look*). In 1960 magazine advertising was estimated at 7.6% of total ad volume; by 1992 it had declined to 5.2–5.4% (the portion of monthlies was only 1.7–1.8%).[1]

In the '80s segmentation translated to specialization as companies increasingly targeted for specific demographics and lifestyle. Despite industry shakeout, more than 2,500 new magazines were launched in the '80s—

two new ones for every failure. By the early '90s there were more than 11,000 periodicals published in the United States (from *TV Guide* to highly specialized titles). The two main categories involved consumer magazines (from *People* and *Time* to *Sports Illustrated* and *Playboy*) and business publications.[2]

The '80s Merger Wave. In the mid-'80s the magazine industry was swept by a wave of acquisitions. As bidders were paying 10 times earnings, debt piled up rapidly.

- In 1985 Ziff-Davis Publishing sold 24 titles to CBS Magazines and News Corp. for a combined $713 million;

- CBS sold *World Tennis* to Family Media, which sold *Ladies' Home Journal* to Meredith Corp. for $92 million;

- S. I. Newhouse, Jr.'s Advance Publications spent $168 million to buy the upscale *The New Yorker*, while spending lavishly in the Condé Nast magazine empire (*Vogue* and *Vanity Fair*);

- in 1987 Peter Diamandis led a $650 million buyout of CBS magazines;

- only a few months later, he sold 7 titles for $240 million and the remainder to Hachette for $712 million;

- in 1988 Murdoch's News Corp. purchased Triangle Publications for $3 billion;

- in 1989 MacFadden Holdings spent $413 million for the *National Enquirer*;

- News Corp. acquired *Soap Opera Digest* for $70;

- New York Times Co. bought into the women's magazines by spending $80 million on *McCall's*.

At the end of the decade, even Capital Cities/ABC had more than 50 shopping guides and real estate magazines, as well as over 75 other specialized publications.

Unsurprisingly, the parents of the nation's large consumer magazines were among the top 10 magazine companies (Time Warner, Reader's Digest, Advance Publications, Meredith, Hearst, News Corp.) (see Table 4-12).

Contraction: Advertising Slump and Debt Crisis. In 1990–91 the slump in magazine advertising stemmed from a sluggish economy, industry competition for ad dollars, and the shift of advertising to other media.

As magazine companies struggled under a crippling debt load, even Rupert Murdoch was forced to divest nine magazines to K-III Holdings. While major publishers hoped that debt-ridden premium magazines would fall into their hands, the selling block was filled with financially ailing magazines that aroused little interest. The owners of premium magazines opted for a recovery.

By 1992 the business was characterized by the revamping of three big

Table 4-12
Top 12 Magazines by Gross Revenues (1988–92)

Rank 92	91	90	89	88	Magazine	Revs. (mil)	Parent
1	1	1	1	1	TV Guide	$938	News Corp.
2	2	2	3	3	People	694	Time Warner
3	3	3	2	2	Time	621	Time Warner
4	4	4	4	4	Sports Illustrated	563	Time Warner
5	5	5	5	5	Reader's Digest	464	Reader's Digest Ass.
6	6	7	7	8	Parade	449	Advance Publications
7	7	6	6	6	Newsweek	412	Washington Post Co.
8	8	9	9	7	Better Homes & Gardens	328	Meredith Corp.
9	10	11	12	12	U.S. News & World Report	295	U.S. News & World Report
10	12	10	11	11	Good Housekeeping	290	Hearst Corp.
11	9	14	20	23	PC Magazine	285	Ziff Communications
12	14	13	10	10	Family Circle	258	New York Times Co.

SOURCE: Reprinted with permission from the August 16, 1993 issue of Advertising Age. Copyright, Crain Communications Inc., 1993.

publishing institutions: *Harper's Bazaar, The New Yorker,* and *Time.* Even the most established franchises' survival was no longer guaranteed.[3]

The industry was dominated by large M&E corporations, which had extensive holdings in other M&E businesses (Time Warner, McGraw-Hill), were part of international media empires (News Corp., Hachette), or controlled by foreign investors (Thomson Corp., Reed International). With the top 5 publishers accounting for about one-third of the total revenues, the magazine business consolidated and matured rapidly.

From 1987 to 1993 the top three magazine companies maintained their dominance. Time Warner's leadership in magazines stemmed from *People, Time, Sports Illustrated,* and *Fortune.* Its magazines boosted the trend toward media packaging. With almost $2 billion in revenues, Time Warner was the undisputable leader of the magazine business. Its major rival, Hearst Corp., generated "only" $1 billion. Hearst's magazines (*Cosmopolitan, Good Housekeeping, Harper's Bazaar*) were its most significant segment; in 1990 new editors were installed at more than half of its 14 titles, and many were revitalized. Advance Publications' *Parade* magazine was the leader in paid circulation, whereas the parent's Condé Nash ranked third in magazines (*Vogue, Glamour, Vanity Fair, The New Yorker*); with virtually no debt, the latter was one of the strongest magazine publishers.

Time Inc.: Magazines in Multimedia Environment. Despite its undisputed leadership, Time Magazine Company in 1991 carried out the most drastic staff reductions in almost two decades (10% of the 6,000 staff positions at *Fortune, Life, Money, People, Sports Illustrated,* and *Time*). Only the two newest Time publications, *Entertainment Weekly* and *Sports Illustrated for Kids,* were spared staff reductions. The changes were followed by *Time's* redesign.[4]

In early 1992 Time Warner's Publishing Ventures Unit launched *Martha Stewart Living,* adopting a new magazine-publishing concept in an effort to rethink the relations between products, channels, and consumers. In the past, publishers placed magazines at the center with ancillary revenue streams positioned as satellites to the core franchise. Whereas by separating the idea (*Martha Stewart Living*) from various satellites, TW's unit engaged in an attempt to target a perceived consumer need via a dizzying array of new channel systems (broadcast, cable, video, book, magazine, other). Eager to develop several revenue streams, the unit molded the editorial concept of the classic magazine publishing model into the marketing concept of the new model.

When Gerald M. Levin replaced N. L. Nicholas Jr. as president and co-chief executive of Time Warner, the executive shuffle intensified at the top. By the fall of 1993 the magazine industry was finally recovering from the contraction and three large magazine groups (Hearst, Condé Nast Publications, New York Times) showed significant gains in ad dollars. Yet Time Warner's 30-title magazine group, the industry leader, found it hard to rebound and all seven core magazines (*Life, Sports Illustrated, Time, People, Entertainment Weekly, Money,* and *Fortune*) lost ad pages. Hence, another dramatic restructuring of operations.

Although the new TW chairman promised to retain the business on which the old Time Inc. was founded, the financial significance of the magazine segment was lower than ever before. Prior to the merger, TW's magazines accounted for 40% of revenue and nearly 45% of profit, whereas in 1992 books and magazines provided less than 24% of TW's total revenue and less than 19% of operating profit.[5] As Time Warner became preoccupied with electronic superhighways for its cable systems and film studio, the publishing segment was no longer a priority.

Role Models: "Hot" Magazines

If TW's magazine division was the industry leader, Advance Publications had *Vanity Fair*, the archetype of the '80s' hottest magazine, and *The New Yorker*, the early '90s' pioneer. Both were redesigned by Tina Brown. As one observer put it in 1993, "In the 10 years she has been in New York, she has almost singlehandedly rewritten the rules for the magazine world, blurring genres, bidding up salaries and fashioning writers into celebrities."[6] Owned by the Newhouse brothers, Condé Nast controlled Advance Publications, one of America's largest privately held M&E giants. With $4.6 billion revenues in 1992, Advance was a major player in magazines, newspapers, cable, and books.[7]

If Tina Brown linked the magazine business with Hollywood agents, costly talent, and high-concept stories, growth in both *Vanity Fair* and *The New Yorker* proved no sure sign of profit. Instead, these highly visible totems attracted the kind of sizzle that Condé Nast's Advance Publications needed for its new ventures in electronic superhighways. With the cable MSOs, Newhouse also was involved in a DBS service, Primetime Partners; a major shareholder, with TCI and Cox, in Discovery Communications, which operated the popular Discovery Channel and The Learning Channel on cable; and was testing Your Choice TV, an interactive "electronic guide" for cable subscribers. Similarly, the book publishing division had sold electronic versions of reference books for years and gotten into the CD-ROM business.

In late October 1993 Newhouse, eager to diversify in entertainment and new media, contributed $500 million to a hostile takeover bid by QVC for Paramount. In January 1994 a new generation took charge at Condé Nast.

The year 1992 saw a relief from the contraction in the magazine industry, infusing more ad pages and ad revenues into the leading U.S. publications. Despite the reversal of past stagnation, growth remained spotty and revenue growth depended on page-rate increases, while newsstand sales continued a downward spiral.

By the spring of 1994 all major magazine companies were catching the interactive wave, which seemed to promise both growth and profits, including Time Warner, Hearst Magazines, Reader's Digest, Ziff-Davis Publishing, International Data Group, News Corp., Advance Publications/Condé Nast Publications, Meredith Corp., McGraw-Hill, and Hachette.[8]

Book Publishing

By 1994 newspapers and periodicals generated over $38 billion and $24 billion, respectively, in annual revenues, while book sales exceeded $20 billion. After the mid-'80s, book revenues had grown three times as fast as newspapers and almost 50% faster than periodicals. The increases stemmed less from growth in unit sales than in consumer expenditures. As a highly segmented industry, book publishing had a market-driven classification system of eight basic categories, with trade (28%) professional (18%), and [college and elementary and highschool] textbooks (25%) accounting for almost three-fourths of total sales (see Table 4-13).[1]

Merger Waves. The post–World War II era witnessed a profound transition in the book publishing business as mass-market paperbacks spearheaded the "democratization" of publishing. At the same time, the fragmented industry was swept by consolidation.[2] During the '60s go-go years, independent publishers were acquired by major conglomerates, such as RCA (Random House), CBS (Holt, Rinehart & Winston), Litton Industries, Time (Little, Brown), ITT (Bobbs-Merrill), and Harcourt Brace Jovanovich (Academic Press). Conglomeratization made available increasing capital resources and brought in a new management generation.

In the early '70s the boom became a bust, due to a worsening economy and declining demographic trends. Consolidation at the top went hand in hand with the proliferation of the bottom level—that is, "small presses." In the '70s the number of publishers in the United States doubled from 6,000 to almost 12,000.

By the late '70s the industry witnessed a new round of mergers, which

Table 4-13
Book Publishing Industry Net Sales (1982–92)*

	1982 ($mil)	1987 ($mil)	1990 ($mil)	1991 ($mil)	1992 ($mil)	(%)	CGR 1987-92
Trade	$1,513	$2,713	$3,893	$4,253	$4,662	27.6%	9.4%
Religious	426	639	788	855	907	5.4	7.3
Professional	1,536	2,207	2,766	2,861	3,107	18.4	6.0
Book Clubs	523	679	725	750	742	4.4	1.1
Mail Order Publications	569	658	731	734	630	3.7	(7.2)
Mass Market Paperback	703	914	1,149	1,244	1,264	7.5	4.9
University Presses	125	171	246	266	280	1.7	6.8
Elementary & Secondary Text	1,108	1,696	2,026	2,054	2,081	12.3	1.4
College Text	1,206	1,550	1,991	2,001	2,084	12.3	2.3
Standardized Tests	70	104	128	134	140	0.8	4.9
Subscription Reference	307	438	541	552	572	3.4	2.9
AV & Other Media	148	213	237	216	198	1.2	(8.5)
Other Sales	162	211	218	225	251	1.5	7.3
TOTAL	$8,397	$12,190	$15,438	$16,143	$16,919	100.0%	

SOURCE: Association of American Publishers, Inc.

added to industry concentration and provided access to major M&E companies (the acquisition of Simon and Schuster-Pocket Books by Gulf + Western, MCA's purchase of Putnam; Coward, McCann & Geogehan; and Berkeley). In the late '80s the fourth national M&A wave resulted in still further consolidation in publishing and went hand in hand with increasing foreign ownership.[3]

- *1987.* The British William Collins PLC acquired one-half of Harper & Row for $156 million; the Canadian Thomson added new properties to its U.S. publishing holdings; Murdoch's News Corp. acquired Harper & Row for $300 million; and Bertelsmann bought Doubleday, Dell, and the Literary Guild for $475 million.

- *1988.* The French Hachette purchased Grolier for $463 million; the late Robert Maxwell's British company acquired Macmillan for over $2.5 billion; the British Pearson PLC bought Addison-Wesley for $284 million.

- *1989.* News Corp. bought the remaining 54% of William Collins PLC for $717 million.

- *1990.* When the Japanese Matsushita acquired MCA, it also got the latter's publishing subsidiary, the Putnam Berkley Group, marking the first time a U.S. publishing company was bought by a non-European entity.

In addition to the "foreign invasion," U.S.-based acquisitions added to industry consolidation, with Time acquiring Sunset Books, Warner buying Mysterious Press, and HarperCollins purchasing Scott Foresman. Finally, Harcourt Brace Jovanovich fell into the hands of General Cinema Corp.

Still, publishing suffered from weakening sales and the industry was shaken by restructuring at Random House, Penguin, and Simon & Schuster. As well-capitalized international publishers struggled for profits, smaller publishers were in trouble. The postrecession industry would be "leaner and meaner."[4]

By 1992 U.S. book publishing was dominated by four publishing houses whose annual sales exceeded $1 billion: Paramount Publishing ($1,524 mil.), Reader's Digest ($1,407 mil.), Time Warner ($1,137 mil.), and Random House ($1,097 mil.). Other major players included HarperCollins, Bantam/Literary Guild, Harcourt Brace, Thomson Publishing, Addison-Wesley, Penguin, and Times Mirror. Each included a number of publishers. Major publishing houses that had been industry leaders for more than a century disappeared, or became units of giant media concerns.

The Postrecession Industry. In 1990–91 the book market's resistance to recession was undermined. While the industry had broadened its readership, the more ephemeral new clients cut back. Swept by the "blockbuster complex," publishers focused on big books and costly deals, at the expense of lesser titles. As "mid-list" books shrank and big publishers recruited the top talent, a number of authors turned to small presses.[5]

Blockbuster deals with strategic talent went hand in hand with consolidation in motion pictures, TV production, and the record and music industry. Just as Hollywood's talent agents encouraged the blockbuster trend in motion pictures (spec auctions), New York's literary agents provided huge advances to presumed bestsellers. Despite restructuring in publishing houses, huge advances continued to be paid even in 1990; the industry did not retrench from the excesses of the '80s until after the contraction. Publishers needed high-priced "brand names" to justify worldwide operations and to sell around the world. They bid defensively, to prevent rivals from signing the talent. The movie-star system had arrived in the publishing industry.[6]

The big publishing houses were owned by major M&E companies, which promoted efforts at synergy to achieve new and added revenue sources, including the exploitation of tie-ins with motion pictures and television. At the same time, the increasing cooperation between Hollywood studios and New York's publishing world contributed to the convergence of traditional publishing operations with the new interactive multimedia technology.[7]

Paramount Publishing (Simon & Schuster). By the turn of the '90s Paramount Communications, the industry leader, had focused its operations on two major businesses, entertainment and publishing. Since the mid-'70s Richard Snyder had turned Simon & Schuster (S&S), a trade publisher of general interest literature, into America's largest educational publisher, as well as a major supplier of information services to lawyers, accountants, and other professionals. The transformation of the publishing unit occurred mainly through acquisitions, such as Esquire, Inc.

(1984), Prentice-Hall and Ginn & Co. (1985), Silver Burdett (1986), Lange Medical Publications (1986), and Master Data Center, Manac Systems, and Charles E. Simon (1988). PCI also acquired Computer Curriculum (1990) and Macmillan Computer Publishing (1991), which catapulted publishing into the forefront of computer-assisted interactive learning and computer book publishing. However, the $750 million bid for Robert Maxwell's Pergamon Press failed narrowly.[8]

Paramount's publishing unit formed a giant corporate juggernaut in which four basic operations—education, consumer, business technical and professional, international—each consisted of several publishing arms (see Figure 4-4).

By the early '90s the education operation generated almost 50% of the publishing arm's total revenues (38% by school and higher education markets), whereas consumer and business/professional brought in 24% and 20%, respectively. International operations accounted for 10% of the publishing arm's revenues (Paramount aimed at about one-third of sales). Snyder committed over $60 million to turn the publishing giant into the first "truly modern" publisher, with the aid of computers and specially tailored software. He hoped to use the education operation's two subsegments (supplementary education, educational technology) to provide schools with "integrated learning systems."

In 1992 S&S remained the quintessential hit-driven house with nearly 20 hardcover bestsellers (e.g., Harvey Penick's *Little Red Book*, Andrew Morton's *Diana*, David McCullough's *Truman*, Rush Limbaugh's *The Way Things Ought to Be*). Though Jack Romanos, S&S's president, signed multimillion-dollar multibook contracts (Judith McNaught, Stephen Coonts, and Mary Higgins Clark), the company also walked away from big authors (Jack Higgins, Douglas Adams), as well as the proposed $16–$20 million Elizabeth Taylor package (an autobiography, two ghostwritten novels, and a TV miniseries). After the flops of Ronald Reagan's memoirs and Joan Collins's *Love, Hate and Desire*, S&S expected "brand-name authors" to perform at spectacular levels just to pay for themselves.[9]

In November 1993 Paramount, S&S's parent, agreed to buy Macmillan, Inc. The 150-year-old company that published writers like Edith Wharton, Ernest Hemingway, and F. Scott Fitzgerald had been put up for sale as part of the liquidation of the bankrupt empire of the late Robert Maxwell. The $553 million deal created the second-largest global book publisher after Bertelsmann.[10]

Since 1989 U.S. publishers had struggled in all product lines except juvenile trade books. By 1992 publishers' sales were expected to rebound, with a number of new start-up publishing houses. Since, however, growth and profits seemed to be in electronic publishing, most Hollywood studios were getting into interactive multimedia (from CD-ROM to virtual reality), either through their publishing operations or recently founded new tech-

Figure 4-4
Paramount Publishing: Operations, Markets, and Publishers (1992)

Operations	Markets	Publishers

Operations	Markets & Publishers
Education Segment	* <u>Elementary</u> Textbooks and related materials (Silver Burdett Ginn) and learning materials (American Teaching Aids, Coronet/MTI Film & Video, Judy/ Instructo, Modern Curriculum Press and Shining Star);
	* <u>Secondary</u> Textbooks and related materials (Prentice Hall and Globe) and vocational materials (Fearon/ Janus/Quercus);
	* <u>Higher Education</u> Textbooks and related instructional and reference materials (Prentice Hall, Allyn & Bacon, Regents/Prentice Hall, Ginn Press, Alemany, Cambridge, Simon & Schuster Workplace Resources and Simon & Schuster Academic Reference);
	* <u>Technology</u> Technology-based learning products and integration of technology in traditional publishing areas (Computer Curriculum Corp., Business & Industry and Advanced Media);
	* <u>Prentice Hall Canada</u> Original Canadian works in the educational, consumer and business markets, and distribution of U.S.-produced Prentice Hall products.
Consumer Segment	* <u>Hardware and Trade Paperback</u> Including Simon & Schuster, Pocket Books Hardcover, Poseidon Press, Touchstone, Fireside, Simon & Schuster Books for Young Readers, Little Simon, Green Tiger Press, and Julian Messner;
	* <u>Mass market paperback</u> Including Pocket Books, Pocket Star Books, Folger Shakespeare Library, Washington Square Press, Archway and Minstrel;
	* <u>Travel information</u> Including American Express, Baedeker's, Frommer's, H.M. Gousha, Mobil, The Unofficial Guide and The Real Guide;
	* <u>General Reference and consumer information</u> Including Prentice Hall General Reference, Arco, Betty Crocker, Burpee, Horticulture, J.K. Lasser and Webster's New World™ Dictionaries;
	* <u>Audiocassettes</u> Sound Ideas and Audio Works.

nology units. By early 1994 the shift led to drastic (and high-profile) restructuring in several publishing houses. Publishing is a *marketplace* of ideas, the new parent companies argued, why should unprofitable books continue to be published?

It seemed as if some secret cabal of publishers had colluded, or as if a philistine contagion had suddenly swept through midtown [Manhattan]. Agents feared that books they believed had been safely signed up would be abandoned or neglected; authors were distraught at the thought of being wrenched away from trusted editors. Some of the most respected writers in the business were involved. . . . Almost everyone in the business wondered whether literary publishing of the kind done at these small, intimate houses had any future at all in dumbed-down America.[11]

Interactive Multimedia: From CD-ROM to Virtual Reality

By the early 1990s entertainment interactive software held enormous sales potential for major M&E groups. While video game software and 16-

Figure 4-4 continued

Operations	Markets	Publishers
Business, Technical and Professional Segment	* <u>Prentice Hall Computer Publishing</u> Personal computer and technical books (Que, Sams, New Riders, Hayden, Brady, Alpha), marketing of computer software (Que Software); * <u>The Bureau of Business Practice</u> Books, videos, loose-leaf services, directories and multimedia training (operations include The New York Institute of Finance); * <u>Appleton & Lange</u> Medical textbooks and health-care related materials; * <u>Prentice Hall Law & Business</u> Information and seminars for the legal community; * <u>Software and Information Services</u> Online information services, document delivery, transaction services and application software in the legal and accounting fields (Prentice Hall Professional Software, Prentice Hall Legal Practice Management and Prentice Hall Legal & Financial Services).	
International Segment	* <u>United Kingdom</u> Academic and professional books (Prentice Hall, Ellis Horwood, Harvester Wheatsheaf, Woodhead-Faulkner); consumer books (Simon & Schuster LTd.); books for children and young adults (Simon & Schuster Young Books); * <u>Australia and New Zealand</u> Educational, professional and consumer books (Simon & Schuster Australia Pty. Ltd.); * <u>Subsidiaries</u> Japan, Mexico, Singapore; * <u>Offices</u> Brazil, Colombia, Denmark, Germany, Greece, Guam, Holland, India, Italy, Korea, Malaysia, Norway, Russia, Spain, Taiwan, Thailand and Turkey; * <u>Co-Publishing Partnerships</u> With publishers in France, Germany, Hungary, Italy, Japan and the Netherlands.	

SOURCE: Paramount Communications, Inc.

bit game systems generated a triple-digit annual growth, computer revenues lagged far behind. The rapid demise of first-generation video games (8-bit systems) reflected the capital-intensive high-risk environment. At $3.6 billion a year, interactive software constituted a small but rapidly growing segment of the total available market for interactive video (from information services and video games to advertising and pay cable) and was estimated at more than $213 billion.[1]

Blurring industry boundaries between Hollywood and Silicon Valley, interactive multimedia represented the convergence of media, entertainment, computers, consumer electronics, and publishing into a huge "umbrella industry." By 1992–93, leading American (Apple, Intel, IBM, Microsoft), Asian (Fujitsu, NEC), and European (Philips) computer and electronics companies were exploring the multimedia technology.[2]

In the short term, investments in interactive multimedia went hand in hand with strategic alliances between Hollywood and Silicon Valley. In the long term, the new technologies required virtually every aspect of traditional M&E businesses to be rethought and redefined.[3] During the 1992–97 period, industry analysts expect the number of multimedia PCs in U.S.

homes to rise from 0.5 million to over 10.8 million, and the unit sales of CD-ROM drives to soar from 1.0 million to 7.9 million.[4]

Push for CD-ROMs

While floppy disks were read by magnetic drives, CD-ROMs' (compact disk-read only memory) laser-based optical disk drives read the digitized data like a CD player. CD-ROM technology combined video images, digital sound, interactive capabilities of a computer, and vast amounts of data. Though CD-ROM was a "read-only" medium, its files could be copied and transferred to the PC's hard drive. Just as CDs pushed the record and music business in the '80s, CD-ROMs were expected to push interactive multimedia in the '90s.[5]

Introduced in 1985, high cost and technology (sluggish drives, issues of incompatibility) served as a barrier to CD-ROMs' entry into the marketplace. By the early '90s prices declined and volume increased, but the standards issue continued to divide warring clusters of companies, including

- MPC (led by Microsoft, the group included over a dozen companies, from Tandy to AT&T and Zenith);
- the CDTV (Commodore's CD-ROM Amiga spinoff);
- and the planned new standard by the shaky IBM-Apple alliance (Apple had a long-standing business relationship with Sony).

Despite uncertainties, Hollywood majors rushed to the emerging marketplace. They created new publishing divisions for CD-ROM titles; licensed characters and properties for interactive CD-ROM games; developed interactive pictures; and repackaged copyrighted material (news, music, movies) for reuse on CD-ROM and digital software; as well as created new entertainment, reference, and educational products for interactive CD-ROM use.

First Mover: Philips' CD-I. In 1991 Philips Interactive Media of America (PIMA), the company's software unit, introduced its CD-I (compact disk-interactive), an $800 home entertainment system that connected directly to a TV set (interacting with a remote, not a keyboard). Despite its first-mover benefits, CD-I did not get off the ground. By 1994 Philips was hunting for a major U.S. interactive software house. To keep pace with Sony and Matsushita, the company was accelerating its move into software, services, and multimedia.[6]

Hollywood Majors and Interactive Multimedia

If Hollywood majors excelled at filming linear stories, new digital studios were experts in graphics and interactivity. While leading M&E companies expected the standardization of formats, software, and hardware prior to entry, major players (Time Warner, Sony) hedged their bets via strategic alliances and establishing multimedia divisions within the corporate structure.[7]

By 1992 the multimedia industry (led by Microsoft, IBM, and Apple) spent an estimated $200 million a year on research and development, hoping to convert PC users and "repurpose" existing materials to CD-ROM. Concurrently, every major M&E company had CD-ROM projects under discussion or in development.

Time Warner. Warner Bros. established Warner New Media as early as 1984. In 1992 TW also bought a 25% stake in SMSG, a multimedia development unit of the thriving Electronic Arts. Warner New Media had a CD-ROM hit, "Desert Storm: The First Draft of History," and Warner Special Products attempted to offer music from Warner Bros. artists to multimedia developers for a low licensing rate. TW also negotiated with IBM to form a super multimedia alliance.

Sony. In 1991 Sony set up Sony Electronic Publishing (SEPC), which served as an umbrella for its interactive ventures. Sony Imagesoft, an SEPC unit, spearheaded the creation of video game adaptations of Sony Pictures Entertainment movie titles (SEPC also developed products for CD-ROM and other formats utilizing its movie and music products), interactive movies and video game versions by SEPC with the motion picture unit, as well as the introduction of a portable multimedia player with a CD-ROM drive.

Matsushita. Like Sony, Matsushita was using MCA/Universal as a software means into the multimedia market. In February 1994 MCA acquired a stake in closely held Interplay Productions, Inc., a small firm that made CD-ROM and video games.

Philips. Philips poured millions of dollars into hardware and software development of CD-I, an international standard established by a joint venture of Philips, Sony, and Matsushita, while Philips' PIMA division produced three "interactive movies" with Propaganda Films.

Disney. At Disney, multimedia issues were dealt with by new technology and development of Disney Pictures and Television.

Paramount. Paramount had several teams exploring various technologies, and Computer Curriculum, a Paramount unit, provided CD-ROM instructional programs.

News Corp. Twentieth Century Fox had a deal with Dark Horse Comics for CD-ROM games based on Fox blockbusters (*Alien, Predator*). While News Corp.'s Fox Cable explored how to tie interactive technology to its programming, News America 900 operated low-tech interactive telephone services for Fox shows and *TV Guide.*

ABC/Turner. ABC News and Turner Broadcasting transformed huge amounts of taped (and copyrighted) archival news material into software for interactive digital and CD-ROM products.

Viacom. Eager to join the Hollywood majors, Viacom launched a "New Media" division of its own.

Smaller high-tech M&E companies sought viable niches in the environment (Lucasfilm Ltd. formed a New Media Group to focus on multimedia for education and entertainment).

In October 1992 major multimedia players (Philips, Tandy, Zenith, Sega) launched a $75 million marketing campaign to introduce the CD-ROM technology to consumers. Despite sluggish sales and incompatibility in different product lines, the competition intensified with Philips enjoying a head start and access to a leading retailer (7.5% stake in Blockbuster video) and the educational market (25% stake in Whittle Communications).

Just as, in the early '80s, adult-oriented videotapes drove the growth of the home video industry, sex was expected to do the same for CD-ROM drives, sound boards, high-resolution displays, and, in the future, interactive TV decoders. It was *Virtual Valerie*, the erotic CD-ROM bestseller, that drove the business.[8]

At Christmas 1993 multimedia emerged as the upscale gift of choice, while shipments of CD-ROM players were expected to more than triple in a year. Concurrently, the new technology began to shatter the world of college textbooks. Indeed, the future was in big nonfiction projects in which the book publishers provided the content and the electronic outfits supplied the technology. CD-ROM editions would be brought out along with conventional books. In May 1994 G.P. Putnam's Sons published *The Haldeman Diaries*, which retailed for $35.95, while the Sony Electronic Publishing Company published a CD-ROM version for $69.95. The former carried 1,000 pages of edited text; the CD-ROM carried all the diaries—2,200 pages of unedited text. Sony estimated there were more than 6 million CD-ROM players in the United States, of which maybe 2 million were in homes. It expected record sales.[9]

If CD-ROM technology provided a bridge to interactive television, virtual reality held the promise of revolutionizing media and entertainment.

Virtual Reality

In the early 1990s virtual reality was the most promising of the new multimedia technologies. Unlike other computer graphics, VR was interactive and conveyed multiple sensory information (sound, touch). VR did not help one to play a video game, it took one inside the video game, literally. A nascent industry pioneered by American researchers, VR had been funded by the Air Force and NASA since the 1960s. Ever since Ivan Sutherland, a computer scientist, built his own head-mounted displays (HMD), the Pentagon's Advanced Research Projects Agency (ARPA) had been one of the big spenders in VR research.

While there was no doubt that VR would eventually be dominated by major M&E and computer/electronics corporations, it started in the mid-'80s with a handful of tiny, mainly California-based, closely held pioneers, such as VPL Research, Sense8, Fake Space Labs, Simgraphics, Greenleaf Medical Systems, and Exos. The field remained marginal until the mid-'80s, when onetime computer hacker Jaron Lanier coined the term "virtual reality."[10]

Jaron Lanier and VPL Research Inc.: The VR Guru. In 1984 Lanier, a self-taught dropout, founded VPL Research. With money he made from programming Moondust, an Atari video game, Lanier made VPL the first company dedicated to VR worlds; he wanted to create an entirely new computer language that used images and sounds instead of alphanumeric codes. A typical Silicon Valley start-up, VPL developed the key VR aids—"EyePhones" (head-mounted stereo screen displays), as well as the "DataSuit" (which enabled VR viewers to convey information to computers with hand signals). These hardware devices were sold to children, and to bigger customers like NASA, Boeing, SRI International, Mattel, Matsushita, and MCA. In 1992 *The Lawnmower Man* was inspired by Lanier's VR philosophy.[11]

Intensifying VR Rivalry. VR has always been seen as the ultimate entertainment technology that might revolutionize the M&E industries. In 1991 then-Senator Al Gore chaired hearings on VR's value to American competitiveness, concluding that America was underinvesting in the emerging technology.

With rising stakes, the nascent VR competition was intensifying. Nintendo's Powerglove, a simpler version of VPL's $8,800 Dataglove, enabled video gamers to play with hand gestures, spawning a host of VR-like video games. At Chicago, the "Battletech Center," Virtual World Entertainment's VR game site, sold 300,000 tickets at $7 each in just three months (the company had two sites in Japan and planned to open 17 more in three years). To penetrate the mass market, a race was on to cut costs. "Virtual reality arcades are already popping up in the U.S. and Europe with space travel games, among others," reported *Fortune.* "The new technology could add a new dimension to publishing as well, in such forms as virtual reality supplements to textbooks on CD-ROMs or laser disks."[12]

By December 1992 VPL's attempts to find financial backing had failed, despite partnerships with major U.S. M&E companies. The venture-capital arm of France's Thomson CSF SA obtained the rights to American patents in VR. It criticized what it perceived as poor management and disorganized research, firing almost the entire staff, including Lanier and his research team (who founded Domain Simulations, which intended to stick to software).[13]

As Disney Studios and Iwerks Entertainment were working in VR, Disney's Imagineering division took the flying carpet from *Aladdin* as the basis for a VR experience. Shamrock Holdings bought controlling interest in Virtual World Entertainment. Paramount had already signed up with Edison Bros. to bring a VR version of *Star Trek: The Next Generation* to shopping centers. "Simulated" VR rides were touted as cost-efficient alternatives for theme parks (e.g., Trumbull's "Secrets of the Luxor Pyramid" entertainment complex in Las Vegas, and Iwerks's Turbotour in San Francisco). Sega planned to build dozens of small (1–5 acres) regional VR theme parks, each costing $10–50 million. Itochu Corp. backed the concept of "Cinetropolis," which combined giant screens and the latest in motion-stimulation and interactive VR rides planned by Iwerks. Concurrently, "cybersex" futurists dreamed of "teledildonics" which would make possible simulated sex with a computerized being, or with another "virtual" person over the phone lines. By May 1993, *Wild Palms*, ABC's six-hour cyberpunk nightmare vision of the future, encompassed film-director Oliver Stone's "event series" of one man's effort to take over the world via network TV; the hallucinatory soap opera brought the VR potential closer to mass market.

Major M&E companies (Paramount, Time Warner, Viacom), telcos (AT&T), video game firms (Sega, Nintendo), entertainment/electronics giants (Sony, Matsushita), toy companies (Hasbro), and VR specialists (Edison Bros.) were betting billions on virtual reality. The new technology was being applied in a wide variety of commercial industries, including selling, design, surgery, manufacturing, education, drugs, and medicine. The increase in performance and decrease in price of semiconductor chips drove VR's development by allowing computer makers to build more sophisticated graphics systems. Stimulated by its potential, government and university laboratories were exploring VR, too. The military hoped to spend more than $500 million on simulations between 1993 and 1997, and an additional $350 million, eight-year contract to create an advanced network for battlefield simulations.

By the early '90s entertainment was only one of VR's many attractions, but the new technology's potential had hardly been touched yet.[14]

Major Studios

TIME WARNER: STRUGGLE FOR CONTROL

On March 4, 1989, Time Inc. and Warner Communications, Inc. announced they planned to merge to form "the largest media and entertainment conglomerate in the world." The two had different histories, management styles, and corporate cultures.

Two Corporate Cultures

The Old Time Inc.

In 1923 *Time* magazine was started by Henry Robinson Luce, the son of foreign missionaries. In the '30s the newsweekly was augmented with two new magazines, *Fortune* and *Life*. By the '60s Time Inc. operated in publishing (magazines, books), broadcasting (TV and radio), cable (minority investments) and pay-TV (a 20% interest in Sterling, precursor of HBO). Remaining Time's largest single stockholder, Luce controlled the company through the board, family, trusts, directors, and officers.[1]

In 1969 another reorganization came as industry veterans were replaced by professional managers and Luce designated Hedley Donovan, *Fortune*'s managing editor, as his successor. In operations, the rise of broadcast TV went hand in hand with the demise of magazines (decline of *Life*, folding of *Look*). In 1974 Time introduced *People*, which (like *Sports Illustrated*) benefited from TV, which created a lot of its subject matter. Meanwhile, it struggled to remain a print company: it sold its five broadcast stations, as well as (mainly unprofitable) cable holdings to ATC, a major MSO; it also integrated backward on the print side, merging with Temple Indus-tries, a Texas-based forest-products company; finally, it raised to 79% its stake in Sterling (dissolved when HBO and Manhattan Cable became Time's wholly owned subsidiaries). Operated largely as four separate di-visions (magazines, books, TV, and Temple-Eastex), Time reinforced a whole that was less valuable than the sum of its parts.

Toward Transition

With Donovan's retirement in 1979, J. Richard Munro was named pres-ident and CEO, while Munro's protégé, Nicholas J. Nicholas, Jr., replaced him as president in 1986. Unlike Munro who had served on the publishing side, Nicholas came from cable TV operations. It was a sharp break with Time's corporate past. Publishers were succeeded by managers.

What the old leadership had acquired, the new one began to divest, including publishing operations (the *Washington Star, TV-Cable Week*), Time-Life Films, and the forest-products group. The shrinking process did not involve the cable business (which generated two-thirds of Time's pre-tax income in 1982).

Despite Luce's opposition, Time had debated buying into Hollywood since the mid-'60s. While a merger attempt with United Artists failed, a 5% stake in MGM was eventually sold off.[2] With HBO, ATC strengthened and Manhattan Cable became a solid moneymaker. Time also continued to explore DBS, while reexamining opportunities in pay-per-view and home video. In 1980 Cinemax was launched to complement HBO's op-erations. Two years later HBO partnered with CBS and Columbia to form Tri-Star Pictures. Pay cable would be Time's avenue into M&E operations.

Time, Inc.: Business Segments

From 1983 to 1988, Time's revenues grew from $2.7 billion to $4.5 billion. It operated in four core businesses. It was the world's largest mag-azine publisher; it generated the third largest book revenues in the United States; it was the biggest premium cable programmer; and it was the sec-ond largest multiple cable-system operator. By 1988 programming (HBO, Cinemax, HBO Video) and cable revenues (ATC) accounted for more than two fifths of Time Inc.'s total revenues (see Table 5.1).

As Time's 1990 *Annual Report* (signed right before the official an-nouncement of the Time Warner merger) put it, refocusing was not enough.

Whether American or European or Asian, all of these [mid-'90s global giants] have a common denominator. They are vertically integrated: that is, large enough to create, market and disseminate their products worldwide, and smart enough to amortize costs across as many distribution outlets as possible.

Time Inc. is one of them.

At Time Inc. vertical integration and globalization meant a major acquisition.

Warner Communications, Inc.

With Goldman, Sachs, Harry, Albert, and Jack Warner took over Vitagraph, an important studio, in 1925, just two years after the incorporation of Warner Bros.; and with Western Electric's technical aid, the Warners pioneered the sound motion picture (*The Jazz Singer*, 1927). As Warner Bros. began diversifying into the music business, vertical integration increased with expansion into exhibition. By the early '30s it was one of Hollywood's Big Five studios.[3]

During the Great Depression, Warner launched a strict cost-cutting policy. The strategy was consistent with Harry Warner's fiscal conservatism and politics, even though the films dealt with "serious" political and social themes. Warner's success continued in the '40s, with movies like *The Sea Hawk* (1940), *The Maltese Falcon* (1941), *Yankee Doodle Dandy* (1942), *Casablanca* (1943), and *The Big Sleep* (1946).

The problems followed in the late '40s and mid-'50s, when the Paramount decrees forced the company to divest its theatre circuit. Harry and Albert Warner retired and put their controlling interest up for sale. By 1966 Warner's value lay in its land, old films, and television production.

Acquisition by Seven Arts. In November 1966 Jack Warner retired and sold his shares to Seven Arts, which also operated record companies, such as Atlantic, Warner, and Reprise. The resulting combination became known as a TV distributor.

Acquisition by Kinney. In July 1969 Warner Bros.-Seven Arts was taken over by Kinney National Services, Inc., a New York-based conglomerate engaged mainly in parking lots, car rentals, construction, and funeral homes. The purchase was preceded by Kinney's acquisition of the Ashley Famous Agency and followed by related M&E purchases. In 1971 Kinney also acquired three large cable TV operations. Building an M&E empire with borrowed funds, Kinney's Steven Ross foresaw the rise of cable, which led him to MTV Music Television and Nickelodeon (later both were sold).

In February 1972 Kinney split into National Kinney, which reflected the conglomerate's original interests with construction and maintenance firms; and Warner Communications, Inc. (WCI), an entertainment group with interests in film, music, television, and publishing. Steve Ross was elected to head WCI. At Kinney, Ross had been associated with the murky world of several alleged mobsters ("Caesar" Kimmel, "Longie" Zwillman, Judson Richheimer). Although he insulated himself from direct contact with such things, businessmen fronting for organized criminals managed to bribe his closest assistants in the notorious Westchester Premiere Theater scandal.[4] Steven Ross, the "magnetic visionary," would dominate Warner until he died of cancer in December 1992.

Warner Communications: Growth by Acquisition

Through the 1970s Ross cultivated a stable of actors and recording artists. While he invested in cable TV, home video, and CDs before his competitors, WCI continued M&E acquisitions, including Atari (video games), QUBE (an advanced cable system), David Wolpe Productions, and Knickerbocker Toy Company. In the early '80s WCI made most of its income with Atari, but waning public enthusiasm and increasing competition in video games brought great losses. In 1983 WCI also became Rupert Murdoch's takeover target. To escape News Corp.'s bid, Ross made a deal with Chris-Craft's Herbert J. Siegel. Seeking to deflect Murdoch, both bought blocks of stock in each other's company.

Despite problems, WCI's financial fortunes improved in the '80s. To a great extent, this was due to films like *Arthur* (1981), *Gremlins* (1984), *Tightrope* (1984), *The Color Purple* (1985), as well as the *Superman* sequels.

Ross maintained his top executives' loyalty with lavish compensations and a highly decentralized decision system that empowered them with great autonomy. Though a "genius in the art of deal-making," he paid a price for his aggressive high-risk management style (a stock sellout of the Atari division, a stock fraud, the kickback scandal at the Westchester theater).

Warner Communications Inc.: Business Segments

From 1984 to 1988 WCI's operating revenues doubled, from $2 billion to $4.2 billion, while operating income more than tripled from $185 million to $608 million. WCI operated in film entertainment, recorded music and music publishing, cable and broadcasting, and (to a lesser extent) publishing and related distribution. By 1988 WCI's filmed entertainment and music operations continued to account for 86% of operating revenues (see Table 5-1).

From Takeover Struggle to Debt Reduction and Strategic Alliances

Having restructured the company in the early '80s, Time's top executives began to design a vertically integrated company at the end of the '80s. Despite rapid growth, Time did not own any significant copyrights in video (it was not *producing* entertainment). The M&E industries were diversified and global, whereas Time was sufficiently neither. Finally, be-

Table 5-1
Time Inc. and Warner Communications, Inc.: Premerger Business Segments (1984-88)

TIME INC.: BUSINESS SEGMENTS (1983-88)

	Total	Magazines	Books	Programming[2]	Cable
Revenues ($mil)					
1988	$4,507[1]	$1,752	$891	$1,122	$812
1987	4,193	1,621	954	904	714
1986	3,762	1,576	663	886	637
1985	3,404	1,482	552	786	584
1984	3,067	1,321	491	745	510
Income from Operations ($mil)					
1988	$683	$287	$104	$116	$176
1987	646	283	88	125	150
1986	464	162	73	111	118
1985	479	176	85	121	97
1984	454	188	65	118	83

WARNER COMMUNICATIONS, INC.: SEGMENTS (1984-88)

	Total	Filmed Entert.	Recorded Music and Music Publ.	Cable and Brdctng	Publishing and Related Distribution
Operating Revenues ($mil)					
1984	$2,024	$1,090	$818	–	$116
1985	2,235	1,201	912	–	122
1986	2,848	1,251	1,139	$326	133
1987	3,404	1,356	1,531	387	130
1988	4,206	1,571	2,040	456	139
Operating Income ($mil)					
1984	$185	$150	$90	$(71)	$16
1985	278	160	113	(9)	14
1986	350	172	151	16	11
1987	448	176	214	46	12
1988	608	203	319	75	11

1. Includes intersegment elimination ($70 million).
2. Includes intersegment revenues.

SOURCES: Time Warner, Inc.

cause of the variability of the company earnings, Time's stock was traded only at a fraction of its theoretical breakup value on Wall Street.[5]

To survive consolidation, Time would have to merge with another media giant. Hence the talks with Gannett, CBS, Paramount, and Capital Cities/ABC. By 1987 Munro and Nicholas narrowed merger candidates to two Hollywood studios: Paramount (Gulf + Western), and Warner Communications, Inc. WCI was perceived as the more profitable and a better strategic match. WCI had significant (production) interests in filmed entertainment, recorded music and music publishing, cable, broadcasting, and publishing; its record business had greater growth potential; it owned

100% of its movie distribution business; 38% of its total revenues came from overseas; and WCI had 1.6 million cable subscribers who would add muscle to ATC's 4.3 million subscribers. After two years of talks, the official announcement of the Time Warner merger came in March 1989.

The Merger Struggle

In the original joint-venture proposal, Richard Munro, chairman of Time, and Steven Ross, chairman of Warner, were to be co-CEOs in the new combine, which was to be a merger of equals. Felix Rohatyn, a long-time friend and adviser to Ross, sold the merger to the WCI board. Since the stock-swap merger structure rendered the combination vulnerable, investors criticized the merger as a poor deal for Time's shareholders. In just three months, Time's stock climbed from $105 to $135.

After the merger announcement, many players showed interest in Time, including GE (which owned the NBC network), Cablevision Systems, Capital Cities/ABC, and Charles Dolan (founder of HBO). Also, financiers like the Bass Group, Carl Icahn, Ronald Perelman, and K-III Holdings considered a bid for Time.

Paramount's Bid. In early June 1989, Paramount offered $175 a share ($10.7 billion in cash) for Time and sought to stop the Time Warner merger. Rejecting the offer, Time's board voted to acquire 50% of Warner for $70 a share in cash and to pick up the rest for cash or securities or both. The shareholders' vote on the original merger was postponed. Paramount increased its bid to $200 a share.[6] The stakes had risen dramatically—from no debt (initial plan) to crushing debt (final plan).

In July 1989 the Delaware decision in *Paramount Communications v. Time* concluded that directors, not shareholders, managed the firm; Time's directors acted reasonably in rejecting Paramount's bid because of their long-term strategy to acquire Warner; since neither company held a controlling block in Time Warner, the majority of the stock changing hands did not imply a change of control; and, in certain instances, "corporate culture" served as a valid defense against takeover. Most Fortune 500 companies were incorporated in Delaware, which got 19% of its revenues from being a corporate haven. In exchange, the state gave directors great latitude in determining corporate conduct.[7]

Postmerger Time Warner

By 1993 TW operated in filmed entertainment (31% of total revenues), music (23%), publishing (22%), cable (15%), and HBO/programming (10%). While TW's entertainment segments (studio, cable, programming) brought in more than half of total revenues, each segment was number one or two in its industry (see Table 5-2).

Publishing. Despite restructurings, Time Inc. remained America's largest magazine publisher and a leading direct marketer of music, videos, and

Table 5-2
Time Warner, Inc.: Business Groups (1988-93)

	Total	Publ.	Music	Filmed Entert.	Cable	Programming - HBO	Intersegment Elimination
						---- Entertainment Group ----	
Revenues ($mil)							
1993	$14,544	$3,270	$3,334	$4,565	$2,208	$1,441	(274)
1992r	13,560	3,123	3,214	3,945	2,091	1,444	(257)
1992	13,070	3,123	3,214	3,455	2,091	1,444	(257)
1991	12,021	3,021	2,960	3,065	1,935	1,366	(326)
1990	11,517	2,926	2,931	2,904	1,751	1,266	(261)
1989	7,642	2,918	1,147	1,315	1,224	1,177	(139)
1988	4,507	2,643	–	–	812	1,122	(70)
Operating income ($mil)							
1993	$1,496	$295	$296	$286	$406	$213	
1992r	1,384	254	275	254	400	201	
1992	1,343	254	275	213	400	201	
1991	1,154	174[1]	256	207	334	183	
1990	1,114	301	260	134	249	170	
1989	848	206	146	91	251	154	
1988	664	391	–	–	168	105	

r = restated
1. Includes a $60 million restructuring charge ($36 million after taxes).

SOURCE: Time Warner, Inc.

print products. In addition to some 30 magazines (e.g., *People, Fortune, Sports Illustrated*), the company made *Time* the first national newsmagazine to be available interactively, via America Online. In book publishing, TW (e.g., Book-of-the-Month Club, Time Life Inc., Little, Brown Co., Warner Books) was among the top four players.

Music. The Warner Music Group (Warner Bros., Atlantic, Elektra, Warner Music International) was the world's leading music company. The multinational family of labels had a premier array of artists in the industry (from Enya to R.E.M., from Metallica to En Vogue). The segment was fully vertically integrated, including the world's leading music publisher, manufacturing capabilities, distribution networks, and half ownership of America's largest music and video club.

Filmed Entertainment. As the domestic box-office champion six times in the past 10 years, Warner Bros. was the most consistent movie studio in Hollywood. The segment was the world's leading producer and distributor of theatrical motion pictures, TV programs, and home video programming. In 1993 it also purchased Six Flags Entertainment, the nation's largest regional theme-park company, with more than 20 million annual admissions.

Programming—HBO. HBO continued to be the most successful pay-TV company in the world, in revenues, ratings, and programming awards.

While current growth came from domestic operations, successful product extensions, and expansion into new programming enterprises, future growth was expected from promising pay-TV initiatives abroad.

Cable Television. Growing rapidly, Time Warner Cable maintained cable TV's highest returns on pay-per-view. It was building the information superhighway to the twenty-first century. Including video-on-demand, telecommunications, and a host of interactive multimedia services (home shopping, education, video games), the "Full Service Network" hoped to render obsolete the notion of channels, and to change the way people related to TV.

Transition of Power

After the merger, Ross assumed a crucial role in efforts to add distribution reach. He negotiated long-term home video distribution rights to MGM/UA products; an agreement involving producers Peter Guber and Jon Peters and an exchange of assets with Columbia Pictures; a significant stake in the Six Flags theme parks. Some deals were not passed without conflict (TW's $650 million loan guarantee to MGM/UA).

Co-CEOs Ross and Nicholas encouraged decentralization, which led to more autonomous TW divisions, following the Warner model (Warner executives captured high-level corporate positions). While Nicholas wanted to cut the debt by selling nonstrategic assets, a classic strategy in the '80s buyouts, Ross focused on strategic alliances, which he saw as a means for raising capital, as well as TW's vehicle to realize its potential as a global powerhouse.[8]

With the surge of the equity markets in spring 1991, Ross and others attempted to raise $3 billion, but an unusual rights offering angered shareholders and outstanding shares lost 25% (over $1.5 billion) of their market value. After TW revised its stock offering, it raised $2.8 billion to restructure its debt load. Concurrently, Ross's 1990 compensation was estimated at $78 million. As a result, TW's public image suffered.[9]

Partnership with Toshiba and C. Itoh. Ross, Oded Aboodi, Gerald Levin, and others used more than a year to pursue a major strategic alliance. To come up with $2 billion, they talked with Hitachi, Toshiba, Nippon Life, C. Itoh, and Matsushita. In October 1991 TW signed an agreement for the Toshiba Corp. and C. Itoh & Company to invest $1 billion for a 12.5% stake in Time Warner Entertainment (TWE). The new limited partnership, of which TW hoped to sell up to 50%, would own TW's cable operations, HBO, and Warner Bros. (Prior to the deal, TW had $8.8 billion in debt, of which TWE assumed some $7 billion. Using $1 billion from its Japanese partners to reduce the debt to $800 million, TW acquired greater financial flexibility. Yet the partnership betrayed the initial Time Warner merger motive—the creation of an *American* M&E giant.)

When Steve Ross began treatment for prostate cancer, Levin gained the trust of Oded Aboodi, TW's secretive de facto chief financial officer. (Two years later TW's board retained Aboodi as an adviser, despite his agreement to pay $930,000 in penalties and interest to settle SEC's insider-trading charges.) In March 1992 Nicholas found himself outside the company. As Levin became the sole heir to Ross as TW's head, the stock moved up several points.[10]

By mid-June 1992, when Ross took indefinite leave of absence for additional cancer treatment, Warner's corporate style permeated TW. A revised rights offering began a "re-equifying" process that reduced the debt from $11.2 billion to $8.7 billion. However, Ross's departure hindered TW's ability to find new foreign partners and reduce the huge debt load. Levin was not a dealmaker.

In December 1992 TW decided to sell off some of the $3 billion of investments it held in various nonstrategic businesses, or convert these stakes into cash-generating assets. That meant another betrayal of the initial merger motives.

When Ross died of complications arising from prostate cancer, Levin assumed his position, and a weeklong boardroom struggle ended with the departure of eight directors from TW. Many were key insiders from the Warner camp and among Ross's closest associates. A month later TW promoted its president and CEO to the additional post of chairman. Levin was in charge.[11] In the mid-'70s Levin had contributed to the cable revolution (the launch of HBO). A decade and a half later, he was preparing another revolution—the interactive age.

High-Tech and Telco Alliances

Unlike the deal-oriented Ross, Levin had a techie bent, which became evident as TW shifted from its search of strategic alliances to integration of new technology. In 1991–92 TW spent months with IBM on a joint venture called Gemini, which drew on TW's software and IBM's expertise in switches and video servers. As IBM became consumed by its own problems, it lost interest in a proposed $500 million stake in TW's entertainment assets.

In January 1993 TW announced plans to build an "electronic superhighway," a high-capacity, computerized network to deliver movies on demand, interactive games, home shopping and telephone services. Thus began a web of ties with computer and telecommunications companies.[12]

In May Levin agreed to sell a 25% stake in TW to US West, to bring programming to subscribers over a cable superhighway. Of the $2.5 billion stake, US West invested $1 billion to upgrade the cable systems, while the remaining $1.5 billion was a direct investment in TW. Time Warner Entertainment would spend an additional $4 billion to upgrade systems across the country by 1998. Warner Bros. planned to spend $2

Figure 5-1
Time Warner: New Corporate Structure (1993)

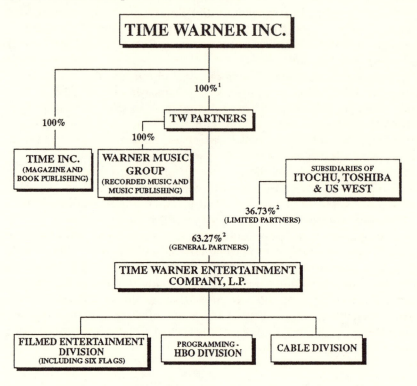

billion to launch a fifth broadcast network in 1994, to protect its TV production capability and insure in-house products for HBO and other cable programming services, and to fuel the superhighway (see Figure 5-1).

The ensuing deals were far smaller than the US West linkup. TW teamed up with TCI and Sega to start a cable network offering interactive video games; Levin gave AT&T a contract for a high-speed switch for the Orlando cable system (where TW was building the world's first fully interactive cable system); Toshiba bid to supply advanced converter boxes to TW's Orlando cable system; Silicon Graphics and 3DO were developing technology that could be used to make interactive video games or cable converter boxes.

The Seagram Stake. After the US West deal, Seagram Company, a $6.1 billion global spirits and juice maker, acquired 5.7% (about $700 million) of TW, planning to increase its stake to 15%. Confronted with falling U.S. liquor consumption, Edgar Bronfman, Jr. had refocused Seagram on upscale brands, made major acquisitions, cut staff, shed the old guard, and installed his own team. In the '60s he had controlled MGM; in the '70s he had produced movies. Dissatisfied with TW's management, CAA's Michael Ovitz hooked Bronfman up with Allen & Co., an investment bank that ultimately advised him to invest in TW. Seagram compared the investment to the 24% friendly stake it had in DuPont (it controlled a fourth of DuPont's board). In January 1994 TW's board adopted defensive measures against the company. TW would not be "Tisched."[13]

In June 1994 Edgar Bronfman, Jr. replaced his father as CEO of Seagram. Still, he could not increase the 15% stake in TW without TW's approval.

"Synergy, schmynergy!" headlined *Variety* in a March cover story in 1994. "Externally, Time Warner is often criticized for a lack of synergy. But despite intra-division roughhousing that Levin likens to corporate 'Darwinism,' Time Warner executives argue that their company's organizational chart may be the model for future media conglomerates."[14]

TW's new strategy was highly capital-intensive. In a year it had sold big minority interests in valuable entertainment assets for prices that averaged 13 times cash flow (while bidding for Paramount rose from a multiple of 18 to 21). Some estimates put TW's theoretical losses at $2 billion.[15] It still carried $10.1 billion in debt from the merger. Strategic alliances with high techs and telcos were driven as much by financial pressures as strategic opportunities. Putting aside the public rhetoric of "electronic superhighways," the fire sale was reminiscent of a debt-reduction strategy masquerading as a high-tech strategy. Despite Levin's efforts to rise above the takeover rumors, the war of attrition intensified in the spring of 1994.[16]

PARAMOUNT: A GLOBAL POWERHOUSE?

With profits from "talkies" in the late 1920s, Paramount began its first era of major diversification (music division, a 50% interest in CBS). Paramount also purchased 500 independent theatre circuits in just nine months. With the Depression, losses from the theatre chain forced Paramount to enter bankruptcy. Adolph Zukor remained chairman of the board and Barney Balaban was the new president, but investment bankers invaded the board.

Despite two reorganizations and substantial financial losses, the '30s were immensely profitable at the newly named Paramount Pictures, which evolved into a huge multinational, diversified corporation holding ownership of 194 listed subsidiaries, including film-processing laboratories, land facilities for production of shorts and newsreels, control of 42 film exchanges, distribution of films via 43 subsidiaries throughout the world, operations in music publishing, and, occasionally, underwriting plays on

Broadway. The company also owned, leased, and/or operated some 1,200 theatres, more than any other studio.

Paramount's vertical integration and acquisitions were monitored closely by the Justice Department. Starting in 1948 the Paramount decrees required the studio to divest its exhibition segment. (United Paramount Theaters, which encompassed a theatre chain and one TV station, merged with ABC.) The company retained the studio and its sales organization, as well as 380 theatres in foreign countries (mainly Canada), the old films, the stock in Dumont (the beleaguered fourth network), and the TV station KTLA in Los Angeles. In 1958 the company sold all rights to its 1929–49 feature films to MCA. The classic Paramount was gone.

After the mid-'60s the company fended off a takeover attempt by two Broadway producers, Cy Feuer and Ernest Martin. Both were in partnership with Herbert Siegel, a former talent agent (and the future CEO of Chris-Craft). When George Weltner, Paramount's then-president, sent off his aide, Martin S. Davis, to find a "white knight" to block the takeover, Davis came up with Charles Bluhdorn, chairman and CEO of Gulf + Western (G + W).

From Gulf + Western to Paramount

Starting from a one-time auto parts distribution business, Bluhdorn, an Austrian immigrant, had built a huge conglomerate. By the mid-'60s Gulf + Western had $182 million in sales. Funded by borrowed money, Bluhdorn's buying spree was boosted by the third M&A wave.[1] Far above the stock price at the time, G + W acquired Paramount Pictures Corporation. Bluhdorn also spent $20 million for Desilu Productions (*I Love Lucy*).

With few hits, Paramount moved into television, which provided a more consistent source of revenues. By the mid-'70s Bluhdorn had hired two young programmers, Barry Diller and Michael Eisner, from ABC. The Diller-Eisner team became the most successful one in Hollywood, bringing the studio its years of success (1974–84). Paramount was creatively and financially astute, focusing on low-budget pictures and using money from outside limited partners to reduce financial risk. Hence its blockbusters, from *Saturday Night Fever* and *Grease* to Spielberg's Indiana Jones films, *An Officer and a Gentleman*, and *Beverly Hills Cop*. The studio introduced popular TV shows, revolutionized the first-run syndication market (*Solid Gold, Entertainment Tonight*), and pioneered price slashing on video cassettes to promote the emerging sell-through market.

With an assortment of unrelated companies from sugarcane fields to consumer loan offices, G + W was a quintessential conglomerate. Changes began in February 1983, when Bluhdorn died of a heart attack. G + W president David Judelson and chairman John Duncan were seen as obvious choices for a successor, as well as Barry Diller (who declined). Although Martin Davis was a distant fourth, he succeeded Bluhdorn.

With Davis, G + W adopted a more formal atmosphere. He considered both Diller and Eisner overpaid and overrated. When Frank Mancuso was appointed Paramount chairman (Mel Harris, a Paramount veteran, was installed as president of the studio's TV group), Diller left for Fox, while Eisner and Jeff Katzenberg moved to Disney, followed by some 30 other Paramount executives at the VP level or higher—almost half of Paramount's senior management. Davis's first major decision at Paramount had nearly decimated the studio.

The Restructuring Era (1983–89)

In the 1980s, conglomerates had lost favor on Wall Street, which favored "synergies," "vertical integration," and companies that were "lean and mean." At a frantic pace, Davis divested about 50 businesses with total sales of $1.3 billion (from building products and racetracks to manufacturing), unloading a $900 million stock portfolio. The divestitures were followed by a dramatic move in 1985, when Davis cut nearly 40% of G + W's operating earnings by selling the $2.7 billion-a-year consumer and industrial products group to Wickes Companies for $1 billion in cash. What Bluhdorn had acquired in three decades, Davis divested over the next few years.[2]

In 1982 G + W's earnings stood at $36 million, and its stock was at about $8 a share. Davis refocused the conglomerate into entertainment, publishing/information, and financial services. With earnings at $385 million in 1988, the new entity's stock boomed to $49.50. Meanwhile, Davis fought off two potential raiders, Carl C. Icahn and Carl H. Lindner. Even Ivan Boesky tried to lure Davis into a deal with promises of $100–$200 million in profits.[3]

By 1989, of the 100 companies that Bluhdorn had assembled, Davis had dismantled some 65, cutting G + W's payroll from 113,000 to just 19,000. The proceeds of the asset sales were used to retire debt and buy back 45 million shares of stock. In the second half of the decade, G + W spent about $1.5 billion on 40 acquisitions in publishing and information services.

"Conglomeration is dead," Davis declared in interviews, attacking G + W's very principle that diversity provided added value and protection. "Two plus two *does* equal four—it doesn't equal five."

Entertainment Diversification

By the end of the 1980s Paramount's studio was the industry leader in TV production, syndication and home video. The studio's movie library included more than 2,000 episodes of popular network TV series (e.g., *Cheers* and *Family Ties*). Davis saw increasing opportunities in international

TV markets, where deregulation and new technology incited demand for filmed entertainment. Hence the increasing diversification in the M&E business.

In June 1987 Paramount owned half of the USA Network, a basic cable channel (whose other half belonged to MCA). The following January it sold 50% interest in its domestic movie theatre chain to Warner Communications. In January 1989 it invested in broadcasting, spending $10 million on an option to acquire the five-station TVX Broadcast Group (the stake would be purchased over four years from Salomon Brothers). Concurrently, the company was considering expansion into broadcast network ownership, contingent upon the relaxation of the fin-syn rules.

High prices hindered Davis's expansion plans. While foreign rivals, such as the Japanese Sony, the German Bertelsmann AG, or the French Hachette Publications were rapidly driving up prices for M&E properties, Paramount did not have cheap dollars and huge capital reserves.

While Davis rejected many potential acquisitions that he found too expensive (a bid for Time, efforts to purchase publishing companies), he himself contributed to the price hikes, via brand-name products. Like Disney, G + W paid significant attention to product development and marketing that built renewable assets. If mass products sold better with brand names, the theory went, branding was an intrinsic aspect of product strategy. Hence, G + W's high-price contracts with best-selling authors (Jackie Collins, Bob Woodward), top talent (Eddie Murphy), and producers (Don Simpson and Jerry Bruckheimer). G + W saw itself as a company creating products that competitors could not replicate and that were proprietary. But as Paramount invested in human capital, it boosted the bargaining power of talent—which, in turn, inflated production costs. In 1987 Paramount's *Coming to America*, an Eddie Murphy vehicle, led to a long legal struggle between Paramount and Art Buchwald, the celebrated columnist who claimed the studio had stolen his idea. None of the studios enjoyed the public scrutiny of Hollywood's "creative accounting practices."[4]

Selling of Finance Subsidiary. By fiscal 1988, 46% of G + W's operating income came from consumer/commercial finance, while entertainment accounted for 31% and publishing/information for 23%. G + W's Associates First Capital Corporation was the nation's third largest independent finance company as measured by total capital funds. It provided a broad range of consumer finance, specialized commercial finance and leasing, as well as related insurance products. In 1988 the Associates' gross revenues were almost $2.1 billion, with $372 million in operating income—more than entertainment or publishing/information.

By April 1989 Davis had consolidated G + W's seven business segments into just three and announced the sale of G + W's financial subsidiary. G + W took the name Paramount Communications, Inc. (PCI). Davis intended to use the expected $3–$5 billion to build and expand the publishing and entertainment segments into a world-class M&E giant.[5]

In Search of a Partner

By the end of the '80s Davis claimed G + W was still primarily interested in friendly acquisitions, or a stock-for-stock merger with another domestic or foreign concern. While he remained interested in joint ventures and explored various options with Sony, Matsushita, and other major corporations, Wall Street speculated on merger candidates like NBC, CBS, Tribune, MCA (which already had some ventures with G + W), and McGraw-Hill.

In the past, the financial subsidiary's steady stream of revenues protected the company against the volatility of the entertainment and publishing businesses. Even though its market value was estimated at some $5 billion, the new Paramount was more vulnerable. Yet Davis had no intention of becoming a takeover target. In the case of a hostile takeover, Paramount Communications, Inc. would be the raider. Two months after the sale of the financial unit, PCI launched a hostile bid for Time Inc.

Paramount's Bid for Time

In March 1989 Time and Warner announced they would merge in a friendly stock swap to form the world's largest M&E concern. A month later Paramount unveiled its new focus strategy intending to sell the consumer-finance subsidiary. Two weeks before the proposed Time Warner merger in June, PCI offered to pay $175 a share, almost $11 billion in cash, for Time. After the Delaware Supreme Court refused pleas by Paramount and some Time shareholders to block the Time Warner merger, PCI terminated its offer. After the failed bid (which cost $80 million), PCI tried to buy its way into the network business.

Effort at the "Fifth Network"

The attempt to develop a fifth network evolved from a three-year agreement by MCA TV and Paramount Domestic TV to combine their barter sales divisions into a joint-venture barter sales company. Announced in September 1989, the venture, Premier Advertiser Sales, was to be the fifth-largest national TV advertising source in the nation, behind the Big Three and FBC. The MCA/PCI plan failed because of strong opposition by the syndicators and FBC.[6]

After the mid-'70s, PCI's entertainment group had passed through two distinct phases: years of success (1974–84), and a transition (1984–89). The late '80s were followed by financial conservatism. The studio resorted to runaway product, nonunion labor, and coventures, instituting comprehensive five-year planning for the studio. Despite its cost-conscious production program, PCI still failed to control rapidly rising costs.[7]

After the bid for Time Inc., Paramount's stock began to decline, due to the concern that the company had engaged in several high-cost films, including *Harlem Nights, Another 48 Hours, Days of Thunder, The Two Jakes,* and *Godfather III.* Megabudgets did not generate megahits. As entertainment companies no longer traded on asset values but on earnings performance, Paramount's spending became an issue. As fundamentals mattered more, the focus on entertainment and publishing rendered PCI vulnerable to the volatility of these businesses. Hence the 1990 management shakeout, and the demise of high-priced talent relationships (Eddie Murphy, Simpson and Bruckheimer). PCI had become "lean and mean," but, amid consolidation, that was no longer enough.

Paramount Re-Targeted. Unlike most of its rivals, PCI entered the '90s increasingly vulnerable and without a major (Asian or European) financial partner, despite rumors on its potential mergers, acquisitions, and joint ventures. As Davis explored various options only to reject them as too expensive, what used to be called "caution" came to be seen as "timidity."

Courting of Japanese Giants. After more than a year of exploring how to invest over $2 billion in cash reserves, PCI was negotiating with several Japanese firms, among them such electronic giants as Toshiba and Hitachi, as well as trading houses like Sumitomo.

In January 1991 Davis emphasized that PCI would be a buyer rather than a seller and wanted to engage in transactions that would make it a stronger U.S. concern. As a result, Paramount was expected to acquire mid-sized independent TV stations or seek a merger with a major network, such as Capital Cities/ABC, or a studio like MCA or Sony. As nothing happened, *Forbes* argued that Paramount had become "a wallflower in the corporate mating dance," stuck in a "Mr. Lonelyhearts" position.[8]

Paramount Communications, Inc.: Business Segments

By the early '90s Paramount Communications had operations in entertainment and publishing. Prior to its sale, the portion of consumer/commercial finance had brought in the most revenues and even more in operating income. After the sale of the financial subsidiary, entertainment brought in 61% of PCI's revenues and publishing accounted for the remaining 39%. In operating income, however, entertainment operations brought in 99% of the total, while publishing accounted for only 1%.

Half of PCI's entertainment revenues consisted of movie production and distribution (via United International Pictures, jointly owned by PCI, MCA, and MGM) and theatres (via Cinamerica, jointly owned with Time Warner), while TV and home video accounted for 25%, and sports/entertainment (Madison Square Garden) accounted for another 20%. The

Table 5-3
Paramount Communications, Inc.: Business Segments (1986–92)*

	Entertainment	Publishing/ Information	Total	Consumer/ Commercial Finance
Revenues ($mil)				
1992	$2,657	$1,608	$4,265	–
1991	2,380	1,515	3,895	–
1990	2,447	1,422	3,869	–
1989	2,072	1,320	3,392	–
1988	1,862	1,194	3,056	$2,052
1987	1,850	1,074	2,924	1,778
1986	1,154	949	2,103	1,687
(%)				
1992	62%	38%	100%	–
1991	61	39	100	–
1990	63	37	100	–
1989	61	39	100	–
1988	36	23	100	40%
1987	39	23	100	38
1986	30	25	100	45
Operating Income ($mil)				
1992	$280	$182	$462	–
1991	66	156	222	–
1990	213	156	369	–
1989	252	2	254	–
1988	252	180	432	$372
1987	297	162	459	324
1986	129	141	269	290
(%)				
1992	61%	39%	100%	–
1991	30	70	100	–
1990	58	42	100	–
1989	99	1	100	–
1988	31	42	100	46%
1987	38	35	100	41
1986	23	52	100	52

* Year ended Oct. 31.

SOURCE: Gulf+Western Inc.; Paramount Communications, Inc.

new station segment (three FBC affiliates, three indies) generated about 8% (see Table 5-3).

By 1992 Paramount Publishing was the world's largest educational publisher; a major consumer publisher; and a leader in select business, technical, and professional publishing segments. While education brought in almost half of the publishing revenues, consumer books accounted for 25% and business/technical/professional for the remaining 20%.

In the past, the proceeds of the divestitures had been used to retire debt, buy back stock, and invest in core businesses. From 1983 to 1992 PCI repurchased some 51 million shares, reducing its debt-to-capital ratio from 38% to 17%. Concurrent to the restructuring, PCI launched an aggressive acquisition program. From 1983 to 1992 it invested $2.8 billion in acquisitions, especially in publishing, where it grew from a $200 million unit to a $1.6 billion publishing powerhouse. In 1991 PCI acquired six broadcast TV stations; the following year it entered into the regional theme-park business. In addition, PCI also acquired Computer Curriculum (1990) and Macmillan Computer Publishing (1991), which catapulted the publishing operations into the forefront of computer-assisted interactive learning and computer book publishing.

By February 1994 Paramount Publishing was completing its $553 million purchase of Macmillan. It reorganized divisions, reduced the number of imprints and published titles, and laid off up to 1% of each company's combined workforce of 10,000. The acquisition gave Simon & Schuster about $2 billion in annual revenues, assuring its position as the largest publisher in the United States and the second largest in the world behind Bertelsmann AG.[9]

Acquirer or Target?

In early 1993 the company's breakup value was estimated at $60–$70 a share, but its stock traded in the $40 range (the price had peaked at about $66 in 1989).

Paramount Pictures had been ridden with instability. In a surprise move, Davis named Stanley Jaffe president and COO. In the past, Jaffe, a veteran indie producer, had reported to Frank Mancuso, the chairman of PCI's Paramount Pictures unit, who now reported to Jaffe. After some turmoil, Mancuso was fired, while his successor Brandon Tartikoff, NBC's legendary programmer, lasted only 15 months. Concurrently, write-offs stalled earnings growth. Despite long-term woes, PCI was one of the best-positioned M&E companies. It had excellent assets, some $1.2 billion in cash, and relatively low debt.

Notoriously tight with a budget and difficult as a CEO, Davis's ego got in the way during several takeover talks with MCA and Time. Rumored talks with PolyGram Records and Virgin Music Group went nowhere. The longer Davis explored his options, the quicker his targets were bought by his rivals. Yet speculation continued on PCI's talks with Viacom, GE's NBC unit, Turner Broadcasting, or a linkup with Capital Cities/ABC. Any deal with a network, however, was unlikely without the removal of the fin-syn rules.

Despite his cost-conscious approach, Davis himself earned more than $4 million in salary and $7.5 million in long-term compensation at the peak of PCI's trading, although he owned less than 2% of the stock. Trusted by few, liked by fewer, he was running out of time. A major raid could easily find his board turning against him very quickly.

In March 1993 Wisconsin's public pension fund was leading an effort to unseat four PCI directors because of the company's lagging stock performance and high executive compensation. The action reflected Wall Street's perception that a major merger was the only solution to Paramount's tepid performance. Also, there were concerns about succession. The 66-year-old Davis had not groomed an heir, even if Stanley R. Jaffe served increasingly as his right-hand man. PCI's nearly $1 billion in cash continued to earn paltry interest. Finally, the company's net income plunged in 1992, mainly because of the decline resulting from a weak film lineup—things changed drastically a year later with films like *The Firm, Addams Family Values,* and *Wayne's World 2.*[10] "Deal mania is a disease," argued Davis.

In mid-September 1993 Paramount's board approved a merger with Viacom in a deal valued at $69 a share. The ensuing combine was to be one of the new diversified, multinational M&E giants.

Just a week later QVC, the home shopping channel, proposed to acquire Paramount in a deal valued at $80 a share. That triggered the kind of a long and bitter takeover battle that Davis could least afford. (On Viacom's takeover struggle for Paramount and merger efforts with Blockbuster, see Chapter 6.)

WALT DISNEY: THE TEFLON KINGDOM

Initially The Walt Disney Company was known as Laugh-O-Gram Films, a Kansas City partnership with Ub Iwerks that produced animated shorts. In 1926 Walt and Roy Disney moved to a new studio in the Silverlake district of Los Angeles, forming Walt Disney Studio (later Walt Disney Productions). The first Mickey Mouse cartoons followed only two years later.[1]

Disney's first feature-length cartoon, *Snow White and the Seven Dwarfs,* was released in 1937. It was followed by other classics, such as *Pinocchio* and *Bambi.* Many of these features were blockbusters, except for *Fantasia,* which forced Disney to go public to raise more capital. Unlike the big studios, Disney did not prosper during the war years, even if it turned out numerous films for the U.S. government.

In 1930–32 Walt Disney films were distributed in the United States by Columbia Pictures; thereafter, by United Artists and RKO Radio Pictures. When, in 1954, Howard Hughes began to dismantle RKO, Disney formed Buena Vista Distribution Company, Ltd. to distribute its films.

The "New" Diversified Disney

In the '50s and '60s Disney continued to release blockbusters, such as *Cinderella, Alice in Wonderland, Peter Pan, Lady and the Tramp, Sleeping Beauty,* but none of these repeated the success of *Bambi,* not even *Mary Poppins.*

By the '70s *The Love Bug* and *The Aristocrats* illustrated the studio's artistic decline. Disney would not have survived without diversification into network TV, which began with *The Mickey Mouse Club* (1955). Concurrently, *Disneyland* became the longest running network series. When films slumped, the theme parks kept Disney in the black. In 1955 Disneyland opened in Anaheim, California; in 1971 it was followed by Disney World in Orlando, Florida.

Fraternal Rivalry

Incorporated in 1929, Walt Disney Productions was reincorporated a decade later. Despite a productive period, the stock division anticipated a destructive fraternal rivalry. While Walt Disney tended the creative side, Roy Disney managed the business operations. One represented idealism, the other realism. Division at the top permeated lower ranks, to the functional departments. The staffs of financial, legal, accounting, and administrative departments were all "Roy men," whereas marketing and sales, and creative divisions such as the studio and the parks, were filled with "Walt men."

After the death of Walt Disney in 1966, Roy Disney became chairman of the company, while Donn B. Tatum assumed the title of president and E. Cardon Walker that of executive VP in charge of operations. In 1971–72 the "Disney Troika" boosted revenues from $116 million to $250 million. The pressure to complete Walt Disney World took its toll on Roy Disney. He died three months after Disney World opened on October 1, 1971. After his death, his son, Roy E. Disney, VP of Disney's animation division, was the principal shareholder, while Walker became president. Unlike his father, Roy E. Disney was much more interested in the creative side of the business, arguing that the film division should encourage innovation rather than repetition of old-fashioned and outdated formulas. Because Walker resisted changes, he left the company in 1977 but stayed on the board. A group of Disney animators also felt Disney's artistic standards had deteriorated. Led by Don Bluth, they defected in 1979.

Disney films went from generating over half the company's revenues in 1971 to only 20% in 1979. Half of this came from the periodic reissue of the animated classics. For all practical purposes, the Disney studio had ceased to exist.

From Synergic Diversifications to Financial Magic

Representing the "Roy" faction, Walker became Disney's CEO and appointed Ron Miller, Walt Disney's son-in-law, as president and COO in 1980. With the opening of Epcot Center in Florida two years later, Miller became CEO and started Touchstone Pictures to produce films like *Splash*, Disney's first hit since *The Love Bug*. Buena Vista served the traditional

Disney audience, whereas Touchstone reached for the contemporary "young adults." As segmentation and attempts at renewal accelerated, losses accumulated. In 1983, when Wall Street was swept by the bull market, the value of Roy E. Disney's stock actually dropped from $80 million to about $50 million. Even though it generated more than $1 billion a year, Disney had never had a business plan.

Steinberg's Takeover Attempt

In June 1984, right before Donald Duck's official 50th birthday, Saul Steinberg, the corporate raider, announced from his Reliance Group Holdings in New York his attempt at a hostile takeover of Walt Disney Prods. By the mid-'80s a bulk of Disney's stock was in the hands of institutional investors. Since Steinberg was prepared to buy the stock at more than $10 per share higher than it was trading before takeover speculation, institutional investors were willing to sell. A few months later, Steinberg was bought out, at a greenmail profit of some $31 million.[2]

After the takeover struggle, Roy E. Disney formed an alliance with the Bass brothers of Fort Worth, Texas. Although he had sold most of his stock and did not hold a board seat anymore, the group still had 18% of Disney's stock. Roy E. Disney and the Bass brothers bought a controlling interest, replacing the old management with new CEO Michael Eisner (Paramount) and president Frank Wells (Warner Bros.).

If Eisner was responsible for Disney's creative and corporate renewal and Gary Wilson for the company's financial structure in the mid-'80s, Jeffrey Katzenberg, CEO of the Walt Disney Studios, played a critical role in filmed entertainment.

The New Walt Disney Studios

Eisner and Katzenberg revived Disney's "sleepy little studio," applying and systematizing ideas they had experimented with at Paramount. At the turn of the '90s, Hollywood Pictures, still another subdivision, complemented Touchstone's operations. Both were slated to produce (cost-effective) "high-quality" films, which kept production costs 30% below the industry average, earning Disney a reputation of a "Scrooge." With releases like *The Little Mermaid, Beauty and the Beast,* and *Aladdin*, animated features captured the imagination of young and old alike, whereas "Touchstone's fare appealed to adult audiences (from *Three Men and a Baby* to *Good Morning, Vietnam*).

Just as Paramount had focused on low-budget movies, using money from outside limited partners to reduce financial risk, Disney replicated the strategy. Just as Paramount had resorted to balance-sheet tricks to offset occasional losses from big-budget failures, Disney took advantage of off-balance-sheet financing in film production. Like Paramount, Disney focused on story and talent, favored multipicture deals, and integration of TV and film production. Katzenberg's experiments with high-cost, big-star action vehicles such as *Dick Tracy* proved disastrous and led to a "return to basics."

Synergic Diversification

By the early 1990s Disney viewed itself as "a diversified international company engaged in family entertainment." The new management team had turned around the company that operated in theme parks and resorts, filmed entertainment, and consumer products. What made Disney so efficient was its synergic diversification. Three divisions "cross-fertilized" each other in myriad ways. The movies presented universally lovable characters, which played a major function in the theme parks, which then sold consumer products inspired by these characters. Hence the design of more rides, attractions, and shows around popular titles such as *Dick Tracy, The Little Mermaid, Who Framed Roger Rabbit?* and *Honey, I Shrunk the Kids.* To maintain and expand cross-fertilization, Disney needed a steady stream of characters to keep its parks attractive enough for the growing number of repeat visitors.

Financial Magic

If Michael Eisner was the architect of Disney's corporate turnaround and the "creative side" of the business, Gary L. Wilson, the former CFO of Marriott Corporation, raised the company's financial profile in the late '80s, vis-a-vis creative asset management and shrewd financial techniques. Wilson pushed Disney to divest itself of the real estate company Arvida Corporation, while greatly expanding Disney's hotel development; he refined Silver Screen Partnership's funding of motion pictures; sold future revenues from the Tokyo Disneyland theme park that Disney operated in exchange for cash; and devised the complex Euro Disney stock offering.[3]

"The Disney franchise is the finest consumer franchise in the world," Wilson acknowledged.

Most assets show up on the balance sheet—films, parks, hotels—all of which you can put a value on. But some of Disney's key assets are not on the balance sheet. . . . Disney's cash flows can be projected with relative certainty for a much larger period than, say, those of a disco or a restaurant concept. The restaurant may be unique and popular, but how long can you project those cash flows before the fad dies? Five years, six years, ten years? Mickey Mouse has endured for 60 years.[4]

As Marriott's CFO Wilson rethought several traditional assumptions about ownership and control; at Disney he applied the lessons in imaginative deals. Unlike its competitors, Marriott sold its hotels and contracted simply to manage them, which allowed the chain to expand rapidly without tying up capital in low-return real estate assets. Similar "off-balance-sheet financing" was later used in Euro Disney's financial structure. Wilson also devised a hedging plan to protect the income from Tokyo Disneyland royalty sources from fluctuations in the yen/dollar exchange rate.

Search for Low-Cost Capital. As Gary Wilson argued, a CFO created value just like skillful marketing and operating executives, by creativity. In finance, that meant creativity in deal-structuring and balance-sheet management.

There are two key things on which a strategic CFO must focus: first, investing the company's assets productively to achieve its strategic objectives, and second, financing the assets at the optimum cost of capital. So on the left-hand side of the balance sheet, we must invest in assets to provide growth at our targeted returns, and on the right-hand side, we must finance the assets in a way to optimize the cost of capital. Optimizing the cost of capital means a generous sprinkling of relatively low-cost debt, because it's the cheapest form of financing.[5]

In the late '80s, film financing exemplified Disney's search for the optimum cost of capital. In 1991 Disney discovered still another vehicle to raise low-cost capital: it sold bonds to the public to finance its network TV business. Like limited partnerships in film financing, the (seemingly attractive) zero coupon bonds created a "win-win" situation for Disney.

Though Wilson left Disney in 1989, he was followed by an imaginative dealmaking corps. Widely admired for its creative financings, the group was responsible for a $2.25 billion convertible debt issue (the largest in U.S. history) of liquid yield option notes (LYONs) to finance Euro Disney. In 1990 they raised $600 million in a debt-and-equity film financing package known as Touchwood.

Disney/Silver Screen Partnerships: $1 Billion of Low-Cost Capital. Until 1976, limited partnership structures served as significant tax-shelter vehicles in the United States. During the 1976–86 period, tax-code changes allowed only the amount at risk to be written off against income by film "owners," while investment tax credits (ITCs) were to be accrued from the date of initial release. The ITCs were a major cash source for movie and TV series producers until the Tax Reform Act of 1986 (which resulted in the demise of ITCs). After 1986, Silver Screen Partners raised $1 billion for 80 Disney movies. (Except for Silver Screen partnerships, investing in movies was a low-return high-risk business.)[6]

- Silver Screen Partners I raised $83 million in total capital (1983);
- Silver Screen II generated $193 million (1985);
- Silver Screen III raised $300 million (1987);
- Silver Screen IV brought in a whopping $400 million in total capital (1988).

All Silver Screen offerings were profitable, while the stakes grew rapidly and returns declined, from a high of $949 per $1,000 invested in 1987 (19 pictures including *Good Morning, Vietnam, Three Men and a Baby*, and *Who Framed Roger Rabbit?*) to $125 in 1988. Of the $1.7 billion of film financing raised via partnerships through the '80s, *more than half* went to Disney. While Disney financed its films off-balance-sheet at a relatively low cost, investors were paid a rate of 13–18% interest. Later, with the Touchwood-produced films, the investors lost their recoupment protection and cross-collateralization benefits, while principal guarantees were paid in noninflation-adjusted dollars—the basic terms were rewritten to better serve Disney's interests. Moreover, with the tax revision of 1986 and the crash of October 1987, investor interest declined.

After stalling negotiations with Silver Screen, Disney began looking for low-cost capital in Japan. In September 1990 Disney made an agreement with Nomura Babcock & Brown (NBB), a unit of Nomura Securities, to finance pictures made for Disney by Interscope, the independent production company that had made *Three Men and a Baby* and several other hits.[7]

Touchwood Pacific Partners I, L.P. In mid-September 1990 Disney replaced the U.S. limited partnerships with a financial package of more than $600 million spearheaded by Japanese institutional investors. Touchwood Pacific Partners was estimated to be the largest single such financing in Hollywood history and the largest infusion yet of Japanese money into a major studio short of acquisition. While other Hollywood studios were expected to follow Disney's lead to access the Japanese market, Japanese investors enjoyed tax benefits not available to U.S. investors, even when taxed both in the United States and Japan.[8]

The Japanese government, however, was about to treat tax proceeds from the investment as any investment in stock. With Touchwood, Disney was paying out at most about 6% to Japanese investors (instead of the 15% return to U.S. investors in the Silver Screen partnerships) who had little chance of fully recouping their initial $191 million investment.

The Touchwood affair taught Japanese investors that it was very risky to get an equity position in the film but not the company. It made Japanese investment capital cautious.

Toward a Production Kingdom?

After the mid-'80s Disney seemed invulnerable. By the 1990–91 contraction, however, attendance at theme parks fell by as much as 18%, while the studio released a series of duds, from *Scenes from a Mall* to *The Marrying Man*. Even Katzenberg's famous memo unwittingly contributed to anxiety about the company's future: "we are entering a period of great danger

Table 5-4
The Walt Disney Company: Business Segments (1985–93)

	Theme Parks and Resorts	Filmed Entertainment	Consumer Products	Total
Revenues ($mil.)				
1993	$3,441	$3,673	$1,415	$8,529
(%)				
1993	40%	43%	17%	100%
1992	44	42	14	100
1991	47	42	12	100
1990	52	39	10	100
1989	57	35	9	100
1988	60	33	7	100
1987	64	30	6	100
1986	70	24	6	100
1985	74	19	7	100
Operating Income ($mil.)				
1993	$747	$622	$355	$1,725
1993	43%	36%	21%	100%
1992	45	35	20	100
1991	50	29	21	100
1990	60	23	17	100
1989	64	21	15	100
1988	64	21	15	100
1987	71	17	13	100
1986	77	10	14	100
1985	74	10	16	100

SOURCE: Industry reports.

and even greater uncertainty. Events are unfolding within and without the movie industry that are extremely threatening to our studio."[9]

Amid the contraction, Disney enjoyed the support of the Bass brothers. After 1984 the Basses had some 25% of Disney, at the cost of almost half a billion dollars. Despite the brothers' breakup, their stake in Disney remained 18.6% in 1991. Though 6% smaller, the stake's worth had soared to $2.8 billion.[10]

Walt Disney: Business Segments

With the opening of Walt Disney World and the '70s decline in film revenues, the economic importance of theme parks and resorts rose rapidly. Synergy went hand in hand with a cost leadership strategy. "At the core of [Disney's] philosophy is the idea of synergy—a word Eisner is credited with introducing and applying," noted one observer. "Disney executives now use it so frequently that it is often accompanied by an apology. In lieu of synergy, it might also be called the blood-out-of-the-turnip approach: If there's a drop left, it will be found and exploited."[11] In the early '90s Disney's theme parks and resorts remained its core business (see Table 5-4).

Theme Parks and Resorts. Disney owned and operated theme parks and resorts at Disneyland (Anaheim, California) and at Walt Disney World (Orlando, Florida). In addition, it earned royalties on the Tokyo Disneyland theme park and was an equity investor in Euro Disney. Under the new Disney team, theme parks began a massive expansion in the mid-'80s, focusing on the previously neglected hotel niche. A major factor in the increasing profitability of the theme parks was Disney's eagerness to exploit price hikes (which made the parks vulnerable to price sensitivity and economic contraction). With new entrants in theme parks (MCA/Universal, Sony/Columbia, Time Warner), competition in the theme-park business grew tighter. From 1985 to 1993 revenues from theme parks and resorts enjoyed a double-digit growth, but the segment portion declined steadily from 74% to 40%. Disney's resorts business, with 12,400 rooms, became an increasingly important component of the total segment, growing from 24% of segment revenues to 33% during 1988–92.

Filmed Entertainment. Starting with movie production, Disney got into movie distribution and television programming in the mid-'50s. Three decades later it paid increasing attention to in-house distribution and marketing, developed a pay-TV programming service, and acquired a TV station in the Los Angeles market. From 1985 to 1992, Disney's filmed entertainment revenues grew almost 39% annually, while the segment portion increased steadily from 19% to 43% (the income segment grew from 10% to 36%).

Consumer Products. Disney's merchandise licensing around the world was a significant contributor of revenues and operating income. From 1985 to 1993, revenues from consumer products grew almost as fast as those from filmed entertainment. Just as Disney pioneered the shift from rentals to sales in home video, seeking to exploit mass-merchandising, a shift in the consumer products mix reflected Disney's focus on retailing and efforts to eliminate the middleman. In 1987 the company started selling its licensed merchandise (from T-shirts, caps, jackets, to toys and videos) in its own retail stores; by 1993, with its 250 retail outlets, Disney was the dominant player in the business.

To Disney the best antitakeover defense was to manage the business in such a way that it had a high market multiple. By 1989 Disney's market value had risen to $15.5 billion; by the early '90s the $19 billion Disney was by far the highest capitalized M&E concern. As Disney invested capital through acquisitions in existing lines of business, it could also afford to be patient and conservative, refraining from overpaying.

When Wall Street cracked the 3,000 mark in April 1991 and the stock market entered a new boom era, Disney was among the few stocks included in the Dow Jones Industrial Average. (In February 1992 Disney declared a 4-for-1 split of its common stock, the first one since a similar split in January 1986.)

By 1993, however, the company's mixed profit picture was puzzling analysts. On the one hand, there was Disney's unglamorous summer film lineup, poor performance at theme parks, Euro Disney's huge losses (by late 1993 Euro Disney's first-year loss amounted to about $930 million), the refusal to participate in the new M&A wave, and certain burdensome tax laws; on the other hand, there were some promising new films and a video release (*Aladdin*) that could bring in more than $300 million.[12]

From Acquisition Plans to Software Factory

At this point Disney seemed to prepare for a takeover of a major studio, network, or TV station. Such rumors first surfaced in spring 1990, when *Forbes* suggested that Disney was willing to acquire CBS. Soon thereafter, Disney raised $980 million in LYONs to garner the $3 billion it needed for a major acquisition. Since Paramount would have posed a significant antitrust problem (both were major distributors), Disney considered ABC. As long as Washington debated the fin-syn rules, the company's more immediate interest was WWOR-TV, which MCA was about to spin off as a separate company.[13]

At Disney, however, the 1990–91 contraction was a watershed. It highlighted the impact of cyclical fluctuations and structural problems of the U.S. economy in the company's revenue formation. It coincided with the eclipse of the honeymoon between the trade press and the new Disney team as controversies mounted over financial partnerships, inflated compensation packages, as well as adverse labor relations. Finally, the recession led to a reconsideration of Disney's corporate strategy: acquisition plans were bypassed, and the company would stand aside as rivals rushed to digital alliances with computer and telecommunications companies— Disney placed its bets on software.

Unlike most of its rivals, "Disney" had a universal cachet, which neither few duds nor contraction could harm. Mounting competition forced the studio to reinvent its animation factory, with fresh themes and new composers—from the popular commercial success of *Aladdin* to Tim Burton's *The Nightmare Before Christmas*, which redefined what was artistically permissible at the studio.[14] Though family entertainment represented some 80% of filmed entertainment operating income, Disney had the market cornered because the rest of the industry had abdicated it. But new rivals were emerging, including Warner Bros., Spielberg's Amblin Entertainment backed by Universal, and Hanna-Barbera (owned by Turner Broadcasting). Poised for renewed growth, the animation investments boosted strengthened ties between Disney and Mattel, both of which targeted children as their primary consumers, especially in the overseas markets.

Product innovation extended from animation (*Beauty and the Beast*) to feature films (*Pretty Woman*). On the one hand, Walt Disney Studios was the highly successful producer of popular family movies from *Honey, I Blew*

Up the Kids to *Sister Act*; on the other, the business match with Joe Roth and the team of James Ivory and Ismail Merchant, as well as with Miramax—an independent distributor of provocative adult films like *The Crying Game, The Grifters*, and *Cinema Paradiso*—brought significant indie niches (and extensive indie libraries) under Disney's umbrella, bringing the number of the company's annual releases to an extraordinary total of some 60 features in 1994.

By 1994 Disney was the last major Hollywood studio not owned by a foreign company or possessing extensive cable holdings. Even Euro Disney took a step away from the brink when a $1 billion plan was worked out with Disney and a steering committee representing creditor banks. Instead of seeking a larger presence in hardware (to combat electronics/entertainment giants like Sony and Matsushita), or strategic alliances with telcos, Michael Eisner and Jeffrey Katzenberg were producing more software, expanding Disney's library of filmed entertainment. As total production costs amounted to a record $1.4 billion, Katzenberg had to moderate hardball tactics; to woo producers and directors, he had to grant them unprecedented freedom.[15]

In 1993 Disney's profit fell 63%. Still, Eisner made $203.1 million (mostly in long-term compensation), the highest pay in history for any chief executive of a public corporation—and 68% of Disney's annual profit.

In April 1994 Disney's president Frank G. Wells died in a helicopter-skiing accident. Eisner took on Wells's titles of president and chief operating officer—which meant dramatically more work.

Even if everybody else seemed to enter the highly expensive battle for the new circuits of digitized entertainment, Disney bet that the copyrights on these properties would wind up being the most profitable cachet of all. The strategy would be put to a test when the indie stations that carried *The Disney Afternoon*, a profitable syndicated animation block, would become part of a fifth network.[16]

Though the company did not rule anything out (including major acquisitions or extensive distribution networks), it held that delivery systems became obsolete, unlike the entertainment that traveled through them. It was the product, as well as its synergic cross-fertilization, that ensured success in the new environment. In February 1994, for instance, Disney brought to Broadway a $10 million-plus stage production of *Beauty and the Beast*, betting that stage versions could bolster the long-term values of its animated features.[17] Just as *Snow White* and *Bambi* outlived the glamorous theatre halls, Disney hoped to beat its rivals by sticking to the basics. As the saying went, "It's the product, stupid!"

Faced with a weak economy, declining profit growth, flops at the box office, and troubles at its theme parks, Disney could no longer expect to achieve a 20% annual earnings growth. To reinvent itself, the company intended to cultivate the high-growth foreign markets, explore new technologies, and expand the responsibilities of the company's senior executives.[18] Change translated into rising costs—as well as increasing tension and dissension at the top.

NEWS CORP./FOX: EXPANSION, DEBT CRISIS, EXPANSION

In 1935 Fox Film Corporation merged with Darryl Zanuck's Twentieth Century Pictures, changing its name to Twentieth Century Fox Film Corp. In the postwar era, rising theatre attendance enabled Zanuck to build a small roster of stars. In the mid-'50s, however, changing Hollywood and personal troubles compelled him to move to Europe as an independent producer. He was succeeded by a slate of studio chiefs.[1]

During the production of the costly *Cleopatra*, the Fox board voted Zanuck, the majority stockholder, president of Twentieth Century Fox. Zanuck gave an executive position to his son, Richard, who was named president of Twentieth Century Fox Film Corp. in 1968. Two years later the studio was about to default on a $25 million loan and owed $75 million to its New York banks. Although a major U.S. corporation, it was managed like a mom-and-pop operation. Richard Zanuck assumed the throne as president, but Fox's board soon asked for his resignation, whereas Darryl Zanuck continued as company chairman and CEO.

In March 1971 Fox's financial officer Dennis Stanfill was made president of the restructured company. He closed the Fox New York headquarters, cut studio overhead, and sold off studio assets. Fox's fortunes were reversed in the mid-'70s, when Alan Ladd, Jr. was named president of the studio. Fox also formed a new entertainment group with a record division, a TV production operation, and a music publishing company. In turn, Ladd brought to Fox writer-director George Lucas, whose *Star Wars* (1977) became the most profitable movie made ever ($194 million in domestic rentals). Overwhelmed by Ladd's creative success, Stanfill replaced him with Alan J. Hirschfield, who drew many of his former colleagues at Columbia to Fox.

When Darryl Zanuck died in December 1979, Fox was busy fighting off a takeover attempt by Chris-Craft Industries. A year later Twentieth Century Fox Film Corp. was a diversified media conglomerate, comprising movie and TV businesses: a 63-acre studio lot in West Los Angeles, a record and music publishing division, a film-processing laboratory, movie theatres in Australia and New Zealand, soft-drink bottling operations, the Aspen Ski Corporation, a home-video company, a luxury resort, and other real estate in Pebble Beach, California.

From LBO Plans to Marvin Davis's Privately Held Fox
(1980–84)

Although Fox was selling at about $35 a share, the value of its assets was probably worth three–four times more. When Chris-Craft raised its stake in Fox to almost 25%, Stanfill developed a plan to ward off a potential hostile takeover by converting Fox into a privately owned corporation. When the plan unraveled in 1981, it made the studio vulnerable on Wall Street.

When Stanfill launched another attempt to take Fox private, the company was circled by sharks like Sir James Goldsmith, Saul Steinberg, and Kirk Kerkorian, as well as Chris-Craft's Herbert Siegel. Marvin Davis reduced the risk of owning Fox by bringing in a silent partner—Marc Rich, the notorious commodities trader. In February 1981 Davis made a $79-a-share offer (over $700 million). For the first time since 1925, Fox became a privately owned company, with Hirschfield as chairman and CEO.[2]

Davis bought the studio with two partners: Aetna Life and Casualty Company, and the silent partner—the secretive brokerage firm Richco of the Netherland Antilles, headed by a group of investors led by Marc Rich. He had borrowed $550 million. Davis and Rich looted Fox's assets.

In the early '80s Fox's most successful films were sequels of *Star Wars: The Empire Strikes Back* and *Return of the Jedi*. The hits also included *9 to 5*, *The Cannonball Run*, and *Porky's*. By the mid-'80s Fox released hits like *Mr. Mom*, *Romancing the Stone*, and *Cocoon*, but lost its creative edge.

Davis and Rich used little of the profits to repay the studio's bank debts, most of which was refinanced and shifted onto the studio. In 1983 Rich fled the United States; he was being charged in the biggest tax evasion case in American history. As the studio's long-term debt nearly doubled in a year, banks pressured Davis to bring in new management.

In early 1984 Barry Diller, a Paramount executive, wanted to purchase half of Fox. Davis offered him a fourth and a lucrative deal to run the studio; Lawrence Gordon, an independent producer, was named president of the newly formed entertainment group. When Diller began a dramatic restructuring, he was in open warfare with Davis, who sold part of his stake to Rupert Murdoch (who, in turn, gave Fox an additional $88 million to get the studio going). Both Murdoch and Diller wanted to get rid of Davis.

News Corp. and Fox

A few years after his father's death in 1952, Rupert Murdoch took over his father's newspaper business in Sydney (the *Mirror*) and entered the Australian television industry. No longer a regional player, he broke into the tightly regulated and lucrative big-city markets. In the mid-'60s Murdoch launched a national newspaper (the *Australian*) that would enhance his operations with increasing political influence. Determined not to repeat his father's mistake, he would retain control over the business and use leverage to finance expansion. "The way to operate," he would say, "is with OPM—other people's money."[3]

In the late '60s Murdoch moved to London to internationalize his operations. The highly profitable *News of the World,* the largest among the Sunday newspapers, heralded the beginning of acquisitions in the United Kingdom. It was followed by the purchase of the daily *Sun* and a controlling interest in London Weekend Television. In the early '70s Murdoch returned to Australia and bought the *Telegraph* for its goodwill value of $17.5 million. While the deal expanded Murdoch's Australian media empire, its significance lay in the manipulation of local accounting rules.

By 1973 Murdoch's growing media empire comprised about 80 newspapers, 11 magazines, TV and radio stations, and printing, paper, and shipping companies in the United Kingdom, Australia, and New Zealand. These holdings were controlled by two major companies: News International (Europe) and News Limited (Australia).

To become a truly international player Murdoch moved his family to New York City, to break into the American market.

Murdoch's Entry into the U.S. Market

To tap into the *National Enquirer* readership of 5 million, Murdoch developed a lower cost weekly tabloid, the *National Star* (his first entirely new publication) and purchased the *New York Post.* Exploiting the accounting differences between the United States and Australia, he presented the *Post*'s estimated goodwill value to Australian banks to raise money for the purchase. With his 1977 acquisitions (*New York* magazine, the *Village Voice*), the Australian mogul gambled his way to the big leagues of American newspaper publishing.

Reorganization: Fox Inc. In March 1984 Marvin Davis sold his remaining 50% of Fox to Murdoch for $162 million (the entire cash outlay was significantly higher). Interest payments forced John Kluge to sell Metromedia's TV and radio stations for Murdoch, despite a $1.6 billion LBO. After the purchase of his new film library and a distribution and production arm, Murdoch bought jointly with Marvin Davis seven Metromedia TV stations for a total of $2 billion. To ensure entry into television, Murdoch applied for U.S. citizenship in May 1985; he wanted to build a fourth network. In November he consolidated the studio and the TV stations under a new corporate parent, Fox Inc. By the early '90s, the corporate structure had evolved into Twentieth Century Fox Film Corp. (movie, TV, home video, and film processing operations), Fox Broadcasting Company (TV network), and Fox Television Stations (TV stations). Legally, the entities had to be separated by "Chinese walls"; a network (15 hours of prime-time programming a week by the FCC definition) would not be allowed to remain in TV syndication, where Fox made much of its money.

The Creation of HarperCollins. In January 1986 Murdoch, who had been publishing books in Australia, entered the industry in the United States (Salem House, Merrimack Publishers Circle). In 1987–88 Murdoch acquired controlling stakes, took over, and merged into one entity (HarperCollins) the Harper & Row and the (British) William Collins & Sons. Like Bertelsmann, Hachette, and Paramount, Murdoch was pushing globalization of publishing operations.[4]

Meanwhile, a bitter strike in British newspaper publishing prompted concern over Murdoch's ability to manage his investments in London and debt burden in the United States.

Building Fox Broadcasting Company. Diller took charge of Fox's movie division, station group, planning for the new network, and hired youthful managers (Jamie Kellner, Scott Sassa, David Johnson, Garth Ancier) who shared his vision. The Fox Broadcasting Company (FBC) was launched with *The Late Show Starring Joan Rivers.* By mid-summer 1989 FBC beat the Big Three in three different time slots (*Married . . . with Children, America's Most Wanted, Totally Hidden Video*). In 1990 Fox posted its first 12-month profit. The secret in FBC's growth lay in the expansion of its distribution and its product innovation.

Between February 1986 and December 1991, FBC's affiliates grew from 9 stations to 138 (93% coverage). As half of the 180 station members of the Association of Independent Television Stations became Fox affiliates, FBC undid the effort by Paramount and MCA to launch Premiere, the "fifth network." Fearing that cable affiliates would be favored over traditional broadcasters, the courtship between FBC and TCI concerned FBC's broadcast affiliates. (In 1993 these concerns resurfaced as Fox launched a basic cable network.)[5]

Initially, product development strategy involved risk-taking in program content (*Married . . . with Children*). The strategy also took into account audience diversity (*In Living Color, True Colors, Roc*), while seeking for increased segmentation (*21 Jump Street, The Simpsons, Beverly Hills, 90210*). Bart Simpson became FBC's first licensing and merchandising hit. Ultimately, product development focused on costs. Fox's new program economics led to a proliferation of "reality-based" programming, which stemmed from tabloid journalism (*A Current Affair, Reporters*), law-and-order programs (*Cops, America's Most Wanted*), and confrontational talk shows (*Morton Downey, Jr. Show*). By 1991–92 *Studs*, another product of Fox Television Stations unit, was setting new standards for "relationship shows," as well as for inexpensive programming costs.[6]

Fox's production arm passed a difficult period before the appointment of Joe Roth to head the studio. In the '70s it held a theatrical-film market leadership three times; in the '80s, only once. By mid-1989 restructuring signaled a new emphasis on motion pictures. Under Roth, Fox's market share increased from 6% to 14%, with hits like *Broadcast News* and *Working Girl*. With its expanding production objectives, Fox joined the increasing number of Hollywood studios and production firms seeking financial backing from Japan. In August 1991 a Swiss insurance company agreed to invest $80 million toward the production and advertising of eight consecutive Fox films, for a one-third interest in each film.

From Globalization to Debt Problems

After the mid-'80s Murdoch focused on the consolidation of his global M&E empire in the United States, the United Kingdom, Australia, and the Orient.

Acquisition of Triangle Publications

In 1988 Murdoch continued his acquisition spree in the United States and purchased Triangle Publications (including the highly profitable *TV Guide*) from Walter H. Annenberg, for $3 billion. While the purchase raised the asset value of Murdoch's empire to $11 billion, its debt soared from $237 million to $7 billion (1983–88). Hence the divestitures of underperforming assets, real estate, and a half interest in *Elle* magazine.

It was the European DBS venture that almost destroyed Murdoch, causing News Corp. to suffer a 60% drop in profits in 1989. Moreover, Murdoch lost out to Qintex after bidding for MGM/UA.

"Pyramiding of Leverage"

While debt served as an inflation hedge (price level gains during inflationary times), interest (unlike dividends) was considered an expense and, therefore, tax deductible. Through most of the '80s Murdoch had debt capital readily available. He borrowed from Australian banks against his holding company, and took advantage of different tax and accounting laws in Australia, the United Kingdom, and the United States.

"Pyramiding of leverage" worked as long as the cash flow from the acquired properties covered the debt service. An overlapping partnership structure allowed Murdoch to reinvest profits back into operations, instead of paying dividends to shareholders. From 1985 to 1989, News Corp.'s revenues nearly quadrupled and net income increased sixfold. As a result of the M&A spree, total assets grew 11-fold, to almost $21 billion. Concurrently, long-term debt increased twice as fast, up to $7.2 billion. With the leverage crisis, Murdoch did cut the debt. Still, the debt ratio soared from 30–45% to more than *110%*.

Although News Corp. enjoyed credibility in the United States, banks were suspicious of its heavy reliance on accounting policies that employed a controversial revaluation practice, which boosted asset values and rein-

Table 5-5
News Corp.: Business Segments (1984–93)

Year	Total	News-papers	Maga-zines	Tele-vision	Filmed Entert.	Book Publ.	Comm. Printing	Other
Revenues (A$mil)								
1994	A$11,621	A$2,894	A$1,654	A$2,103	A$3,093	A$1,597	–	A$280
1993	10,686	3,070	1,656	1,614	2,623	1,513	–	210
1992*	10,189	2,955	1,644	1,235	2,424	1,453	–	479
1991	10,971	3,088	1,308	1,331	2,199	1,555	A$495	993
1990	8,763	3,016	1,445	1,172	1,265	–	516	1,350
1989	7,880	2,904	1,172	745	1,208	–	473	1,378
1988	6,019	2,569	610	564	1,184	–	260	832
1987	5,318	2,020	571	687	1,388	–	177	475
1986	3,823	1,965	512	351	550	–	148	296
1985	2,447	1,600	340	194	–	–	121	193
1984	1,866	1,253	226	135	–	–	113	138
Operating Income (A$mil)								
1994	A$1,597	A$436	A$339	A$466	A$141	A$208	–	A$7
1993	1,702	671	402	373	53	202	–	2
1992	1,591	591	382	260	127	204	–	28
1991	1,558	522	281	123	211	205	A$55	161
1990	1,357	650	319	7	109	–	57	215
1989	1,452	687	276	100	121	–	50	219
1988	1,030	479	106	83	121	–	22	218
1987	847	360	103	115	172	–	19	79
1986	534	153	97	54	77	–	17	135
1985	164	80	55	9	–	–	7	14
1984	154	76	40	8	–	–	6	25

* In 1992, News Corp. eliminated its segment of commercial printing, whereas magazines became magazines and inserts. The change affected the results in "magazines" and "other" segments.

SOURCE: News Corp. (various issues).

forced Murdoch's borrowing power. Moreover, bankers had become wearier of risk.[7]

Diversification

In the early '90s News Corp. was a holding company, with principal subsidiaries in the United States (News America Holdings, Inc.), in the United Kingdom (News International PLC), in Australia and the Pacific Basin (News Limited). It operated in newspapers, magazines, television, filmed entertainment, and book publishing. In the United States the focus was on TV and entertainment (Table 5-5).

Between the mid-'80s and 1994, revenues from News Corp.'s TV segment grew almost sixteenfold, representing about 18% of total (29% of operating income). The segment's operating income fluctuated dramatically, due to FBC's initial losses and the European satellite ventures. In filmed entertainment, revenues more than doubled in 1986–87 and since 1989 they have risen to 27% of the total. While operating income has fluctuated drastically, high costs have reduced the segment's operating income, which remained less than 9% of the total in 1994.

From Print Media to Electronic Media. Since the mid-'80s Murdoch had steered News Corp. away from newspapers, which he thought were in long-term decline, toward electronic media, where he saw the prospect of long-term growth. In reality, fortunes went hand in hand with business cycles. From 1984 to 1987, electronic media revenues (TV, filmed entertainment) increased from 8% to 39% of total, plunging to 24–28% in 1988–90. After two market crashes and a severe economic contraction, electronic media revenues resumed their growth, increasing to 45% of total in 1994—as against 53% from newspapers, magazines, and book publishing.

Operating income from electronic media reveals a more volatile pattern. In 1993 it lingered at 25%; a year later it jumped to 38%. Meanwhile, the portion of publishing revenues declined from 75% to 62%. Like the Japanese, Murdoch took the long view: "We don't deal in market share," Murdoch once remarked. "We *create* the market."[8] In the midst of contraction and uncertainty, such a strategic posture was synonymous with financial masochism, but amidst growth and stability it supported visionary prospects.

As shareholders gave Murdoch a mandate to raise equity through new classes of shares that would not dilute his controlling stake, he negotiated a new financing agreement that eased the cash crunch. With the plunge in stock prices, Murdoch also cut back dramatically on spending by merging Sky TV, the British satellite broadcasting venture, with its major competitor, British Sky Broadcasting.[9] Still, News Corp. had to wipe $6 billion from its balance sheet to comply with U.S. regulations governing the valuation of assets. The write-down confirmed the suspicion that the company's book value was overstated.

Debt Pact. In the late '80s News Corp.'s acquisitions, ventures, and investments were financed primarily with short-term bank debt because the funding cost was relatively low, bank loans were available, and the refinancing of such loans at maturity was not expected to be difficult. When the company entered its debt crisis, banks were suffering a liquidity crisis of their own and Murdoch found it hard to refinance maturing bank facilities and meet working capital requirements. In February 1991 News Corp. reached a three-year banking agreement with 146 financial institutions. The agreements committed amounts of some $7.8 billion of $8.2 billion in debts. Under the agreement, News Corp. received a $600 million bridge loan to cover its current cash squeeze. To Murdoch, the pact gave operating flexibility, without watering down the family holdings.[10]

News Corp.'s rapid expansion and rising debt had strained Murdoch and highlighted weaknesses in the corporate structure. In September 1990 he quietly moved longtime CFO Richard Sarazen to a new post as senior executive VP, promoting deputy CFO David DeVoe to CFO. When the debt pact was announced in February 1991, August Fischer was appointed the new CFO. Another round of executive shuffle began in 1992, when

Barry Diller stunned Hollywood by resigning as chairman of Fox. He and Murdoch had clashed over who would run Fox, or own it.[11]

Having left the running of his newspapers to others and sold most of his U.S. publications, Murdoch assumed Diller's title and duties at Fox. When Joe Roth, Fox's film division president, left for Disney, Murdoch moved his main base of operations from New York to Los Angeles. Financial turmoil and executive shuffle brought to a halt the FBC plan to globalize its operations. Looking to older viewers for stability, the network had to expand the audience if it wanted to keep advertising revenues growing.[12]

In November 1993 FBC suffered from demographic decline and 8 of the 10 returning shows showed a ratings drop.[13] Only a month later it beat out mighty CBS for the National Football League's broadcasts. The $1.56 billion bid topped CBS's by some $100 million a year. While industry observers expected annual losses of $150 million, the football package enhanced FBC's clout in the network rivalry.

An Era of Cost-Cutting

In 1991 News Corp.'s massive deleveraging effort continued with the sale of nine of News Corp.'s U.S. consumer publications to K-III Holdings, controlled by Kohlberg, Kravis, Roberts, for $600 million. Murdoch also issued 65 million additional shares, hoping to put News Corp. on sounder financial footing as it strove to reduce debt. In 1992 the deleveraging effort continued with still another $300 million debt offering as part of its ongoing financial restructuring, as well as a planned global issue of $1.7 billion of debt and equity securities. The ensuing financial stability enhanced News Corp.'s repositioning in the United States and Europe.[14]

In September 1992 News Corp. posted a strong return to profitability. Through asset sales and news offerings of debt and equity, Murdoch had raised nearly $2 billion, while working on refinancing $2.4 billion.

By 1993 Murdoch was systematically remaking Fox in his own image, hiring veteran News Corp. executives who shared his economic credo and populist sensibilities. Concurrently, he began another round of global empire building.[15]

In July, after being blocked in an attempt to buy a 22% share of Hong Kong's biggest TV station, News Corp. acquired 64% of Star TV, a major player in Asia's fast-growing satellite TV industry (through which he hoped to ensure access to 45 million viewers in 38 countries), for $525 million in cash and stock. The sum nearly equaled the market value of Murdoch's stake in the *South China Morning Post*, Hong Kong's principal English-language newspaper and a highly profitable unit (he was negotiating a sale of his 50% controlling interest in that paper).

The year 1993 witnessed a flurry of deals, including:

- an expanded slate of programming for British Sky Broadcasting, the largest satellite and cable service in the United Kingdom and Europe, of which News Corp. was half owner;
- the acquisition of Delphi Internet Services, a U.S.-based on-line data services firm;
- a joint venture with British Telecom and the cellular communications firm Cellnet to develop an information superhighway for the British market;
- the launch of a Latin American cable TV service;
- the launch of the new Fox cable channel, FX (1994);
- the acquisition of 15% stake in Australia's Seven Network for $408 million;
- the creation of originally programmed "global channels," (e.g., open university, arts channel);
- a joint venture with Pro 7, a German satellite channel with close ties to Germany's Kirch Group media empire, for the launch of a premium service and minipay package in Germany (January 1994);
- an agreement with Mexico's Grupo Televisa S.A., the world's largest Spanish-language broadcaster, to coproduce 500 hours of programs annually;
- the coming introduction of a second sports channel to supplement Sky Sports· in the United Kingdom;
- a plan to create a common digital satellite system for global use.[16]

At the core of the expansion was Fox, Inc., News Corp.'s U.S.-based film and TV production company, which provided a critical building block for entertainment services across different media and across the globe. Or, as Murdoch put it, in News Corp.'s 1992 *Annual Report,*

The more we think about our business, and the more we look at the whole communications industry in all its facets, the more we define ourselves as a global supplier of what is now called "software." For us, the hardware developments that attract so much attention are secondary to our real business.[17]

In May 1994 New World Communications Group, Inc., controlled by financier Ronald O. Perelman, dumped all 12 of its network affiliations (8 of them with CBS), and, instead, signed on with Murdoch's Fox. In exchange, Murdoch agreed to invest $500 million for a minority stake in New World. Although the "midnight raid" vaulted Fox into the same league as the Big Three, it was a costly strategy. The Australian mogul thought dominance in broadcast distribution was critical in the coming electronic superhighways.[18]

But, sooner or later, even the graying Murdoch, who remained constantly on the move, would have to face realities. In a global corporation, autocratic rule obstructed change and innovation. Just as family businesses thrive in entrepreneurialism, a global scale has its requirements. A global corporation was not a "one-man show."

SONY/COLUMBIA: HARDWARE/SOFTWARE COMBINE

Without capital resources, Columbia Pictures lacked theatre ownership; without exhibition, it could not become vertically integrated; and without vertical integration, it could not compete against the Big Five studios. It would long be one of the Little Three. Under the leadership of Jack and Harry Cohn, Columbia Pictures was the only Poverty Row studio that evolved into a major corporation.[1]

Columbia Pictures

Without debt and theatres, Columbia was spared from the Depression. With Frank Capra's comedies (*It Happened One Night, Mr. Smith Goes to Washington*), it made profits. By the mid-'30s it was a Wall Street favorite; and by the '40s it operated in movie production, foreign and domestic distribution, as well as film processing.

Columbia had its best years in the postwar period (*A Song To Remember, The Jolson Story, Gilda,* and *All the King's Men*). Even in the '50s the studio made hits (*From Here to Eternity, The Bridge on the River Kwai*). As the Cohns left the company, transition followed. Going into the red, it was saved by TV production. As early as 1952, Columbia established a subsidiary, Screen Gems (Columbia Pictures Television in 1976), to produce and distribute TV programs (*The Ford Theater, Father Knows Best*).

In the early '60s Columbia had popular hits (*Guns of Navarone, Lawrence of Arabia*), but profit margins were declining. By the end of the decade, *Funny Girl*, starring Barbra Streisand, was Columbia's only major U.S.-made hit.

Columbia Pictures Industries

In 1968–69 Columbia Pictures Corporation was reorganized as Columbia Pictures Industries, Inc. (CPI). When CPI's debt ratio exceeded 90% in 1973, Allen & Co., an investment banking house, came in as Columbia's financial adviser and its largest shareholder. A new management team (Alan Hirschfield, David Begelman, and Peter Guber) restored Columbia's financial health with hits like *Shampoo, Murder by Death, Taxi Driver, The Deep,* and *Close Encounters of the Third Kind.* When a major embezzlement scandal forced Begelman to resign, it hurt both CPI and the entire industry, prompting still another executive shuffle. The new chairman, Herbert Allen, Jr., the scion of Allen & Co., replaced Hirschfield with Fay Vincent as CPI's president and Frank Price succeeded Begelman as head of movie production.[2]

As major M&E companies diversified into other businesses, CPI decided it needed a strong parent company to inject the necessary capital. In June 1982, the Coca-Cola Company acquired all of CPI's outstanding capital stock.

Coca-Cola and Columbia

When Roberto Goizueta took over Coca-Cola, it operated in a single industry. Since 1965 the flagship soft drink had been losing market share in the United States against Pepsi-Cola; by the mid-'80s soft drinks generated over 80% (earnings were higher) and foods less than 20% of Coca-Cola's net operating revenues. When Arthur D. Little suggested that Coca-Cola should buy into entertainment, CPI was a natural target with its 1,800 movies. The studio had made several hits (*Kramer vs. Kramer, Stir Crazy, Stripes, Tootsie, Gandhi*); and its earnings growth was impressive. Coca-Cola hoped to employ CPI in marketing, as well as to lessen heavy exposure to overseas markets. CPI became the flagship of Coca-Cola's Entertainment Business Sector (EBS).[3]

From Tri-Star Pictures to Columbia Pictures Entertainment

In November 1982 CBS, Home Box Office, and CPI formed a new major producer/distributor. It was conceived in discussions between Fay Vincent and Victor Kaufman, who became Tri-Star Pictures' chairman and CEO. The new entity had three major areas of business: it produced and acquired motion pictures for distribution in foreign and domestic markets; it commenced TV production, distribution, and syndication following the sale by CBS of its interest in the company; and it acquired the Loews theatre circuit. In December 1987 the combination of EBS and Tri-Star prompted the latter to change its name to Columbia Pictures Entertainment, Inc. (CPE).

From 1978 to 1989 CPE had four different chiefs: Frank Price, an MCA-trained corporatist; Guy McElwaine, an ex-agent; David Puttnam, a preachy British producer (whose era remained the shortest in recent Hollywood history); and Dawn Steel, a veteran of the Paramount production wars. While Coca-Cola took good care of CPE's TV division, the studio began to post deficits. As the anticipated synergies failed to materialize, CPE was no longer a strategic asset. Coca-Cola renounced its diversification plans and divested itself of several subsidiaries. In November 1989 Sony bought Coca-Cola's stake in CPE for $1.55 billion.[4]

Sony Corporation: From Electronics to Entertainment

In the three decades after World War II, Sony became world famous for its product innovation, a world leader in the development, manufacture, and sale of consumer electronics, as well as video technology.[5]

In 1946 Akio Morita, Masaru Ibuka, and Tamon Maeda (Ibuka's father-in-law) incorporated Tokyo Telecommunications Engineering (TKK). TKK's personnel grew over tenfold in the '50s and four times in the '60s; unlike established Japanese companies, it was not bound by old corporate traditions and relied little on the government and banks; it began internationalizing well before the rivals.

In 1955, a year after beginning transistor production, TKK launched one of the world's first transistor radios. These were followed by the first Sony-trademarked product, a pocket-sized radio, as well as transistor television and videotape recorder. (By the mid-'60s the company launched its first eight-inch set, electronic desktop calculator, video recorder, solid-state condenser microphone, and integrated circuit-based radio.)

In 1958, TKK changed its name to Sony Kabushiki Kaisha—Sony Corporation.

Sony: Global Company, Quality Products

In the United States, Morita founded the Sony Corporation of America. In 1963 he moved to New York to better understand the U.S. market and to oversee the U.S. expansion. With its quality products, Sony assumed leadership in new electronics markets. In the '70s Morita was promoted to Sony's president as well as to chairman and CEO.

Focusing on breakthrough products, Sony sought "new and different" solutions. When, for example, color television began invading the U.S. market in 1964, most manufacturers operated under RCA's "shadow mask" system; in 1967 Sony introduced Trinitron. The new color picture tube employed a one-gun, three-beam electron gun system. In a year, Trinitron dominated the small-screen market in Japan.

By fiscal 1974 Sony's overseas net sales exceeded domestic sales; in 1980 foreign sales climaxed at 75%. Intense growth slowed in the early '80s, when Sony faced two major setbacks: the struggle over the VCR standard and the decline in sales. Both accelerated the shift to software.

The Beta Failure. In 1956 the first practical videotape recorder (VTR), the Quadruplex, was introduced by Ampex, an American company. By 1965 Sony developed its first home use VTR, the CV-2000. Since open-reel tapes were not good in the home market, the company also developed the first videocassette recorder (VCR), the Sony U-Matic. In 1974 Sony completed a prototype Beta VCR and showed it to its competitors (as it had with U-Matic) to persuade them to agree on a standard industry format. Despite resistance (Matsushita considered the one-hour playing time inadequate), Morita introduced Beta to the marketplace, whereas Matsushita developed a VHS format that could record for two hours. In early 1977 Sony announced a two-hour Beta recorder, but Matsushita responded with a four-hour design. Sony was defeated in the marketplace.[6]

Slowdown in Sales. In the early '80s Sony produced two new examples of product innovation: the Walkman sound system and the Mavica all-electronic still-camera system. But the electronics industry was maturing, which reduced sales. Although total net sales grew from the early '70s to the early '80s, net income often showed negative growth. The pioneering spirit that had made Sony known worldwide was turning against the company (high R&D costs, first-mover expenses, and risks).

In the early '80s, Sony's top executives decided to reposition the company. Morita's successor, Norio Ohga, Sony's president and COO, would mastermind the new strategy. (Ohga and Morita first combined their efforts to introduce the CD.) Instead of hardware innovations, the new Sony would make money by selling its technology as well as diversify in what it considered audio- and image-based software.

Software Acquisitions

Initially, the motion picture industry objected to the new VCR technology, fearing that it would pose a threat to theatres. In reality, VCRs revived the movie business and caused the home video boom. Initially, too, the record industry objected to the new CD technology, fearing retailers would not carry both records and CDs. Yet, by the early '80s, the hardware (CD) and software (music) drove each other's sales.

Acquisition of CBS Records. From 1982 to 1986 revenues for CBS Records grew from almost $1.1 billion to $1.5 billion, while profits soared from $22 million to $192 billion. In 1988 Sony acquired CBS Records for $2 billion, which provided Sony with headway for the diversification of its operations in the United States. Now the company needed "image-based software" to augment its audio-based software, and both to complement its electronics hardware.[7]

Acquisition of Columbia Pictures Entertainment. In September 1989 Sony approved a $3.4 billion offer for all outstanding shares of Columbia. Walter Yetnikoff, head of CBS Records, played a major role in the deal (with his friends Peter Guber and Jon Peters, the producers of Warner Bros.' *Batman*). Sony was expected to use Columbia's library of 2,700 feature films and 23,000 episodes of 260 TV series episodes to push new forms of hardware, such as Sony's 8mm video format, laser discs, and HDTV telecasts and cassettes. The acquisition was followed by Warner Bros.'s $1 billion suit against Sony and Guber-Peters. Sony countersued, charging WB with trying to sabotage its acquisition and hurt its efforts to enter the U.S. movie business. By mid-November the parties reached a hefty billion-dollar settlement. Sony overpaid for its acquisition, heavily.

On January 1, 1991, CBS Records, Inc. was renamed Sony Music Entertainment, Inc. Under CBS the unit had been in the record business; under Sony the subsidiary was to produce music and image-based software to feed the parent's electronics operations, especially audio equipment. Similarly, the motion picture holdings were consolidated into Sony Pictures

Entertainment, Inc. While, financially, the Columbia purchase preceded the burst of Japan's bubble economy and overheated stock market, it made Sony a prime scapegoat of the Japanese buying activities in the United States.

A New Corporate Mission

In the late '80s Sony's corporate mission shifted from a product orientation to a customer orientation. As Theodore Levitt noted in a classic essay on "Marketing Myopia" (1960), American railroads "defined their industry wrong . . . because they were railroad-oriented instead of transportation-oriented; they were product-oriented instead of customer-oriented." The point was as familiar to Peter Guber and Jon Peters as it was to Sony itself.[8] While the concept of the hardware/software combination derived from the mid-'80s, the implications became apparent in the early '90s.

A Strategic Dichotomy. Since entertainment was not closely related to its traditional core strengths, Sony sought control of CBS Records and Columbia, which retained full autonomy. With hardware, however, Sony sought competitive strength through extensive access to outside resources; it was content with partial control on the basis of ongoing mutual adjustments, seeking merely to share risks. In electronics (hardware), strategic alliances; in entertainment (software), strategic acquisitions.

Reorganization of U.S. Operations

Prior to its U.S. acquisitions in the late '80s, Sony had been a 100% electronics operation; by the early '90s the split was 70–30 between hardware and software. With CBS Records and Columbia, operations were refocused from Tokyo to New York and Los Angeles.

Rewarded for his role in the U.S. acquisitions, Michael Schulhof had been deputy president of Sony USA and vice-chairman of Sony Corp. of America. Rewarded for his role in the U.S. acquisitions, he became president of Sony USA, Inc. and the first American to be named to Sony's board. His new task was to integrate Sony's various businesses in the United States and to seek synergies. In spite of the restructuring and Schulhof's rise, the power at the company remained centralized. Sony was still run by its chairman, Akio Morita, and its president and CEO, Norio Ohga. In the United States, Sony USA, Inc. oversaw the Japanese company's consumer electronics, motion picture, and recorded music operations, while Ohga served as Sony USA's chairman, and Masaaki Morita (Akio Morita's brother) as its executive vice-chairman and CEO.[9]

In January 1991 Sony created a new U.S.-based company, Sony Software Corporation, which put film, music, and electronic publishing under one umbrella. Schulhof was named president. Previously, he had reported to

Figure 5-2
Sony's U.S. Operations (1991)

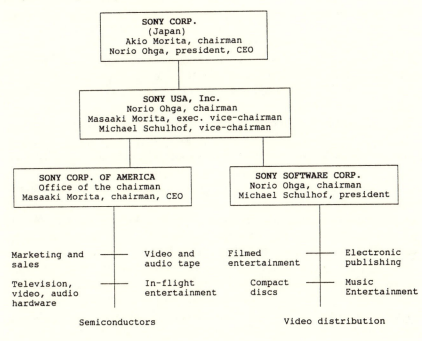

SOURCE: Company reports.

Masaaki Morita; in his new post, he reported directly to Ohga (see Figure 5-2).

Sony Corp.: Business Segments

By fiscal 1993 Sony's sales amounted to $34.4 billion, with $27.3 billion from electronics and $7.2 billion from entertainment. Electronic operations consisted of four basic segments:

Video Equipment. Home-use VTRs, laserdisc players, video equipment for broadcast and professional use, HDTV-related equipment, and videotapes.

Audio Equipment. CD players, minicomponent stereos, hi-fi components, radiocassette tape recorders, headphone stereos, digital audio tape players, radios, car stereos, audiotapes, professional-use audio equipment, ultra-small digital micro recorders, and transmission receivers.

Televisions. Color televisions/monitors, HDTV-related equipment, satellite broadcast reception systems, projectors, professional-use displays, and large color video display systems.

Other Products. Semiconductors, electronic components, information-related equipment, telecommunications equipment, computers and peripherals, and factory automation systems.

Sony remained a hardware vendor, with electronics bringing in 75% of revenues and about half of operating income. It was strong in several key technologies that powered next-generation products: magnetic and optical storage, including CD-ROM formats, semi-conductors, and wireless communications. It was already the world leader in consumer electronics, professional broadcast equipment, CD-ROM disks, as well as airline video systems.

Entertainment operations comprised two basic segments:

Music Entertainment. Represented by Sony Music Entertainment, Inc., which included Columbia, Epic, Epic/Associated, Chaos, Sony Classical, Sony Music Video Enterprises, Sony Kids' Music, Sony Kids' Video, Soho Square, and Associated Labels; and Sony Music Entertainment (Japan) Inc.

Filmed Entertainment. Represented by Sony Pictures Entertainment, which comprised Columbia Pictures, TriStar Pictures, Columbia Pictures Television Distribution, TriStar Television, Merv Griffin Enterprises, Columbia TriStar Home Video, Columbia TriStar International Releasing Corp., and Loews Theatre Management Corp.

On the software side, much depended on the success of the two-year-old Sony Electronic Publishing, where efforts in multimedia and interactivity converged. It sold video games for Sega and Nintendo systems, many of which were based on films produced at Sony Pictures and used soundtracks from Sony Music. The unit's goal was to double sales annually, which would make it a half-billion-dollar enterprise by 1996.

Sony had been a Japanese electronics giant for more than 40 years. Still, consumer electronics was a maturing business (see Table 5-6).

With the acquisition of CBS Records and Columbia, Sony's huge product groups formed an electronics business (video equipment, audio equipment, TV sets, other products) and an entertainment business (music entertainment, filmed entertainment). The mix changed, but not as rapidly as anticipated. Between 1988 and 1994 the portion of Sony's electronics sales declined from 97.5% to 78.8%, whereas that of entertainment grew from 2.5% to 21.1%. Despite high start-up costs and massive investments, however, the latter increased just 2.6% between 1990 and 1994. Prior to its U.S.-based acquisitions, Sony had hoped for a 60–40 split between hardware and software.

Integration of Electronics and Entertainment

High acquisition prices and costly legal struggles consumed Sony's financial resources, due to the burst of Japan's bubble economy, and the plunge of the stock market.

By the fall of 1991 Walter Yetnikoff, the head of Sony Music, as well as

Table 5-6
Sony Corp.: Business Segments (1985–94) [Sales as % of total]

		Electronics				Entertainment	
Year*		Video Equip.	Audio Equip.	TV Sets	Other Prods.	Music Entert.	Filmed Entert.
1994		-------	78.9%	--------------		-----	21.1%	----
1992		-------	80.2	--------------		-----	19.8	----
1990		-------	81.4	--------------		-----	18.6	----
1988		-------	97.5	--------------		-----	2.5	----
1994	$36,250	17.9%	22.5%	16.6%	21.9%	12.3%	8.8%
1993	34,422	20.8	23.2	15.9	19.3	11.2	9.6
1992	29,439	22.8	24.1	15.1	18.2	11.4	8.4
1991	26,176	24.6	23.9	14.9	16.7	12.9	7.0
1990	18,760	25.2	24.5	15.1	16.6	15.5	3.1
1989	16,678	26.7	26.2	15.9	15.3	15.9	-
1988	11,655	29.0	30.8	20.3	17.4	2.5	-
1987	3,820	30.9	31.2	21.2	16.7	-	-
1986	8,309	33.1	28.6	22.8	15.5	-	-
1985	6,788	36.3	23.8	25.7	14.2	-	-

> *   U.S. dollars, translated from yen, for convenience only, at the
> approximate Tokyo foreign exchange market rate as at the final day
> in each respective fiscal year.
> In fiscal 1985 and 1986 year ended October 31, whereas in 1987
> and thereafter year ended March 31; years 1986, 1987, 1988 have
> been restated (five-month fiscal period in 1987).

SOURCE: Sony Corp.

Jon Peters and Frank Price, Columbia's cochairman and chairman, were all gone. Like the acquisitions, the departures were not cheap. In the end, Sony kept only Peter Guber, who had the least problems in adjusting to its corporate family; but even Guber reported to Schulhof, who continued to bridge gaps between Japanese and American corporate culture, software and hardware, Los Angeles and New York, the "creative types" and the "corporate suits." By 1992 both Columbia and TriStar were folded into Sony Pictures Entertainment, while cost-cutting became the norm.[10]

The new corporate mission was hardly an instant success. Since the late '80s, suspicion had been building between Sony's electronics and entertainment operations. The price-driven electronics business felt upstaged by the less profitable but flashier and hit-driven movie and record businesses. Divided corporate structure threatened to undermine potential synergies, especially in cross-marketing and coordinated product introductions (the digital audio tape, the Data Discman).

In 1993 the $60 billion *Last Action Hero* was a test in Sony's cross-marketing and product tie-ins. With Schwarzenegger, the epic infomercial featured Sony's recording artists, a new sound system, new electronics products, and footage for a video game and amusement ride. Exploiting Columbia for marketing purposes, the feature was an exercise in déja vu (a decade earlier, Coca-Cola turned Bill Cosby's *Leonard Part VI* into a similar flop).

Toward Electronic Superhighways

While "sonyizing" its new possessions, the image of Sony itself was being "resonyized." In March 1993 Norio Ohga conducted classical music in a benefit concert for the Lincoln Center Consolidated Corporate Fund. The AT&T building in mid-Manhattan was being remodeled for Sony, while more outlets, emulating the new "Sony Plaza," were being planned nationwide. "We are an entertainment company," Schulhof insisted, hopefully rather than realistically. "We make films, we make music, we showcase talent—*and* we make electronic equipment."[11]

By summer 1993 Sony consolidated its U.S. electronics and entertainment operations under Sony Corp. of America and named Schulhof president and CEO of the unit (which accounted for $13.5 billion of Sony's worldwide $34.4 billion in sales). The de facto integration of Sony Corp. of America and Sony Software Corp. meant Schulhof's personal victory, another step in organizational integration, as well as increasing centralization of power under Norio Ohga in Sony.[12]

When, two years earlier, Sony tried to raise $2–$3 billion in Japan and the United States, the poor response highlighted the weakness of Tokyo's stock market. With increased competition, Akio Morita conducted himself more as an elderly statesman than corporate leader. By summer 1993 Morita wrote to the G-7 leaders proposing lowering of "*all* economic barriers between North America, Europe, and Japan," to create a new world economic order that would include a "harmonized world business system."[13] With far more global operations than its rivals, Sony had the most to gain from free trade.

Cutting capital spending and squeezing more profitability out of its electronics operations, Sony was striking up more alliances, especially with computer firms like Apple, IBM, and Microsoft. With Disney as its model, Sony was moving into theme parks, consumer products and retailing, licensed merchandise, professional sports, as well as video games.

Over the last few years, Sony had invested more than $8 billion to buy into entertainment. Now it looked at ways to raise outside capital. Although the studio had the top market share of the box office, it had suffered from an abundance of problems, from the flop of the big-budget *Last Action Hero* to allegations that some studio executives were involved in Hollywood's prostitution scandal, not to speak of the Michael Jackson scandal (Sony had staked over $50 million in his production concern).

At the end of November 1993, Sony signed new long-term contracts with top executives of its filmed entertainment, music, and electronic publishing units. The move signaled its commitment to the entertainment business and reassured Hollywood on management stability, despite the Tokyo-based parent's problems.

By late 1993 Schulhof met with top U.S. telco executives to discuss a strategic alliance, which Sony hoped would also inject capital into the company. It contemplated the sale of a 25% stake in its ($6–$8 billion) motion picture and ($6 billion) music operations, to bring in $3–$4 billion of badly needed capital.

In the electronic superhighways, Sony sought to create the software, transmit it, and make the equipment to bring it into the home. Like Disney, Sony was not interested in the pipeline, as long as there was open access to the delivery systems; unlike Disney, Sony was interested in both software (M&E production) and hardware (M&E electronics) and struggled to integrate both.[14]

In December 1993 Morita suffered a cerebral hemorrhage that forced his withdrawal from Sony. Although he had not been actively involved in daily operations since 1989, he was Sony's psychological backbone. The absence came as the company was facing tough periods: both sales and operating profits were declining or plunging, due to the strong yen and recessions in Japan and the United States. True, the company was managed for the long term, but its debt burden amounted to over $14.6 billion, while its net income declined from $902 million to $149 million in 1992–94. In the new competitive environment, Sony was vulnerable—and would soon have to face a $3.2 billion write-off.

MATSUSHITA/MCA: THE GREAT COPYCAT

In 1912, after a costly legal fight against The Trust, Carl Laemmle, a German-Jewish immigrant, and his partner, Robert Cochrane, formed Universal, through a merger of several independents. In classic Hollywood, the economic power was held by the oligopoly of the Big Five studios. Universal was the largest of the Little Three.[1]

From Universal to MCA

In the 1930s Universal disposed of its theatre circuit and went into receivership as Standard Capital Corporation took control. In the postwar period, Universal sought survival through strategic alliances with the British J. Arthur Rank and International Pictures. By the late '40s profits declined again, the studio went back into the red, and revived its low-cost production strategy. In 1951 Decca Records purchased Rank's holdings in the studio, which garnered substantial profits (from *The Glenn Miller Story* to *Spartacus*). But when the decline in box-office attendance resulted in losses at Universal, Music Corporation of America, Inc. (MCA) acquired a controlling interest in Decca.

MCA: The Octopus Years

Starting with bands and packaging talent, Jules Stein expanded MCA into a major U.S. corporation, which encompassed a band-booking agency, a motion picture actors' agency, a radio performers' agency, and a movie studio. The company's monopolistic tendencies conflicted so often with the Justice Department's antitrust division that one judge called MCA "the Octopus—grasping everything in show business."[2]

In 1946 Stein became chairman of the board, while VP Lew Wasserman, then 33, was named MCA's president and CEO. Through its powerful talent representation, MCA contributed to the demise of the old studio contract system. By 1952 a controversial "blanket waiver" deal turned MCA's Revue Productions into the nation's biggest producer of TV shows.[3]

In 1959 MCA underwent a major reorganization. All units were brought under a single publicly owned corporate structure, MCA, Inc. When it purchased Decca Records (which owned 90% of Universal), it already controlled 80% of TV talent and program production.

From Divestiture to Hollywood's Powerbroker. In 1962 MCA was forced to divest its talent agency. With more than 50% of Decca and Universal, it became the owner of a TV production company (Revue); a studio facility and one of the major distributors (Universal); and a record label (Decca Records).

As a privately held talent agency and radio/TV producer, MCA had been little affected by politics; as a major diversified entertainment corporation, its interests were affected by government. From the '60s to early '80s, the old "Octopus" expanded its clout in political parties (Stein worked for Reagan, while Wasserman supported mainstream Democrats), local politics (Los Angeles's downtown business; Wasserman's friendship with Jerry Brown), government (Wasserman's friendships with Johnson and Carter; and Stein's with Republican presidents), industry (Wasserman's role as "industry leader"), unions (Wasserman's powerful role as the main negotiator in labor conflicts), and—allegedly—organized crime (Stein's and Wasserman's business links with Sidney Korschak).[4]

In 1966, MCA was burdened by an $80 million debt and became a target for Westinghouse Electric Corporation. While the Department of Justice undid the merger, the takeover attempt caused a power struggle between Stein and Wasserman. Another merger proposal followed from Firestone Tire and Rubber Company, but Wasserman did not support the merger with the tire company, which, unlike Westinghouse, did not own TV and radio stations.

In 1970 Wasserman promoted his protégé, Sidney J. Sheinberg, to new president at Universal-TV (two years later he became MCA's executive VP). Three years later Wasserman succeeded Jules Stein as MCA's chairman, while Sheinberg became new president of MCA and Frank Price was appointed the president of Universal Television. Concurrently, Universal thrived with the star-studded *Airport*, followed in 1973 by *American Graffiti* and *The Sting*; and by the mid-'70s the unit pioneered the blockbuster era, with Steven Spielberg's *Jaws*. Even the TV division flourished. In 1976, for the first time in its history, the company grossed $100 million. As MCA became more attractive, its board of directors insulated the company against a possible takeover by amending bylaws.

Operation Prime Time. In 1977 a cooperative of independent stations launched an effort to finance the production of prime-time programs. With Paramount Pictures, the syndication arm of Universal TV (MCA-TV) joined the consortium to create Operation Prime Time (OPT), an ad hoc "fourth network." As an ongoing venture, OPT was limited by the scarcity of indie starions and the high risk of programs with network-scale budgets.

After the network failure, MCA sought transformation into a hardware/software combination—more than a decade before the Japanese invasion of Hollywood. In 1976 Universal and Disney filed a copyright lawsuit against Sony's Beta VCRs in a case that took over seven years and ended with Sony's legal victory. In 1978 Magnavox, a subsidiary of Philips, introduced DiscoVision (the Philips/MCA System), but failed against Sony and RCA. A year later MCA formed a joint venture with IBM to produce and market videodisks. In 1982 MCA sold its videodisk operation; it had lost nearly $100 million. The first attempt at a software/hardware combination was a disaster. In April 1981 the 85-year-old Stein died of a heart attack amid a costly corporate crisis.

On Golden Pond precipitated Universal's turnaround. In 1982 Spielberg returned to Universal with the industry's mega-hit—*E.T.: The Extra-Terrestrial* grossed over $700 million worldwide, with $229 million in domestic rentals. (Six years later the videocassette was released for home video; with 15 million units sold, it returned another $225 million to MCA.) *E.T.*'s enormous popularity was augmented by the success of other Universal features (from *The Best Little Whorehouse in Texas* to *Conan the Barbarian* and *Sophie's Choice*). Although Universal continued to release hits, none were as profitable as *E.T.*

MCA's Strategic Shift

In 1979 MCA bought ABC Records to augment its profitable records division. To reduce dependence on movies (which comprised 84% of its profits in 1980), Wasserman also embarked on real estate development. Problems seemed to subside with the advent of the Reagan administration, which permitted vertical combinations. By 1986, however, MCA had become even more dependent on its movie group: the TV production business had lost its dominant position; the defection of Irving Azoff, the head of the record division, was expected to drag down the unit's profits; and diversification into the theatrical exhibition (Cineplex Odeon) led to financial problems.

In 1986 entertainment lawyer Tom Pollock began to turn the studio around, but, despite several box-office hits, new deal structures threatened the studio's ability to recoup its investment. Meanwhile, the decline of one-hour shows on the network and in syndication caused problems for MCA's TV group, which excelled in that format (from *Magnum, P.I.* to *Miami Vice* and *Murder, She Wrote*). After an aggressive move into sitcoms, Universal's TV shows climbed in the ratings in the late '80s.

The Search for an M&A Partner

Although its stock was selling at $10 a share below its asset value, MCA avoided takeover games (and high leverage) until 1985, when the Golden Nugget, Inc. (Stephen Wynn's gambling concern in Las Vegas and Atlantic City) obtained 5% of MCA stock, at $95 million. By the summer Wasserman also discussed the possibility of RCA acquiring MCA until GE acquired RCA. In effect, the company prepared itself for a software/hardware combine, via piecemeal vertical integration:

- In 1984 MCA increased its interest in USA Network to a 50/50 partnership with Paramount Pictures;
- in 1986 MCA got into the exhibition business, through a 49% equity interest in Canadian-based Cineplex Odeon;
- outbidding Westinghouse in 1987, MCA purchased an independent station in New York from RKO for $387 million (WWOR became a major force in the industry);
- in 1989 MCA-TV and Paramount Domestic TV tried to combine their barter sales divisions into a joint venture (with WWOR-TV as one cornerstone), to form the "fifth network";
- in 1990 MCA divested LJN Toys (which had cost $99.5 million over the past three years);
- that same year, Universal opened the $630 million, 444-acre Universal Studios Florida, close to the Disney Studios (like Disney, MCA also negotiated on theme parks in foreign sites);
- as the record business consolidated, MCA Records repositioned itself in spring 1990, when it bought Geffen Records, a major independent label, for $600 million.

By fall 1990 MCA had few interests without an organic role in the vertical company (e.g., Yosemite National Park). In the past the company had been placed in buyout negotiations with Sony, Philips, and Disney. In 1987, while Sidney Sheinberg, president of MCA, ran the company on a day-to-day basis, the 77-year-old Wasserman's postsurgery complications almost caused his death. The surgery and the ensuing stock manipulation forced Wasserman to look for a buyer. By the '90s the studios would have to eat or be eaten. "We're a 200-pound gorilla in a game with 1,000-pound gorillas," Wasserman told one MCA shareholder. "We've got to become a 1,000-pound gorilla, or get out of the game."[5]

In 1989 Mike Ovitz, Creative Artists Agency's powerful chairman, had recommended MCA to Sony, which found its stock too expensive. That year, too, MCA and Paramount failed to negotiate a merger.

MCA Inc.: Business Segments

From 1980 to 1989 MCA's revenues grew from $1.3 billion to $3.3 billion. As a diversified company, MCA engaged in filmed entertainment, music entertainment, retail and mail order, book publishing, as well as broadcasting and cable. It also had a substantial investment in theatrical exhibition.

In the '80s MCA's dependence on filmed entertainment declined from over 60% to about 50% of total revenues, while the portion of the music segment rose from 11% to 23%. Still, filmed entertainment was far more profitable (see Table 5-7). After Sony acquired Columbia, Ovitz consulted another Japanese company. It, too, was interested in an American studio. Its name was Matsushita.

Matsushita: Software Acquisitions

By the early '90s Sony was far better known in the United States than Matsushita, whose brand names (National, Panasonic, Quasar, Victor, Technic) were more recognizable than the company itself.[6]

Konosuke Matsushita founded his business in the 1920s. It nurtured a highly decentralized divisional structure, not unlike DuPont's in the United States. With the recovery of the Japanese economy, Matsushita's business expanded rapidly, meeting rising demand for consumer electric and electronic products, from washing machines and refrigerators to black-and-white televisions. In 1952 the company got into TV-set production.

Matsushita also developed a unique corporate strategy. Instead of trying to recoup investments rapidly, Matsushita cut its prices quickly, preferring long-term profits; instead of established retail channels, it set up its own distribution networks, going directly to retailers; it offered innovative trade financing for retailers; and, instead of using the Matsushita name, the company promoted its various brands.

In 1957 Matsushita opened its first American office, Matsushita Electric Corporation of America (MECA) in Manhattan. Four years later it established its first international manufacturing subsidiary in Thailand and began overseas production. Growth continued through the '60s and '70s, when the company expanded its product range to include color television receivers, hi-fi components, videotape recorders, air conditioners, microwave ovens, industrial equipment, communication and measuring equipment. Unlike Sony, Matsushita rarely pioneered new technologies; it got ahead by skillful imitation; the VHS format, which defeated Sony's Beta-

Table 5-7
MCA, Inc.: Business Segments (1982–89)

Year	Filmed Entert.	Music Entert.	Retail/ Mail Order	Book Publ.	Broadctng and Cable	Toys	Others	Total
Revenues ($mil)								
1989	$1,739	$765	$275	$189	$172	–	$243	$3,382
1988	1,484	661	313	176	132	–	135	2,900
1987	1,316	477	320	159	88	–	118	2,479
1986	1,311	386	302	132	2	208	101	2,230
1985	1,169	326	296	138	2	77	92	2,021
1984	870	275	311	117	–	–	79	1,651
1983	909	206	288	106	–	–	75	1,584
1982	995	176	248	90	–	–	77	1,586
(%)								
1989	51%	23%	8%	6%	5%	9%	7%	100%
1988	51	23	11	6	5	4	5	100
1987	53	19	13	6	4	–	5	100
1986	59	17	14	6	0	–	5	100
1985	58	16	15	7	0	–	5	100
1984	53	17	19	7	–	–	5	100
1983	57	13	18	7	–	–	5	100
1982	63	11	16	6	–	–	5	100
Operating Income ($mil)								
1989	246	57	6	24	31	–	126	$489
1988	223	60	0	23	13	–	52	372
1987	149	41	10	18	3	–	44	265
1986	78	34	16	17	4	28	37	181
1985	144	25	1	18	(0)	12	14	203
1984	59	11	7	12	–	–	10	99
1983	163	(7)	19	9	–	–	3	186
1982	212	25	12	7	–	–	(1)	250
(%)								
1989	50%	12%	1%	5%	6%	15	26%	100%
1988	60	16	0	6	3	6	14	100
1987	56	15	4	7	1	–	17	100
1986	43	19	9	9	2	–	20	100
1985	71	12	0	9	(0)	–	7	100
1984	60	11	7	12	–	–	10	100
1983	88	(4)	10	5	–	–	2	100
1982	85	10	5	3	–	–	(0)	100

SOURCE: Matsushita Electric.

max, was an exception to the rule. If Sony created innovative products, Matsushita made them better and cheaper. Hence the latter's Japanese nickname "Maneshita," copycat.

By the mid-'80s financial problems in Japan, labor shortages, and a protectionist backlash in the United States and Europe accelerated Matsushita's efforts to increase overseas production and internationalize the company. In 1986 Akio Tanii became Matsushita's new president. His rise coincided with the company's attempt to break away from its cautious strategies. Tanii turned the company into a major force in industrial equipment and semiconductors; he consolidated Matsushita's 87 companies in Japan and almost as many abroad. By 1988 Matsushita's results began to show recovery, aided by Japan's expanding domestic economy. As Sony's product-innovation strategy and Matsushita's mass-production strategy eclipsed, both opted for vertical integration. Again, the great copycat emulated Sony.

By 1990 Matsushita had integrated production and sales, both in Japan and overseas, to become "one global body" with 200,000 employees. It was the largest manufacturer in Japan, and one of the largest producers in the world of consumer electronic and electric products. It needed software to sell the new TV technologies.

The MCA Deal: Acquisition Process

In April 1989 Konosuke Matsushita died at the age of 94. When Sony, later that year, purchased Columbia, Matsushita contacted Mike Ovitz, CAA's chairman (its JVC had already invested $100 million in a joint venture with Hollywood producer Lawrence Gordon). Of three potential targets, Matsushita rejected Orion and Paramount. In spring 1990 Ovitz suggested MCA, which was big enough, eager to sell, and had the right mixture of business. Despite secretive orchestration, things got out of control.

By fall 1990 MCA President Sidney Sheinberg informed the board that the company was dealing with Matsushita; he also talked to David Geffen, who had sold his record company to MCA (when MCA's stock soared, the worth of Geffen's shares increased to $660 million, almost twice their value three months before). The story was leaked to the *Wall Street Journal*, which reported that Matsushita and MCA were negotiating on a $7 billion merger deal.[7] After the leak, MCA's stock jumped 60%. Matsushita believed the leak had come from MCA. As the price dropped to $74 a share in mid-November, both companies prepared for a major round of talks.

In the past, MCA's asset value had been estimated at $90–$100 a share; now Wasserman expected to get $75 a share. Though the recession affected the pricing, it kept out possible competing bids. After intense negotiations, the deal was sealed in November 1990 at $66 a share, in a $6.6 billion, all-cash transaction. The merged entity's revenues topped $51 billion, nearly doubling those of Sony/Columbia. To combat political opposition to the sale, MCA mobilized its board members and enlisted top lobbyists to promote the sale. It was a profitable deal to most American parties (MCA's top executives, investment banks). Ovitz alone earned an estimated $40 million fee.[8]

The acquisition prompted several divestitures. Because of restrictions on foreign ownership of U.S. broadcast stations, MCA spun off WWOR. In the United States, public debate escalated on foreign ownership in Hollywood, whereas in Japan, the purchases were seen as new milestones in a long-standing feud between Sony and Matsushita. Vertical integration was blurring the notion of entertainment as the "quintessentially American industry." "It's going to be one world, though I'm not going to live to see it," Wasserman noted. "[The Japanese] have the money. Isn't that what we're talking about? It's impossible to have a savings rate of fourteen per cent in Japan and three per cent here and for us to be competitive."[9]

Matsushita Electric Industrial: Business Segments

From 1980 to 1990 Matsushita's revenues nearly tripled to $38 billion. In the early '80s its long-term debt stayed around 2–6% of invested capital; by 1990 it amounted to 24% ($7.5 billion).

Prior to MCA's acquisition, Matsushita was engaged mainly in production and sales of electric and electronic products (video equipment, audio equipment, home appliances, communication and industrial equipment, electronic components, batteries, and kitchen-related products). The attempt at a software/hardware combination presumed that software (programming, films) would support hardware (HDTV, VCR), and that both would feed each other. The evolution of the video category, for example, had a critical role in Matsushita's acquisition of MCA. In fiscal years 1985–93 the portion of video equipment sales declined from 37% to 21%. In 1988–91, entertainment formed just 1% of sales, but the acquisition of MCA raised the segment portion to 9%. While Sony had a 7:3 hardware/software ratio, Matsushita's remained lower than 9:1 (see Table 5-8).

The Postmerger Matsushita/MCA

Initially, Universal's *Mr. Baseball* was to be a comedy about a baseball player (Tom Selleck) who leaves the New York Yankees, joins a team in Japan, and clashes with the Japanese culture. After Matsushita acquired MCA, Universal's parent, the film evolved into a romantic tale of an athlete coming to accept himself and Japan. In 1991 the shift illustrated MCA's new role as Matsushita's entertainment *subsidiary*.[10]

In contrast to Sony, which remade its studios (Columbia, TriStar) in its image, renaming them Sony Pictures Entertainment, Matsushita adopted a low-key approach, even if it was expected to increase control in two–four years. Unlike Sony, which relied on high-profile coverage, Matsushita remained silent on virtually everything concerning MCA. No longer publicly traded, analysts had virtually no access to financial information on MCA.[11]

In just half a year, relations between the two companies were strained—partly because of cost-cutting measures at Matsushita and MCA, partly because of MCA's reversal of fortunes.

The Loss of Virgin Records. Tensions stemmed from December 1991, when MCA sought to expand its record business internationally by bidding for

Table 5-8
Matsushita Electric Industrial: Business Segments (1986–94) [sales][3]

	Video	Audio	Home	Com/ind	Elect/comp	Batt.	Entert.[1]
($mil)							
1994	$12,683	$5,222	$8,132	$15,926	$8,051	$3,366	$5,697
(¥bil)							
1994	¥1,306.3	¥537.9	¥837.5	¥1,640.3	¥829.3	¥346.7	¥586.8
1993	1,441.3	594.1	945.9	1,697.8	835.4	365.8	607.9
1992	1,699.8	631.7	982.2	1,678.6	862.8	367.8	626.4
1991	1,694.3	597.9	899.5	1,553.4	841.7	349.4	62.9
1990	1,579.4	561.1	802.4	1,374.9	781.2	312.1	59.0
1989	1,550.5	515.1	776.8	1,104.4	726.5	283.0	49.0
1988	1,479.3	507.1	754.6	957.6	637.2	257.9	50.7
1987[2]	531.6	163.5	213.4	278.1	195.7	82.3	na
1986	1,559.5	507.3	738.2	827.7	563.2	231.8	na
(%)							
1994	19.7%	8.1%	12.6%	24.8%	12.5%	5.2%	8.9%
1993	22.2	9.2	14.6	26.2	12.9	5.6	9.4
1992	24.8	9.2	14.3	24.5	12.6	5.4	9.1
1991	28.2	10.0	15.0	25.9	14.0	5.8	1.0
1990	28.9	10.3	14.7	25.1	14.3	5.7	1.1
1989	31.0	10.3	15.5	22.1	14.5	5.7	1.0
1988	31.9	10.9	16.2	20.6	13.7	5.6	1.1
1987[2]	36.3	11.2	14.6	19.0	13.4	5.6	na
1986	35.2	11.5	16.7	18.7	12.7	5.2	na

Video = Video equipment. Audio = Audio equipment. Home = Home appliances. Com/ind = Communication and industrial equipment. Elect/comp = Electronic components. Batt. = Batteries and kitchen-related products. Entert. = Entertainment.

1. A new product category, "entertainment," was created beginning with fiscal 1992. Certain video and audio software products previously included in "Video equipment" and "Other" have been transferred to this new category. The figures of fiscal 1988 through 1991 have been restated to reflect these classifications.
"Entertainment" includes sales of MCA Inc., JVC Co., as well as MCA Music Entertainment Group.
2. Figures for 1987 represent operations for the four months and 11 days, due to a change of fiscal period.
3. "Other" category not presented.

SOURCE: Matsushita Electric Industrial.

the British-based Virgin Records, a key to MCA Records' foreign distribution. Matsushita refused to support the $600 million bid. The episode was revealing in still other respects. MCA's entrepreneurial style was at odds with Matsushita's slow bureaucratic style; the two were separated by a language barrier; unlike Sony (which had had a joint venture with CBS Records since the '60s), Matsushita had no exposure to creative ventures; the episode also spelled the demise of Wasserman as the industry leader. In the end, Virgin was bought by Thorn-EMI. As Universal was having one of its worst years, MCA froze salaries and bonuses after a disappointing year.[12]

Matsushita was quite vague on the purpose of the newly launched "entertainment arts division," which was created in Osaka in March 1992 to interface with MCA. The launch of the new division, coupled with the parent's increasing requests for extensive financial data from MCA, invited suspicion. Apparently, the plans involved a joint-venture Japanese theme park and mutual interests in new technology, HDTV, and movie distribution. (In January 1994, MCA announced it would build a $1–$2 billion theme park in Osaka.)

Executive Shake-up, Restructuring, and Sales Rumors

In February 1993 Matsushita President Akio Tanii resigned unexpectedly, saying he was taking responsibility for certain "unfortunate events." The resignation came amid one of Matsushita's worst fiscal years. As Tanii engaged in restructuring operations, Matsushita had covered over $150–$200 million of bad debt racked up by a financial subsidiary. Even more damaging were engineering flaws that sent 400,000 defective refrigerators back for repairs. Finally, critics were questioning Matsushita's ability to integrate MCA-Universal.

At Matsushita the 1993 downturn foreshadowed a fundamental change in the economic and social orders. The company's response was the "management innovation plan," which followed two precepts: manufacture products that created new markets (prioritize risk-taking and next-generation products); and build a leaner, stronger management structure (streamline operations, expand selectively, and effectively utilize management assets).

Tanii may well have been shunted aside by the 80-year-old chairman Masaharu Matsushita. He was succeeded by Yoichi Morishita, a no-nonsense marketing expert, whom chairman Matsushita was expected to replace by his son, the Wharton-educated Masayuki. The elderly Matsushita was solidifying family control of the $64 billion company.[13]

The U.S. studio was identified as a major reason for Matsushita's reduced profits and heavy drain on resources. Unlike Tanii, who had a long association with entertainment due to his involvement in the successful VCR division, Morishita had never visited Hollywood, had no personal interest in movies, and did not speak English.

Despite its past poor results, industry analysts considered MCA a great long-term asset to Matsushita. Moreover, Universal's summer release, *Jurassic Park*, became a landmark test for the parent's exploitation of synergies.

In late 1993 Sony was mulling a sale of 25% of its entertainment operations. Once again, Matsushita emulated its rival. In November Keiya Toyonaga, a senior managing director, was introduced to TCI's John Malone by Allen & Co. Malone talked with Toyonaga about acquiring a 50% stake in MCA. The meeting angered Sheinberg, who was told of the discussions only after they had taken place.[14] Yet there was little MCA could do. No longer an independent corporation, it was a subsidiary of a foreign electric giant—a mere shadow of its past grandeur.

PART II

TOWARD ELECTRONIC SUPERHIGHWAYS

The Struggle for Distribution

NEW GOVERNMENT POLICIES

Despite the Clinton administration's high-tech activism, much of the "national information infrastructure" was overtaken by events that took place between 1992 and 1994. The government lacked the funds to launch the infrastructure and corporate America was not willing to wait for one to be built. Electronic superhighways were being put in place prior to new government policies and legislative changes by leading telcos, cable operators, computer companies, and Hollywood studios.

Toward the National Information Infrastructure (NII)

During the 1992 campaign, Bill Clinton and Al Gore vowed to rebuild America. One of their policy priorities was the creation of "a national information network to link every home, business, lab, classroom, and library by the year 2015 . . . .To expand access to information, we will put public records, databases, libraries, and educational material on line for public use."[1]

The Clinton administration regarded the new commercial Internet as a prototype of the information infrastructure that the telcos and cable companies were racing to build. As a national priority, the administration regarded the information network as critical as defense conversion, renovation of transportation, and environmental technologies. But the debate over the proposed infrastructure was preceded by a more fundamental debate on the impact of government policy on industry competition.

America's Industrial Policy

Unlike its European and Asian rivals, America has never had a comprehensive industrial policy. As long as growth was a given in the U.S. economy, there was little discussion on industrial policy. Despite major efforts since the 1960s, such objectives were set aside during the 12-year Republican era, even if the Reagan administration acknowledged that government promoted some economic sectors over others. Even in the mid-'70s, when major industrial sectors were in trouble, the Council of Economic Advisers focused on large aggregates and did not gather data on sectors. Yet both figured in America's de facto industrial policy—an amalgam of public and private efforts without center or coordination.[2]

The industrial policy (IP) debate commenced in the late 1970s and continued after 1984 under the rubric of "international competitiveness." The Reagan and Bush administrations, however, associated concern about U.S. industrial structure with pessimism about America. In 1993 the *Economic Report of the President*, the last one of the Republican era, argued that "America still has the largest and strongest economy in the world. It is neither deindustrializing, nor losing some overall economic competition with other countries."[3]

Since the triumph of U.S. media and entertainment worldwide seemed to reinforce the administration's point of view, it was cited as a case example of continuing growth. "If the most efficient way for the U.S. to get steel is to produce tapes of 'Dallas' and sell to the Japanese," noted Herbert Stein, the former chairman of the Council of Economic Advisers, "then producing tapes of 'Dallas' is our basic industry."[4] By the late '80s, however, foreign (Japanese, European) investors and corporations controlled critical pieces of U.S. M&E businesses. Though still in American hands, U.S. media and entertainment was no longer owned by Americans.

Ultimately, the issue came down to the question that U.S. Trade Representative Mickey Kantor posed to his fellow cabinet members in spring 1993: "Who are my clients—American companies or American workers?" The debate divided the Clinton administration. While Labor Secretary Robert B. Reich believed it no longer mattered much whether foreigners or Americans owned companies doing business in the United States, Council of Economic Advisers Chair Laura D'Andrea Tyson thought national ownership made a lot of difference.[5]

Public/Private Partnerships

The Clinton administration extended its regulatory reach and stepped up antitrust enforcement. While, for example, the cable industry faced federal mandates to roll back rates and improve quality, the new administration's selective deregulation was reminiscent of the Carter years in communications.[6]

The new White House encouraged pragmatic partnerships between government and industry, relying on European-style industrial policies. Just as it forged a partnership with the big three automakers to produce a clean, fuel-efficient car, it planned to help the U.S. electronics industry to establish a business base in flat-panel displays. Similarly, the Clinton team released a blueprint for a "national information highway" to connect businesses, schools, and homes. It had no fears of "picking winners and losers"—an approach that was bound to lead to allegations of "favoritism" (e.g., resource allocation in the rejuvenated National Institute of Standards and Technology, the FCC's "pioneer" policy).[7]

The concept of a national information network reflected the views of Vice President Al Gore, long active in communications and a high-tech advocate. If the United States was going to compete effectively in a global economy, argued Gore, a fast and flexible information network was as essential to manufacturing as steel and plastic. He was the administration's point man in the efforts at a national information highway, just as his father had been a principal architect of the interstate highway system. On January 14, 1994, Gore held a live interactive news conference on an international computer network. It reminded many of President Franklin D. Roosevelt's appearance at the 1938–39 New York World's Fair on a newfangled contraption called television.[8]

Behind the facade loomed a far more influential organizational and ideological catalyst. Just as the conservative Heritage Foundation had served as the ideological idea shop of the Reagan administration, the Progressive Policy Institute (PPI) (a research arm of the centrist Democratic Leadership Council [DLC]) cultivated intellectual soulmate ties to the Clinton White House. After the 1992 election, the DLC and PPI served as a source of transition personnel.[9]

Scenarios

In July-August 1992, DLC's think tank encouraged the telcos to build broadband, fiber-optic networks without granting the Baby Bells the right to own and transmit video programming. The PPI proposed that the telcos enter joint ventures with public utility companies to build the network; since both were regulated by state and local authorities, consumers would not be unduly burdened by the national fiber-optic infrastructure whose price was put at $300–$400 billion.[10]

By December PPI urged the administration to foster the development of the information network that "could mix video, voice, text, and data transmissions, turning the family television set into an interactive 'telecomputer.' " Instead of public funds, the PPI suggested "the new President should press for regulatory changes that encouraged electric utilities to become investors in this new system, along with the local phone companies and perhaps cable television companies."[11]

At the Economic Summit of December 1992, Clinton seemed determined to unlock the potential of the new media. While Gore suggested the national information infrastructure should be built by the government, Robert E. Allen, CEO of AT&T, disagreed. The widening dispute witnessed a rift into two camps.[12]

Seeking to avoid competition from a more advanced network they did not control, AT&T and other long-distance carriers argued that the electronic superhighways should be built, owned, and operated by private companies. The proponents of a private venture included traditional free-market advocates and budget-deficit hawks who contended the venture was too costly for government. In contrast, Gore argued that the private sector would not gamble on such a risky investment; and that if it did, it would not build a superhighway accessible to all, but a sort of private toll-road open to a business and scientific elite. In addition to public-interest advocates, such as the nation's librarians and educators, the public venture camp included the Baby Bells and computer manufacturers (IBM, Apple, DEC), which hoped to gain from the increased demand for new computers.

With the administration's start-up problems, the issue was put aside until Clinton announced a broad new high-tech initiative a month after unveiling his economic program. This initiative revived the infrastructure debate.

Clinton's High-Tech Initiative

Seeking to generate new government-industry consortiums and help the beleaguered semiconductor industry, the new initiative encouraged government and industry cooperation to create new technologies and nurture innovative small companies. Emulating goals sketched by Clinton with executives of Silicon Valley companies during the election campaign, the initiative called for spending $17 billion over four years and included financing research leading to a national high-speed computer network, and $718 million in "seed money" through 1998, to start construction of a national broadband communications superhighway.[13]

The high-tech initiative reflected a substantial break with the policies of the Bush administration and the biggest change in federal technology policy since World War II. Modeled after European-style industrial policies and current strivings to "reinvent the government," the Clinton plan aimed to redesign existing programs and agencies to render them more responsive to industry and the economy. The ideas were not new; the determination to implement them was.[14]

Jockeying for position, the telcos took a more visible role in the rush to the new marketplace. In March, in a rare display of unity, the CEOs of local and long-distance telephone companies called for the White House to let private companies build and manage most of the national high-speed fiber-optic network.

Due to fiscal realities, the government could not build a national information infrastructure. As the new administration saw it, its task was not so much to interfere with the rivalry as to keep the playing field competitive. In return for their new markets, U.S. corporations would carry the financial burden of the costly infrastructure.

A Delicate Balancing Act: Public Goals, Private Objectives

In September 1993 the Clinton administration released a vision statement, "The National Information Infrastructure: Agenda for Action." Arguing that the local telephone and cable markets were "dominated by monopolies," the administration promised to work with Congress to enact legislation in 1994 that would open the markets to more competition. Through a collection of initiatives, the Clinton team sought to foster a "seamless web" of high-capacity networks and information services interconnecting the nation's homes and businesses; it would invest $1–$2 billion a year to fund research and development of transmission and information technologies, to "quicken the pace" of infrastructure construction.[15]

Meanwhile, the interagency Information Infrastructure Task Force, established by the Clinton team within months of taking office, released its report pledging that the administration would rely on the private sector to build the information superhighway. The government's role was to devise investment incentives, to insure affordable universal service, to keep the highway democratic, and to protect both privacy and intellectual property rights.

In the coming months, lofty principles gave rise to heated debates. First studies confirmed Vice President Gore's doubts. When the telcos began wiring the information highway, they seemed to bypass poorer neighborhoods and minority populations, engaging in "electronic redlining." Although the real issue was whether, after the testing stage, the new services would still be targeted at the affluent areas, public goals (universal access) were not easily matched with private objectives (profits, growth).[16]

By December 1993 the administration was poised to make broad changes in communications policy and was supporting legislation that would break down the legal barriers that separated the telephone and cable industries. Concurrently, Vice President Gore gave two major speeches for permitting greater competition between cable and telephone industries, and for moves to relax restrictions that barred local telcos from competing in long-distance service. Unable to pay for network construction, the government hoped to influence events by reducing regulatory barriers obstructing competition and promoting new standards that allowed different networks to communicate with each other. In brief, the administration tried to navigate between the rival goals of promoting private investment and market competition while championing the broader public interest.

As Washington advocated the most far-reaching changes in telecommunications policy since the AT&T breakup in 1984, and as bipartisan efforts in Congress were accompanied with a new level of agreement in the fractious M&E industries, computers, and telecommunications, the stars were finally aligned for historic legislation in 1994—a major rewrite of the nation's communications laws, some of which dated half a century back to the Communications Act of 1934.[17] Then, in less than a half year, major players were mugged by reality.

Phone and cable companies blamed Washington for conflicting policies, outdated regulations, and insensitive bureaucrats: the FCC had held back more than a dozen requests for interactive network tests; federal Judge Harold H. Greene held sway over virtually every move AT&T and the Baby Bells made toward the interactive era; and the Justice Department seemed to take a harder line in reviewing such combinations as AT&T-McCaw and, before its collapse, Bell Atlantic-TCI.[18] "Come to think of it, Al Gore really does look like a state highway cop," lamented the *Wall Street Journal* in April 1994. "Put a helmet and mirrored aviator glasses on the Vice President and you're looking at the guy whose Federal Communications Commission is setting up radar traps and roadblocks all along the Information Highway."[19]

Speed slowed on the electronic superhighways. In May 1994 Vice President Gore urged the nation's largest local and long-distance telephone companies to put aside their differences. While cable and broadcasting officials shared Gore's enthusiasm for the superhighway bills, Baby Bells opposed revisions that kept them from immediate entry into the long-distance business, just as long-distance carriers were concerned about a House bill that would enable the Bells to deliver long-distance services in less than five years.[20] Strategic groups struggled for the place in the sun.

NEW STRATEGIC GROUPS AND ALLIANCES

By the early 1990s the Big Three TV networks, major cable operators, and Hollywood studios were subsidiaries of giant U.S. and foreign corporations. The proposed electronic superhighway translated into increasing rivalry. Eager to join distribution, new strategic groups represented three different industries:

- direct broadcast satellites (PrimeStar, Hughes/Hubbard);
- computers (American hardware and software companies, foreign integrated-electronics firms);
- telecommunications (Baby Bells, long-distance carriers, foreign distributors)

In search for vital growth markets, each entered into strategic alliances with major M&E companies.

Direct Broadcast Satellites

Direct broadcast satellite (DBS) transmits TV signals to dishes at subscribers' homes, which use a TVRO antenna to receive signals directly from a high-power domestic communications satellite. Eliminating the TV station as intermediary, DBS could pose a threat to broadcasters and cable systems.[1]

By the early '90s, modest DBS services, which offered 3–14 channels, were operating in the United Kingdom and Japan. Despite high start-up costs, they proved moderately successful. Due to the rapid growth of cable, the concept did not take off in the United States (where the acronym for DBS stood for "Don't Be Stupid"). In America, DBS evolved in four distinct phases. Each meant rising costs and growing capital requirements.

Failure of Pioneers: Birth of Industry

In 1980 the Communications Satellite Corporation (Comsat) attempted to launch a DBS system providing three channels of programming, at $250–$750 million. Instead of competing head-on against the Big Three, the service targeted unserved audiences. Without partners to share the high entry costs (CBS and Paramount nearly signed on), Comsat abandoned the venture in 1984. Still, it persuaded the FCC to set aside a spectrum for DBS and establish regulations for the new medium.

Backed by Prudential Insurance, United Satellite Communications (USCI) in 1983 inaugurated the first American DBS service in Indianapolis. Since a rural audience could not recoup $180 million in costs, USCI tried to expand beyond its initial market. Staying alive with TCI's support, it folded in 1985.

Skyband was Rupert Murdoch's first and short-lived attempt to break into U.S. satellite broadcasting (which did not require U.S. citizenship). In fall 1983 he signed a $75 million long-term lease with the now defunct Satellite Business Systems (jointly owned by Aetna, IBM, and Comsat), planning to launch a five-channel service. Later, the plans were dropped.

Transition: Increasing Stakes

In Murdoch's U.S. operations, the Skyband failure signaled a shift to higher stakes in broadcast TV. Due to the failure of the Pan-European four-channel Sky Channel and the high start-up costs of the British Sky TV ($120 million in the first five months), Murdoch opted for a less-aggressive entry into the United States. Instead of launching his own DBS system, he participated in a joint venture, Sky Cable.

In the mid-'80s a substantial DBS project was also put together by Time

Inc. and General Electric, which joined forces in Crimson Satellite Associates, a partnership of their subsidiaries (HBO and GE Americom). Eventually, Crimson sold the satellite at a loss to a Luxembourg-based satellite broadcaster, Astra.

New Rivals, New Realignments: Intensified Competition

The year 1989 saw the emergence of several DBS projects: K Prime Partners, SkyPix, Dominion Video Satellite, Sky Cable, U.S. Satellite Broadcasting, Advanced Communications, Continental Satellite, and TVN Entertainment. With new rivals came new realignments, as major players struggled for market dominance. Throughout the '80s, nearly 20 different companies sought the FCC's authority to provide DBS service, though most gave up their efforts (CBS, RCA, Western Union Telegraph).

K Prime Partners. Controlled by giant MSOs (TCI, Time Warner, and others), the K Prime group planned to launch a medium-power 10-channel service in 1990. With K Prime's service, TCI planned to shift to TCI-Tempo's high-power system in the mid-'90s. K Prime remained under scrutiny by the U.S. Justice Department and a task force questioned the MSO's monopolistic role.[2]

The Sky Cable Partners. In February 1990 Murdoch's News Corp., NBC, Cablevision Systems, and General Motors's subsidiary Hughes Communications announced plans for a high-power DBS. As the largest supplier of commercial satellites in the United States, Hughes developed the technology for the venture. Together, the Sky Cable partners planned to invest nearly $1 billion in DBS services (108 channels, HDTV potential), but the effort collapsed.[3]

In mid-1991 United States Satellite Broadcasting (USSB) paid $50 million to Hughes Communications to build and launch at least one high-power direct broadcast satellite by mid-1994.[4]

With the third wave, giant MSOs captured the DBS business. K Prime was driven by nine cable operators, Viacom loomed behind USSB, and TCI behind Tempo. When TCI acquired a stake in Netlink USA and purchased Tempo Enterprises, Malone claimed the idea was to ensure fair pricing and access to programming. Yet satellite competitors complained to Washington regulators that TCI tried to strangle satellite TV as a rival to cable.

Fourth Wave: From Hughes/Hubbard to Primestar Partners

In June 1993 a $4.8 million antitrust settlement between seven of the largest U.S. cable companies and 40 state attorneys general won satellite broadcasting access to cable. While the settlement spurred new DBS services, including the Hughes/Hubbard venture, it also greenlighted the development of Primestar Partners, a medium-power satellite broadcasting service owned by GE and seven cable companies (Comcast, Cox, Continental Cablevision, Newhouse, TCI, Time Warner, Viacom).

The Hubbard/Hughes Venture. In December 1993 Hubbard's USSB and DirecTV, a division of Hughes Communications, carried DBS-1, the first of two DBS satellites into orbit. In 1994 the $1 billion venture planned to provide 20 digital channels of programming to U.S. homes equipped with an 18-inch backyard dish. While USSB was offering a package of cable channels, DirecTV's total DBS capacity would ultimately range from 150 to 200 channels; it expected to break even with 3 million customers by late 1996.[5]

In 1985 General Motors bought Hughes Aircraft, a defense contractor whose profits had declined with the end of the Cold War. When C. Michael Armstrong took over as CEO of Hughes in 1992, he embarked the company on a risky turnaround strategy. Hollywood replaced the Pentagon.[6]

In May 1993 Stanley Hubbard, founder and president of USSB, testified in Congress that there was no immediate need to build an expensive fiber-optic information superhighway because an "equally good" DBS system was already in place. In reality, the DBS system had deficiencies of its own, including monthly fees, the high cost of the satellite receivers and set-top converters, and inability to deliver local programming. Unlike DBS, the telco/cable alliances offered two-way interactive capabilities. Ultimately, the Hughes/Hubbard venture would have to compete with PrimeStar, which intended to increase its 10 channels to 70 channels using new digital transmission technology.[7]

Despite Hubbard's lofty rhetoric, DBS was evolving into a niche service for unserved audiences (compare Figure 6-1).

Star Wars in Satellite Communications?

In March 1994 Craig O. McCaw, who built McCaw Cellular Communications into the world's largest cellular telephone company, and William H. Gates, the billionaire behind Microsoft, the biggest software company in the world, announced the formation of Teledesic Corporation to develop a global satellite communications network. The two proposed to build a $9 billion system with *840* small satellites, providing service by 2001. Teledesic would transport information from telephone calls to high-resolution computerized medical images and two-way video conferences to and from virtually any spot on the planet. The $9 billion global cellular dream was the brainchild of Edward F. Tuck, who met McCaw in late 1989, who, in turn, called Gates. Although the two high-tech luminaries each put up $5 million for 30% stakes, Gates eschewed any operating role.[8]

The project was ambitious, but not unique. Motorola was already building a $3.3 billion satellite telephone system named Iridium that would use 66 spacecraft, aimed at mobile users; and it had managed to raise $800

Figure 6-1
Targeting the Satellite-to-Home Market (Spring 1994)

| Programing Package | Overview |

C-band

A wide variety of unscrambled programing - about 75 channels - is available at no extra cost to anyone who owns a receiving dish. Many packages of scrabled programing are available from a variety of companies and typically carry a $22-$23 monthly basic subscription cost. Among the many packages offered: Showtime Satellite Networks, $29.55 monthly; National Programing Service, $18.95 monthly; Showtime/TMC or HBO/Cinemax combos may be added for $15 each.

More than 3.6 million households in the U.S. now receive TV programing via 7-10-foot wide C-band dishes; 1.7 million of those are equipped with decoders that enable users to receive pay TV services. A dish, with installation, usually costs $1,700-$1,800.

Medium-Power Ku-band DBS

PRIMESTAR   Basic - $25-$35 monthly (price set locally)

Includes C-SPAN, CNN, HLN, Prevue Guide, TNT, TBS, TDC, TLC, USA, FAM, Cartoon, TNN, CMT and often Disney Channel and 6 digital audio. Multiplex HBO and Cinemax usually cost extra $9.95 each. Multiplex Encore usually extra $3.95-$5.95. Three channels of PPV movies cost $3.95-$4.95 per title.

Future Basic - $25-$35 monthly (set locally)
By midyear, Primestar's package will expand to include 15 regional sports networks, several cable channels, and 10 PPV channels.

Debuted in late 1990 in 40 markets and rolled out nationally in July 1991. Primestar, currently provides service to 70,000 customers, has just switched to digital compression and plans to move to a stronger satellite. Primestar is owned by subsidiaries of GE American Communications and 6 large cable system owners: Comcast, Cox, Continental, Newhouse, TCI and Time Warner. Customers do not own receiving equipment but do pay installation cost of $100-$200.

High-Power Ku-band DBS

DIRECTV   Personal Choice I - $21.95 monthly.

Includes A&E, CNBC, ESPN, TBS, TNN, C-SPAN, CNN, TLC, Sci-Fi, TNT, Court, Cartoon, TDC, CMT, E!, TWC, HLN, TCM, USA, FAM, Disney, Encore and Bloomberg Direct. Also includes one $3.95 PPV credit per month and a PPV preview channel.

Personal Choice II - $21.95 monthly
(Available when 2nd DBS satellite is launched in fall 1994)
Includes CNN, ESPN, Cartoon, TNN, TRIO, TCM, USA, TBS, TNT, C-SPAN, HLN, TDC and Bloomberg. Also includes 7 multiplex channels from Encore or 10 or the more than 20 remaining services. Also provided at no extra cost are Disney (east and west), 30 digital audio channels from Digital Cable Radio, the PPV preview channel and one $3.95 PPV credit each month.

Total Choice - $29.95 monthly
(Also available upon launch of 2nd satellite)
Includes all of the Personal Choice selections plus the 7-channel Encore multiplex, Disney (east and west), the DCR channels and two $3.95 PPV credits per month.
PPV movies for all DIRECTV packages will be $1.95-$3.95 per title. Other PPV pricing, including sports, TBA.

Beginning next month, the first paying customers for high-power DBS expected to come on board. Eventually, households will be able to receive more than 150 channels via 18-inch home dishes, including some 40 channels of PPV movies and 30 channels of PPV sports. More than 29 channels will come from USSB, the Minneapolis company launched by terrestrial broadcast pioneer Hubbard Broadcasting. The remainder of the channels will come from DIRECTV, a unit of GM Hughes Electronics. Hughes Space and Communications Group owns the satellites that transmit DIRECTV and USSB. Home receiving equipment. starts at a cost to the consumer of about $700.

USSB   Basic - $7.95 monthly

Includes MTV, VH-1, Nickelodeon, Nick at Nite, All News Channel, Comedy Central and Lifetime.

Showtime Plus - $23.95 monthly
Basic plus 3-channel multiplex of Showtime, the Movie Channel and Flix.

HBO Plus - $34.95 monthly
Basic plus 5-channel HBO multiplex and 3-channel Cinemax mltiplex.

Premium Plus - $34.95 monthly
Basic with Showtime Plus and HBO Plus. USSB will offer Premium Plus free for one month.

SOURCE: *Broadcasting & Cable*, March 28, 1994, p. 51.

million. Unlike traditional high-orbit satellite communications, Iridium and Teledesic planned to use fleets of low-orbit craft. In mid-April 1994 McDonnell Douglas won a $400 million agreement to launch 40 satellites for the Iridium project.[9] There were also other minor projects (Global-Star, Odyssey, Ellipsat). In addition, Teledesic would have to compete with conventional phone networks, which were rapidly moving toward efficient high-speed digital fiber-optic highways.[10] After considerable initial hype, the Teledesic plan drew skeptical reviews. It had not addressed significant technical, financial, and political issues.

IBM, Apple, and Microsoft in Hollywood

In the mid-1980s the erosion of America's leadership in technology intensified with the overvalued dollar, the collapse of U.S. international competitiveness, and a trade deficit in high-tech sectors. As video games entered children's rooms, computing markets changed the landscape of business. The key question was "whether there will be a market for *digital, interactive, multimedia* computer technologies in the home."[1]

By the early '90s U.S. computer companies were extending PC wars into the Japanese market long impenetrable to them, whereas Japanese electronics behemoths (Hitachi, Matsushita, Toshiba, NEC, and Fujitsu) had grown too big, too slow, and too cautious. Their margins were being squeezed by lean and mean U.S. computer and chip manufacturers, as well as upstarts from South Korea, Taiwan, and Southeast Asia.[2]

New Computer Industry Economics

Electronics had become the largest manufacturing segment of the U.S. economy, ranging from computers and industrial electronics, telecommunications equipment, military electronics, and electronic components to consumer electronic products. The industry was maturing. By 1991 personal computers (PCs) accounted for 47% of total computer revenues and 93% of all industry shipments.[3] The rise of personal computers took place at the expense of classic products, such as supercomputers, mainframes, midrange systems, and workstations.

Industry Transition. The computer industry had been dominated by mainframe and minicomputer manufacturers (IBM, Unisys, DEC, and others), which prospered by exploiting proprietary hardware and operating systems software. Due to high switching costs, each dominated its niche and the industry remained fragmented. The transition came with the microprocessor. By the late '70s a slate of entrepreneurial small firms (Apple, Tandy, Commodore) introduced personal computers. As rapid advances in microprocessor technology (by Intel and Motorola) increased the equalization of power between PCs and minicomputers, major players announced new operating systems, whereas IBM expected to deflect new rivals, as it had in the past.

With flat sales, plummeting profits, and intense price wars, most companies began to suffer. In 1991 computer revenues actually declined—for the first time in the industry's brief history.[4]

In the late '80s PCs and microprocessor chips revolutionized the economics of the computer industry. The industry moved from proprietary, mainframe-based computing (IBM's classic products) toward network-based processing that utilized lower priced nonproprietary PCs, workstations, and midrange computers.[5]

From Company Standards to Open Standards. In the past, standards were set and owned by big companies that used them to lock in customers and lock out competitors. One firm's software was incompatible with the other's. In the new industry, proprietary standards were replaced by "open" standards. Software became more compatible.

Commodity Business. At one time the industry was typified by proprietary mainframe-based computing, high entry barriers, and high profit margins. The new industry was exemplified by nonproprietary networking utilizing ever-lower priced PCs, low entry barriers, and low margins.

Strategic Alliances. IBM dominated the old industry. The new industry was typified by strategic alliances as companies hedged bets in competition characterized by a growing number of rivals, rapid technological change, and substantial uncertainty.

From Vertical Integration to Horizontal Layers. Through vertical integration, IBM and a few other big firms (DEC, NCR, Wang, NEC) dominated the industry's value chain from manufacturing to marketing, whereas the new rivalry was characterized by intense rivalry in (relatively open) horizontal layers (see Figure 6-2).

Until the early '90s, PC users had only two alternatives in selecting a new computer and operating system: an Intel-based DOS and Windows, or an Apple Macintosh and Macintosh operating system. By 1994 the available processors included Intel's Pentium, the PowerPC (IBM, Apple, Motorola), and DEC's Alpha (in which Capital Cities/ABC acquired a minority stake). Operating systems comprised MS-DOS and Microsoft's Windows NT, IBM's OS/2, and various Unix versions. Meanwhile, ever-faster processors continued to blur the line that separated PCs and workstations (many of the special effects of the 1993 blockbuster *Jurassic Park* were created with Silicon Graphics workstations).[6]

At $360 billion in 1992 (35% in the United States, 35% in Europe, and 19% in Japan), the worldwide information technology industry had become the world's largest industry. Fueled by PC sales, it was a critical component of the U.S. economy.[7]

New Industry Leaders. Three U.S. firms (IBM, Apple, and Microsoft) dominated a significant market share in computer platforms, operating-system

Figure 6-2
Computers: Industry Transition (Early 1990s)

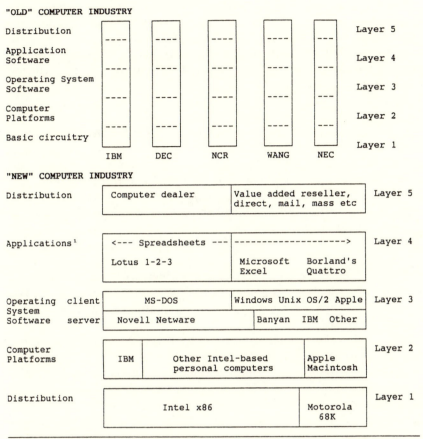

"OLD" COMPUTER INDUSTRY

Distribution						Layer 5
Application Software						Layer 4
Operating System Software						Layer 3
Computer Platforms						Layer 2
Basic circuitry	IBM	DEC	NCR	WANG	NEC	Layer 1

"NEW" COMPUTER INDUSTRY

Distribution	Computer dealer	Value added reseller, direct, mail, mass etc	Layer 5
Applications[1]	<--- Spreadsheets --- Lotus 1-2-3	---------------------> Microsoft Borland's Excel Quattro	Layer 4
Operating System Software client / server	MS-DOS / Novell Netware	Windows Unix OS/2 Apple / Banyan IBM Other	Layer 3
Computer Platforms	IBM Other Intel-based personal computers	Apple Macintosh	Layer 2
Distribution	Intel x86	Motorola 68K	Layer 1

1. Several markets, i.e., spreadsheets (presented), word processors, graphics, database, E-mail.
2. Operating-system software is divided between the basic software needed to run client machines in a network or stand-alone PCs (presented), as well as the software needed to operate the central server of a network.

SOURCE: 1993 The Economist Newspaper Group, Inc. Reprinted with permission.

software, and applications. By the early '90s, computer firms that inhabited these horizontal layers played a leading role in strategic alliances with major M&E companies. As large consumer electronics players, foreign companies were industry leaders in other computer segments (mainframes, midrange systems, workstations). Better positioned in low-cost production than entrepreneurial innovation, they boosted commodification.

Of the U.S. players, the huge mainframe-driven IBM found it hard to adjust to new realities, whereas the PC-oriented Apple was more responsive to the new environment. Microsoft was the real beneficiary of the shift toward software. Overall, the companies that benefited most were those whose hardware and/or software was adopted as the industry standard (Microsoft, Intel).

As computer firms entered U.S. media and entertainment, new strategic alliances coincided with industry transition and the ensuing restructuring among leading players themselves.

The Beleaguered IBM

With $65 billion in revenues, IBM was a shrinking giant. To hedge its bets, it entered a number of alliances. In mid-1991, to take on Microsoft and Intel, IBM and Apple announced a wide alliance to create a new operating system. In December 1991 IBM announced a $3 billion reorganization; in 1992 it took a staggering $6 billion charge; in January 1993 CEO John Akers resigned. Big Blue had become "like a music-publishing company run by deaf people."[8]

Strategic Alliances in Media and Entertainment. In spring 1992, seeking growth markets, IBM launched a decisive effort to enter the M&E business and began courting cable MSOs (Time Warner, TCI); other computer companies (Apple, Digital Equipment); Hollywood majors (Disney, MCA); and influential players (Steven Spielberg, George Lucas, Michael Ovitz). Concurrently, IBM tested new technologies with Canada's largest cable provider and new information services with BellSouth. In July 1992 it delivered a new breed of supercomputer, speeding up the production of special effects in Hollywood. It also became a minor backer of the Apple-led research consortium.

In November 1992 IBM's Lucie Fjelstad unveiled a blitz of multimedia products and strategies, earmarking over $100 million in five years to nurture interactive multimedia. Determined to become a major player in Hollywood, IBM began working with GE's NBC on a pilot scheme to provide businesses with "news on demand." In February 1993 IBM announced it would back James Cameron (*Terminator*) in a visual-effects studio to develop new film techniques and entertainment software; with 50% of Digital Domain, IBM intended to compete with Lucas Digital Services, Sony, and smaller shops.[9]

The New IBM. When Louis V. Gerstner, Jr. took charge of the $62 billion company, IBM began layoffs, for the first time in its history. From 1986 to 1993 it took some $28 billion in write-offs. Ordering new layoffs and cost-cutting, Gerstner began to mold IBM into a customer-driven company. By spring 1994 the company embarked on a fresh bid for the desktop software market that Microsoft dominated. (In 1993 IBM's software revenues amounted to $11 billion.) Resorting to a high-stakes gamble, Gerstner's modified play-to-win strategy relied on internal IBM efforts, the aid of partners, and potential acquisitions to get into applications software. The new strategy entailed an expansion into new consumer markets, including interactive television.[10]

The old IBM could not get its multimedia projects going. It talked with Time Warner and TCI on interactive cable TV, but negotiations withered with mounting internal problems.

Despite the dismantling of Fjelstad's proposed multimedia empire in mid-1993, IBM redoubled its efforts in the business. In addition to a $10 million stake in Digital Domain, it operated IBM Multimedia Publishing Studio (CD-ROM titles), Fireworks Partners ($50 million in business multimedia projects), and IBM Watson Research Laboratory (sale of computers and software to movie producers). IBM retained Kaleida, a joint multimedia venture with Apple, and negotiated with Blockbuster on joint ventures.[11]

In January 1994 IBM reported its first quarterly profit in more than a year. While Gerstner struggled to change the ingrained IBM culture, he also sketched out six "strategic themes" for IBM's future. The company would push its core technology across product lines; become a player in client/server computing; offer network services to large companies; reengineer the sales force to cut costs; jump into new geographic markets (Asia); and leverage IBM's size and scale. When, a few months later, the company consolidated its $400–$500 million in worldwide advertising at Ogilvy & Mather Worldwide, the news rocked Madison Avenue.[12] Despite a low public profile, IBM had more entrance ramps onto the heavily hyped information superhighway than any other firm.

The Revitalized Apple

Founded by Steven Jobs and Stephen Wozniak in 1976, Apple Computer was among the handful of PC companies that ignited the PC boom. Unlike its rivals, Apple made hardware and software to proprietary designs. With sales at $117 million in 1980, it went public; four years later, armed with the popular Macintosh, it challenged IBM. Incorporating a graphical user interface (inspired by Xerox's Alto), Macintosh created a linkage between computers and entertainment. When Wozniak departed from Apple, Jobs hired John Sculley from Pepsi as president. In 1985 it was Jobs's turn to leave. After the power struggle, Apple moved into the office market, ushering in the desktop-publishing revolution.[13]

By the early '90s the pursuit of high margins was replaced with lowering prices to expand market share. With the industry shift to software, Apple reversed its decision to spin off Claris, a software subsidiary. It entered a number of strategic alliances to produce the Macintosh PowerBook notebook (with Sony); Newton, a pen-based personal digital assistant (Sharp); as well as new software and hardware designs (with IBM).[14]

Sculley blended the original Apple visions of "computing for the masses" with a sophisticated appeal that gave the company access to corporate markets.

Apple in Hollywood. Starting in 1980–90, Apple Television, a state-of-the-art TV production center in California, used Macintosh as the technical interface between the production team and the TV process.

In mid-1991 Apple and IBM announced an alliance, which included Kaleida, the joint venture in multimedia. A year later Apple continued its thrust into consumer electronics by joining Toshiba (which had a joint venture with IBM and an equity stake in Time Warner) on joint development of products that combined sound and video with computers (especially CD-ROM).

The first effort to size up the demand for the new multimedia technology took place in October 1992, when 11 of the nation's largest computer and telephone companies (including IBM) formed an alliance to distribute multimedia into U.S. homes.

The New Apple. By 1992 Apple was the world's second-largest manufacturer of PCs, with almost $7 billion in revenues. As a leading industry spokesman for the interactive convergence, Sculley predicted the new "single market" would have revenues of $3.5 trillion a year. After Newton, Apple's first personal digital assistant (PDA), the company promised to introduce electronic books, on-line services, electronic TV guides, and interactive TV. In practice, new products suffered from delays, and new markets had not evolved.

While other computer firms formed links with M&E and telco companies (Time Warner/Silicon Graphics, Time Warner/US West, Time Warner/TCI/Microsoft), Apple was absent from dealmaking, in spite of talks with AT&T, US West, and Turner. It sold more computers than before, but its PC sales grew more slowly than those of its rivals, largely because of aggressive price cuts by IBM and Compaq. And while the new Mac technology (PowerPC), developed by IBM and Motorola, was expected to restore margins, it would not be ready until 1994.

In June 1993, a few weeks before Apple announced a $188 million third-quarter loss, Sculley relinquished the title of CEO to the president Michael Spindler. In October, after a surprising fourth-quarter profit, Sculley stepped down as chairman and was replaced by A. C. Markkula Jr. (Apple's chairman from 1977 to 1988). It was Apple's turn to face layoffs. It would take a year of chaos, restructuring, and reengineering to get the company back on track.

The Rise of Microsoft Corporation

By the early '90s the largest independent software company was Microsoft, headed by William Gates whose personal wealth was estimated at $7 billion. Its financial strength stemmed from a near-monopoly in PC operating systems, which accounted for about 40% of its revenues.[15]

Microsoft's explosive growth was boosted by two IBM actions. In 1969 a court decision forced IBM to unbundle its software (sell hardware and software separately), which led to the emergence of the software industry and independent software companies. In the early '80s IBM chose Microsoft to write the software for its PC, which turned the IBM-compatible MS-DOS into a huge success and the standard operating system. (Microsoft's applications also contributed to the success of Apple's Macintosh.)

In 1984 Microsoft's sales exceeded $100 million. Two years later Gates took the company public. Unlike the IBM-driven MS-DOS, Microsoft's Windows provided the DOS operating system with an easy-to-use graphical user interface (GUI) operating environment that featured pull-down menus and icons. After the launch of its highly successful Windows 3.0, Microsoft announced it intended to dominate all major PC applications software categories. Hence the development of Windows NT, capable of running on a variety of computer platforms, whose making took six years and cost $150 million.

From Windows to Hollywood. In mid-1990 Microsoft introduced an upgraded Windows GUI for the DOS operating system, which became available for IBM and IBM-compatible PCs. As the sole major software company with a variety of Windows applications, Microsoft enjoyed the benefits of near-monopoly in major software segments (word processing, spreadsheets). Although Gates launched a start-up to research the multimedia market, Microsoft did not join the alliance craze. Still, *Forbes* published a report on "Gates goes Hollywood," when he had lunch with Michael Ovitz of CAA. "The notion that I would invest in a film company is absolute fiction," commented Gates.[16]

In fiscal 1993 applications accounted for 58% of Microsoft's revenues (as opposed to 34% in operating systems). While operating software cost little to market and sell, applications software meant both increased development costs as well as hefty marketing and ad budgets. Gates expected the small but rapidly growing multimedia-driven consumer division to be the firm's biggest in five years. To extend Microsoft's multimedia range, Gates was negotiating with Hollywood producers and British publishers.

To reduce the risk and development costs of new Windows versions for everything from personal digital assistants to combined PC-TVs, Gates entered a slate of joint ventures. The cable box sitting atop TV sets had become a battleground for computer, telephone, and cable companies as major players jockeyed for position through strategic alliances. Microsoft focused on hardware decoders and software interfaces that enabled viewers to navigate in the coming electronic superhighways.

In March 1993 Microsoft demonstrated a prototype "user interface"—that is, a computer-programmed TV picture whose multiple windows and options guided viewers through the complexity of the proposed 500-channel environment. In May, Microsoft, Intel, and General Instruments announced plans to develop a cable converter that would have a built-in PC. By June Microsoft closed an alliance with Time Warner and TCI to create the equivalent of software for cable TV. "Cablesoft" was expected to establish an industry standard for the transmission of interactive programs. The joint ventures included deals with Compaq and Intel, which hoped Windows Telephony would become the standard software to integrate telephones with PCs.[17]

As the software business matured, falling prices began to bite Microsoft. In the struggle for market share, the rising cost of developing new products could be offset only by selling them in huge volumes, followed by upgrades of software over several years. Gates reckoned three-quarters of Microsoft's software revenues would eventually be generated by upgrades, compared with only one-quarter in 1993.[18] Also, seeking to extend its reach, in January 1994 Microsoft announced it would supply portions of the basic software for controlling Sega's new video game machine.

In seizing the mantle of the industry leadership from IBM, Microsoft was earning power and influence as well as the kind of antitrust headaches that contributed to IBM's downfall. By August 1993 it had been investigated for 38 months by the FTC on accusations that it had locked customers into using its MS-DOS program, had created incompatibilities for competitors, and had unfairly linked its applications to its operating system. After the FTC's futile investigation, the Justice Department decided to pursue its own inquiry.[19]

Controlling almost 80% of the market for PC operating systems, Microsoft was a very different competitor from IBM. It was not interested in vertical integration; it was a dealmaker and obsessed with creating a multitude of industry alliances. While the objective was to establish industry standards in new-generation technologies (which ensured monopolistic benefits), the alliances limited the damage of prolonged investigations, especially in interactive cable TV.

In May 1994 Microsoft made its long-anticipated entry into the nascent multimedia market, introducing its new software (Tiger) for delivering movies on demand. Based on the Microsoft Windows NT Advanced Server operating system, Tiger ran on computer servers. The software giant planned interactive cable ventures with TCI, the U.S. cable giant, and Rogers Cablesystems Ltd., Canada's largest cable TV company.

Toward the Home Market

There were two powerful motivations for increasing cooperation between the PC industry and the M&E business. The home market emerged as the next battlefield for PC sales; and the future of the business was in multimedia computing.

In March 1994 Novell, Inc. paid $1.4 billion in stock for WordPerfect Corporation. Indeed, a sweeping consolidation was under way in the software industry, with half a dozen big companies and hundreds of smaller ones struggling for shelf space. In just half a year, Adobe bought Aldus for $516 million; Electronic Arts acquired Broderbund for $400 million; Tribune bought Compton's Multimedia Publishing Group for $57 million; and Intuit acquired Chipsoft for $281 million.[20] In some cases the mergers failed. Overall, however, industry forces reinforced consolidation in the software business.

By December 1993 several computer companies (Intel, General Instrument, Zenith) announced tests linking PCs to cable TV lines to retrieve data nearly 1,000 times faster than over phone lines. The cable-PC connection was part of a broad overhaul of existing communications networks.[21]

Into Cyberspace: The Internet Model

In 1984 virtual-reality programmers fell in love with William Gibson's *Neuromancer.* The science-fiction author's story was about Case, an interface cowboy who ran a computer matrix until he double-crossed the wrong people. "The matrix has its roots in primitive arcade games, in early graphics programs and military experimentation with cranial jacks," wrote Gibson, who envisioned the vast information pathway to PC users worldwide:

Cyberspace. A consensual hallucination experienced daily by billions of legitimate operators, in every nation, by children being taught mathematical concepts.... A graphical representation of data abstracted from banks of every computer in the human system. Unthinkable complexity. Lines of light ranged in the nonspace of the mind, clusters and constellations of data. Like city lights, receding.[22]

A decade later, cyberspace was no longer science fiction.

Internet. Internet was cyberspace's real-life precursor. In 1964 Paul Baran, a researcher at the Rand Corporation, designed a computer-communications network that had no hub, no central switching station, no governing authority. The concept took root in the computers that showed up in universities and government research laboratories in the late '60s and early '70s and became the technological underpinning of Internet. In the mid-'80s the National Science Foundation (NSF) built the high-speed, long-distance data lines that formed Internet's backbone in the United States. The major costs of operating the network were shared by its primary users: universities, national laboratories, high-tech companies, and foreign governments. Internet was neither owned nor controlled by any single organization.[23]

By the early '90s the network comprised over 9,000 interlocking networks communicating over existing telephone lines and reaching 10 million people in over 100 countries. In 1991 the NSF lifted restrictions against commercial use of the Internet, which the Clinton team made its starting point for the "national information infrastructure."

As NSF's contribution shrank to 10% of the total cost of the network (the agency phased out its support in 1994), a cottage industry of private companies emerged, offering Internet access to businesses and individuals, while commercial computer networks dismantled the walls that used to separate their private operations from the public Internet.

By spring 1994 Internet's cyberspace began to suffer from overcrowding. "In the computer-age equivalent of the Gold Rush, thousands of people are signing up each month for access to the worldwide web of computer networks and electronic information," reported the *New York Times*. "Lured by triple-digit annual growth rates, hundreds of businesses are emerging to offer services, ranging from billion-dollar corporations that want to provide entertainment, shopping and information networks, to technically savvy teen-agers who are among those providing the computer and phone line connections needed for individuals and businesses to link up."[24]

On-Line Computer Services. In 1992–93 the on-line subscriber base of North American users grew to 4.2 million (of the 31 million home-PC owners), while the nascent industry's revenues amounted to $600 million. The business was dominated by an oligopoly of computer networks, such as Prodigy, a joint venture by Sears and IBM (2.0 million subscribers); H&R Block's CompuServe (1.7 million subs.); and America Online (600,000 subs.). The rivalry heated up with new entrants (News Corp., Continental Cablevision, AT&T), redesigned services (Prodigy), and targeted services (Ziff, Apple's E-World). Intelligent computer networks (General Magic's Telescript) were expected to boost the demand for on-line services.[25]

By the spring of 1994 the stock of America Online, the hottest of the new commercial on-line services, was valued at more than *100* times earnings. Between 1994 and 1997 the subscriber base of North American users is expected to increase from 6.6 million to 19.5 million.[26]

Following the collapse of the Bell Atlantic-TCI deal, and all the hype about the information superhighway, on-line services enjoyed a new burst of popularity; they were viewed as critical means to the brave new interactive world. The anarchistic feel of an electronic frontier was giving way to a commercial Internet—a kind of a suburban cybermall.

Telephone Monopolies and Cable Giants

The history of U.S. telecommunications consists of two eras separated by widely differing notions of competition, regulation, and antitrust policies. The third one is arriving with electronic superhighways.

The Bell System

In the traditional era, which lasted from the 1870s to early 1970s, the telecommunications marketplace was regarded as a "natural monopoly."

In the late 1870s the Western Union Telephone Company retreated to telegraphy and the Boston Bell Patent Association to telephone service. In exchange for shareholder equity, Bell issued local franchises; a manufacturer, Western Electric, was acquired in 1882; and a long-distance company, American Telephone and Telegraph Company (AT&T), was founded in 1885. A vertically integrated system was in place. The status quo was maintained by regulatory oversight (private ownership subject to public regulation), which insulated the Bell System from antitrust statutes.[1]

In the early 1920s a patents struggle led to a polarization between telephone companies (AT&T and its manufacturing subsidiary Western Electric) and radio companies (GE, RCA, Westinghouse). As arbitration decided most issues in favor of the radio group, AT&T withdrew from broadcasting (it did obtain a monopoly of providing wire interconnections between stations).

In 1948 the Bell System's vertical integration came under an antitrust attack. The conflict marked an end to the peaceful coexistence of private monopoly and regulatory oversight. The '60s signaled further erosion of past regulatory frameworks. When state public utility commissions (PUCs) and telephone companies resisted regulatory changes, the FCC encouraged selective market access. The struggles between the FCC, the PUCs, AT&T, and Congress resulted in an administrative gridlock.

The Breakup of AT&T

With its vertical machine, Bell was the world's largest corporation in 1974. Prompted by MCI, the Justice Department filed an antitrust suit alleging AT&T had suppressed competition. After eight years of legal struggle, AT&T reached an out-of-court settlement with the Department of Justice.

The Modified Final Judgment led to the breakup of AT&T as of January 1, 1984. Barred from local telephone service, AT&T would provide long-distance service and manufacture telecommunications equipment (and computers). AT&T's 22 Bell operating companies (BOCs) were spun off into seven regional holding companies ("Baby Bells"): Ameritech, Bell Atlantic, BellSouth, Nynex, Pacific Telesis, Southwestern Bell, and US West. Barred from long-distance service and manufacturing equipment, each provided local phone service.

In a massive restructuring, AT&T's $148 billion in assets were cut to $39 billion. What AT&T lost the Baby Bells gained. Each local telco generated $7–$10 billion in annual revenues.

Long-Distance Service. After the 1984 divestiture, the long-distance business was carved away from the traditional AT&T monopoly. The interexchange business consisted of interstate and international calls, with gross revenues at $47 billion at the end of the '80s. Although there were 270 interexchange service providers in the long-distance market, more than

93% of the market was dominated by three dominant carriers: AT&T (71%), MCI Communications (13%), and US Sprint (9%), an 80%-owned subsidiary of United Telecommunications.

Cellular (Mobile) Service. The cellular business remained in an emergent stage in the late '80s, but was expected to evolve into a household commodity. The industry's heavy merger activity ceased in 1990. The prospect of growth held strategic significance for the Baby Bells, which dominated the cellular market.

Local Telephone Service. At the end of the '80s, 93% of U.S. households were receiving telephone service. With $89 billion in revenues in 1989, the local segment was the largest of the three markets. The competitors consisted of Baby Bells and the remaining 1,300 independent telephone companies (mainly privately held mom-and-pop operations), but Baby Bells and General Telephone and Electronics (GTE) dominated the business. These eight companies owned and operated about 85% of the 135 million access lines in the United States.

The new marketplace was a dynamic one. The number of equipment manufacturers multiplied; the long-distance segment was served by several carriers; businesses linked with alternative carriers bypassing local service. To find new revenue sources, Baby Bells sought entry in cable TV, a promising vehicle for diversification and a critical window into media and entertainment.

Telcos and Cable

In 1989–90 Baby Bells launched ventures in foreign cable markets (which had low cable penetration, few relevant competitors, and promising growth prospects). To reduce risks and learn more of the U.S. cable business, telcos used partnerships with American MSOs to enter foreign markets.[2] Similarly, cable operators wanted to learn the telephone business.

By the late '80s *all* Baby Bells struggled to be freed from the antitrust restrictions and sought increasing flexibility from state and federal regulators. However, the 1990–91 contraction saw a rash of fines against the Baby telcos, which allegedly overcharged their customers by $30 billion from 1984 to 1991.[3]

When the telcos intensified their campaign to enter TV distribution and production, broadcasters and cablers opposed such entry. Both feared the telcos' financial resources. Revenues for Baby Bells were 3.5 times higher than those for an average cable company; while a telco earned $1.25 billion in net income in 1990, a major cable company generated a deficit of $221 million; cablers' debt ratio increased to 86%, whereas telcos' stayed around 40–42%; cablers' payout ratio was less than 3%, whereas telcos' amounted to 64%.[4]

By mid-1992 the FCC allowed telcos to transmit TV programming to homes over their telephone lines. Supporters argued the rule could lower cable TV prices and speed construction of a nationwide network of fiber-optic cables to transmit TV images.[5]

Despite regulatory changes, telcos needed time to complete fiber-optic networks. In the past, they had stumbled in diversification; they had little or no experience in the M&E business; they had to find program producers and were exploring opportunities in information services and multimedia.[6] Ironically, as telcos entered the television business, their own business was losing its invulnerability.

Toward the "Second Bell Breakup"

Since 1984 local telcos had struggled to lift the restrictions in the Modified Final Judgment; to open the local telephone monopoly to competition; and to restructure regulatory plans for a more competitive environment (from rate-of-return regulation to incentive/alternative regulation). The transition heralded the opening up of the local service to direct competition—the "second" breakup of the old Bell System.

Personal Communications Networks. In February 1991 the FCC approved applications by three major cable companies to build experimental telephone networks that enabled consumers to use wireless telephones small enough to be carried in shirt pockets. "Personal communications networks" (PCNs) used cellular technology, but the phones were ultra-small and the transmitters covering service areas were much closer together. Cox Enterprises, Cablevision Systems, and Continental Cablevision planned to use their cable networks to tie together scores of low-powered radio towers scattered throughout a town or city.[7]

TCI and US West: Video-on-Demand. As cable and telephone industries prepared to battle over each other's business, the alliances of TCI and US West (1991) stunned both industries, heralding even wider strategic alliances. The Denver experiment in video-on-demand was the first part of a relationship between these two strange bedfellows. (It was followed by a joint venture to build and operate cable systems in the United Kingdom, Sweden, Norway, and Hungary; and a cable/telephone experiment in the United Kingdom.) Video-on-demand was not a new concept. What was unique was the alliance between the two companies, with AT&T providing the equipment.[8]

Bypass and TCI/Teleport. In May 1991 upstart rivals gained on local telcos as the FCC backed a rule that forced the Baby Bells to let rivals plug directly into local telephone systems. The upstarts, led by Teleport (Merrill Lynch, Metropolitan Fiber Systems), hoped to compete head-to-head against the telcos on a full range of services. With beachheads in large cities, the industry included several regional companies. With cable reregulation, TCI poured funds into fiber optics and entered telco businesses. Determined to cut into the Baby Bells' marketplace, TCI bought a 49.9%

stake in Teleport.[9] By 1992 bypass operations cost the Bell companies an estimated $3 billion in lost annual revenues.

Toward Electronic Superhighways

After the breakup of the Bell system, AT&T had taken $10 billion in network writeoffs, whereas in the early '90s it was the Baby Bells's turn to reorganize. Pressure from Wall Street to increase dividends, coupled with lagging profits, pushed payout ratios from 67% to 84% (as opposed to AT&T's 50% or MCI's 10%). High payout rates left little cushion for downturns or capital for reinvestment at a time when the Bells's networks required massive investments in digital switches, fiber, and marketing.[10]

Prompting the changes was a rapidly developing array of technologies, alliances, and communications networks and services that blurred traditional industry distinctions. In November 1992 AT&T decided to team up with McCaw Cellular Communications. If AT&T expanded wireless communications, Baby Bells feared it would cut into their local phone business—just as cablers sought to get into the $100 billion local telco business.

Although both the local and long-distance industries struggled to dominate the new telecommunications, the two strategic groups had very different ideas on the coming electronic superhighways.[11] While the telcos needed cablers to build the information infrastructure, they were intent on retaining control; after all, they had the financial muscle. Whereas the entire cable industry generated $21 billion in sales and just $6 billion in cash flow, the Baby Bells grossed about $82 billion a year ($33 billion of which counted as operating cash flow).

As the Clinton administration seemed to favor telecommunications and cablers lacked financial muscle, the latter were bound to play second fiddle in the ensuing strategic alliances.

Demise of Regulatory Hurdles, Rise of Strategic Alliances

By fall 1993 local and long-distance telcos were exploring ways to deliver interactive multimedia services to the home market. For years local telcos had argued that, to upgrade their networks to handle digital video and other data, they had to have the right to distribute *and* produce programming. Neither the 1991 ruling, which allowed Baby Bells to participate in information services, nor the 1992 "video dial tone" ruling, which permitted local telcos to construct video pipelines to homes, were adequate to prompt investments into the U.S. M&E businesses. The remaining regulatory barriers began to fall in August 1993, when a federal court struck down the section of the 1984 Cable Act that barred the Baby Bells from creating, owning, and packaging M&E programming distributed within their telephone service regions. Though the watershed ruling applied only to Bell Atlantic (it had filed the lawsuit), the rationale was expected to provide ammunition for other telcos as well.

The Baby Bells's rush to Hollywood was set off in May 1993, when US West announced it would invest $2.5 billion for a 25% stake in Time Warner's entertainment unit. Under the alliance, it would help TW rebuild its cable-TV systems for interactive video and phone service. Next, Southwestern Bell announced it would spend $650 million to buy two cable systems outside Washington, D.C., from Hauser Communications. In October a $33 billion merger between Bell Atlantic and TCI set the stage for a revolution in U.S. media and entertainment.

From May 1993 (US West-Time Warner investment) to February 1994 (the collapse of the Bell Atlantic-TCI deal), all aggressive telcos wanted a piece or total control of the cable business. The Baby Bells were swept by a high-tech "gold rush."

Bell Atlantic and TCI. When Raymond W. Smith took charge of Bell Atlantic in 1989, the company already owned a $1.2 billion stake in New Zealand's phone company, and $1 billion in a Mexican cellular network. Two years later the $12.7 billion telco colossus challenged legal restrictions that barred it from providing information services.[12] By mid-1993 Smith decided that getting into the cable was not enough. "What do we need to do," he asked, "to change the nature of this business?" Bell Atlantic needed a cable partner, and cable giant TCI was an obvious candidate. "We have three information instruments in the home—the telephone, the television and the computer—and they are all coming together to communicate on a full-service network. The time is not far off when you will be answering your television set and watching your telephone."[13]

In August 1993 Bell Atlantic won the right to offer cable service in its local telephone market. In October it announced it would acquire TCI in a $33 billion transaction. While Smith would steer the new entity, TCI's John Malone would become its vice-chairman. More than any of the hundreds of new alliances, the Bell Atlantic-TCI merger outlined the potential of a national data highway and heralded a wave of strategic alliances between telcos and cablers.

Behind the facade of visionary rhetoric and rosy high-tech utopias, TCI continued to lose money and Bell Atlantic's revenues grew only 1% a year (it had to book $11 billion in goodwill and write that off against earnings).[14]

In December 1993 Bell Atlantic announced an aggressive plan for launching the information highway. In a five-year, $15 billion effort, it would deliver interactive services to almost 9 million American households. It selected a prototype controller for movies on demand and electronic shopping. Sitting on top of TV sets, the boxes allowed viewers to navigate through hundreds of programs and on-line services, shopping and ordering movies. The telco also teamed with with Oracle to develop video on demand and other interactive TV services. By January 1994 Bell Atlantic sought approval to provide long-distance services as part of its proposed acquisition of TCI.

US West and Time Warner. Offering local service in 14 western states, US West had ventured furthest from its home market. It had helped build a cellular-phone system in Hungary, and invested in phone systems in the former Soviet Union. In February 1993 the $10.3 billion telco announced it would spend $1.4 billion to build a voice and video network by 1995.

In May 1993 US West bought a 25% stake in Time Warner's entertainment division. Agreeing to help upgrade TW's cable networks to carry interactive video, data, and voice services, US West offered customers a one-stop shopping source for local cable and telephone service. By October 1993 the telco teamed up with 3DO for an interactive television trial in Omaha, Nebraska. In January 1994 US West announced it would build new multimedia networks in 20 cities over the next five years, starting with a $750 million effort in four markets.[15]

BellSouth: From QVC to Prime Management. The largest and most profitable of the Baby Bells, the $15.2 billion BellSouth, would have captured $1.5 billion of QVC if the latter had won the Paramount takeover war. A major provider of paging service nationwide, BellSouth owned a stake in Latin American cellular services. Aside from the bidding war, it had a critical separate joint venture with QVC to develop interactive multimedia, set up much like the TW/US West deal. In October 1993 BellSouth also acquired a 22.5% stake in Prime Management, the 24th largest cable operation in the nation. Ultimately, the transaction could exceed $1 billion.[16]

Unlike the risktakers, Southwestern Bell and Nynex took a more cautious approach.

Southwestern Bell: From Cable Systems to Partnership with Cox. In 1986, SW Bell offered $1.4 billion to acquire Metromedia's cellular and paging operations. In 1990 it joined forces with a consortium of Mexican businesses and France Telecom to purchase a controlling 5% interest ($486 million) in Mexico's national phone company (later it doubled the stake). In February 1993 the $10 billion SW Bell bought two cable systems from closely held Hauser Communications for $650 million. Amid restructuring, it cut costs, developed new technology, and invested in a British cable video system. In December 1993 SW Bell and the privately held Cox Enterprises (which had agreed to contribute $500 million toward QVC's offer for Paramount) formed a cable partnership, with $4.9 billion in assets. The operation intended to become the nation's third largest MSO.

Nynex: From Overseas Ventures to Viacom. In October 1993 the $13.2 billion Nynex invested $1.2 billion in Viacom, intensifying the latter's struggle for Paramount. For years, Nynex's bad service, lagging technology, and high prices had alienated profitable customers. Operating in the nation's most competitive region (the Northeast and New York City area), Nynex struggled to fight off upstart phone services that were luring away its business. Focusing on overseas ventures, the largest telco owner of British cable-TV/phone systems was building a new phone system in Thailand. At home, intense competition was taking its toll. By January 1994 Nynex planned to cut 22% of its payroll and took $1.6 billion in charges against its fourth-quarter earnings.

Pacific Telesis and Ameritech, as well as GTE, the independent giant, observed M&E alliances from outside.

Pacific Telesis: A $16 Billion Upgrade. In the past the $9.9 billion telco had engaged in costly diversification. In 1993 it spun off its cellular phone business into a separate public company, decided to reduce its workforce by 10,000 over four years, and to take a $665 million after-tax charge. In November 1993 Pacific Bell, PT's phone unit, planned to spend $16 billion to roll out a fiber optic upgrade in California. AT&T would be a prime beneficiary in the seven-year effort, receiving orders of $5 billion and serving as the systems integrator of the project. Pacific Bell also held an option to buy small cable operations in Chicago.

Ameritech: Toward New Markets. The $11.2 billion Ameritech had no substantial investments in the cable business. Focusing on its core Midwestern telephone business, it explored other options and invested in New Zealand's phone company. Amid dramatic restructuring in early 1993, it announced plans to open its local market to competitors, in return for permission to enter cable TV (it was rumored to be in talks with QVC) and long-distance service. In December 1993 it announced it would invest $472 million in a new data-services venture with General Electric's information services subsidiary.

GTE: New Information Technologies. In 1990, with Hollywood studios, the $20 billion GTE inaugurated experimental voice and video tests in Cerritos, California; unlike Prodigy, GTE was providing information to homes via cable TV rather than PCs. Since its operations were not geographically concentrated, it bypassed the alliance frenzy. In January 1994 GTE planned to offer interactive TV services in a test market, with AT&T. The company also announced 17,000 job cuts, forcing a $1.8 billion charge. Four months later GTE announced that it planned to build a video network linked to 7 million homes and competing with the cable TV industry. It intended to invest $250 million by the end of 1995 to build a new fiber-optic and coaxial cable video network for 550,000 homes in the four initial markets. By 2003 GTE expected to deliver broadcast, cable, and interactive television programs in 66 cities and bring in $1 billion in annual revenues.

Long-Distance Telcos

National in scope and eager to provide international service, long-distance leaders (AT&T, MCI, Sprint) saw themselves as critical players in the struggle for electronic superhighways. If the 1980s witnessed foreign invasion in U.S. media and entertainment, the 1990s began with similar developments in U.S. telecommunications (the BT-MCI alliance, BCE's stake in Jones Intercable).

AT&T: "Anytime, Anywhere" Communications. Between the late 1980s and early 1990s, chairman Robert Allen put in place a vision of "anytime, anywhere" communications, a high-tech system that tracked people down with AT&T's intelligent long-distance network as the backbone. In August 1993 AT&T announced it would take over McCaw Cellular Communications for $12.6 billion in new stock. The purchase was the most recent one in a slate of acquisitions. It was also secretly testing interactive multimedia content and services (VinnieVision). Betting the electronic super-highways would begin via on-line entertainment, AT&T invested in a virtual reality player, an interactive multimedia developer, an on-line interactive network, a multimedia educational software company, and video game companies.

By fall 1993 AT&T held talks with major MSOs about linking their customers into one big interactive, multimedia network, which it was testing separately with Time Warner and Viacom (which would soon take over Paramount).[17]

MCI: From BT Alliance to Multimedia Network. In spring 1993 MCI was talking to several cable TV and entertainment companies about partnerships. In June, British Telecommunications (BT) invested $4.3 billion in MCI; the two planned to pour $1 billion into a new joint venture. The BT-MCI alliance was an assault on AT&T's plans to offer global services to multinational corporations. Yet MCI remained vulnerable on its own turf as local telcos sought to enter the $60 billion U.S. long-distance market.

In December 1993 MCI unveiled its plan to spend over $1 billion to construct local networks in major U.S. cities; with the aid of giant MSOs (TCI, Time Warner), it intended to bypass the Baby Bells. In January 1994 it announced a $2 billion plan to invade the local telephone market, and an effort to team up with unspecified partners on a $20 billion attempt to upgrade its long-distance network for an array of voice, video, and high-speed data communications. In March MCI announced it would spend $1.3 billion for a 17% stake in wireless upstart Nextel Communications—the push forced rivals to position themselves in the coming free-for-all for wireless customers.[18]

Sprint: A Link with Internet. In June 1993 Sprint announced it would link business customers over Internet, with Microelectronics and Computer

Technology. As financial disagreements broke off merger talks with GM's EDS computer service in May 1994, Sprint announced a $4 billion linkup with France Telecom and Deutsche Telekom, which would share a 20% stake in the company. The proposed global triumvirate faced political, technical, and marketing obstacles.

BCE and Jones Intercable. In December 1993 the $15 billion BCE, Inc., the largest public company in Canada, agreed to pay $400 million for a 30% stake in Jones Intercable, Inc. and an option to eventually buy control of the entire company. The transaction enabled BCE to enter the U.S. cable market. Selling its troubled financial services and real estate businesses, BCE had completed a three-year drive to refocus on telecommunications and grow internationally. With Bell Canada Ltd. and a 25% stake in Northern Telecom Ltd., it was eager to position itself in America's information superhighway.

By late 1993 the reversals in international investment flows enabled many major U.S. M&E and telecommunications firms (including TCI, Pacific Telesis, and Motorola) to acquire significant equity holdings in Japanese cable and telecommunications concerns. All hoped to ensure a competitive edge in a new generation of global information services.[19]

In the United States most telcos had strategic alliances with major MSOs and more were anticipated with the remaining cablers (Continental Cablevision, Comcast, and Cablevision Systems).

With BellSouth's stake in Prime Management, the spotlight turned to midsize cable companies (Century Communications, TCA Cable TV). If aggressive telcos were taking chances by spending billions of dollars on MSOs and building expensive networks, the Baby Bells that remained uncertain on their strategy or did not line up big cable partners risked becoming second-tier players in a maturing business.

Meanwhile, the cable and telco industries prepared to struggle with one another. In December 1993 the leading members of the cable TV industry announced a joint venture that would enable the cablers to compete directly with the phone companies for a variety of local services.

Increasing intra- and interindustry competition, the demise of the old regulatory regime, as well as the rush to the electronic superhighways, prompted severe restructuring in the telcos. Between November 1992 and February 1994, major telcos announced they would cut a total of 85,100 positions. The pace of restructuring climaxed *prior to* the collapse of the Bell Atlantic-TCI deal (see Table 6-1).

The telcos engaged in restructuring not only—and, perhaps, not even primarily—to prepare for the information highway, but to gain efficiency, to install the highly advanced digital technology, and to meet the demands of an increasingly deregulated, capital-intensive industry. As the desire for

Table 6-1
Telco Job Cuts: November 1992–February 1994*

Date announced		Company	Jobs
November 6,	1992	BellSouth	8,000
August 21,	1993	Ameritech	up to 1,500
September 3,	1993	GTE	2,600
September 7,	1993	Southwestern Bell	1,500
September 17,	1993	U.S. West	9,000
November 12,	1993	Southern New England Tel.	up to 1,500
November 10,	1993	BellSouth	2,200
January 7,	1994	Pacific Telesis	10,000
January 13,	1994	GTE	17,000
January 24,	1994	Nynex	16,800
February 10,	1994	AT&T	up to 15,000
Total			85,100

* If these figures were supplemented by job cuts at computer
companies (IBM 35,000, Apple 2,500, AST Research 1,000), the
total would amount to almost 125,000.

SOURCE: Company reports; industry analysts.

leadership in the new high-tech markets went hand in hand with competitive costs, a deep gap surfaced between the emerging realities of electronic superhighways and the new rhetoric of job creation.

Telcos and Cablers: End of Honeymoon

In mid-July 1993, Bell Atlantic and TCI agreed to pursue a merger, even though the plan was kept secret until mid-October. This megamerger, estimated at $33 billion, heralded a period of intense competition, restructuring, job cuts, strategic alliances, and merger activity. As late as February 2, 1994, the *Wall Street Journal* reported that Ray Smith of Bell Atlantic and John Malone of TCI hoped to "sign a definitive agreement within two weeks."[20]

In reality, the negotiations suffered from recurrent abortive agreements, and when the FCC announced new cable rate cuts, the parties could no longer wrap things up. While the action was bound to reduce TCI's cash flow from its cable system subscribers, the cable giant considered the problem a short-term one, whereas the telco contended that its price for TCI should drop by about $1.7 billion. As neither TCI nor Bell Atlantic were willing to renegotiate the agreement, the deal was off. The price disagreement was only the tip of the iceberg. A cultural clash defeated the megamerger.

What Smith saw as accountability (reporting earnings and paying dividends), Malone viewed as aversion to risk (building or acquiring new properties). As a utility, Bell Atlantic paid hefty reported earnings and generous dividends, whereas the cable MSO paid no dividends and reported almost no net income, after paying interest on loans. To Malone, traditional corporate goals meant siphoning off money that should be plowed back into more growth-oriented corporate goals.

Smith grew weary of his cable partner: Malone was too eager to stake Bell Atlantic's shareholders' money on TCI's high-tech dreams. TCI was militantly antiunion; Bell Atlantic was largely unionized. The cable giant was notorious for its miserly customer service; the telco remained steeped in phone company traditions. What Malone viewed as a high-cost, slow-moving bureaucracy, Smith saw as a prudish, growth-oriented enterprise. In brief, it was a bad match.

After Bell Atlantic and TCI had touted the benefits of the proposed combination for four months, infatuation faded away, and the wedding was off. The collapse of the megamerger was a terrible embarrassment for both companies and an unaccustomed setback for the two executives. Publicly, both blamed the FCC and Washington, even though rate cuts simply highlighted the cultural mismatch and the tension over pricing.[21]

Despite the collapse of its megamerger with TCI, Bell Atlantic moved forward, tapping AT&T and General Instrument to equip its new $11 billion multimedia network. The project aimed to deliver interactive voice, data, and video services to 1 million homes by the end of 1995 and almost 9 million by the end of the decade. The agreement gave AT&T the largest supply agreement in telecommunications history. While the project exemplified the most aggressive Bell strategy, Bell Atlantic was still regrouping after the collapse of its proposed merger with TCI. (In May 1994 Arthur A. Bushkin, the principal architect of Bell Atlantic's plunge into interactive TV, resigned.)

Although joint ventures between the telcos and the cablers were still considered an inevitable long-term strategy, the rush to the superhighways slowed down, and carefully negotiated strategic alliances replaced risky merger propositions. In a month the collapse of the Bell Atlantic-TCI deal heralded the failures of other similar merger efforts—just as it had, a half a year earlier, inspired the very same activities.

In March 1994 Jones Intercable and BCE renegotiated a $400 million deal to reduce initial investment; in early April Southwestern Bell and Cox Enterprises called off their $4.9 billion joint venture; BellSouth was renegotiating the price of a $500 million deal with QVC (it had failed in its attempt to take over Paramount); U.S. District Judge Harold H. Greene called time out on AT&T's $12.6 billion plan to buy McCaw Cellular Communications, the nation's biggest cellular phone company. Meanwhile, the cable industry began a major legal campaign to delay the telcos' plans to enter the television business.[22]

By summer 1994 the House of Representatives had taken the lead in legislative activity with the proposal of two resolutions, while the Senate had formulated its own bill. The critical issue in the legislative debate was whether or not to allow the Baby Bells into long-distance services.

The Baby Bells were no longer going to serve as the sugar daddies for the debt-laden cable companies, allowing them to raise billions of dollars to upgrade services. Instead, they slowed down investment in video networks. New alliances were narrower in scope, limiting the cooperation to certain cities or technologies. Working on existing partnerships and seeking new cable properties, Baby Bells pursued smaller-scale regional strategies. Exceptions confirmed the rule: eager to shed its conservative Baby Bell past, Ameritech explored joint ventures (with Disney, Capital Cities/ ABC, and Sony) to jump onto the information superhighway.[23]

A passionate love affair, with its characteristic tantrums of rage and desire, was replaced by a calculated infatuation and cautious dating—after all, it was the 1990s.

VIACOM AND PARAMOUNT'S TAKEOVER STRUGGLE

As major corporate players jockeyed for position in the evolving digital media and entertainment business, the rush to the new marketplace cast a shadow on the more traditional M&E merger proposals, including the infamous struggle for Paramount Communications, Inc.—the last remaining autonomous studio.

Merger Bids

During the years 1989–93 Martin S. Davis had a series of futile talks about a merger of some sort. He found target companies too expensive or not for sale. He flirted with Reed, the British publisher; after the $4 billion merger fell through, he toyed with the idea of buying 25% of Elsevier, a Dutch media company; then he began talks with record companies, such as PolyGram, Bertelsmann, and Geffen (prior to its purchase by MCA). When a proposed $4.5 billion partnership with Thorn-EMI fell through, there were talks with Sony, a brief courtship of McGraw-Hill, Gannett, AT&T, Matsushita—and, of course, Time. Afterward, Davis explored mergers with major TV networks. But CapCities/ABC was not interested, the purchase of CBS fell on regulatory hurdles, and the acquisition of NBC (what was to become "The Paramount Broadcasting System") blew apart at the last moment. Time went by and Paramount remained without strategic alliances.

In 1989 the company generated $3.4 billion in revenues and was among the leading Hollywood studios, such as Disney ($4.6 billion) and MCA-Universal ($3.3 billion). In the postmerger environment, the giant shrank. In 1993 Paramount's revenues amounted to $4.3 billion, but now it competed with increasingly capital-intensive businesses, such as Time Warner ($13.1 billion) and Sony ($34.4 billion).[1]

In 1993 Paramount was the last studio in play. After the demise of the NBC deal, Davis decided Paramount would no longer have to be the buyer—it could be the seller. With the blessing of TCI's John Malone, Davis met with Ted Turner on the merger of Paramount and Turner Broadcasting. In April he negotiated with Sumner M. Redstone, Viacom's chairman, while talking with Malone about a quasi-merger that called for TCI to acquire 17% of Paramount. By May Paramount's board was presented with several possible merger scenarios (TCI, Turner, and Viacom).

In July Viacom and Paramount signed confidentiality statements, but the talks collapsed. Meanwhile, QVC's Diller signed an agreement with Comcast and Liberty Media in a plan to purchase the Home Shopping Network.

Viacom's Bid. In late July Davis told Barry Diller (whom he considered a mere facade for TCI's Malone) that Paramount was not for sale and threatened him with defenses against hostile takeovers. By mid-September Davis agreed to a merger. Redstone, the billionaire owner of Viacom, was to acquire Paramount in a $8.2 billion stock-and-cash deal ($69.14 a share).

With its 7 cable networks and 12 broadcast stations, Paramount-Viacom would be unrivaled in national TV distribution, the world's leading cable programmer, with networks such as MTV and Nickelodeon; the leading book publisher; and a major Hollywood studio. With cash flow of more than $1 billion and just $3.3 billion in debt, the new entity seemed to be well positioned to capitalize on multimedia technology.

QVC's Bid. A week after Viacom's bid, QVC announced an $80-a-share $9.5 billion hostile bid for Paramount. Its two main shareholders, Comcast and Liberty Media (TCI), each put up $500 million to back QVC's offer. Without high-quality programming, the distribution technologies were but high-tech plumbing. With its film library, movie studio, TV programs, publishing house, and sports teams, Paramount had what QVC needed: the content to fill the new electronic pipelines.

"In the American cable industry, one man has . . . seized monopoly power," argued Redstone, a former antitrust lawyer, in Viacom's antitrust suit against TCI. "Using bullyboy tactics and strong-arming of competitors, suppliers and customers, that man has inflicted antitrust injury on . . . virtually every American consumer of cable services and technologies. That man is John C. Malone."[2] With the antitrust suit, Redstone hoped to kill two birds with one stone: to bring down Malone, a longtime adversary, and win Paramount. In fact, the adversarial relationship between Paramount and QVC revived talks with Viacom.

A Hostile Battle

After the two bids, the stakes rose in the takeover battle. Although Paramount's board authorized management to meet with QVC, no meeting was held. Davis would not talk to QVC without "evidence of financing." In late September 1993 Viacom obtained $600 million from Blockbuster to sweeten the bid. In early October it got an additional $1.2 billion commitment from Nynex to further sweeten the bid.

Meanwhile, TCI announced it would buy Liberty Media, its former programming subsidiary, while Bell Atlantic announced plans to buy both TCI and Liberty. The deal added financial muscle to QVC's bid for Paramount, especially as Advance Publications and Cox Enterprises decided to back QVC's offer with $500 million each.

The highly complex $33 billion Bell Atlantic-TCI deal altered the controversial $10 billion Paramount scenarios. While it seemed to solidify Diller's prospects to buy Paramount, Malone distanced himself from the takeover battle. Even though he supported Diller, he expressed interest in buying financial stakes in hardware/software giants, such as Sony or Matsushita. Still focusing on the Bell Atlantic-TCI deal, Malone had come to consider the QVC bid "peripheral" and the Paramount bid a "small investment."

In late October 1993 both QVC and Viacom raised their bids for Paramount. In November BellSouth invested $1.5 billion in QVC, while Liberty agreed to divest its QVC investment. As QVC raised the cash part of its bid to $90 a share, which Paramount's board rejected as too conditional, Delaware Chancery Court ruled Paramount directors should have considered the higher QVC bid (the decision was upheld by the Delaware Supreme Court).

Auction Process

By mid-December 1993 Paramount withdrew its support of the Viacom bid and opened an auction. When QVC disclosed a bid of $11 billion ($88.50 a share), Paramount's board recommended a merger with QVC but left Viacom a chance to increase its bid. Meanwhile, Chris-Craft Industries and Paramount finalized a new Paramount network pact aimed at stopping Diller from scuttling their fifth network plan if QVC were to beat back Viacom's new offer.

In early January 1994 Viacom announced a $8.4 billion merger with Blockbuster and Viacom offered $105 a share in cash for 50.1% of Paramount's stock with the rest to be purchased with Viacom's stock. Though the offer was more cash-rich, traders still preferred the QVC bid.[3]

At first, the synergies of Viacom-Blockbuster were seen mainly on the balance sheet (the video retailer had a debt-free financial structure), whereas operational synergies were vaguer. Viacom's Sumner Redstone, who would retain a 61% of the vote in the new entity, needed the merger to win Paramount, whereas Blockbuster's Wayne Huizenga saw Viacom as a way to exit home video, an industry bound to decline with the electronic superhighways. The major retailer of music and video was eager to get into video game retailing.

The End of the Bidding War

On January 12, 1994, Paramount's directors rejected Viacom's revised $9.3 billion takeover bid and stuck to their earlier endorsement of QVC's higher $9.9 billion offer. A week later, Redstone made yet another offer: $107 a share cash for 50.1% plus security that rose in value if Viacom stock did not rise. Paramount's board terminated its merger agreement with QVC and endorsed the revised Viacom bid.[4]

On February 12, 1994, QVC gave in with a brief statement: "They won. We lost. Next." The exit of QVC and Barry Diller cleared the way to the $10 billion entertainment giant Viacom Paramount—after a bitter five-month takeover struggle.[5]

The combined Viacom-Paramount-Blockbuster would be headed by Sumner Redstone and his long-time second-in-command, Frank J. Biondi, Jr., who would serve as CEO. With their transition teams, the two would lead the consolidation of Paramount and Blockbuster into the new parent company. In other words, Martin Davis, Paramount's chairman, and his No. 2., Stanley Jaffe, were out. When the acquisition was completed, Redstone controlled 61% of the votes in the new entity. As the video retailer's steady and strong cash flow was critical in servicing the debt of the new combination, Wayne Huizenga, Blockbuster's chairman, pressured Viacom to sweeten the terms of its offer, while Nynex wanted to "restructure" its investment in Viacom.

By mid-March Viacom named Jonathan Dolgen, president of the Sony Motion Pictures Group since 1991, to run the movie and television divisions of Paramount. Widely respected in Hollywood, Dolgen had a reputation as a tough businessman and a steely negotiator. Speculation on Paramount's future caused nervousness even in the $2 billion publishing empire.

Viacom had paid an astonishing premium for Paramount, whose studio was in disarray following a slate of flops. The price was almost $2 billion higher than Viacom agreed to pay in September when the two struck a friendly merger agreement. Both Wall Street and Hollywood expected Viacom to shed some Paramount assets to raise cash (e.g., Madison Square Garden, half-interest in USA Network).

On March 11, 1994, Viacom took control of Paramount Communications. In a month or two it stepped up a campaign to cut costs and sell nonstrategic assets. In late April Viacom's $2 billion Paramount Publishing unit announced it intended to sell several (Prentice Hall) units in its software and information division. Two months later Viacom dismissed Richard E. Snyder as chairman and CEO of Simon & Schuster, the publishing company he had built into a giant over the last 33 years. The abrupt dismissal stunned the consolidated publishing industry, which was now powered by executives with no background in book publishing. Concurrently, Viacom negotiated with TCI on broad ties in cable and pay-TV, despite its massive antitrust lawsuit against TCI.

As the value of Viacom's shares plunged, the prospects clouded for the acquisition of Blockbuster. In May 1994 Huizenga sent a letter to his shareholders saying there "could be no assurance the board could recommend a transaction" with Viacom. (In spite of the apparent breakdown in the merger agreement, Viacom did not have the right to break off the merger until September 30.) As Huizenga acted more like an interested investor than a decisive player, his stockholders became worried about how much Blockbuster might lose on its Viacom investment.[6]

Venturing further into the video dialtone business, Viacom joined Nynex in exploring video-on-demand possibilities for the vast Viacom and Paramount film and TV libraries. It also began to create interactive versions of Viacom's cable networks (MTV, Nickelodeon, VH-1) and to develop multiplayer video games.

Even if Viacom's original deal with Blockbuster was not going to happen as planned, it did not jeopardize the acquisition of Paramount—which was complicated by what came to be called the "blockbummer" deal.

The Great Convergence

NEW CHANNEL STRUCTURE

From the late 1940s to the mid-1980s, U.S. media and entertainment had been dominated by the Hollywood studios and the Big Three broadcast TV networks, which controlled the production and distribution pipelines. By the late '80s a multitude of competitive forces—technological (digital electronics, fiber optics, compression), industrial policies (deregulation, new antitrust, and tax policies), corporate governance (the fourth national M&A wave, foreign invasion of U.S. private sector), and economic changes (twin deficit, capital disadvantage)—were bringing about revolutionary changes in the environment.

Nostalgia of the Past

Even the press and industry observers were caught by the pace of events. Although, for example, TCI's John Malone played a leading role in most developments, the cable giant steered through the "Booming Eighties" with relatively few wounds, despite allegations ranging from monopolizing to TCI executives' links with the notorious BCCI. As American broadcasting and cable went through a dramatic metamorphosis, public scrutiny focused on the least significant players in the new competitive environment. The years of 1986–90 witnessed a proliferation of books on the demise of CBS and its historic pioneers—including A. M. Sperber's *Murrow: His Life and Times* (1986), Lewis J. Paper's *Empire: William S. Paley and the Making of CBS* (1987), Peter McCabe's *Bad News at Black Rock: The Sell-Out of CBS News* (1987), Ed Joyce's *Prime Times, Bad Times: A Personal Drama of Network Television* (1988), Bill Leonard's *In the Storm of the Eye: A Lifetime at CBS* (1987), Peter J. Boyer's *Who Killed CBS? The Undoing of America's Number One News Network* (1988), Robert Slater's *This Is CBS: A Chronicle of 60 Years* (1988), and Sally Bedell Smith's *In All His Glory: The Life of William S. Paley* (1990). Meanwhile, not a single work has been written on either John Malone or TCI. It was the nostalgia of the past that engaged the critics, not the promise of the future.

Complexity in Electronic Superhighways

Although the White House was speeding up a high-tech vision of partnership between the government and the private sector, the Clinton administration found much of its "national information infrastructure" overtaken by events. True, the telephone system (in the '30s) and the interstate highways system (in the '60s) had roles to play as major metaphors for the "national information infrastructure." But the leading telcos, cable operators, computer firms, and Hollywood studios were already putting a great variety of information highways in place.

The wholesome images of an orderly twentieth century laying of telephone lines and interstate highways under government support were inaccurate metaphors. A more proper analogy for the great rush to the twenty-first century digital marketplace derived from the railway free-for-all of the nineteenth century. Like the robber barons, the new corporate chieftains seized any means available to position themselves and, thereby, brought order and stability amid chaos and change.

The Clinton administration termed the new environment the "national information highway." The term was mistaken, in two ways. First, to define the new environment vis-a-vis "information" was reflective of the government's purposes and objectives, but associated a certain kind of content with the coming structure. Since it was the private sector that would build the new pipeline, "information" was bound to play a secondary role to "entertainment." Moreover, while the new pipeline would evolve as a "system," it would not be a "single" highway. Since several major U.S. corporations would take part in the construction of the new environment, it would be a "pluralistic system"—that is, a multitude of electronic superhighways. (As a result, I've used the notion of "national information highway" in sections dealing with the government's purposes, and "electronic superhighways" elsewhere. Although the two are not identical, they are not mutually exclusive either.)

In the course of my research, I became acutely aware of the complexity of the "research field." Certain issues in management, finance, and competitive environment indicate that our traditional theoretical formulations may be part of the problem—as much up to date as the church prior to the Copernican revolution.[1]

In a classic essay, "Managing our way to economic decline" (1980), Robert H. Hayes and William J. Abernathy argued that, during the previous two decades, American managers had increasingly relied on principles that prized analytical detachment and methodological elegance over insight, based on experience, into the subtleties and complexities of strategic decisions.[2] As a result, maximum short-term financial returns became the overriding criteria for many companies. (Hence, too, the financial games of the "Booming Eighties.")

Today the conventional wisdom in business has (or at least should have) become open to debate—especially in finance, management, and competitive strategy.[3] As persistent doubt has replaced pompous self-certainty, some researchers have turned to the theory of "chaos" or "complexity" to make sense of the difficult phenomena. Concurrently, historians are detailing the obscurity of premises that business schools still advocate as ultimate axioms (e.g., Peter L. Bernstein's *Capital Ideas*).[4]

STRATEGIC ALLIANCES: DIGITAL CAPITALISM

As major M&E corporations, computer companies, and telcos jockey for position in the evolving electronic superhighways, they hedge their bets. New markets evolve through a battle of complex alliances, which spread costs and risks and establish technical standards. Strategic groups of corporations are held together through cross-shareholding that dominate Japanese industry. The rapid pace of change blurs industry boundaries. As TCI's John Malone put it, the big players are "octopuses all with their hands in each other's pockets. Where one [industry] starts and the other stops will be hard to decide."[1]

It was Malone's TCI that pioneered the model of American digital keiretsu—that is, a U.S. version of Japan's multitiered, manufacturer-controlled distribution networks. From joint ventures with telcos to a proposed computer cable channel with Microsoft, TCI's strategy meant flexibility, speed, and highly opportunistic dealmaking. Instead of owning the layers of the value chain, the new corporate giants were content with participating in different parts of the value chain.

Unlike the old trusts, driven by monopolistic dreams, the new giants were willing to cooperate in one arena while banging heads in another, in return for spreading costs and risks. The new order favored neither a lone hero nor a wild bunch. If oligopolistic rivals conducted themselves like monopolists (they no longer were), retaliation and isolation were bound to follow. In May 1994, for example, IBM and Blockbuster launched a joint venture to store and download music CDs on demand, without obtaining the approval of the major record companies. The problem was not technological, but political. "My objection to the Blockbuster/IBM announcement is that here's someone else who wants to be the gatekeeper," said MCA's Al Teller. "We, as record companies, are already in the distribution business. Why would we empower somebody else to do that? To take over our distribution business? We should own that."[2] The Blockbuster/IBM venture was a textbook case of how *not* to form a strategic alliance.

The compelling drive toward alliances exemplified a new stage in American capitalism, and only time will tell whether it represents a fleeting phase or a permanent characteristic of the evolving landscape.

Since the decline of the powerful industrial trusts in the early twentieth century, giant corporations had built their empires through acquisitions and internal expansion. By the 1990s things were different. With the decline of the U.S. economy, the end of the Cold War, and the advent of global competition, American companies searched for common goals and common ownership. Mighty new oligopolies were boosted by significant changes in regulation and antitrust policies, as well as the Clinton administration's faith in industrial policies and partnerships between the government and private industry. Like U.S. corporations, the White House viewed electronic superhighways as a way to recapture momentum in global high-tech competition, after two decades of erosion in U.S. technology leadership.[3]

TRANSFORMATIONS OF COMPETITIVE ENVIRONMENT

In the early twentieth century, the Big Five Hollywood studios (Paramount, Loew's, Twentieth Century Fox, Warner Bros., and RKO), and the Little Three (Universal, Columbia, United Artists) pioneered U.S. media and entertainment, along with a few newspaper empires. As major studios adapted to sound, they also positioned themselves in the nascent record and music industry. Both Hollywood majors and newspaper chains diversified in radio, whereas the competitive environment in book publishing remained more fragmented. Major magazine owners (Time) became significant players only in the '50s and '60s when they diversified into other M&E industries (newspapers, broadcast and cable television).

The Network Era

The golden era of Hollywood majors ended with the Paramount decrees, which forced the vertically integrated studios to divest their theatrical segments. Concurrently, the rise of broadcast television, as well as shifts in demographics and lifestyle, led to Hollywood's demise and the growth of the independents. As classic Hollywood lost its exhibition pipeline, more extensive distribution emerged through the explosive growth of broadcast television. With their vast film libraries, the studios survived as production houses in broadcasting, just as they would (later) thrive in syndication and foreign markets. (see Figure 7–1A)

As the Big Three broadcast networks gained the role of the Big Five studios in Americans' lives, Hollywood studios were taken over by diversified conglomerates.

By the early '70s the networks lost control of production. Despite their long struggle against the financial interest and syndication rules, the Big Three failed to reenter production. Since viewership was forged by brand identification with the shows rather than with the networks, the status quo translated to a growing shift of bargaining power to suppliers (Hollywood studios, independent TV producers).

In the network era, capacity encompassed only 10 channels. This barrier enhanced the oligopoly of the Big Three. Until the '80s, NBC, CBS, and ABC remained as invulnerable as once Detroit's three automakers were— *and* as arrogant and complacent.

The Transition Era

Since the networks thrived on mass-audience products, segmentation was bound to further the broadcast networks' erosion. In the early '80s the Big Three dominated over 90% of the prime-time audience; by the end of the '80s only 50–60%. The proliferation of new cable channels translated into a transition from mass markets to segmentation (see Figure 7–1B).

With alternative outlets, advertisers no longer accepted broadcasters' price increases. Operating in a maturing business, the beleaguered Big Three broadcast networks were taken over in less than a year in 1986–87. Concurrently, deregulation unleashed the growth of cable, boosting the expansion of multiple station operators and cable networks. Some were "pure" cable networks (Turner), or multiple system operators with growing stakes in cable programmers (TCI); others became subsidiaries of Hollywood majors (Warner's ATC) or media conglomerates (Capital Cities/ABC, Viacom-Paramount). The MSOs' rising bargaining power stemmed from their critical technologies: as local cable systems sent their programming menus through coaxial lines to converters, they acquired control of distribution head ends in the information infrastructure.

Meanwhile, channel offerings increased almost tenfold. Cable programming narrowed rapidly as program creators focused on lucrative niche markets. In a decade, cable captured a third of network viewership, even if ratings for distinct cable channels remained less than 1%. The industry garnered a significant portion of revenues, but broadcasting remained the dominant mode of (mass) distribution.

If the '80s meant turmoil in broadcasting and consolidation in cable, market proliferation in entertainment boosted the wealth of Hollywood

Figure 7-1
The Evolution of Distribution in U.S. Media and Entertainment

A. Network Pipeline: From 1950s to Late 1970s

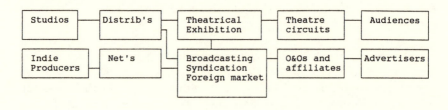

Producers -> Wholesalers -> Markets -> Retailers -> Buyers

B. Transition Pipeline: From Early 1980s to Early 90s

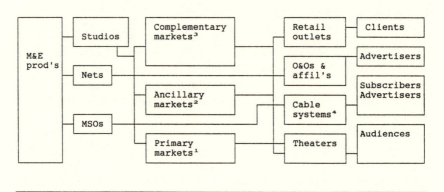

Producers -> Wholesalers -> Markets -> Retailers -> Buyers

majors. To survive in a highly capital-intensive business, they lost their corporate identity in the M&A wave. But, unlike the Big Three, the studios were not confined to maturing markets. Reintegrating their primary market (theatrical exhibition), they thrived in ancillary markets (home video, syndication, foreign markets), and complementary markets—from theme parks, toys, video games and licensed merchandise, record and music industry, publishing (newspapers, magazines, books) to interactive multimedia (from CD-ROM to virtual reality).

Toward the Electronic Superhighways Era

As advancements in technology (digital electronics, fiber optics, compression) boosted the fortunes of cable MSOs and consolidated home

Figure 7-1 continued

C. Toward Electronic Superhighways: The Mid-1990s

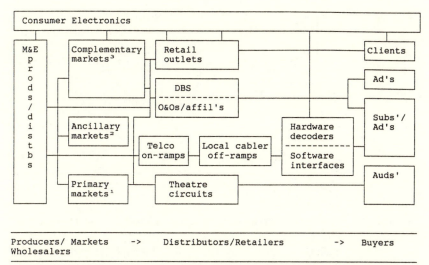

Producers/   Markets   ->   Distributors/Retailers   ->   Buyers
Wholesalers

1. Primary markets: theatrical exhibition, broadcasting. 2. Ancillary markets: home video, syndication, foreign markets. 3. Complementary markets: theme parks, toys, video games, licensed merchandising, record and music industry, publishing (newspapers, magazines, books), interactive multimedia (from CD-ROM to virtual reality). 4. Cable systems: basic cable, pay cable, pay-per-view (and video-on-demand).

shopping networks, electronics giants (Asian consumer electronics firms like Sony and Matsushita) and computer companies (mostly U.S.-based firms such as IBM, Apple, and Microsoft) entered M&E markets. By the early '90s they were followed by local telephone companies (Baby Bells, GTE) and long-distance carriers (AT&T, MCI, Sprint), motivated by the maturing of their own business and growth prospects in the electronic superhighways (see Figure 7–1C).[1] Due to the breakdown of old regulatory barriers and outmoded antitrust policies, major players engaged in strategic alliances or outright mergers starting in the mid- and late '80s.

New Producers/Distributors

By the early '90s half a dozen major M&E companies owned large film libraries and controlled existing TV shows—that is, Time Warner, Sony (Columbia), Viacom-Paramount, News Corp. (Fox), Disney, Matsushita (MCA-Universal), and Turner Broadcasting (New Line, Castle Rock, MGM library). Most of these companies had significant interests in TV shows and dominated the distribution of new products. The overall industry de-

Table 7-1
Video-on-Demand Revenues to Studios (1994E)

Number of Subs. (millions)

		10	20	30	40	50	60
Rentals	1	$240	$480	$720	$960	$1,200	$1,440
Per	2	480	960	1,440	1,920	2,400	2,880
Month	3	720	1,440	2,160	2,880	3,600	4,320
Per Sub	4	960	1,920	2,880	3,840	4,800	5,760
(millions)	5	1,200	2,400	3,600	4,800	6,000	7,200
	6	1,440	2,880	4,320	5,760	7,200	8,640

SOURCE: Richard P. Simon and Stephen G. Abraham, "Movie Industry Update - 1994," Goldman Sachs Entertainment/U.S. Research, April 4, 1994, p. 8.

mand for filmed entertainment resulted from the rollout of full-service networks or networks that offered adequate video-on-demand channel capacity—that is, 300–500 channel system as well as DBS (DirecTV). In 1994 a national survey found video-on-demand (VOD) the most appealing of the proposed interactive services; some 44% of Americans were ready to pay for it.[2] Based on VOD household levels of 10–60 million and monthly usage rates of 1–6, Goldman, Sachs estimated the overall revenues to the studios (see Table 7–1).

The Big Three broadcast networks still had a role to play in the new competitive environment. Although the demise of fin-syn rules in 1993 increased their opportunities in production and syndication, it would take years to get back into the business. Still, broadcast networks remained the principal sources of financing for new TV shows.

When Fox, in May 1994, signed eight CBS stations, the networks entered an intense and uncertain competitive environment. While the Big Three sought to protect their core business, they were also quietly pursuing interactive ventures (on-line market, CD-ROMs) to avoid being left behind by the new media. To secure distribution pipelines in the post-fin-syn environment, a number of powerful industry players were considering a "fifth network," or maybe more. Seeking a competitive edge in the new environment, major M&E companies explored how to meld TV station groups, program producers, and cable systems into hybrid networks. To succeed, any new network had to reach 80–90% of all TV households; as no station groups could form a fifth network alone, strategic alliances were inevitable. While Warner Bros. and Paramount intended to launch their networks in 1995, others considered similar distribution pipelines (e.g., Chris-Craft Industries, Tribune, QVC, Turner Broadcasting, SCI Television, Silver King Communications).

In addition to Hollywood studios and TV networks, the new producers/ distributors encompassed all companies, or, more precisely, strategic groups of companies, able and willing to fill the electronic pipeline with entertainment or information, including cablers, home shopping channels *as well as* retailers, on-line services, news organizations and information services, electronic publishing, and libraries.

Transformed by the 1960s' conglomeratization and the 1980s' mergers and divestitures, only the vertically integrated Hollywood majors had access to most M&E markets. Whereas in the new environment, telcos and cablers would control the distribution pipeline. Each could not afford to build the information infrastructure entirely alone; complementing one another, they improved service within existing infrastructure, focusing on their core competencies. While local telcos would take care of "on-ramps" distribution, their existing copper phone lines to the home were inadequate for video. Local cable systems were needed to complete the distribution headends.

Telco "On-Ramps"

Telco "on-ramps" encompassed most of the seven Baby Bells (Ameritech, Bell Atlantic, BellSouth, Nynex, Pacific Telesis, Southwestern Bell, US West). They were building the fiber-optic infrastructure and had the signal switch and billing technology needed to track megachannel services. GTE, long-distance telcos (AT&T, MCI, Sprint), and foreign entrants (Canadian BCE) used a greater variety of strategies to find a new mission (compare Table 7–4).

Local Cabler "Off-Ramps"

Local cabler "off-ramps" consisted of the MSOs that partnered with local telcos in 1993, including TCI, Time Warner Cable, Continental Cablevision, Comcast, Cablevision Systems, Cox Cable, Jones Intercable/Spacelink, Newhouse Broadcasting, Viacom, and others. They were building and upgrading fiber-optic lines to neighborhood converters that squeezed the signal into the "last mile" of existing coaxial cable. Meanwhile, increasingly powerful signal compression technology kept pace with channel growth—from video conferences and CD encyclopedias to realistic-looking video games to Mariah Carey recordings on Sony's pint-sized new MiniDisc. Compression's popularity stemmed from economics: it lowered the cost of storage and transmission by packing data into a smaller space.[3]

Like all technologies superseded by more powerful inventions, television had not readily disappeared from American living rooms, George Gilder argued in *Life After Television*. Yet the analog corpse had become as passé as last century's icebox and ice wagon.

The new system will be the telecomputer, a personal computer adapted for video processing and connected by fiber-optic threads to other telecomputers all around the world. Using a two-way system of signals like telephones do, rather than broadcasting one-way like TV, the telecomputer will surpass the television in video communication just as the telephone surpassed the telegraph in verbal communication.[4]

Prior to the '80s, remote controls were rare in U.S. households. During the transition era Americans got used to remotes, VCRs, and cable converter units. The old hardware represented a relatively basic, one-way technology and left few options to the viewer, irrespective of channel proliferation. In the '90s, with the convergence of television and computer technology, electronic superhighways were expected to multiply viewer options via channel proliferation and two-way interactivity.

Also, many M&E companies scrambled to invest in interactive services that could be used on the PC instead of on the TV. Indeed, many PC makers considered the collapse of TCI and Bell Atlantic's megadeal inevitable. While the top tier of computer companies had jumped into the fray (IBM's set-top box trial with Bell Atlantic, Apple's Macintosh set-top trial), the rest of the pack—which accounted for two-thirds of all computers sold in 1993—treated the information-highway concept with disdain.[5]

Replacing the outmoded cable boxes, new hardware was required to funnel the programming into the new TV set. It was this transformation that accounted for strategic alliances between M&E companies and PC/ software firms. Hardware decoders and software interfaces would be necessary to sort out the new 500–1,000 channel capacity.

Hardware Decoders

PC software companies (Microsoft, Intel/General Instruments, IBM, Apple, Frox, 3DO, Microware Systems, Silicon Graphics) raced to design the "set-top box" (STB), a super-cable converter unit they hoped would become the new central controller. Prototypes resulted in hardware decoders, linked to the video dial tone and voice, games, CDs, and even the VCR.

With hardware decoders, viewers needed software interfaces that sorted out programming, scheduled viewing, and anticipated a variety of new options.

Software Interfaces

As TV sets acquired the intelligence of computers, the difference between the two became blurry; menus served as navigational aids in the new channel environment. By the early '90s, software interfaces were being developed by Microsoft, Apple EZTV, Your Choice TV, and Prodigy. For example, TV Guide On Screen (a joint venture between *TV Guide* magazine and Liberty Media) developed an electronic listing service. Tested in Denver, the system transmitted a full schedule of programming each day over the cable system to a set-top control device. With the schedule, parents could designate the shows they wanted to see, the ones they wanted their VCRs to record, and lock out particular categories.[6]

Even voice-recognition technology was finding its way to TV controls. Later, "smart television" was expected to provide a wealth of information to advertisers, just as viewers could use keyboards and the "mouse" to manipulate sound, image, voice, and text. Ultimately, the potential of the technology could make possible the famous (or infamous) utopias of "cyber-sex," with a private line and the proper software.

Hardware decoders and software interfaces were not the only new high-tech markets to evolve with the electronic superhighways. In January 1994 Bell Atlantic said it would spend $25 million for three new supercomputers as well as software; a new market was opening for giant servers to feed the new interactive services. After all, downsizing ignited the server market, trading mainframes and minicomputers for networks of powerful PCs and workstations. The PC server business was expected to climb from $4.7 billion to $7.4 billion between 1993 and 1996.[7]

The New Universe of Television

In December 1992, John Malone announced that TCI planned to introduce digital compression technology that would let it provide 500 or more channels to cable subscribers. The statement popularized the notion of a "500–channel universe," although the number of channels could well be higher. In theory, digital compression enabled a typical 54–channel cable system to display 540 channels. And if pure fiber systems were linked with compression, a 150-channel system could theoretically deliver 1,500 channels to a home.[8]

Yet, sheer quantity was no guarantee of consumer acceptance. In the late 1970s, blockbuster titles popularized VCRs in U.S. households, just as variety shows and sitcoms had sold the first generation of TV sets in the '50s. Unlike consumer electronics, computers, and telecommunications, Hollywood had a long track record in expanding entertainment choices while keeping them simple enough. Now Tinseltown was expected to find a way to package the new hardware decoder/software interface in a user-friendly format.

The opportunity and the challenges were formidable. Network programming schedules would have to be redesigned. Program services, offered with a tiered pricing system, would range from increasingly fragmented basic cable (with proposed niche channels like the SciFi Channel, the Crime Channel, The Television Food Network, and the Military Channel) and pay cable to pay-per-view. A major portion of the new channels would be used as "multiplex" movie services. Premium services (HBO, Showtime, Encore) would be split into different networks, and dozens of channels would be set aside as an "electronic video store."

Unlike the current shopping channels, the new home-shopping services would evolve into "cybermalls."

Toward a New Value Chain

The evolving electronic pipeline not only suggested the features of the new channel structure, but also the clustering of traditional and new strategic groups around critical nodal points of the new value chain. Industry observers reacted rapidly to changes in the competitive environment. By the spring of 1994, *Advertising Age* began to publish its "Interactive Media & Marketing" section, while *Broadcasting & Cable* followed suit with its "Telemedia Week" supplement focusing on "the interactive world of voice, data and video." By summer 1994, even NBC had lined up major on-line services (Prodigy, America Online, GE's Genie) to carry a new programming and marketing service, NBC Online; CBS Marketing Interactive intended to make use of a variety of interactive media technologies to deliver CBS programming, promos, and advertisers' messages.

The highly capital-intensive distribution rivalry would be dominated by major telcos and Hollywood studios—as evidenced by the surge of video dialtone applications and the increasing number of evolving interactive TV systems (see Tables 7–2 and 7–3).[9]

As suppliers, Hollywood studios operated in primary, ancillary, and complementary markets, while other strategic groups (TV networks, cablers, news organizations) would have businesses in some of them. Mediating between markets and buyers, manufacturers would produce hardware decoders (consumer electronics, telecommunications) and software interface (computer firms) (see Table 7–4). Instead of the old M&E companies, or telephone or computer companies, the new era would witness the birth of the first true, integrated "communications" companies.

If those societal and corporate structures that once corroded American media and entertainment would prevail in the new environment, capital disadvantage and global competition would spare neither the new industries nor the new companies—despite the telcos' financial muscle. Moreover, public goals and private objectives did not always go hand in hand. When the telcos began wiring the information highway, they seemed to bypass poorer neighborhoods and minority populations, engaging in "electronic redlining." It was the government role to insure affordable universal service, as well as to devise investment incentives, to keep the highway democratic, and to protect privacy and intellectual property rights.

Indeed, government policies—from regulation and antitrust to taxation—had a critical role in molding industry evolution in the new environment. "After years of reeling in dollars, the cable television industry, buffeted by Federal regulation, competition and uncertainty about the future, is now simply reeling," reported the *New York Times* amid the in-

Table 7-2
A Sample of Proposed Interactive Television Systems (Spring 1994)[1,2]

Launch date	Location	Status	Test Duration	Number of Customers[3]
Time Warner's Full Service Network (FSN)				
1994/4rd q.	Orlando	Equipment delays	1-1,5 yrs	4,000
US West's Multimedia Network				
1994/3rd q.	Omaha	Under construction	1 year	9,000
GTE's Cerritos Project				
1988	Cerritos, Cal.	In progress	5 yrs	Varies by service
Bell Atlantic's Multimedia Networks				
1993	2 cities and 1 county in Virginia	Waiting for FCC's approval	1 year	2,000
Viacom/AT&T Castro Valley Project				
1994	Castro Valley, Cal.	Network upgrade under way	1,5 yrs	1,000
TCI, AT&T and US West: Viewer Controlled Cable TV				
1992	Denver	In progress	2 yrs	300

1. Other interactive TV systems included Time Warner's 150-channel cable network in Queens New York, Cox Enterprise's and Southwestern Bell's trial test in Omaha, Nebraska; Bell Atlantic's video/telephone network in Toms River, N.J.; as well as trials by Your Choice TV, Ameritech, SNET, Nynex, GTE, Interaxx TV Network, Bell South, IT Network, Sprint, Interactive Network and Pacific Telesis.
2. Most systems' general categories included video on demand, home shopping, video games, education, and information.
3. Market trial [preceded by technical trial].

SOURCES: From "Interactive Media & Marketing," _Advertising Age_, March 21, 1994, pp. IM1-IM4.; Edmund L. Andrews, "With Merger's Failure, an Industry Seeks a Leader," _New York Times_, February 26, 1994, pp. 39, 41.; David S. Jackson and Suneel Ratan, "Play... Fast Forward... Rewind... Pause," _Time_, May 23, 1994, pp. 44-46.

dustry's annual meeting.[10] Yet it was hard to weep for an industry that still rolled up profit margins of 40%. Besides, cable had weathered previous storms, such as the credit crunch of 1990. Having reached maturity, the industry was paying for the early years' aggressive hardball strategy.

While the electronic superhighways continued to be built, the cable companies were increasingly playing a supporting role. As the mighty telephone giants were pioneering the new field, they protected their core business. Yet things were changing.

Even a decade after the breakup of the old Bell system, the seven regional telcos still handled more than 95% of telephone calls in the United

Table 7-3
Video Dialtone Applications at the FCC (April 1994)

Applicant	Location	Homes	Status	
Bell Atlantic	Arlington, VA	2,000	Approved	3/25/93
Nynex	New York	2,500	Approved	6/29/93
SNET	West Hartford, CT	1,500	Approved	11/12/93
US West	Omaha, NE	62,500	Approved	12/22/93
Rochester Telephone	Rochester, NY	120	Approved	3/25/93
NJ Bell Telephone	Florham Park, NJ	11,700	Pending	
NJ Bell Telephone	Dover Township, NJ	38,000	Pending	
Bell Atlantic	MD and VA suburbs of DC	300,000	Pending	
Pacific Bell	Orange County, CA	210,000	Pending	
Pacific Bell	South San Francisco	490,000	Pending	
Pacific Bell	Los Angeles	360,000	Pending	
Pacific Bell	San Diego	250,000	Pending	
US West	Denver	300,000	Pending	
US West	Portland, OR	132,000	Pending	
US West	Minneapolis-St. Paul	292,000	Pending	
Ameritech	Detroit	232,000	Pending	
Ameritech	Columbus/Cleveland	262,000	Pending	
Ameritech	Indianapolis	115,000	Pending	
Ameritech	Chicago	501,000	Pending	
Ameritech	Milwaukee	146,000	Pending	
US West	Boise, ID	90,000	Pending	
US West	Salt Lake City	160,000	Pending	

SOURCE: _Broadcasting & Cable_, April 18, 1994, p. 6.

States, and their local monopolies were likely to avoid a serious challenge for another decade, asserted a study sponsored by AT&T, MCI, and a long-distance industry group. Despite various efforts, new rivals had made scant inroads into the Baby Bells's turf. By the spring of 1994, however, in the pioneering plan of its type in the United States, Time Warner intended to use its cable-TV system in Rochester to provide telephone service to residential and business customers in competition with the local phone company; it reflected the first real sign of direct competition between cable and telephone companies. Meanwhile, Southwestern Bell was seeking to offer local telephone service to cable customers in Bell Atlantic's region, in what would be the first assault by a Baby Bell on a sibling's local phone business.[11]

AMERICA'S ENTERTAINMENT ECONOMY

In the early '90s the U.S. economy was growing and American companies were prospering, but announcements of job cuts were more numerous than ever. As the "jobless recovery" was becoming a more normal one in 1994, U.S. M&E companies served as growth engines in what _Business Week_ called "The Entertainment Economy." "As consumers spend big bucks on fun, companies are plowing billions into theme parks, casinos, sports, and interactive TV. The result: Entertainment is reshaping the U.S. economy."[1]

In 1993 the entertainment and recreation industries added 200,000 workers—more than the health-care industry, the preeminent job creator of the 1980s. Indeed, entertainment and recreation have claimed a steadily increasing share of consumer spending (7.71% in 1979, 9.43% in 1993).[2]

After decades of Cold War, entertainment was replacing defense as the driving force for new technology. Yet electronic superhighways were no guarantee of job growth. As we have seen, prior to the collapse of the Bell Atlantic-TCI deal, major telcos cut more than 85,000 jobs. Citing a new study by the Council of Economic Advisers, however, Vice President Al Gore argued that enactment of the Clinton administration's information superhighway proposals would add $100 billion to the economy during the next 10 years and create 500,000 new jobs by the end of 1996.

Between 1994 and 1999 cable TV and telcos alone are expected to spend some $50 billion building advanced networks. The risks of the telcos' capital expenditures were considered reasonable. In the past, spending had been driven by regulation. Now it was driven by customers and the anticipated competitive landscape. Still, the efforts to acquire cable companies, build high-tech networks, as well as new wireless communications networks, raised concern on Wall Street.[3]

The Price of Bargaining Power

"Right now, the advertiser is the customer," John Malone had said in late 1993. "Entertainment is the lowest common denominator because a programmer has to line up a big audience to see that advertising. This puts the consumer on top. He buys the programming."[4] True, prior to the '80s, buyers of U.S. media and entertainment consisted of advertisers; in the new environment, bargaining power would shift to subscribers, but for a price—consumers would pay for the new services. Interestingly enough, a national survey found more than half of the nation's cable subscribers (54%) interested in interactive services, although two-fifths were ready to drop current cable services to offset the cost of adding them.[5]

Also, the association between bargaining power and quality programming was not a direct one. Despite increasing cable investments in original programming, the networks continued to finance the bulk of new TV products well into the early '90s. Moreover, despite the lofty rhetoric about quality programming, consumer spending in the evolving information highway grew most rapidly in X-rated computer networks and adult software, replicating the home video pattern a decade before. In spring 1994, for example, *Newsweek* reported that "thousands of cyberswingers" were linked together by networks of adult-oriented bulletin

Table 7-4
Electronic Superhighways: Major Players—Diverse M&E Assets (Spring 1994)

	HARDWARE/SOFTWARE							
	Recording playback equipment	Filmed & TV entert	Recorded music	Newsp	Publishing Magaz	Books	Theme Parks	Inter-active softw[1]
CapCit/ABC		x		x				
CBS		x						
GE/NBC		x						
Disney		x	x		x	x	x	x
Matsushita	x	x	x			x	x	x
News Corp.		x		x	x	x		x
Sony	x	x	x				x	x
TCI		x						
Time Warner	x	x	x		x	x	x	x
Turner Brdng		x				x		
Viacom-Par		x	x			x	x	x

	WHOLESALE DISTRIBUTION			RETAIL DISTRIBUTION					
	Cable programming	Broadc net	Radio network	Cable oper	Broadc stats	Radio stats	Theater circuit	Ret[2] oper	DBS
CBS	x	x	x	x					x
CapCit/ABC		x	x	x	x				
Disney	x			x				x	
GE/NBC		x		x	x				x
Matsushita	x			x			x		x
News Corp.		x		x	x				x
Sony							x	x	
TCI	x			x				x	x
Time Warner	x			x			x	x	x
Turner Brdng	x					x			
Viacom-Par	x			x	x	x	x	x	x

1. Includes video games. 2. Includes consumer products, retailing, home shopping, video retailing.

boards with names like KinkNet and ThrobNet. Loaded with libraries of X-rated pictures and interactive adult games like "Pin the Tail on Your Wife," these on-line services draw users to the computer the same way porno videos attracted consumers to VCRs a decade ago."[6]

Advertisers and Consolidation

In the early '90s most of the hype about the information highway focused on technology, whereas advertisers were interested in audiences. If, in the new environment, bargaining power were to shift to subscribers, advertisers—the current buyers of U.S. media and entertainment—would run the risk of simply adapting to changing technologies. If audiences become more program-driven and less channel-driven, advertisers could face the threat of losing access to broad segments of their audiences.

In May 1994 Edwin L. Artzt, chairman-CEO of Procter & Gamble (P&G), energized the advertising community with a significant speech on the future of TV advertising:

Table 7-4 continued

Telcos	Investment Strategies in U.S. Media and Entertainment (Spring 1994)
Ameritech	Upgrading its network for digital video services ($29 bil., 1994-99); effort to rollout video services to over 1.3 1.3 mil. homes; seeking entry to long-distance business.
Bell Atlantic	The most aggressive telco in U.S. media and entertainment; seeking local cable partners; building a $11 bil. multimedia network (1 mil. homes in 1995, another 1.5 mil. each year thereafter); numerous contracts for hardware, video programming, computer hardware.
Bell South	Still articulating its video services strategy; a 22.5% stake in Prime Cable for $1 bil.; seeking to buy additional cable systems; agreed to invest $1.5 bil. in QVC to help in its bid for Paramount.
Nynex	$1.2 bil. investment in Viacom to help it acquire Paramount (access to library and production capability); a new focus on video and multimedia.
Pacific Telesis	Planning major video service trials; constructing a statewide broadband network; prepared to invest $16 bil., 1994-2001, to construct fiber-coaxial hybrid networks.
Southwestern Bell	After the collapse of Bell Atlantic-TCI deal, SW Bell's partnership with Cox cable came asunder; purchased two cable systems from Hauser for $650 mil.; pursuing in-region video plans.
US West	A $2.5 bil. investment in Time Warner Entertainment; solid commitment to multimedia markets via US West Interactive Video Enterprises; invested $10 bil. to upgrade service to every home in its region.
GTE	Experimental voice and video tests; interactive TV services in a test market, with AT&T; building a video network linked to 7 mil. homes; by 2003 expected to deliver broadcast, cable and interactive TV programs in 66 cities and bring in $1 bil. in annual revenues.
AT&T	Takeover of McCaw Cellular Communications for $12.6 bil. in new stock; talks with cablers about linking their customers into one big interactive, multimedia network (with Time Warner and Viacom).
MCI	Planned to pour $1 billion into a joint venture with British Telecommunications (a $4.3 bil. in MCI); spending over $1 bil. to construct local networks in major U.S. cities (with TCI, Time Warner); a $2 bil. plan to invade the local telephone market; an effort to team up with unspecified partners on a $20 bil. attempt to upgrade long-distance network for an array of voice, video, and high-speed data communications; $1.3 bil. for a 17% stake in wireless upstart Nextel Communications Inc.
Sprint	Linking business customers over Internet; after failed merger effort with GM's EDS, plan for global links via an alliance with France Telecom and Deutsche Telekom.

From where we stand today, we can't be sure that ad-supported TV programming will have a future in the world being created—a world of video-on-demand, pay-per-view and subscription television.

Within the next few years—surely before the end of the decade—consumers will be choosing among hundreds of shows and pay-per-view movies. They'll have dozens of home shopping channels. They'll play hours of interactive videogames.

And for many of these—maybe most—no advertising at all.

If that happens, if advertising is no longer needed to pay most of the cost of home entertainment, then advertisers like us will have a hard time achieving the reach and frequency we need to support our brands.[7]

If QVC's Barry Diller could sell 20,000 pairs of earrings in 5 minutes on the home shopping channel, that was terrific for a company that sold impulse items, but P&G had to sell 400 million boxes of Tide annually. Frequency and depth of sale were critical to preserving loyalty to such frequently purchased brands. (Indeed, P&G spent almost 90% of its $3 billion advertising budget on TV.) Hence, advertisers' concern with the apparent demise of broad-reach television.

Artzt's solution? Embrace technology and return to program ownership. The other side of Artzt's solution? A new restructuring wave in Madison Avenue (which had hardly recovered from the booming '80s), increasing consolidation, and the demise of mid-size shops.

The brave new world of Madison Avenue began in May 1994, when IBM, in the largest shift in advertising history, announced it would dismiss more than 40 agencies it had worked with around the world and move its entire account to a single shop, Ogilvy & Mather Worldwide. As one of the world's biggest marketers, the beleaguered computer giant spent half a billion dollars annually on advertising. The decision reverberated for months reflecting sweeping changes in the advertising industry.

By the early 1990s the "truck lanes" that helped U.S. companies conduct business electronically were being set in place. As businesses recognized that a high-speed information infrastructure could play a critical part in speeding the pace of operations and cutting costs, investments accumulated in electronic commerce (e.g., the commercialization of the Internet). For instance, CommerceNet, Silicon Valley's experimental information superhighway for business, was expected to shape a large business infrastructure.[8]

As optimists painted visions of high-tech utopias, pessimists warned that, since the early nineteenth century, there had been three major eras of financial speculation that included communications issues of some sort (in 1825, canals and railroads; in 1873, the telegraph and ticker-tape-machine businesses; in 1929, the radio, gramophone, and talking-picture industries). In each case, speculation in the "information superhighways" of the day was followed by a major market downturn.[9]

In 1992 Barry Diller, a TV veteran of enormous drive and reputation, suggested that speculating on the future of American media and entertainment so early in the game was an exercise in babble-think. A year and a half later, things remained fuzzy:

. . . the picture is murkier. And the reason is that there's been some progress, and that always makes things a little more confusing. We've made enough progress to know some of the words now. Like information superhighway, infobahn, roadkill, on ramps, off ramps—all tasked to a technology that's not there yet. It's even more misleading when it's real than it was as just a big rosy piece of hype.

The truth is, if you separate what's real from what's not, despite a muddled government policy, despite a turndown in the market, despite worries about capital structure, despite Bell Atlantic-TCI, the tracks are being laid.[10]

By the mid-'90s the existing competitive environment in American media and entertainment was rapidly fading away, while the new landscape was in fast formation underneath.

The contemporary was history in disguise. In the electronic highways, the bells rang for the toll-keepers.

Notes

CHAPTER 1. AMERICAN ECONOMY: U.S. MEDIA AND ENTERTAINMENT

1. *The Economist/A Survey of the Entertainment Industry,* December 23, 1989, p. 4.

2. *Building a Competitive America,* Competitiveness Policy Council, March 1, 1992, p. vii.

3. Michael E. Porter, *Capital Choices,* a Research Report Presented to the Council of Competitiveness, the Harvard Business School (1992). See also Michael T. Jacobs, *Short-Term America* (Boston: Harvard Business School Press, 1991); Benjamin M. Friedman, *A Day of Reckoning* (New York: Random House, 1988); Lester Thurow, *Head to Head* (New York: William Morrow, 1992).

FROM SUPPLY-SIDE REVOLUTION TO TWIN DEFICIT

1. Compare Paul Craig Roberts, *The Supply-Side Revolution* (Cambridge, Mass.: Harvard University Press, 1984).

2. Benjamin M. Friedman, *A Day of Reckoning* (New York: Random House, 1988), p. 211.

3. Compare John B. Judis, "The Red Menace," *New Republic,* October 26, 1992, pp. 26–29; Owen Ullman, "No Smoke, No Mirrors," *Business Week,* October 11, 1993, pp. 30–31.

4. Compare Cathie J. Martin, *Shifting the Burden* (Chicago: University of Chicago Press, 1991), p. 107.

5. On tax reforms and M&E companies, see Dan Steinbock, "American Media and Entertainment: The 'Booming' Eighties" (unpublished manuscript).

6. Compare Myron S. Scholes, "Tax Treatment of Short-Term Trading," in Arnold W. Sametz (ed.), *Institutional Investing* (Homewood, Ill.: Irwin, 1991), pp. 150–158; Rick Wartzman, "Foreign Firms' Income in U.S. Is Understated," *Wall Street Journal,* June 4, 1993, p. A2.

7. Anthony S. Ginsberg, *Tax Havens* (New York: New York Institute of Finance, 1991); Peter Bart, "Beached bankers," *Variety,* April 13, 1992, pp. 5, 20.

8. See Steinbock, "American Media and Entertainment."

NEW STOCK MARKET

1. Michael E. Porter, *Capital Choices,* a Research Report Presented to the Council on Competitiveness, the Harvard Business School (1992), pp. 61–62.

2. Marshall E. Blume, Jeremy J. Siegel, and Dan Rottenberg, *Revolution on Wall Street* (New York: W.W. Norton, 1993).

3. Connie Bruck, *The Predators' Ball* (New York: Viking Penguin, 1989), pp. 19–20; E. I. Altman and S. A. Nammacher, *The Anatomy of the High-Yield Market* (New York: Morgan Stanley & Co., 1986); Robert A. Taggart, Jr., "The Growth of the 'Junk' Bond Market and Its Role in Financing Takeovers," in Alan J. Auerbach (ed.), *Mergers and Acquisitions* (Chicago: University of Chicago Press, 1988), pp. 5–24.

4. Larry Light with Leah J. Nathans, "Corporate America Wants Out from under Its Junk Pile," *Business Week,* August 21, 1989, pp. 80–81.

5. Merrill Brown, "Television's Junk-Bond Blues," *Channels,* November 1988, p. 30.

6. Securities Data Co.

7. On the Milken debate, see Joe Queenan, "Prose and Con: The Milken Book Boom," *Barron's,* November 30, 1992, pp. 10–11, 22–23.

8. On individual investors, see Michael Siconolfi, "Individual Investors' Holdings of U.S. Stocks Fall Below 50% of Total Market for the First Time," *Wall Street Journal,* November 13, 1992, p. C1; Susan E. Kuhn, "The New Perilous Stock Market," *Fortune,* December 27, 1993, pp. 48–62. On institutional investors, see Carolyn Kay Brancato, *Institutional Investors and Capital Markets: 1991 Update* (New York: Columbia Institutional Investor Project, September 1991). See also Jay O. Light and Andre F. Perold, "The Institutionalization of Wealth: Changing Patterns of Investment Decision Making," in Samuel L. Hayes III (ed.), *Wall Street and Regulation* (Boston: Harvard Business School Press, 1987), pp. 97–126.

9. See *NYSE: Fact Book 1991* (New York: NYSE, 1991), p. 79.

10. Compare Brett Duval Fromson, "The Big Owners Roar," *Fortune,* July 30, 1990, pp. 66–78.

11. Brancato, *Institutional Investors; Barron's,* September 1, 1986, p. 30; Jeffrey Daniels, "Portfolio Managers: Powerful Wall Street Players," *Hollywood Reporter/ Entertainment Finance,* August 1991, pp. F4, F6, F13.

12. Louis Loewenstein, *Sense & Nonsense in Corporate Finance* (New York: Addison-Wesley, 1991); Dan Steinbock, "American Media and Entertainment: The 'Booming' Eighties" (unpublished manuscript); Paul Noglows, "Black Monday:

The Impact on Media Dealmaking," *Channels*, January 1988, pp. 10–14; *The Report of The Twentieth Century Fund Task Force on Market Speculation and Corporate Governance* (New York: The Twentieth Century Fund Press, 1992).

13. Compare Douglas R. Sease and Steven E. Levingston, "Fickle Market: As Stocks Swing About and Decline Abruptly, Many Investors Suffer," *Wall Street Journal*, August 10, 1992, pp. A1–A2.

14. William Glasgall et al., "The Market's Revenge," *Business Week*, April 18, 1994, pp. 32–40.

TROUBLED BANKING INDUSTRY

1. Compare Neal Gabler, *An Empire of Their Own* (New York: Doubleday, 1988), pp. 133–136.

2. "Commercial Banks and Investment Banking," in J. Peter Williamson (ed.), *Investment Banking Handbook* (New York: John Wiley, 1988), pp. 433–471; "American Finance," *The Wilson Quarterly*, Autumn 1992, pp. 17–45; David M. Meerschwam, "Breaking Relationships: The Advent of Price Banking in the United States," in Samuel L. Hayes III (ed.), *Wall Street and Regulation* (Boston: Harvard Business School Press, 1987), pp. 63–96; Richard H. K. Vietor, "Regulation-Defined Financial Markets: Fragmentation and Integration in Financial Services," in Hayes, *Wall Street and Regulation*, pp. 7–62.

3. Michael T. Jacobs, *Short-Term America* (Boston: Harvard Business School Press, 1991), pp. 143–170.

4. On the historical evolution of U.S. investment banking, see Samuel L. Hayes III, A. Michael Spence, and David V. P. Marks, "Investment Banking Competition: An Historical Sketch," in J. Peter Williamson (ed.), *Investment Banking Handbook* (New York: John Wiley, 1988), pp. 11–33.

5. *Wall Street Journal*, December 28, 1989, p. C1.

6. "Banking in the Fifth Estate," *Broadcasting*, November 13, 1989, pp. 47–76; "Boutiques, up-and-comers and others," *Broadcasting*, November 13, 1989, pp. 66–70; as well as special reports by *Hollywood Reporter*.

7. Paul Noglows, "Focus on workout wizards," *Variety*, November 30, 1992, pp. 79, 88.

8. Paul Noglows and Dennis Wharton, "Showbiz gets a lift as Fed eases up on HLT," *Variety*, January 27, 1992, pp. 69–70.

9. Kenneth H. Bacon, "Banks' Declining Role in Economy Worries Fed, May Hurt Firms," *Wall Street Journal*, July 9, 1993, pp. A1, A5.

10. Cheryl Heuton, "Banks Just Say No," *Channels*, December 17, 1990, p. 14.

11. On the top 500 bank data, see *American Banker* (selected July issues); on Japanese banks' oligopolistic penetration strategies, see Hervé de Carmoy, *Global Banking Strategy* (Cambridge, Mass.: Basil Blackwell, 1990), pp. 125–126.

12. Michael Quint, "Japan's Giant Banks on the March," *New York Times*, October 1, 1989, pp. F1, F12.

13. *Federal Reserve Bank of New York Quarterly Review*, Spring 1992; Michael Quint, "U.S. Banks Cut Global Business as Rivals Grow," *New York Times*, July 5, 1990, pp. A1, D9.

14. On Frans Afman, see Hy Hollinger, "Hollywood's Sugar Daddy," *Daily Va-*

riety, March 6, 1991, pp. F18–F20; on Crédit Lyonnais and Hollywood, see Kathleen A. Hughes and Charles Fleming, "How a French Bank Went to Hollywood and Found Trouble," *Wall Street Journal,* June 19, 1991, pp. A1, A4.

15. See, for example, Peter Gumbel, "Crédit Lyonnais Risky-Loan Exposure Worse Than Admitted, New Book Says," *Wall Street Journal,* February 5, 1993, p. A8.

16. Compare Peter Gumbel, "Crédit Lyonnais Losses Focus Attention on Business Decisions Linked to Politics," *Wall Street Journal,* March 31, 1994, p. A11.

NEW ANTITRUST AND DEREGULATION

1. On the significance of antitrust genesis, see Robert H. Bork, *The Antitrust Paradox: A Policy at War with Itself* (New York: Basic Books, 1978), p. 15.

2. William G. Shepherd, *The Economics of Industrial Organization,* 3rd ed. (Englewood Cliffs, N. J.: Prentice-Hall, 1990), p. 20.

3. Compare F. M. Scherer, "Merger Policy in the 1970s and 1980s," in Robert J. Larner and James W. Meehan, Jr. (eds.), *Economics & Antitrust Policy* (Westport, Conn.: Quorum Books, 1989), pp. 83–101.

4. Compare William J. Baumol, John C. Panzar, and Robert D. Willig, *Contestable Markets and the Theory of Industrial Structure* (San Diego: Harcourt Brace Jovanovich, 1982). For an opposing view, see Walter Adams and James W. Brock, *Dangerous Pursuits: Mergers and Acquisitions in the Age of Wall Street* (New York: Pantheon Books, 1989).

5. Catherine Yang, "Pull the Lever—and Fill the Bench," *Business Week,* October 19, 1992, pp. 107–108.

6. Larry N. Gerston, Cynthia Fraleigh, and Robert Schwab, *The Deregulated Society* (Pacific Grove, Calif.: Brooks/Cole, 1988), pp. 40–63. See also Erwin G. Krasnow, Lawrence D. Longley, and Herbert A. Terry, *The Politics of Broadcast Regulation,* 3rd ed. (New York: St. Martin's Press, 1982), pp. 33–142.

7. See Fred Strasser, "Antitrust Shift Eyed With Doubt," *National Law Journal,* March 9, 1992, pp. 3, 36.

8. Bob Davis and Joe Davidson, "Clinton Team Is Split About Antitrust Policy As Big Mergers Wait," *Wall Street Journal,* October 28, 1993, pp. A1, A14.

9. Compare Clyde Prestowitz, "U.S. Rules, Not Japanese Money, Lost MCA," *Wall Street Journal,* December 3, 1990, p. A14.

10. Compare Harry A. Jessell and Kim McAvoy, "A chairman apart," *Broadcasting & Cable,* March 21, 1994, pp. 12–18; Mark Lewyn, "Clinton's Lightning Rod at the FCC," *Business Week,* May 16, 1994, pp. 86–87.

11. Catherine Yang, with William Spindle, "Commerce Cops," *Business Week,* December 13, 1993, pp. 69–70.

12. Keith Bradsher, "U.S. Sues British in Antitrust Case," *New York Times,* May 27, 1994, pp. A1, D6.

13. Edmund L. Andrews, "Clinton and Technology: Some Policies Clash," *New York Times,* April 11, 1994, pp. D1–D2.

THE FOURTH M&A WAVE: FOREIGN INVASION

1. See John Huey, "America's Hottest Export: Pop Culture," *Fortune,* December 31, 1990, pp. 50–60.

2. Roy C. Smith, *The Money Wars* (New York: Plume, 1990), p. 4.

3. Robert Sobel, *The Rise and Fall of the Conglomerate Kings* (New York: Stein and Day, 1984).

4. Michael Porter, "From Competitive Advantage to Corporate Strategy," *Harvard Business Review*, May–June 1986, pp. 43–59. See also Alfred D. Chandler's *Strategy and Structure* (1962), *The Visible Hand* (1977), *Scale and Scope* (1990), all published by The MIT Press.

5. M&A Data Base, ADP/MLR in *Mergers & Acquisitions*, Volume Twenty-Four, No. 5, March/April 1990, p. 119.

6. David B. Hilder, "Dealmakers Mourn Raiding as a Lost Ark," *Wall Street Journal*, September 27, 1989, pp. C1, C17.

7. Compare Dan Steinbock, "American Media and Entertainment: The 'Booming' Eighties" (unpublished manuscript).

8. "Media companies rebalance the balance sheet," *Broadcasting*, June 17, 1991, p. 52; Michael Siconolfi, "Many Companies Sell Securities to Bolster Their Balance Sheets," *Wall Street Journal*, November 12, 1992, pp. A1, A7.

9. U.S. Bureau of Economic Analysis, *Survey of Current Business* (various issues).

10. Edward M. Graham and Paul R. Krugman, *Foreign Direct Investment in the United States*, 2nd ed. (Washington, D.C.: Institute for International Economics, 1991), p. 24.

11. See Judy Brennan, "Yen Around Play," *Daily Variety*, March 6, 1991, p. F12. See also *Japan M&A Reporter* and *Business Tokyo*, May 1991, p. 15.

12. Compare Bruce Alderman, "NBC, Japanese shop for major," *Variety*, February 14, 1990, pp. 1, 16.

13. Geraldine Fabrikant, "U.S. TV Producers Seek More Foreign Partners," *New York Times*, November 13, 1989, p. D13.

14. Quoted in Steven R. Weisman, "Reagan Sees Virtue in Sale of Studio to Sony," *New York Times*, October 26, 1989, p. A7.

15. Compare "Hill questions foreign ownership of U.S. media," *Broadcasting*, November 20, 1989, pp. 56–58; "Bill Introduced That Would Curb Foreign Ownership of Studios, 'Cultural' Holdings," *Daily Variety*, October 11, 1991, pp. 1, 4.

16. Michael E. Porter, *Capital Choices*, a Research Report Presented to the Council on Competitiveness, the Harvard Business School (1992). See also *A Competitiveness Strategy for America*, Second Report to the President and Congress, Competitiveness Policy Council, March 1993.

17. David Wessel, "Foreign Direct Investment in the U.S. Turns Negative, Reversing Long Trend," *Wall Street Journal*, March 18, 1993, p. A3.

18. Garth Alexander, "Japan: Land of waning tax breaks for pics," *Variety*, March 2, 1992, pp. 73–74.

19. Paul Krugman, *The Age of Diminished Expectations* (Cambridge, Mass.: MIT Press, 1990).

20. Randall Smith, "Merger Activity Shifts into High Gear as the Information Superhighway Opens," *Wall Street Journal*, January 3, 1994, p. R8; Larry Armstrong, with Larry Holyoke, "Look Who's Stuck in the Slow Lane," *Business Week*, March 28, 1994, pp. 28–29; Richard L. Hudson, "Europeans No Longer Scoff at Interactive Multimedia," *Wall Street Journal*, March 2, 1994, p. B4; Peter Gumbel, "France Steers Toward 'Superhighway' With TV-Industry Mergers, a New Law," *Wall Street Journal*, February 25, 1994, p. A9.

CHAPTER 2. BROADCASTING: DECLINE AND REJUVENATION

Network Television

1. On the shift from mass markets to segmented markets, see Susan Strasser, *Satisfaction Guaranteed* (New York: Pantheon Books, 1989); Richard S. Tedlow, *New and Improved* (New York: Basic Books, 1990).

2. Quoted in Richard Levinson and William Link, *Off Camera: Conversations with the Makers of Prime-Time Television* (New York: A Plume Book, 1986), pp. 245–265. See also "How Americans Watch TV: The New TV Viewer," *Channels*, September 1988, pp. 53–62.

3. Peter Passell, "TV Industry Unfazed by Rise in 'Zapping,' " *New York Times*, July 8, 1991, pp. D1, D6.

4. On audience research in the United States, see Erik Larson, "Watching Americans Watch TV," *The Atlantic Monthly*, March 1992, pp. 66–80; John Dempsey, "Nielsen plays monopoly," *Variety*, November 1, 1993, pp. 25, 30; "Research," *Advertising Age* (various issues); Steve McClellan, "TV networks take ratings into own hands," *Broadcasting & Cable*, February 7, 1994, p. 8.

5. Compare N. R. Kleinfeld, "The Networks' New Advertising Dance," *New York Times*, July 1990, pp. F1, F6.

6. See "Group ownership on the rise," *Broadcasting*, February 11, 1991, pp. 69–71.

7. See John Lippman, "Indie-station business regains stability and respectability after turbulence, bankruptcies rocked scene in mid-'80s," *Variety*, January 3, 1990, p. 34.

8. Joe Mandese, "Here come the newest brands: NBC, CBS, ABC," *Advertising Age*, May 17, 1993, pp. 1, 44.

9. See Les Brown, Five Tumultuous Years," *Channels/Field Guide '87*, pp. 8–9.

10. On network takeovers, see Ken Auletta, *Three Blind Mice* (New York: Random House, 1991).

11. Compare Steve McClellan, "The TV networks in play," *Broadcasting*, November 11, 1991, pp. 3–5.

12. Compare Edmund L. Andrews, "F.C.C. Acts to Let the Networks Buy Local Cable Units," *New York Times*, June 19, 1992, pp. A1, D9.

13. See Elizabeth Jensen and Mark Robichaux, "Fifth Network Sparks Interest of TV Industry," *Wall Street Journal*, June 28, 1993, pp. B1, B6; John Dempsey, "WB credo: if you can't sign 'em, create 'em," *Variety*, April 11–17, 1994, p. 45.

14. Richard W. Stevenson, "Foreign Horizons Lure U.S. Broadcast Networks," *New York Times*, November 15, 1993, pp. D1, D10.

15. Elizabeth Lesly et al., "Musical Chairs May Be the Hot New TV Game," *Business Week*, June 6, 1994, pp. 28–29; Joe Flint, "Webs want O&O ceiling lifted," *Variety*, May 30–June 5, 1994, pp. 21, 26.

16. On the networks' new bargaining power, see, for example, Geoffrey Foisie, "Reports of network deaths exaggerated," *Broadcasting & Cable*, March 14, 1994, pp. 6, 14; Elizabeth Jensen, "Major TV Networks, Dinosaurs No More, Tune in to New Deals," *Wall Street Journal*, March 17, 1994, pp. A1, A10; John Dempsey, "Nets' new riddle: buyer be where?" *Variety*, March 28, 1994, pp. 1, 83.

17. See Geoffrey Foisie, "Broadcast TV fortunes on the rise," *Broadcasting & Cable*, April 25, 1994, pp. 14–15.

Network Radio

1. On radio broadcasting, see Christopher H. Sterling and John M. Kittross, *Stay Tuned: A Concise History of American Broadcasting*, 2nd ed. (Belmont, Calif.: Wadsworth, 1990); Jim Ladd, *Radio Waves* (New York: St. Martin's Press, 1991).

2. *Radio Marketing Guide and Fact Book for Advertisers 1992*, Radio Advertising Bureau. See also "Pop Radio Is Suffering a Midlife Crisis," *New York Times*, July 28, 1991, pp. H1, H28.

3. *Trends in Advertising Volume*, the Television Bureau Research Department (McCann-Erickson).

4. Compare Edmund L. Andrews, "A New Tune For Radio: Hard Times," *New York Times*, March 15, 1992, P. E6. See also Edmund L. Andrews, "Too Many Stations, Too Few Buyers and Depressed Prices," *New York Times*, June 30, 1991, p. F10.

5. Anthony Ramirez, "A Compromise on Radio Station Ownership," *New York Times*, August 6, 1992, pp. D1, D2. See also "Network Radio: Special Report," *Broadcasting*, July 13, 1992, pp. 27–36; John Callagher, "Duopoly changes roust the rankings," *Broadcasting*, November 9, 1992, pp. 57–59.

6. Peter Viles, "A new network giant: Infinity to run Westwood and Unistar," *Broadcasting & Cable*, October 18, 1993, pp. 40–41; Peter Viles, "Shamrock's formula for success: patience and good people," *Broadcasting & Cable*, March 29, 1993, pp. 28–30. On the 1993 talk radio phenomenon, see *Time*'s cover story, "Voice of America?" November 1, 1993, pp. 60–66.

7. See "Radio's Top 25 Groups," *Broadcasting & Cable* (various issues).

CAPITAL CITIES/ABC: FROM HUNTER TO HUNTED?

1. On ABC, see Sterling Quinlan, *Inside ABC* (New York: Hastings House, 1979); Sally Bedell, *Up the Tube* (New York: The Viking Press, 1981); Huntington Williams, *Beyond Control* (New York: Atheneum, 1989); Leonard H. Goldenson, with Marvin J. Wolf, *Beating the Odds* (New York: Charles Scribner's Sons, 1991); Timothy S. Mescon and George S. Vozikis, "American Broadcasting Companies, Inc." in Mescon and Vozikis, *Cases in Strategic Management* (New York: Harper & Row, 1988); James L. Baughman, "The Weakest Chain and the Strongest Link: The American Broadcasting Company and the Motion Picture Industry, 1952–60" in Tino Balio (ed.), *Hollywood in the Age of Television* (Boston: Unwin Hyman, 1990), pp. 91–114; Marc Gunther, *The House That Roone Built* (Boston: Little, Brown, 1994).

2. See *Forbes*, July 19, 1982.

3. Dennis Kneale, "Murphy & Burke: Duo at Capital Cities Scores a Hit, but Can Network Be Part of It?" *Wall Street Journal*, January 2, 1990, pp. A1, A6.

4. Compare Ron Suskind, "Legend Revisited: Warren Buffett's Aura as Folksy Sage Masks Tough, Polished Man," *Wall Street Journal*, November 8, 1991, pp. A1, A6–A7; Michael Lewis, "The Temptation of St. Warren," *New Republic*, February 17, 1992, pp. 22–25.

5. Compare Dennis Kneale, "Which TV Executive Would Be So Bizarre as to Air 'Twin Peaks'?" *Wall Street Journal*, April 26, 1990, pp. A1, A7.

6. Quoted in Bill Carter, "For Networks, Is No.1 a Winner?" *New York Times*, September 16, 1991, pp. D1, D10. See also Brian Lowry, "Ad coin rolls to youth," *Variety*, December 27, 1993, pp. 33–34.

7. "Capital Cities/ABC: Networking for a living," *The Economist*, November 21, 1992, pp. 80, 85.

8. "Profile: Capital Cities/ABC," *Electronic Media*, January 10, 1994, pp. 1, 40–52.

GENERAL ELECTRIC/NBC: FROM BOOM TO BUST?

1. On David Sarnoff, RCA and NBC, see Eugene Lyons, *David Sarnoff* (New York: Pyramid Books, 1966); Kenneth Bilby, *The General* (New York: Harper & Row, 1986); Robert Sobel, *RCA* (New York: Stein & Day, 1986).

2. On GE prior to the '80s, see "General Electric: Strategic Position—1981," Harvard Business School case 381–174.

3. On Jack Welch and GE, see Robert Slater, *The New GE* (Homewood, Ill.: Business One Irwin, 1993); Noel M. Tichy and Stratford Sherman, *Control Your Destiny or Someone Else Will* (New York: Doubleday, 1993). See also "General Electric, 1984," Harvard Business School case 385–315 (Revised May 1989); Stratford P. Sherman, "Inside the Mind of Jack Welch," *Fortune*, March 27, 1989; Noel Tichy and Ram Charan, "Speed, Simplicity, Self-Confidence: An Interview with Jack Welch," *Harvard Business Review*, September–October 1989, pp. 112–120.

4. Compare William M. Carley, Michael Siconolfi, and Amal Kumar Naj, "How Will Welch Deal With Kidder Scandal?" *Wall Street Journal*, May 3, 1994, pp. A1, A6.

5. On Wright as NBC's president, see Dyan Machan, "On a roll with the man from GE," *Forbes*, April 17, 1989, pp. 124–127.

6. Compare Bill Carter, "The Man Who Owns Prime Time," *New York Times Magazine*, March 4, 1990, pp. 23–24, 38–40.

7. See David W. Tice, "GE May Not Escape the Woes Affecting Other Big Lenders," *Barron's*, October 22, 1990, pp. 10–11, 32–35.

8. Compare Paul Noglows, "GE Capital's Surge," *Channels*, October 1988, p. 65.

9. Compare Geoffrey Foisie, "A write-down at hand for NBC?" *Broadcasting & Cable*, April 5, 1993, pp. 35–36.

10. Joe Mandese, "NBC splices new, older media," *Advertising Age*, March 15, 1993, p. 8.

11. Quoted in "GE's Brave New World," *Business Week*, November 8, 1993, pp. 64–70; "GE's Money Machine," *Business Week*, March 8, 1993, pp. 62–70.

LOEWS CORP./CBS: END OF THE TIFFANY NETWORK?

1. On Paley and CBS, see Sally Bedell Smith, *In All His Glory: The Life of William S. Paley* (New York: Simon & Schuster, 1990). See also Lewis J. Paper, *Empire: William S. Paley and the Making of CBS* (New York: St. Martin's Press, 1987); Robert

Slater, *This Is CBS: A Chronicle of 60 Years* (Englewood Cliffs, N.J.: Prentice-Hall, 1988); Richard Metz, *CBS: Reflections in a Bloodshot Eye* (New York: Signet, 1976). On Paley's self-mythologies, see his *As It Happened* (New York: Doubleday, 1979).

2. Smith, *In All His Glory*, p. 393.

3. William Boddy, "Building the World's Largest Advertising Medium: CBS and Television, 1940–60," in Tino Balio (ed.), *Hollywood in the Age of Television* (Boston: Unwin Hyman, 1990), pp. 63–89.

4. On the Tisches, Loews, and CBS, see Constance Lynn Irwin, "Loews Corporation," Harvard Business School Case Study, 387–131, 1987; Michael Ozanian and Alexandra Biesada, "America's Most Undervalued Stock," *Financial World*, May 29–June 11, 1990, pp. 22–24; Subrata N. Chakravarty, "Manufacturer needs outlets," *Forbes*, March 5, 1990, pp. 42–43.

5. During the period 1958–60, Loews started by circling around MGM (stock purchases); when it saw an underutilized asset, it acquired a major stake (increased control); finally, full control followed by tightening of operational control (brothers' shared management authority, budget cuts and layoffs, increase in profitability).

6. Compare Joseph Vitale, "Sad News at Black Rock, Good News From the Field," *Channels/1988 Field Guide*, pp. 36–37.

7. John Lippman, "Running CBS' New Game Plan," *Los Angeles Times/Calendar*, December 30, 1990, pp. 5, 77–78, 86.

8. Jonathan Clements, "Loews Hasn't Kept Up with Tobacco Rivals . . ." *Wall Street Journal*, November 19, 1993, p. C2.

9. Compare Thomas Jaffe, "Will Larry Tisch look good in mouse ears?" *Forbes*, December 24, 1990, pp. 168–169.

10. Andrew E. Serwer, "CBS: To Beat the Odds, Stay the Course," *Fortune*, September 6, 1993, pp. 70–72.

11. Elizabeth Lesly, with Suzanne Woolley, "Loews Could Be Worth More Dead Than Alive," *Business Week*, December 13, 1993, pp. 104–107.

12. Elizabeth Lesly et al., "Musical Chairs May Be the Hot New TV Game," *Business Week*, June 6, 1994, pp. 28–29.

CHAPTER 3. CABLE: GROWTH AND CONSOLIDATION

THE RISE OF CABLE

1. On cable, see "History of Cable," Research & Policy Analysis Department, National Cable Television Association. See also Andrew F. Inglis, *Behind the Tube: A History of Broadcasting Technology and Business* (Boston: Focal Press, 1990), pp. 360–391.

Basic and Pay Cable

1. Compare Harvey Solomon, "Refranchising: Cities Fight Back," *Channels*, March 1989, pp. 46–49.

2. See Nielsen Television Index and Cable TV Facts.

3. Stuart Miller, "Kagan controversy brews over cable marketing study," *Variety*, February 22, 1993, p. 76.

4. Kevin Goldman, "Cable-TV Networks Strive to Stand Out from the Crowd with Original Programs," *Wall Street Journal*, December 17, 1990, pp. B1, B5.

5. Compare Walter Adams and James W. Brock, *Antitrust Economics on Trial* (Princeton, N.J.: Princeton University Press, 1991), pp. 72–73. See also Rich Brown, "New cable networks ready for launch," *Broadcasting & Cable*, April 11, 1994, p. 24.

6. Elizabeth Jensen, "Cable Concerns Explore Export of Programs," *Wall Street Journal*, April 18, 1994, pp. B1, B6.

7. See *U.S. v. Columbia Pictures Industries, Inc.*, 507 F.Supp. 412 (1980), at p. 421, footnote 16. See also Michele Hilmes, *Hollywood and Broadcasting* (Chicago: University of Illinois Press, 1990), pp. 176–181.

8. Mark Robichaux, "Premium Cable Channels Gain Viewers with Original Programs, Package Deals," *Wall Street Journal*, March 24, 1993, pp. B1, B6.

9. Johnnie L. Roberts and Mark Robichaux, "A New Player Is Rattling the World of Pay Television," *Wall Street Journal*, October 1, 1993, pp. B1, B8.

10. See National Cable Television Association, based on Paul Kagan Associates data and U.S. Copyright Office data.

11. Mark Robichaux, "Cable-TV Firms' Higher-Priced 'Tiers' Bring Cries of Outrage From Consumers," *Wall Street Journal*, January 15, 1992, pp. B1, B7.

12. Paul Kagan Associates, Inc.

13. Quoted in Bill Carter, "Cable May Get Its Wings Clipped," *New York Times*, July 10, 1989, pp. D1, D7.

14. Mark Robichaux, "How Cable-TV Firms Raised Rates in Wake of Law to Curb Them," *Wall Street Journal*, September 28, 1993, pp. A1, A12.

15. Compare Bill Carter, "Networks' New Cable Channels Get a Big Jump on Competition," *New York Times*, March 14, 1994, p. D7.

16. On the additional rate cuts, see Elizabeth Kolbert, "F.C.C. Orders Cuts in Cable TV Rates of 7% on Average," *New York Times*, February 23, 1994, pp. A1, D2.

Pay-Per-View

1. On the pay-per-view market, see "Special Report: Pay-Per-View," *Variety*, July 22, 1991, pp. 47–52; "Special Report: Pay-Per-View," *Electronic Media*, March 30, 1992, pp. 16–26; Lisa Gubernick and Amy Feldman, "Money talks," *Forbes*, June 8, 1992, pp. 114–115.

2. See Paul Kagan Associates, Inc.

3. Kevin Goldman, "Pay-Per-View Fine-Tunes Focus to Rock'n'Wrestling," *Wall Street Journal*, December 19, 1989, pp. B1, B6.

4. Rich Brown, "Study shows PPV revenue up in 1993," *Broadcasting & Cable*, November 15, 1993, pp. 35–36.

Home Shopping

1. On the early evolution of the home shopping industry, see *Channels/Field Guide* (various issues from 1985 to 1990).

2. Compare Glenn Ruffenach, "Home Shopping Network Stumbles in Upscale Move," *Wall Street Journal*, July 31, 1989, pp. B1.

3. Laura J. Zinn and Antonio N. Fins, "Home Shoppers Keep Tuning In—But Investors Are Turned Off," *Business Week*, October 22, 1990, pp. 70–72.

4. Seth Lubove, "King of the startups," *Forbes*, November 8, 1993, pp. 186–190.

5. Laurie M. Grossman, "Home Shopping Talks to QVC About Merger," *Wall Street Journal*, February 28, 1992, pp. B1, B10.

6. Ken Auletta, "Barry Diller's Search for the Future," *The New Yorker*, February 22, 1993, pp. 49–61.

7. Mark Robichaux, "Liberty Media Bid on Home Shopping Hits Antitrust Snag," *Wall Street Journal*, January 8, 1993, p. A9B; Johnnie L. Roberts and Mark Robichaux, "Scandal Channel," *Wall Street Journal*, May 14, 1993, pp. A1, A4.

8. Geraldine Fabrikant, "QVC Network Wins Court Round in Its Bid to Take Over Paramount," *New York Times*, November 25, 1993, pp. A1, D6.

9. See Laura Zinn et al., "Retailing Will Never Be the Same," *Business Week*, July 26, 1993, pp. 54–60; Teri Agins, "Clothing, TV Shopping May Be Tough Fit," *Wall Street Journal*, March 31, 1993, pp. B1, B6.

10. Patrick M. Reilly, "Home Shopping: The Next Generation," *Wall Street Journal*, March 21, 1994, p. R11.

TELE-COMMUNICATIONS, INC.: THE DEAL MACHINE

1. On TCI and John Malone, see Christopher Knowlton, "Want This Stock? It's Up 91,000%" *Fortune*, July 31, 1989, pp. 97–104; L. J. Davis, "Television's Real-Life Cable Baron," *New York Times/The Business World*, December 2, 1990, pp. 16, 38–53; Johnnie L. Roberts, "Cable Cabal: How Giant TCI Uses Self-Dealing, Hardball To Dominate Market," *Wall Street Journal*, January 27, 1992, pp. A1, A4.

2. L. J. Davis, "Television's Real-Life Cable Baron," *New York Times Magazine*, December 2, 1990, pp. 16ff.

3. Ronald Grover, "The Second Empire of John Malone," *Business Week*, January 25, 1993, p. 46.

4. Compare Kate Maddox, "TCI improves, but old image lingers," and William Mahoney, "How TCI responded to this story," in *Electronic Media*, November 4, 1991, pp. 1, 41, 43.

5. On TCI and BCCI, see Kate Oberlander, "Magazine ties TCI executives to BCCI," *Electronic Media*, August 19, 1991, p. 18; Thomas Petzinger, Jr. and Peter Truell, "U.K. Audit Points to Larger BCCI Role By Two Top U.S. Cable-TV Executives," *Wall Street Journal*, January 17, 1992, p. A4; Peter Truell and Thomas Petzinger, Jr., "TCI Officers' Links to BCCI Are Detailed," *Wall Street Journal*, July 31, 1992, p. A2.

6. Johnnie L. Roberts and Laura Landro, "King of Cable," *Wall Street Journal*, September 27, 1993, pp. A1, A16.

7. Mark Robichaux, "Need More TV? TCI May Offer 500 Channels," *Wall Street Journal*, December 3, 1992, pp. B1, B3; Rich Brown, "TCI kicks off $2 billion fiber upgrade," *Broadcasting & Cable*, April 19, 1993, p. 50.

8. J. Max Robins, "Mega-Malonia may reshape TV scape," *Variety*, April 26, 1993, pp. 1, 89.

TURNER BROADCASTING SYSTEMS: THE MAVERICK AND HIS SHADOW PARTNERS

1. On Turner and TBS, see Porter Bibb, *It Ain't As Easy As It Looks* (New York: Crown Publishers, 1993); Hank Whittemore, *CNN: The Inside Story* (Boston: Little, Brown, 1990), pp. 4–5. See also Scott Ticer, with William C. Symonds, Peter Finch, and David Lieberman, "Captain Comeback," *Business Week*, July 17, 1989, pp. 98–106.

2. Whittemore, *CNN: The Inside Story*, pp. 29–31. See also Philip Revzin, Peter Waldman, and Peter Gumbel, "Ted Turner's CNN Gains Global Influence and 'Diplomatic' Role," *Wall Street Journal*, February 1, 1990, pp. A1, A6.

3. Compare Mark Hertsgaard, *On Bended Knee: The Press and the Reagan Presidency* (New York: Farrar, Straus and Giroux, 1988), pp. 3, 29, 78–79.

4. Compare "High cost of Gulf news slows CNN's expansion cruise," *Variety*, October 15, 1990, pp. 3, 94; Kate Oberlander, "Top MSOs OK money to aid CNN," *Electronic Media*, February 4, pp. 3, 34.

5. Peter Fuhrman, "All-news orgy, anyone?" *Forbes*, November 22, 1993, pp. 54–60.

6. Peter Boyer, "Taking on the World," *Vanity Fair*, April 1991, pp. 92–106, 114–116.

7. Priscilla Painton, "The Taming of Ted Turner," *Time*, January 6, 1992, pp. 34–39.

8. Compare Laura Landro, "Time, TCI Mull Plan for Turner Assets," *Wall Street Journal*, April 6, 1993, pp. B1, B3.

9. Compare Johnnie L. Roberts and Rochelle Sharpe, "Turner Deal Will Provide Steady Flow of Feature Films," *Wall Street Journal*, August 23, 1993, p. B3.

10. Anita Sharpe, "Ted Turner Sees into His Future, Spies a Network," *Wall Street Journal*, February 4, 1994, pp. B1, B3.

11. Anita Sharpe and Mark Robichaux, "Turner Broadcasting, Home Shopping Discuss Possible Combination," *Wall Street Journal*, March 29, 1994, p. A2.

VIACOM: SEARCH FOR GROWTH

1. On Viacom, see Geraldine Fabrikant, "When Leverage Works," *New York Times*, December 24, 1989, pp. F1, F8; Kevin Pearce, "The Emerging Giant," *Television Business International*, June 1990, pp. 16–20.

2. On Summer Redstone, see Christopher Vaughn and Rich Zahradnik, "Redstone's Arsenal," *Channels*, May 1988, pp. 46–52; Mark Lander, with Geoffrey Smith, "The MTV Tycoon: Sumner Redstone Is Turning Viacom into the Hottest Global TV Network," *Business Week*, September 21, 1992, pp. 56–62.

3. Compare Anne B. Fisher, "The Big Drive to Reduce Debt," *Fortune*, February 10, 1992, p. 118–124.

4. Mark Landler, "I Want My MTV—Stock," *Business Week*, May 18, 1992, p. 55.

5. See Joseph M. Winski, " 'Addicted to research, Nick shows strong kids' lure," and "Netting the numbers," in *Advertising Age*, February 10, 1992, pp. S2, S22; Kathleen Murray, "Tuned in to Kids, She Takes Nickelodeon to the Top," *New York Times*, March 14, 1993, p. F8; "Special Report: Nickelodeon," *Variety*, December 20, 1993, pp. 41–52.

6. Lander, with Smith, "The MTV Tycoon."

7. Paul Noglows, "Is Redstone studio-prone." *Variety*, January 13, 1992, pp. 1, 85–86.

CHAPTER 4. ENTERTAINMENT: MARKET
MULTIPLICATION

ENTERTAINMENT CONGLOMERATES

1. Compare Calvin Sims, "An Economic Hooray for Hollywood," *New York Times*, August 2, 1993, pp. D1, D6; Christian Moerk and John Evan Frook, "Studios brace for billion-dollar makeover," *Variety*, July 19, 1993, pp. 1, 82–83.

Hollywood Studios

1. U.S. Department of Commerce, *National Income Supplement to the Survey of Current Business*, in Fredric Stuart, "The Effects of Television on the Motion Picture Industry: 1948–1960," in Gorham Kindem (ed.), *The American Movie Industry* (Carbondale: Southern Illinois University Press, 1982), pp. 257–307.

2. Quoted in David J. Jefferson, "Movie-Making Cost Record $28.8 Million in '92, Valenti Tells U.S. Theater Owners," *Wall Street Journal*, March 10, 1993, p. B5.

3. Compare Peter Bart, "Numbing numbers," *Variety*, March 14–20, 1994, pp. 3, 70.

4. "Col's Billion Dollar Man sets new standard in H'wood," *Variety*, November 29, 1989, pp. 1, 4. See also Nina J. Easton, "Will the Good Times Always Roll?" *Los Angeles Times/Calendar*, July 8, 1990, pp. 5, 84.

5. "Katzenberg's Bottom Line Strategy for Disney," *Daily Variety*, January 31, 1991, pp. 18–23.

6. Lawrence Cohn, "1990's midsize pix had compact earnings," *Variety*, March 4, 1991, pp. 3, 21; John Brodie, "Are Majors Losing Middle?" *Variety*, April 11–17, 1994, pp. 1, 171.

7. Marcy Magiera, "Madison Avenue hits Hollywood," *Advertising Age*, December, 10, 1990, pp. 24–26.

8. Geoffrey Foisie, Rich Brown, and Joe Flint, "One of tv's best-kept secrets: how ABC, CBS and NBC have taken the bite out of program costs," *Broadcasting*, December 9, 1991, pp. 3–4.

9. Compare Bill Carter, "Big Shifts in Network-Studio Relationships," *New York Times*, April 27, 1992, p. D8.

10. Charles Fleming, "March of the mobile moguls," *Variety*, November 2, 1992, pp. 1, 109; Alan Citron, "The Hollywood That Can't Say No," *Los Angeles Times*, December 13, 1992, pp. D1, D8.

Talent Agencies

1. Judy Brennan and Andy Marx, "Biz bows to ten-percenters," *Variety*, November 15, 1993, pp. 1, 54.

2. Whitney Stine, *Stars & Star Handlers: The Business of Show* (Santa Monica, Calif.: Roundtable Publishing, 1985); *Hollywood Reporter/Talent Special Report,* May 1990.

3. Connie Bruck, "The World of Business," *The New Yorker,* September 9, 1991, pp. 38–73.

4. Cleveland Horton, "Coke/CAA draws flak," *Advertising Age,* September 30, 1991, pp. 1, 50.

5. David Kissinger, "Legal eagles rule the roost," *Variety,* July 25, 1990, pp. 1, 65–66.

6. Anne Thompson, "Hollywood Agents on the Hard Streets," *New York Times,* November 15, 1992, p. F27.

7. Ronald Grover, with Mark Landler and Michael O'Neal, "Ovitz," *Business Week,* August 9, 1993, pp. 50–55.

8. Bernard Weinraub, "Ovitz Riddle Roils Hollywood," *New York Times,* April 13, 1994, pp. D1, D15.

9. Brennan and Marx, "Biz bows to ten-percenters."

PRIMARY MARKET

1. Compare Les Brown, "The Growing Back End," *Channels,* May 1988, p. 40.

Domestic Theatrical Exhibition

1. A. D. Murphy, "Winter, spring, summer or fall, b.o.'s now a year-round ball," *Variety,* March 15–21, 19089, pp. 1, 26.

2. Thomas R. King, " 'Strange Beings! Rarely in Theaters!' New Films Lure Infrequent Moviegoers," *Wall Street Journal,* July 22, 1993, pp. B1–B2.

3. On the post–World War II changes in U.S. exhibition, see Richard Gold, "No exit? Studios itch to ditch exhib biz," *Variety,* October 8, 1990, pp. 1, 84; Suzanne Mary Donahue, *American Film Distribution* (Ann Arbor, Mich.: UMI Research Press, 1987), pp. 103–142.

4. On the *Paramount* case, see *Federal Trade Commission v. Paramount Famous-Lasky Corp.,* 57 F.2d 152 (2d Cir. 1932), at 158–159; *U.S. v. Paramount Pictures* (1948), 68 S.Ct. 915, at 931–934. See also Gerald F. Phillips, "The Recent Acquisition of Theatre Circuits by Major Distributors," in John David Vera and Robert Thorne (eds.), *1988 Entertainment, Publishing & The Arts Handbook,* pp. 227–250.

5. Computed with the following: 1943–44 exhibition revenues from *U.S. v. Paramount Pictures* (1948), 68 S.Ct. 915, at p. 925; 1987 exhibition revenues from Richard P. Simon, "Movie Industry Update—1990," *Goldman Sachs/Investment Research,* March 19, 1990, p. 2; the number of domestic screens from *Variety* (various issues) as based on data from the Motion Picture Association of America and the Motion Picture Export Association of America.

6. Compare Geraldine Fabrikant, "Tough Times for Movie Theaters," *New York Times,* December 2, 1991, p. D7.

7. Robert Marich, "2nd-tier titans of exhibition on roll despite profit squeeze," *Hollywood Reporter,* February 5, 1991, pp. 1, 93–94.

8. Paul Noglows, "Screen sobers studios," *Variety,* March 9, 1992, pp. 1, 69.

9. Compare Richard Turner, "Movie Magic," *Wall Street Journal*, April 6, 1992, p. R15.

Home Video

1. On the VCR victory over the videodisc and Beta-VHS wars, see Andrew F. Inglis, *Behind the Tube* (Boston: Focal Press, 1990), pp. 444–447; James Lardner, *Fast Forward* (New York: Mentor, 1987).

2. "New Variety chart tracks vid rentals," *Variety*, December 14, 1992, p. 42; Marc Berman, "Studios miss boat on vid demographics," *Variety*, September 14, 1992, p. 15.

3. Richard Turner, "Disney Leads Shift from Rentals to Sales in Videocassettes," *Wall Street Journal*, December 24, 1992, pp. 1, 30.

4. On Blockbuster's rise, see Alan Citron, "Blockbuster vs. the world," *Los Angeles Times*, July 22, 1990, pp. D1, D7.

5. Eric J. Savitz, "An End to Fast Forward?," *Barron's*, December 11, 1989, pp. 13, 43–46; Lee J. Seidler, "Blockbuster: The Accountants Earn Their Pay," *Investment Research/Bear Sterns*, May 8, 1989.

6. Gail DeGeorge, with Jonathan B. Levine and Robert Neff, "They Don't Call It Blockbuster for Nothing," *Business Week*, October 19, 1992, pp. 113–114.

7. On Huizenga and Blockbuster in the early '90s, see Pat Jordan, "Wayne Huizenga," *New York Times Magazine*, December 5, 1993, pp. 54–57; James Bates, "Wayne's World," *Los Angeles Times*, June 6, 1993, pp. D1, D5.

Syndication

1. On syndication, see *Syndication 1995* (C. C. Publishing, 1989). See also Franklin M. Fisher, "The Financial Interest and Syndication Rules in Network Television: Regulatory Fantasy and Reality," in Franklin M. Fisher (ed.), *Antitrust and Regulation: Essays in Memory of John J. McGowan* (Cambridge, Mass.: MIT Press, 1985), pp. 263–298.

2. Compare Dennis Kneale and Mary Lu Carnevale, "In TV Rerun Ruling Hollywood Interests Prove Special Indeed," *Wall Street Journal*, April 10, 1991, pp. A1, A10.

3. Wilkofsky Gruen Associates (*Channels*, October 1989, p. 40). See also Neal Weinstock, "Syndication's Hot 20 Outfits," *Channels*, February 1990, pp. 76–82.

4. Jill Abramson and Dennis Kneale, "Hollywood and TV Networks Are Slugging it Out in Capitol over $3-Billion-a-Year Issue of Reruns," *Wall Street Journal*, March 30, 1990, p. A18.

5. Elizabeth Jensen, "Networks Gain in Syndication Dispute, But Many See Rerun of Battles Ahead," *Wall Street Journal*, November 9, 1992, pp. B1, B8.

6. "2-Pronged Offensive: Fin-Syn Battlefront Shifts to Court After FCC Ruling," *Daily Variety*, October 25, 1991, pp. 1, 28; Joe Flint, "Networks win, Hollywood winces as fin-syn barriers fall," *Broadcasting & Cable*, November 22, 1993, pp. 6, 16.

7. "ASTA at NATPE," *Advertiser Syndicated Television Association*, January 17, 1994, p. 1.

8. Compare Bill Carter, "Hollywood Isn't Smiling at an ABC Comedy Tactic,"

New York Times, April 4, 1994, pp. D1, D6. See also Bill Carter, "ABC's ownership of its fall lineup is raising eyebrows in Hollywood studios," *Wall Street Journal*, May 16, 1994, p. D6.

9. "Who's selling series?" *Advertising Age*, April 25, 1994, p. 46.

10. Brian Lowry, "Webs and studios get cozy with new alliances," *Variety*, May 23–29, 1994, pp. 1, 62.

COMPLEMENTARY MARKETS

1. On complements, see Michael Porter, *Competitive Advantage* (New York: The Free Press, 1985), pp. 416–425.

Theme Parks

1. Compare Harold L. Vogel, *Entertainment Industry Economics* (New York: Cambridge University Press, 1990), pp. 273–274.

2. On the Orlando studio wars between Disney and MCA, see Robert Wrubel, "Jaws vs. Mickey Mouse," *Financial World*, May 16, 1989, pp. 24–25; Charles Leehrsen, "A Real Kongfrontation," *Newsweek*, June 11, 1990, pp. 66–67; Amy E. Gross, "The Battle of the Florida Movie Theme Parks," *Adweek's Marketing Week*, June 18, 1990, pp. 41–44.

3. Laura Landro, Patrick M. Reilly, and Richard Turner, "Clash of Titans," *Wall Street Journal*, April 14, 1993, pp. A1, A7.

4. Christian Moerk, "Theme parks taking reality for a ride," *Variety*, June 22, 1992, pp. 3, 17; James R. Norman and Nikhil Hutheesing, "Hang on to your hats—and wallets," *Forbes*, November 22, 1993, pp. 90–98; Andrew Pollack, "Sega Takes Aim at Disney's World," *New York Times*, July 4, 1993, pp. F1, F6.

5. On the Disney-MCA struggle over foreign theme park business, see Terry Ilott and Michael Williams, "MCA plays catch-up in global parks," *Variety*, March 18, 1991, pp. 1, 110.

Toys, Video Games, Licensed Merchandise, and Retail Chains

1. Joseph Pereira, "Playful After 1992 Gains, Toy Makers Are Ready to Unveil a Slew of Products," *Wall Street Journal*, February 5, 1993, pp. B1, B6.

2. *Toy Industry Fact Book* (annual); Sidney Ladensohn Stern and Ted Schoenhaus, *Toyland: The High-Stakes Game of the Toy Industry* (Chicago: Contemporary Books, 1990).

3. Joseph Pereira, "Hasbro Enjoys Life off the Toy-Market Roller Coaster," *Wall Street Journal*, May 5, 1992, p. B4.

4. See Calvin Sims, "Fisher-Price To Be Bought by Mattel," *New York Times*, August 20, 1993, pp. D1, D4; Eric Schine, "Mattel's Wild Race to Market," *Business Week*, February 21, 1994, pp. 62–63.

5. Compare David Sheff, *Game Over* (New York: Random House, 1993).

6. Christian Hill, "Nintendo-Atari Zapping Contest Goes to Washington," *Wall Street Journal*, December 8, 1989, pp. B1, B5.

7. On the U.S. software companies' reentry into the video game market, see

Richard Brandt, "Creeping Up on the Mario Bros.," *Business Week*, July 30, 1990, pp. 74–76.

8. Joseph Pereira, "Nintendo, Sega Zap Prices as Video-Game War Heats Up," *Wall Street Journal*, May 5, 1992, pp. B1, B8.

9. Richard Brandt, "Clash of the Titans," *Business Week*, September 7, 1992, p. 34.

10. Pamela Sellers, "Licensed to Play: From Silver Screen to Home Screen," *VideoGames & Computer Entertainment*, December 1990, pp. 50–58, 102.

11. Jeffrey Jolson-Colburn and Anita M. Busch, "Studio no strangers to software profits," *Hollywood Reporter*, July 30, 1991, p. 5.

12. Andrew Pollack, "Sega Takes Aim at Disney's World," *New York Times*, July 4, 1993, pp. F1, F6; John Battelle and Bob Johnstone, "Sega's Plan for World Domination," *Wired*, December 1993, pp. 73–76, 128–131.

13. Lindsey Gruson, "Video Violence: It's Hot! It's Mortal! It's Kombat!" *New York Times*, September 16, 1993, pp. B1, B8. On Acclaim's post-Mortal Kombat world, see Veronica Byrd, "Is There Life After *Mortal Kombat?*" *Business Week*, May 16, 1994, p. 76.

14. Rick Tetzeli, "Videogames: Serious Fun," *Fortune*, December 27, 1993, pp. 110–116.

15. Neil Gross and Richard Brandt, "Sony Has Some Very Scary Monsters in the Works," *Business Week*, May 23, 1994, p. 116; Joseph Pereira, "PC Games Could Capture Sega, Nintendo Customers," *Wall Street Journal*, April 27, 1994, pp. B1, B9; Kate Fitzgerald, "Videogame market explodes," *Advertising Age*, May 23, 1994, pp. 1, 52.

16. John Brodie and Andy Marx, "Agents and studios face off in new contest for videogame profits," *Variety*, December 27, 1993, pp. 1, 74.

17. *The 1990 Marketer's Resource to Licensing*, Advertising Supplement/Advertising Age, May 28, 1990, pp. L1–L12.

18. On licensing and merchandising, see Cy Schneider, *Children's Television* (Lincolnwood, Ill.: NTC Business Books, 1989), pp. 111–159; Stern and Schoenhaus, *Toyland*.

19. *Toy Industry Fact Book* (various issues).

20. Marcy Magiera, " 'Batman Returns'—licensees cheer," *Advertising Age*, June 1, 1992, pp. 1, 29.

21. On sports merchandise see Calvin Sims, "It's Not Just How Well You Play the Game . . . " *New York Times*, January 31, 1993, p. F5.

22. "Special Report: The Business of Jurassic Park," *Variety*, December 27, 1993, pp. 57–68.

23. Jonathan Berry, with Lori Bongiorno, "Wilma! What Happened to the Plain Old Ad?" *Business Week*, June 6, 1994, pp. 54, 58.

24. On major M&E conglomerates and retail operations, see Patrick M. Reilly, "New Retailers May Find Selling Isn't Mickey Mouse," *Wall Street Journal*, October 21, 1993, pp. B1, B12; Adam Sandler and Andy Marx, "Move over, movies!" *Variety*, December 6, 1993, pp. 1, 50.

Record and Music Industry

1. On the U.S. recording industry, see the annual Statistical Overview of the Recording Industry Association of America, Inc. (RIA); "An Overview of the U.S.

Recording Industry," in U.S. Congress, Office of Technology Assessment, *Copyright & Home Copying: Technology Challenges the Law,* OTA-CIT-422 (Washington, D.C.: U.S. Government Printing Office, October 1989), pp. 89–100; Marc Eliot, *Rockonomics: The Money Behind the Music* (New York: Franklin Watts, 1989); Russell Sanjek and David Sanjek, *American Popular Music Business in the 20th Century* (New York: Oxford University Press, 1991). See also Robert Hilburn and Chuck Philips, "Rock's Top 40," *Los Angeles Times/Calendar,* November 29, 1992, pp. 7–10, 58–59; and "A Survey of The Music Business," *Economist,* December 21, 1991, pp. 1–20.

2. "Compact Disc: The 10th Anniversary," *Billboard,* September 26, 1992, pp. CD1–CD28.

3. Richard D. Hylton, "Recordings Off? CDs Miss the Message," *New York Times,* August 25, 1991, p. F6; Michael Lev, "Music Industry Bets on CD Sets," *New York Times,* September 4, 1991, pp. D1, D4.

4. Patrick M. Reilly, "Skeptics Question Development Progress of Two New Digital-Recording Systems," *Wall Street Journal,* January 8, 1992, pp. B1–B2.

5. Bob Tannenbaum, "A Bumpy Ride for TV's High Flyer," *Manhattan, Inc.,* August 1989, pp. 74–79. See also Michael Shore, *The Rolling Stone Book of Rock Video* (New York: Quill, 1984).

6. On VJN, see Peter Newcomb, "Music video wars," *Forbes,* March 4, 1991, pp. 68–70; Peter Ainslie, "On the Jukebox Network, You Make the Call," *Rolling Stone,* May 2, 1991, p. 48, 63.

7. Mark Landler, "I Want My MTV—Stock," *Business Week,* May 18, 1992, p. 55; Mark Landler, "Will MTV Have to Share the Stage?" *Business Week,* February 21, 1994, p. 38.

8. Adam Sandler, "Tracking a lost generation," *Variety,* November 29, 1993, pp. 1, 74.

9. Meg Cox, "Rock Is Slowly Fading As Tastes in Music Go Off in Many Directions," *Wall Street Journal,* August 26, 1992, pp. A1, A4.

10. "A Survey of the Music Business," pp. 7–11.

11. Stephen Holden, "Breakup of Pop Music Audience Leaves Top 40 Radio Tuned Out," *New York Times,* March 23, 1993, pp. C13, C18.

12. Robert G. Woletz, "Technology Gives the Charts a Fresh Spin," *New York Times,* January 26, 1992, pp. H26, H32.

13. Compare Subrata N. Chakravarty, "Revenge of the antisuits," *Forbes,* December 11, 1989, pp. 49–52; Richard Behar, "A Music King's Shattering Fall," *Time,* September 17, 1990, p. 64.

14. Quoted in Bill Holland, "CBS' Yetnikoff Testifies at Hearing on U.S. Competitiveness," *Billboard,* November 25, 1989, p. 84.

15. Compare Sony Corp. 1989 *Annual Report,* pp. 2–3.

16. William Knoedelseder, *Stiffed: A True Story of MCA, the Music Business and the Mafia* (New York: HarperCollins, 1993). See also Fredric Dannen, *Hit Men: Power Brokers and Fast Money Inside the Music Business,* 2nd ed. (New York: Vintage, 1991).

17. "An Overview of the U.S. Recording Industry," pp. 94–95. See also Jon Pareles, "When the Business of Music Becomes Even Bigger," *New York Times,* March 19, 1990, p. C17; Michael Lev, "Can All Those Upstart Record Labels Survive," *New York Times,* January 5, 1992, p. F5.

18. See, for example, Stephen Holden, "Big Stars, Big Bucks and the Big Gamble," *New York Times,* March 24, 1991, pp. H24–H25; Kevin Zimmerman, "The

misleading megadeals," *Variety*, April 27, 1992, pp. 91–93; Geraldine Fabrikant, "The Recording Industry Hedges Its Bets and the Superstars Sign On," *New York Times*, October 25, 1992, p. E16.

Publishing: Newspapers, Magazines, Books

1. U.S. Department of Commerce, Bureau of the Census, International Trade Administration (ITA).

Newspapers

1. On the new newspaper business, see James D. Squires, *Read All About It! The Corporate Takeover of America's Newspapers* (New York: Random House, 1993). See also Ben H. Bagdikian's classic *The Media Monopoly*, 2nd ed. (Boston: Beacon Press, 1987); Edwin Emery and Michael Emery, *The Press in America*, 6th ed. (Englewood Cliffs, N.J.: Prentice-Hall, 1992); Ernest C. Hynds, *American Newspapers in the 1980s* (New York: Hastings House, 1980); "Don't Stop the Presses," *Barron's*, March 2, 1992, pp. 8–9, 25–29.

2. Martha Groves, "Bad News for Newspapers," *Los Angeles Times*, December 15, 1991, pp. D1, D3, D7.

3. Squires, *Read All About It!*, pp. 21–22.

4. "Don't Stop the Presses."

5. "Good News for Newspaper Stocks," *Barron's*, June 21, 1993, pp. 8–9, 24–32.

6. Patrick M. Reilly and Gary Putka, "Times-Globe Deal Looks Good—on Paper," *New York Times*, June 14, 1993, pp. B1–B2. On the flagship's journalistic shifts, see Edwin Diamond, *Inside the New New York Times* (New York: Villard Books, 1994).

7. William Glaberson, "The Los Angeles Times Steps Back from a 'Sky's the Limit' Approach," *New York Times*, December 13, 1993, p. D6.

8. Christy Fisher, "Newspaper call to arms in fight over classified," *Advertising Age*, April 26, 1993, pp. S1–S2.

9. William Glaberson, "Newspapers' Adoption of Color Nearly Complete," *New York Times*, May 31, 1993, p. L41.

10. John Markoff, "17 Companies in Electronic News Venture," *New York Times*, May 7, 1993, pp. D1, D15.

11. Jeff Jensen, "Newspapers do it their way in broadcast experiments," *Advertising Age*, April 26, 1993, pp. S10–S11. See also Richard A. Melcher, with Ronald Grover, "Chicago's Tribune Co. gets the multimedia bug in a big way," *Business Week*, March 28, 1994, pp. 56–60.

12. Patrick M. Reilly, "Publishers Design Electronic Newspapers To Keep Control of Information Delivery," *Wall Street Journal*, April 26, 1993, pp. B1, B7; William Glaberson, "Newspapers Race for Outlets in Electronic Marketplace," *New York Times*, January 17, 1994, pp. D1, D6.

13. George Garneau, "Financial prospects of interactive services explored," *Editor & Publisher*, March 12, 1994, p. 30; Michael Conniff, "Truck Stops on the Information Superhighway," *Editor & Publisher/Telecommunications and Interactive Newspapers*, February 12, 1994, pp. 4–6, 28.

Magazines

1. "Magazines in America," *Advertising Age*, October 6, 1991. On the magazine industry, see John Tebbel, *The American Magazine: A Compact History* (New York: Hawthorn Books, 1969); James Playsted, *Magazines in the United States* (New York: Ronald Press, 1971).

2. Compare Magazine Publishers of America.

3. Compare Scott Donaton, "Magazines: Survival of the hippest," *Advertising Age*, October 19, 1992, pp. S1, S14; Laura Noro, "Heavy hitters gamble on launches," *Advertising Age*, October 19, 1992, pp. S13–S14.

4. Deirdre Carmody, "Layoffs at Time Inc.'s Magazines," *New York Times*, September 20, 1991, pp. D1–D2; Scott Donaton, " 'Fortune's move to ignite 1993 magazine war," *Advertising Age*, November 23, 1992, p. 13.

5. Meg Ox, "Time Inc. Begins a New Chapter on Its Restructuring," *Wall Street Journal*, September 20, 1993, p. B3.

6. Elizabeth Kolbert, "How Tina Brown Moves Magazines," *New York Times Magazine*, December 5, 1993, pp. 66–72, 85–87, 97–99.

7. Meg Cox, "Newhouse Family Starts to Peer into Electronic Future," *Wall Street Journal*, October 21, 1993, p. B4.

8. Compare "Magazine companies catch the interactive wave," *Advertising Age*, March 7, 1994, p. S12.

Book Publishing

1. *Book Industry Trends 1992*, Book Industry Study Group.

2. On book publishing, see John P. Dessauer, *Book Publishing: A Basic Introduction*, 2nd ed. (New York: Continuum, 1990); John Tebbel, *Between Covers: The Rise and Transformation of Book Publishing in America* (New York: Oxford University Press, 1987); Kenneth C. Davis, *Two-Big Culture: The Paperbacking of America* (Boston: Houghton Mifflin, 1984).

3. On the M&A activity in book publishing, see Albert N. Greco, "The Growth in Mergers and Acquisitions in the United States Publishing Industry: 1984–88," the 39th Annual Conference of the International Communication Association, May 1989, San Francisco.

4. Edwin McDowell, "Publishers Worry After Fiction Sales Weaken," *New York Times*, October 30, 1989, p. D12. See also Meg Cox, "Book Publishers Face a Painful Austerity After Lavish Spending," *Wall Street Journal*, November 21, 1989, pp. A1, A11.

5. Roger Cohen, "Jitters in a 'Recession-Proof' Trade," *New York Times*, December 17, 1990, pp. D1, D11; Roger Cohen, "Weak Sales Put a Damper on an Annual Book Party," *New York Times*, May 27, 1991, pp. L33, L37.

6. Edwin McDowell, "Dell Pays Ken Follett $12.3 Million for 2 Books," *New York Times*, June 28, 1990, pp. C13, C17; Roger Cohen, "Publishing World Is Shaken as Advances for Books Soar," *New York Times*, July 16, 1990, pp. D1, D6; Esther B. Fein, "Book Lists Dwindling as Publishers Cut Fat," *New York Times*, March 30, 1992, pp. D1, D8.

7. Lisa See, "The Hollywood Connection," *Publishers Weekly*, April 5, 1991, pp. 8–11; Daniel Max, "Publishers take a page from the studios," *Variety*, October 14, 1991, p. 248.

8. See Paramount Communications, Inc.'s annual reports and 10–K's, as well as Roger Cohen, "Profits—Dick Snyder's Ugly Word," *New York Times*, June 30, 1991, pp. 1, 4.

9. D. T. Max, "Par publisher seeks synergy," *Variety*, April 26, 1993, pp. 1, 88.

10. Geraldine Fabrikant, "Paramount to Acquire Macmillan," *New York Times*, November 11, 1993, pp. D1, D20.

11. Rebecca Mead, "Dumbing Down *or* Wising Up?" *New York*, February 28, 1994, pp. 57–61.

Interactive Multimedia: From CD-ROM to Virtual Reality

1. Morgan Stanley Research, *Hollywood Reporter/Interactive Home Media*, October 27, 1992, p. S12.

2. See also "Special Report: It's a PC, It's a TV—It's Multimedia," *Business Week*, October 9, 1989, pp. 152–166; "Multimedia: Special Report," *Variety*, September 28, 1992, pp. 76–77.

3. On Hollywood majors and interactive multimedia, see Robert Marich, "A Piece of the Inter-Action," *Hollywood Reporter/Interactive Home Media*, October 27, 1992, pp. S31, S42.

4. Compare Richard Turner, "Hollywired," *Wall Street Journal*, R1, R6.

5. On CD-ROM and the U.S. market, see Mark Alpert, "CD-ROM: The Next PC Revolution," *Fortune*, June 29, 1992, pp. 68–73.

6. Gail Edmondson et al., "Philips Needs Laser Speed," *Business Week*, June 6, 1994, pp. 46–47.

7. Charles Paikert, "Majors check in to ROM with view," *Variety*, March 9, 1992, pp. 1, 73; "Special Report: The CD-ROM Frontier," *Variety*, March 9, 1992, pp. 51–53; "Special Report: Multimedia," *Variety*, September 28, 1992, pp. 76–77.

8. Suzanne Stefanac, "Sex & the New Media," *NewMedia*, April 1993, pp. 38–46.

9. See Meg Cox, "Technology Threatens To Shatter the World of College Textbooks," *Wall Street Journal*, June 1, 1993, pp. A1, A5; James M. Perry, "Can't Get Enough of a Book? Buy a CD-ROM," *Wall Street Journal*, May 23, 1994, pp. B1, B6.

10. Howard Rheingold, *Virtual Reality* (New York: Summit Books, 1991), pp. 154–174; Joan O'C. Hamilton, "Going Where No Minds Have Gone Before," *Business Week*, October 5, 1992, p. 104. On virtual reality, see also Michael Benedikt (ed.), *Cyberspace* (Cambridge, Mass.: MIT Press, 1992); Linda Jacobson, *Cyberarts* (San Francisco: Milton Freeman, 1992); Ken Pimentel and Kevin Teixeira, *Virtual Reality* (New York: Intel/Windcrest, 1993); Bob Cotton and Richard Oliver, *Understanding Hypermedia* (London: Phaidon Press, 1993).

11. Gene Bylinsky, "The Marvels of 'Virtual Reality'," *Fortune*, June 3, 1991, pp. 138–150.

12. See Matt Rothman, "H'wood 'voomies' or bust?" *Variety*, December 14, 1992, pp. 3, 6.

13. G. Pascal Zachary, " 'Virtual Reality' Patents Gained by French Firm," *Wall Street Journal*, December 7, 1992, pp. B1, B6; Joan O'C. Hamilton, "Trials of a Cyber-Celebrity," *Business Week*, February 22, 1993, pp. 95–97.

14. On the VR potential, see Joan O'C. Hamilton et al., "Virtual Reality—How a Computer Generated World Could Change the Real World," *Business Week*, October 5, 1992, pp. 97–105.

CHAPTER 5. MAJOR STUDIOS

TIME-WARNER: STRUGGLE FOR CONTROL

1. On Henry Robinson Luce and Time Inc., see Robert T. Elson, *Time Inc.: The Intimate History of a Publishing Enterprise, 1923–41* (New York: Atheneum, 1968); Robert T. Elson, *The World of Time Inc.: The Intimate History of a Publishing Enterprise, 1941–1960* (New York: Atheneum, 1973); Curtis Prendergast with Geoffrey Colvin, *The World of Time Inc.: The Intimate History of a Changing Enterprise, 1960–80* (New York: Atheneum, 1986). See also Hedley Donovan, *Right Places, Right Times* (New York: Touchstone, 1989); George Mair, *Inside HBO* (New York: Dodd, Mead, 1988); Connie Bruck, *Master of the Game* (New York: Simon & Schuster, 1994).

2. On Time's early attempts to buy into broadcast TV (1950s), movies (1960s), and cable (1970s), see Prendergast with Colvin, *The World of Time Inc.*, pp. 214–215, 381–393.

3. On Warner, see Robert Gustafson, " 'What's Happening to Our Pix Biz?' From Warner Bros. to Warner Communications Inc.," in Tino Balio (ed.), *The American Film Industry* (Madison, Wisc.: University of Wisconsin Press, 1985), pp. 574–586.

4. On Steven Ross and the mob allegations, see Bruck, *Master of the Game*.

5. Compare Bill Saporito, "The Inside Story of Time Warner," *Fortune*, November 20, 1989, pp. 164–210.

6. See David Lieberman, "A Nice, Simple Time-Warner Deal Was Too Good to Last," *Business Week*, June 19, 1989, pp. 38–39. See also George Lucas, "World Market Is the Last Crusade," *Wall Street Journal*, July 13, 1989, p. A14.

7. Compare Bill Saporito, "A Legal Victory for the Long Term," *Fortune*, August 14, 1989, pp. 56–59.

8. Connie Bruck, "The World of Business," *The New Yorker*, July 6, 1992, pp. 34–56. On leverage and the postmerger TW, see Susan Duffy, "Time Warner: Debt Burden? No Problem," *Business Week*, October 22, 1990, pp. 82–83.

9. Compare Mark Landler and Christopher Power, "Is This Any Way for Time Warner to Raise Cash," *Business Week*, June 24, 1991, p. 43.

10. Ann M. Morrison, "After the Coup at Time Warner," *Fortune*, March 23, 1992, pp. 82–90; Richard M. Clurman, "The Iceman Goeth," *Vanity Fair*, May 1992, pp. 60–72.

11. On Ross's legacy, see Connie Bruck, "A Mogul's Farewell," *The New Yorker*, October 18, 1993, pp. 69–93.

12. Johnnie L. Roberts and Mary Lu Carnevale, "Time Warner Plans Electronic 'Superhighway'," *Wall Street Journal*, January 27, 1993, pp. B1, B10.

13. Eben Shapiro, "Seagram Heir, Advised By His Show-Biz Pals, Circles Time-Warner," *Wall Street Journal*, December 17, 1993, pp. A1, A10.

14. Compare Sharon Moshavi, "Fire Sale," *Forbes*, November 8, 1993, pp. 96–98.

15. John Brodie and J. Max Robins, "Synergy, Schmynergy!" *Variety*, March 21–27, 1994, pp. 1, 70–71.

16. Laura Landro and Johnnie L. Roberts, "Time Warner's Levin Tries to Rise Above the Takeover Talk," *Wall Street Journal*, March 25, 1994, pp. A1, A5.

PARAMOUNT: A GLOBAL POWERHOUSE?

1. On Charles Bluhdorn, see Robert Sobel, *The Rise and Fall of the Conglomerate Kings* (New York: Stein and Day, 1984, pp. 101–126.

2. Laura Landro, "Gulf & Western Plans to Sell Finance Firm, Build a Media Giant," *Wall Street Journal*, April 10, 1989, pp. A1, A8.

3. "Boesky Bid for Paramount Alleged," *New York Times*, June 8, 1990, p. D4.

4. On the Buchwald case, see, for example, Laura Landro, "Hollywood's Accounting in Spotlight," *Wall Street Journal*, March 21, 1990, pp. B1, B6.

5. See Bill Carter, "Paramount Chairman's Advice: 'Do Something'," *New York Times*, June 7, 1989, p. D5.

6. "Never mind: Fifth network deep-sixed," *Broadcasting*, October 30, 1989, pp. 31–32.

7. Jesse Kornbluth, "Why Hollywood Hates Martin Davis," *Vanity Fair*, May 1991, pp. 60–72.

8. Kathryn Harris, "Mr. Lonelyhearts," *Forbes*, February 4, 1991, pp. 39–40.

9. Sarah Lyall, "Paramount Publishing to Cut Jobs and Books," *New York Times*, January 24, 1994, p. D8.

10. Kathryn Harris, "Days of Reckoning at Paramount," *Los Angeles Times*, June 20, 1993, pp. D1, D5.

WALT DISNEY: THE TEFLON KINGDOM

1. On Walt Disney and the Walt Disney Co., see Marc Eliot, *Hollywood's Dark Prince* (New York: Birch Lane Press/Carol Publishing Group, 1993); Leonard Mosley, *Disney's World* (Chelsea, Mich.: Scarborough House, 1985); Ron Grover, *The Disney Touch* (Homewood, Ill.: Business One Irwin, 1991); Joe Flower, *Prince of Magic Kingdom* (New York: John Wiley, 1991).

2. Compare John Taylor, *Storming the Magic Kingdom* (New York: Ballantine Books, 1987).

3. Geraldine E. Willigan, "The Value-Adding CFO: An Interview with Disney's Gary Wilson," *Harvard Business Review*, January–February 1990, pp. 85–93.

4. Ibid.

5. Ibid.

6. See "Limited partnerships and tax-shelters," in Harold L. Vogel, *Entertainment Industry Economics*, 2nd ed. (New York: Cambridge University Press, 1990), pp. 66–70. See also Geraldine Fabrikant, "Silver Screen's Tie With Disney," *New York Times*, September 11, 1990, p. D8; Paul Noglows, "Death Knell for financing partnerships," *Variety*, November 5, 1990, pp. 1, 31.

7. Richard W. Stevenson, "The Fine Art of the Disney Deal," *New York Times*, September 14, 1990, pp. D1, D4; Paul Noglows and Garth Alexander, "Touchwood: A turnoff?" *Variety*, April 8, 1991, pp. 1, 53, 86.

8. Compare Paul Noglows, "Did Disney design a Mickey Mouse deal?" *Variety*, November 26, 1990, pp. 1, 75; Lisa Gubernick, "Mickey Mouse's sharp pencil," *Forbes*, January 7, 1991, p. 39.

9. Richard Turner, "Disney Hits Bad Patch After Eisner's Six Years of Giddy Expansion," *Wall Street Journal*, November 12, 1991, pp. A1, A10.

10. Peter Elkind, "The Breakup of the Bass Brothers," *New York Times Magazine*, November 24, 1991, pp. 34–42, 77–78.

11. Betsy Sharkey, "Michael Eisner: Disney's Big Thinker Is Free of Guile," *Adweek's Marketing Week*, September 4, 1989, pp. 3–5.

12. Andy Marx and Max Alexander, "Disney slips the street," *Variety*, October 4, 1993, pp. 1, 78. See also Peter Gumbel and Richard Turner, "Fans Like Euro Disney But Its Parent's Goofs Weigh the Park Down," *Wall Street Journal*, March 10, 1994, pp. A1, A12.

13. Compare Subrata N. Chakravarty, "Manufacturer needs outlets," *Forbes*, March 5, 1990, pp. 42–43.

14. See also Richard Turner, "Disney, Using Cash and Claw, Stays King of Animated Movies," *Wall Street Journal*, May 16, 1994, pp. A1, A8.

15. Ronald Grover, "Jeffrey Katzenberg: No More Mr. Tough Guy?" *Business Week*, January 31, 1994, pp. 78–79.

16. Richard Turner and Thomas R. King, "Disney Stands Aside as Rivals Stampede to Digital Alliances," *Wall Street Journal*, December 24, 1993, pp. A1, A5; Jim Benson, "Fifth net not kid stuff to Disney," *Variety*, November 15, 1993, pp. 1, 55.

17. Compare Greg Evans, "Booty and 'The Beast'," *Variety*, April 11–17, 1994, pp. 1, 170.

18. Compare Calvin Sims, "Walt Disney Reinventing Itself," *New York Times*, April 28, 1994, pp. D1, D9.

NEWS CORP./FOX: EXPANSION, DEBT CRISIS, EXPANSION

1. On Twentieth Century Fox, see Marlys J. Harris, *The Zanucks of Hollywood* (New York: Crown Publishers, 1989); Tony Thomas and Aubrey Solomon, *The Films of 20th Century Fox* (Secaucus, N.J.: The Citadel Press, 1985); Stephen M. Silverman, *The Fox That Got Away* (Secaucus, N.J.: Lyle Stuart, 1988); Aubrey Solomon, *Twentieth Century Fox* (Metuchen, N.J.: The Scarecrow Press, 1988); William Shawcross, *Murdoch* (New York: Simon & Schuster, 1993).

2. On Marvin Davis, see Alex Ben Block, *Outfoxed* (New York: St. Martin's Press, 1990), pp. 1–5; Michael Schroeder and Maria Mallory, with Jon Templeman, "Making Marc Rich Squirm," *Business Week*, November 11, 1991, pp. 120–122.

3. Quoted in Jerome Tuccille, *Rupert Murdoch* (New York: Donald I. Fine, 1989), p. 57. On Rupert Murdoch and News Corp., see also Thomas Kiernan, *Citizen Murdoch* (New York: Dodd, Mead, 1986); Harold Evans, *Good Times, Bad Times* (New York: Atheneum, 1984); Piers Brendon, *The Life and Death of the Press Barons* (New York: Atheneum, 1983); Michael Leapman, *Arrogant Aussie* (Secaucus, N.J.: Lyle Stuart, 1985); William Shawcross, *Murdoch* (New York: Simon & Schuster, 1993).

4. On Murdoch's global publishing operations, see Meg Cox, "Murdoch Puts Global Imprint on Books," *Wall Street Journal*, May 4, 1990, B1, B4.

5. Compare Sharon Moshavi and Steve Coe, "Fox, affiliates aim for dual revenue stream," *Broadcasting*, November 25, 1991, pp. 4–5.

6. Compare Rita Koselka, " 'He was an octopus . . . ' " *Forbes*, October 26, 1992, pp. 192–194.

7. Karene Witcher, "News Corp. Prepares to Upvalue Assets," *Wall Street Journal*, July 27, 1990, p. B3B; Dennis Kneale, "With Debt to Match Its Global Ambitions, News Corp. Squirms," *Wall Street Journal*, October 19, 1990, pp. A1, A12.

8. Quoted in Roger Cohen, "Rupert Murdoch's Biggest Gamble," *New York Times Magazine*, October 21, 1990, pp. 30–33, 64, 72–75.

9. Roger Cohen, "Satellite TV Battle Ends in Britain," *New York Times*, November 3, 1990, pp. 33, 37; Don Groves, "Sky's the limit for B-SKY-B," *Variety*, October 19, 1992, pp. 49–57.

10. Barnaby J. Feder, "Murdoch Obtains Accord on Most of News Corp. Debt," *New York Times*, February 2, 1991, pp. 29, 35; Mike Harris, "News Corp., Murdoch: A Family Affair," *Variety*, October 28, 1991, p. 66.

11. Compare Ronald Grover, "Now Playing, Rupert Murdoch in *Mogul*," *Business Week*, March 9, 1992, p. 30.

12. Elizabeth Guider, "Fox Global gets guarded reaction," *Variety*, October 21, 1991, pp. 39–40; Elizabeth Jensen, "Fox Looks to Older Viewers for Stability," *Wall Street Journal*, March 26, 1993, p. B7.

13. Ronald Grover, with Mark Landler, "How Fox Outfoxed Itself," *Business Week*, December 20, 1993, p. 48.

14. Kathryn Harris, " 'A big dose of realism'," *Forbes*, September 2, 1991, pp. 40–42; Paul Noglows, "News Corp. pares its debt," *Variety*, October 28, 1991, pp. 65–66.

15. Compare Meg Cox, "How Do You Tame a Global Company? Murdoch Does It Alone," *Wall Street Journal*, February 14, 1994, pp. A1, A6.

16. J. Max Robins and John Brodie, "Murdoch's makeover," *Variety*, April 12, 1993, pp. 1, 93; Adam Dawtrey, "What Murdoch didn't say: How he'll rule the world," *Variety*, September 13, 1993, pp. 1, 46.

17. News Corp., *Annual Report 1992*, p. 7.

18. Elizabeth Lesly et al., "Musical Chairs May Be the Hot New TV Game," *Business Week*, June 6, 1994, pp. 28–29.

SONY/COLUMBIA: HARDWARE/SOFTWARE COMBINE

1. On Columbia, see Bob Thomas, *King Cohn* (New York: McGraw-Hill, 1967); Clive Hirschhorn, *The Columbia Story* (Hong Kong: Crown Publishers, 1990); Bernard F. Dick (ed.), *Columbia Pictures* (Lexington: University Press of Kentucky, 1992). See also Andrew Yule, *Fast Fade* (New York: Delta, 1989).

2. David McClintick, *Indecent Exposure: A True Story of Hollywood and Wall Street* (New York: Dell Publishing, 1982).

3. Timothy S. Mescon and George S. Vozikis, "The Coca-Cola Company," in Mescon and Vozikis, *Cases in Strategic Management* (New York: Harper & Row, 1988), pp. 683–713; Samuel C. Certo and J. Paul Peter, "Coca-Cola Company," in Certo and Peter, *Selected Cases in Strategic Management* (New York: McGraw-Hill, 1990), pp. 489–514. See also Anthony Ramirez, "It's Only Soft Drinks at Coca-Cola," *New York Times*, May 21, 1990, pp. D1, D3.

4. See Lawrence Cohn, "Exec shifts make Columbia the gem of commotion," *Variety*, November 22, 1989, pp. 1, 16.

5. On Akio Morita and Sony Corp., see James Brian Quinn (1986) "Sony Corporation," in James Brian Quinn, Henry Mintzberg, and Robert M. James, *The Strategy Process* (Englewood Cliffs, N.J.: Prentice-Hall, 1988), pp. 725–749; Akio Morita, *Made In Japan* (New York: E. P. Dutton, 1986). On Norio Ohga, see David E. Sanger, "Sony's Norio Ohga: Building Smaller, Buying Bigger," *New York Times Magazine*, February 18, 1990, pp. 22–25, 61–70.

6. James Lardner, *Fast Forward: Hollywood, the Japanese, and the VCR Wars* (New York: A Mentor Book, 1987).

7. Subrata N. Chakravarty, "Revenge of the antisuits," *Forbes*, December 11, 1989, pp. 49–52; Peter J. Boyer, "Hollywood Banzai," *Vanity Fair*, February 1990, pp. 131–139, 189–194.

8. Compare Nina J. Easton and Alan Citron, "Sony's Sunshine Boys," *Los Angeles Times/Calendar*, March 10, 1991, pp. 1, 8–9, 83–87. On "Marketing Myopia," see Theodore Levitt, *The Marketing Imagination* (New York: The Free Press, 1986), pp. 141–172.

9. Andrea Rothman, with Ronald Grover and Robert Neff, "Media Colossus," *Business Week*, March 25, 1991, pp. 64–74.

10. Maggie Mahar, "Adventures in Wonderland: Sony's Fling in Show Biz Is Proving a Costly One," *Barron's*, October 7, 1991, pp. 8–9, 26–28; John Lippman, "At Sony Pictures, Dolgen-omics Rules," *Los Angeles Times*, December 27, 1992, pp. D1, D7.

11. Allan Kozinn, "Sony's President Takes the Podium," *New York Times*, March 24, 1993, C15–C16.

12. Akio Morita, "Why Japan Must Change," *Fortune*, March 9, 1992, pp. 66–67; Akio Morita, "Partnering for Competitiveness: The Role of Japanese Business," *Harvard Business Review*, May–June 1992, pp. 75–91; Akio Morita, "Toward a New World Economic Order," *The Atlantic Monthly*, June 1993, pp. 88–98.

13. Patrick M. Reilly, "Sony Combines U.S. Operations Under Schulhof," *Wall Street Journal*, May 25, 1993, pp. B1–B2.

14. David P. Hamilton and Laura Landro, "Sony Loses Services of Visionary Founder at a Critical Juncture," *Wall Street Journal*, December 3, 1993, pp. A1, A6; Seth Lubove and Neil Weinberg, "Creating a seamless company," *Forbes*, December 20, 1993, pp. 152–157. See also Joe Flower, "The Americanization of Sony," *Wired*, June 1994, pp. 94–98, 134–135.

MATSUSHITA/MCA: THE GREAT COPYCAT

1. On Universal, see *Hollywood Reporter/Universal 75th Anniversary Salute*, June 1990.

2. Dan E. Moldea, *Dark Victory* (New York: Viking Penguin, 1986), pp. 48–51.

3. See David F. Prindle, *The Politics of Glamour* (Madison: University of Wisconsin Press, 1988), pp. 78–81.

4. Compare Moldea, *Dark Victory*, pp. 268–269. On Wasserman as Hollywood's power broker, see Ronald Brownstein, *The Power and the Glitter: The Hollywood-Washington Connection* (New York: Pantheon Books, 1990), pp. 184–185.

5. Quoted in Richard Turner, "Missed Opportunities Old-Fashioned Style Push MCA to Merge," *Wall Street Journal*, September 26, 1990, pp. A1, A6.

6. On Matsushita, see James Brian Quinn (1985) "Matsushita Electric Industrial Company," in James Brian Quinn, Henry Mintzberg, and Robert M. James, *The Strategy Process* (Englewood Cliffs, N.J.: Prentice-Hall, 1988), pp. 422–438.

7. Compare Connie Bruck, "The World of Business," *The New Yorker*, September 9, 1991, pp. 38–74. See also Clyde Prestowitz, "U.S. Rules, Not Japanese Money, Lost MCA," *Wall Street Journal*, December 3, 1990, p. A14.

8. Richard Turner and Randall Smith, "MCA's Sheinberg to Receive $21 Million as Bonus in 5-Year Matsushita Contract," *Wall Street Journal*, December 3, 1990, p. A8. On lobbying fees, see Martin Tolchin, "MCA Goes Calling on Capitol Hill," *New York Times*, November 19, 1990, pp. D1–D2.

9. Quoted in Bruck, "The World of Business," pp. 71–72.

10. Steven R. Weisman, "Japanese Buy Studio, and Coaching Starts," *New York Times*, November 20, 1991, pp. A1, C21.

11. Alan Citron and Leslie Helm, "Matsushita Plays a Low-Key Role at MCA for Now," *Los Angeles Times*, November 17, 1991, pp. D1, D8.

12. Geraldine Fabrikant, "The Osaka Decision," *New York Times*, May 3, 1992, pp. F1, F6.

13. Garth Alexander and Paul Noglows, "Osaka shakeup rattles MCA," *Variety*, March 1, 1993, pp. 1, 77; Neil Gross, "Matsushita's Urgent Quest for Leadership," *Business Week*, March 8, 1993, p. 52.

14. Geraldine Fabrikant, "Talks About Sale of MCA Angers Company President," *New York Times*, November 12, 1993, p. D5.

CHAPTER 6. THE STRUGGLE FOR DISTRIBUTION

Toward the National Information Infrastructure (NII)

1. Bill Clinton and Al Gore, *Putting People First* (New York: Times Books, 1992), pp. 9–11.

2. On the U.S. industrial policy debate, see Otis L. Graham, Jr., *Losing Time: The Industrial Policy Debate* (Cambridge, Mass.: Harvard University Press, 1992).

3. *Economic Report of the President*, January 1993, pp. 19–34.

4. Quoted in "Don't Fall for Industrial Policy," *Fortune*, November 14, 1983, p. 78. Compare Graham, *Losing Time*, pp. 120–121, 324 n.7.

5. Compare Paul Magnusson, "Why Corporate Nationality Matters," *Business Week*, July 12, 1993, pp. 142–143. For Reich's argument, see his *The Work of Nations* (New York: Random House, 1991); for Tyson's argument, see her *Who's Bashing Whom?* (Washington, D.C.: Institute for International Economics, 1992).

6. Bob Davis and Bruce Ingersoll, "Clinton's Team Moves To Extend Regulation in Variety of Industries," *Wall Street Journal*, April 13, 1993, pp. A1, A10.

7. John Carey et al., "Bill's Recipe," *Business Week*, October 18, 1993, pp. 30–31. On criticism, see Peter Passell, "F.C.C. 'Pioneer' Policy Under Attack," *New York Times*, January 31, 1994, pp. D1, D7; Bob Davis, "An Old, Quiet Agency Has Suddenly Become a High-Tech Leader," *Wall Street Journal*, April 5, 1994, pp. A1, A12.

8. Peter H. Lewis, "Gore Preaches, and Practices, the Techno-Gospel," *New York Times*, January 17, 1994, pp. D1, D4.

9. Compare Will Marshall and Martin Schram, The Progressive Policy Institute (eds.), *Mandate for Change* (New York: Berkley Books, 1993). On President Clinton and PPI, see Paul Starobin, "Aspiring to Govern," *National Journal*, May 9, 1992, pp. 1103–1110.

10. Steven R. Rivkin and Jeremy D. Rosner, *Shortcut to the Information Superhighway: A Progressive Plan to Speed the Telecommunications Revolution* (Washington, D.C.: Progressive Policy Institute, 1992).

11. Doug Ross, "Enterprise Economics on the Front Lines: Empowering Firms and Workers to Win," in Marshall and Schram, *Mandate for Change*, pp. 51–80. See also Robert B. Cohen, "The Impact of Broadband Communications on the U.S. Economy and on Competitiveness" (Washington, D.C.: Economic Strategy Institute, 1992).

12. J. Max Robins and Paul Noglows, "Wise men of media at dogpatch pow-wow," *Variety*, December 21, 1992, pp. 1, 81. On the private/public dispute, see John Markoff, "Building the Electronic Superhighway," *New York Times*, January 24, 1993, pp. 3/1, 6.

13. John Markoff, "Clinton Proposes Changes in Policy to Aid Technology," *New York Times*, February 23, 1993, pp. A1, A18.

14. Compare David Osborne and Ted Gaebler, *Reinventing Government: How the Entrepreneurial Spirit Is Transforming the Public Sector* (New York: Viking, 1992).

15. Harry A. Jessell, "Clinton promises open info highway," *Broadcasting & Cable*, September 20, 1993, pp. 42–43.

16. Compare Daniel Pearl, "Debate Over Universal Access Rights Will Shape Rules Governing the Future of Communications," *Wall Street Journal*, January 14, 1994, p. A12; Ken Auletta, "Under the Wire," *The New Yorker*, January 17, 1994, pp. 49–53. On the initial wiring efforts and the issue of universal access, see Steve Lohr, "Data Highway Ignoring Poor, Study Charges," *New York Times*, May 24, 1994, pp. A1, D3. On the legal aspects of the strategic alliances, see Victoria Slind-Flor, "Paving the Data Highway," *The National Law Journal*, August 2, 1993, pp. 1, 36–37.

17. Edmund L. Andrews, "New Tack on Technology," *New York Times*, January 12, 1994, pp. A1, D5; John Carey and Mark Lewyn et al., "Yield Signs on the Info Interstate," *Business Week*, January 24, 1994, pp. 88–90.

18. John J. Keller et al., "Washington Slows Speed on Information Superhighway," *Wall Street Journal*, April 8, 1994, pp. B1, B6.

19. "Blocking the Information Highway," *Wall Street Journal*, April 8, 1994, p. A14.

20. Kim McAvoy, "Gore to the rescue," *Broadcasting & Cable*, May 9, 1994, p. 9.

Direct Broadcast Satellites

1. On DBS's technology and history, see "A quick look at the other players in the DBS spectrum," *Broadcasting*, February 26, 1990, pp. 30–31.

2. On the TCI-Tempo project, see "TCI next into DBS race," *Broadcasting*, March 5, 1990, p. 34.

3. Compare Mark Lewyn, with Dori Jones, "Satellite Broadcasting: Stuck on the Launchpad?" *Business Week,* December 3, 1990, p. 158.

4. "Hubbard's DBS dream: 10 years in making," *Broadcasting,* June 10, 1991, p. 36.

5. On Hughes/Hubbard DBS venture, see "Special Report: Countdown to DBS," *Broadcasting & Cable,* December 6, 1993, pp. 30–68.

6. Eric Schine with Kathleen Kerwin, "Hughes Bets on Another Kind of Bird," *Business Week,* March 15, 1993, p. 65.

7. Sean Scully, "Hubbard says DBS is highway enough," *Broadcasting & Cable,* May 24, 1993, p. 72. See also Schine and Kerwin, ibid.

8. Mark Lewyn, "He's No Mere Satellite-Gazer," *Business Week,* April 4, 1994, p. 39.

9. Edmund L. Andrews, "An Orbiting System Is Planned To Link Most of the Globe," *New York Times,* March 21, 1994, pp. A1, D2.

10. John J. Keller, "McCaw-Gates Satellite Plan Draws Skeptical Reviews," *Wall Street Journal,* March 22, 1994, p. B4; Bradley Johnson, "The interactive super-hype-way," *Advertising Age,* March 28, 1994, pp. 15, 17.

IBM, Apple, and Microsoft in Hollywood

1. Charles H. Ferguson and Charles R. Morris, *Computer Wars* (New York: Random House, 1993), p. 196. On the erosion of America's technology leadership, see Michael L. Dertouzos et al., *Made in America* (New York: HarperPerennial, 1989); Jean-Claude Derian (1990), *America's Struggle for Leadership in Technology,* trans. by Severen Schaeffer (Cambridge, Mass.: MIT Press, 1992).

2. Andrew Pollack, "Now It's Japan's Turn to Play Catch-Up," *New York Times,* November 21, 1993, pp. F1, F6; Kyle Pope and David P. Hamilton, "U.S. Computer Firms, Extending PC Wars, Charge into Japan," *Wall Street Journal,* March 31, 1993, pp. A1, A8.

3. See Dataquest, Inc.

4. On the computer industry evolution, see Ferguson and Morris, *Computer Wars;* Gerald W. Brock, "The Computer Industry," in Walter Adams (ed.), *The Structure of American Industry,* 8th ed. (New York: Macmillan, 1990), pp. 161–182.

5. "Within the Whirlwind: A Survey of the Computer Industry," *The Economist,* February 27, 1993, pp. 5–11.

6. Laurie Hays, "Computer Giants Duel Over Operating Systems," *Wall Street Journal,* November 30, 1993, pp. B1, B8.

7. See International Data Corp.

8. Paul Carroll, *Big Blues: The Unmaking of IBM* (New York: Crown, 1993). See also James Chopsky and Ted Leonsis, *Blue Magic* (New York: Facts on File, 1988); Franklin M. Fisher, John J. McGowan, and Joan E. Greenwood, *Folded, Spindled, and Mutilated: Economic Analysis and U.S. vs. IBM* (Cambridge, Mass.: MIT Press, 1985).

9. James R. Norman, "Lights, cameras, chips!" *Forbes,* October 26, 1992, pp. 260–262; Laurence Hooper, "IBM Unveils Plan to Expand in Multimedia,"

Wall Street Journal, November 11, 1992, p. B5; Richard Turner and Laurence Hooper, "IBM Ventures to Hollywood in Visual Effects," *Wall Street Journal*, February 26, 1993, pp. B1–B2.

10. Ira Sager, "IBM Reboots—Bit By Bit," *Business Week*, January 17, 1994, pp. 82–83; Amy Cortese, "IBM Rides into Microsoft Country," *Business Week*, June 6, 1994, pp. 111–112.

11. Evan I. Schwartz with Bart Ziegler, "Again, IBM Divides To Conquer," *Business Week*, May 24, 1993, pp. 133–135.

12. Ira Sager, with Amy E. Cortese, "Lou Gerstner Unveils His Battle Plan," *Business Week*, April 4, 1994, pp. 96–98; Jonathan Berry, with Ira Sager, "A Big Blue Twister Rocks Madison Avenue," *Business Week*, June 6, 1994, p. 33. On IBM and the information highway, see Bradley Johnson, "Big Blue's best-kept secret," *Advertising Age*, April 18, 1994, pp. 14, 17.

13. On Apple, see Frank Rose, *West of Eden* (New York: Viking, 1989).

14. Lawrence M. Fisher, "I.B.M. Stumbles, While Apple Sets Records," *New York Times*, October 16, 1992, pp. D1, D6; John Markoff, "Beyond the PC: Apple's Promised Land," *New York Times*, November 15, 1992, pp. 3/1, 10.

15. On Bill Gates and Microsoft, see Daniel Ichbiah, with Susan L. Knepper, *The Making of Microsoft* (Rockland, Calif.: Prima, 1991); James Wallace and Jim Erickson, *Hard Drive: Bill Gates and the Making of the Microsoft Empire* (New York: John Wiley, 1992); Stephen Manes and Paul Andrews, *Gates* (New York: Simon & Schuster, 1993). See also Alan Deutschman, "Bill Gates' Next Challenge," *Fortune*, December 28, 1992, pp. 30–41.

16. See Julie Pitta, "Gates goes Hollywood," *Forbes*, February 1, 1993, p. 18.

17. Geoffrey Foisie, "Microsoft demonstrates Windows for TV," *Broadcasting & Cable*, March 29, 1993, p. 44; John Markoff, "Microsoft and 2 Cable Giants Close to an Alliance," *New York Times*, June 13, 1993, pp. 1, 31; "Today Windows, tomorrow the world," *The Economist*, May 22, 1993, pp. 25–27.

18. "The softening of software," *The Economist*, January 8, 1994, pp. 63–64.

19. Amy Cortese, Catherine Yang, and Richard Brandt," Gunning for Microsoft: The Feds' New Weapon," *Business Week*, May 9, 1994, p. 90.

20. G. Pascal Zachary, "Consolidation Sweeps the Software Industry: Small Firms Imperiled," *Wall Street Journal*, March 23, 1994, pp. A1, A6.

21. See Don Clark, "Tests Linking PCs, Cable TV Lines To Be Slated by Several Big Firms," *Wall Street Journal*, December 1, 1993, p. B8.

22. William Gibson, *Neuromancer* (New York: Ace Books, 1984), pp. 5, 51.

23. See Philip Elmer-Dewitt, "First Nation in Cyberspace," *Time*, December 6, 1993, pp. 62–64.

24. Peter H. Lewis, "Even in Cyberspace, Overcrowding," *New York Times*, February 2, 1994, pp. D1, D5. See also Mitchell Kapor, "Where Is the Digital Highway Really Heading?" *Wired*, July 1993, pp. 53–59, 94; Mitchell Kapor and Jerry Berman, "A Superhighway Through the Wasteland?" *New York Times*, November 24, 1993, p. A25.

25. Compare Steve Stecklow, "Computer Users Battle High-Tech Marketers Over Soul of Internet," *Wall Street Journal*, September 16, 1993, pp. A1, A15; "America's Information Highway," *The Economist*, December 25, 1993–January 7, 1994, pp. 35–38. On Internet and U.S. companies, see Mary J. Cronin, *Doing Business on the Internet* (New York: Van Nostrand Reinhold, 1994). On the public sector

and electronic highways, see U.S. Congress, Office of Technology Assessment, *Making Government Work: Electronic Delivery of Federal Services*, OTA-TCT-678 (Washington, D.C.: U.S. Government Printing Office, September 1993).

26. Forrester Research, Inc. See *Wall Street Journal*, March 21, 1994, p. R6.

Telephone Monopolies and Cable Giants

1. On telecommunications, see Manley R. Irwin, "The Telecommunications Industry," in Walter Adams (ed.), *The Structure of American Industry*, 8th ed. (New York: Macmillan, 1990), pp. 244–263; Steve Coll, *The Deal of the Century* (New York: Atheneum, 1986); Peter Temin, *The Fall of the Bell System* (New York: Cambridge University Press, 1987); Robert Britt Horwitz, *The Irony of Regulatory Reform* (New York: Oxford University Press, 1989).

2. Compare Peter Krasilovsky, "Telcos go abroad to build cable systems," *Electronic Media*, December 10, 1990, pp. 60, 64.

3. Peter Coy, Mark Lewyn, with Sandra D. Atchison and Gail DeGeorge, "The Baby Bells Misbehave," *Business Week*, March 4, 1991, pp. 22–23; Anthony Ramirez, "Baby Bells Are Accused of Overcharging," *New York Times*, December 18, 1991, p. D5.

4. See Dan Steinbock, "American Media and Entertainment: The 'Booming' Eighties" (unpublished manuscript).

5. Anthony Ramirez, "TV-Phone Link: Long Way to Go," *New York Times*, November 2, 1991, pp. 37, 50.

6. Kyle Pope, "Multimedia Alliance Is Established by 11 Big Computer and Phone Firms," *Wall Street Journal*, October 7, 1992, B3.

7. See Edmund L. Andrews, "Cable TV In Phone Challenge," *New York Times*, February 28, 1991, D1, D8.

8. Robert Strubel, "Strange Bedfellows," *FW*, September 15, 1992, pp. 44–46.

9. Edmund L. Andrews, "The Local Call Goes Up for Grabs," *New York Times*, December 29, 1991, pp. 3/1, 6.

10. Compare Peter Coy, "Are High Dividends Stunting the Babies' Growth?" *Business Week*, October 5, 1992, p. 134.

11. Compare Edmund L. Andrews, "Cable TV Battling Phone Companies," *New York Times*, March 29, 1992, pp. 1/1, 22.

12. On the Bell Atlantic-TCI deal, see Mark Landler et al., "Bell-Ringer!" *Business Week*, October 25, 1993, pp. 32–36. See also Rosabeth Moss Kanter, "Championing Change: An Interview with Bell Atlantic's CEO Raymond Smith," *Harvard Business Review*, January–February 1991, pp. 119–130.

13. Quoted in Edmund Andrews, "A Baby Bell Primed for the Big Fight," *New York Times*, February 21, 1993, pp. F1, F6.

14. Compare Robert Lenzner and Michael Schuman, "Manipulating the multiple," *Forbes*, November 8, 1993, pp. 40–42.

15. "Cable-Phone Link Is Promising Gamble," *Wall Street Journal*, May 18, 1993, pp. B1, B10.

16. Anita Sharpe and Mark Robichaux, "Bell South to Enter Cable TV by Buying Stake in Prime," *Wall Street Journal*, October 13, 1993, pp. B1, B9.

17. John J. Keller, "AT&T's Secret Multimedia Trials Offer Clues to Capturing

Interactive Audiences," *Wall Street Journal*, July 28, 1993, pp. B1, B6; Bart Ziegler et al., "1-800-GUTS," *Business Week*, August 30, 1993, pp. 26–30.

18. Bart Ziegler with Mark Lewyn, "MCI Takes on the Baby Bells—and Everyone Else," *Business Week*, January 17, 1994, pp. 26–27; John J. Keller, "MCI Is Rich, Ambitious, Heading for Risky Showdown," *Wall Street Journal*, January 28, 1994, p. B4.

19. David P. Hamilton, "Cable, Telecommunications Firms in Japan Attract U.S. Investment," *Wall Street Journal*, October 18, 1993, p. A11.

20. Leslie Cauley, "Bell Atlantic, Tele-Communications Say Pact Is Near for Proposed Combination," *Wall Street Journal*, February 2, 1994, p. B3.

21. On the failure of the megamerger, see, for example, Geraldine Fabrikant, "Merger Talks Fail on $33 Billion Deal in Communications," *New York Times*, February 24, 1994, pp. A1, D6; Dennis Kneale, Johnnie L. Roberts, and Leslie Cauley, "Why the Mega-Merger Collapsed: Strong Wills and a Big Culture Gap," *Wall Street Journal*, February 25, 1994, pp. A1, A16; Steve Lohr, "A Cultural Clash Defeated Bell Atlantic and T.C.I.," *New York Times*, March 23, 1994, pp. D1, D5.

22. Compare Geraldine Fabrikant, "$4.9 Billion Cable Deal Called Off," *New York Times*, April 6, 1994, pp. D1, D20; Bart Ziegler and Mark Robichaux, "Mutual Attraction of Phone and Cable Giants Fades Fast," *Wall Street Journal*, April 7, 1994, pp. B1, B8; Edmund L. Andrews, "In Twist, Consumer Group and F.C.C. Back Cable TV," *New York Times*, May 12, 1994, pp. D1, D21.

23. Diane Mermigas, "Ameritech draws blueprint for superhighway empire," *Electronic Media*, March 28, 1994, pp. 1, 32–40.

VIACOM AND PARAMOUNT'S TAKEOVER STRUGGLE

1. On the Paramount takeover battle, see Geraldine Fabrikant, "QVC's Hostile Bid For Paramount Wins Board Vote," *New York Times*, December 23, 1993, pp. A1, D5; Ken Auletta, "The Last Studio in Play," *The New Yorker*, October 4, 1993, pp. 77–81; Bryan Burrough, "The Siege of Paramount," *Vanity Fair*, February 1994, pp. 66–70, 129–138.

2. Quoted in Johnnie L. Roberts and Laura Landro, "John Malone of TCI Is Formidable Player in Bid for Paramount," *Wall Street Journal*, September 27, 1993, pp. A1, A16.

3. Compare Paul Noglows and J. Max Robins, "Sumner swallows Wayne's world," *Variety*, January 10–16, 1994, pp. 1, 71.

4. Geraldine Fabrikant, "Viacom Revises Its Offer," *New York Times*, January 19, 1994, pp. D1, D5; Geraldine Fabrikant, "Spurning QVC, Paramount Embraces New Viacom Bid," *New York Times*, January 22, 1994, pp. 37, 45.

5. On the end of the takeover struggle, see Laura Landro and Johnnie L. Roberts, "Viacom Is Set to Grow into Media Colossus—Or Burdened Giant," *Wall Street Journal*, February 16, 1994, pp. A1, A9; Mark Landler, with Gail DeGeorge, "Sumner at the Summit," *Business Week*, February 28, 1994, pp. 32–33.

6. Gail DeGeorge and Mark Landler, "Call It Blockbummer," *Business Week*, May 9, 1994, p. 31; Peter Bart, "Viacom-Par going steady," *Variety*, May 9–15, 1994, p. 3.

CHAPTER 7. THE GREAT CONVERGENCE

NEW CHANNEL STRUCTURE

1. On the theory of chaos and complexity, see, for example, James Gleick, *Chaos* (New York: Viking Penguin, 1987); M. Mitchell Waldrop, *Complexity* (New York: Simon & Schuster, 1992).

2. Robert H. Hayes and William J. Abernathy, "Managing Our Way to Economic Decline," *Harvard Business Review*, July–August 1980, pp. 67–77.

3. On crisis and scientific revolutions, see Thomas S. Kuhn (1962), *The Structure of Scientific Revolutions* 2nd ed. (Chicago: University of Chicago Press, 1970).

4. On chaos theory and classic orthodoxies in finance, management, and competition, see David H. Freedman, "Is Management Still a Science?" *Harvard Business Review*, November–December 1992, pp. 26–37; Nancy A. Nichols, "Efficient? Chaotic? What's the New Finance?" *Harvard Business Review*, March–April 1994, pp. 50–60. See also Louis Lowenstein, *Sense & Nonsense in Corporate Finance* (Reading, Mass.: Addison-Wesley, 1991); Robert J. Shiller, *Who's Minding the Store?* (New York: The Twentieth Century Fund Press, 1992); Peter L. Bernstein, *Capital Ideas: The Improbable Origins of Modern Wall Street* (New York: The Free Press, 1992).

STRATEGIC ALLIANCES: DIGITAL CAPITALISM

1. See Stephen Kreider Yoder and G. Pascal Zachary, "Digital Media Business Takes Form as a Battle of Complex Alliances," *Wall Street Journal*, July 14, 1993, pp. A1, A4.

2. "Future Shocks: The End of the Music Business As We Know It," *Musician*, December 1993, pp. 34–49.

3. See Jacob M. Schlesinger et al., "Japan's Tech Giants Wake Up to Big U.S. Acquisition," *Wall Street Journal*, October 15, 1993, p. A6; Richard L. Hudson, "Europe Lingers in the Wake of U.S. Multimedia Might," *Wall Street Journal*, November 2, 1993, p. B4.

TRANSFORMATIONS OF COMPETITIVE ENVIRONMENT

1. Compare "The 500 Channel Future," *The Hollywood Reporter*, August 31, 1993, pp. S1–S32.

2. Harry A. Jessell, "Cable ready: The high appeal of interactive services," *Broadcasting & Cable*, May 23, 1994, pp. 75–78.

3. Peter Coy, "Invasion of the Data Shrinkers," *Business Week*, February 14, 1994, pp. 115–116.

4. George Gilder, *Life After Television* (New York: W. W. Norton, 1990), pp. 30–31.

5. Kyle Pope, "Many PC Makers Steer Clear of Information Highway," *Wall Street Journal*, February 28, 1994, pp. B1, B5. See also John Markoff, " 'I wonder what's on the PC tonight,' " *New York Times*, May 8, 1994, pp. 3/1, 3/8.

6. Compare Edmund L. Andrews, "A Chip That Allows Parents to Censor TV Sex and Violence," *New York Times,* July 18, 1993, p. 14.

7. Gary McWilliams, with Robert D. Hof, "They Can't Wait To Serve You," *Business Week,* January 24, 1994, p. 92; Peter Burrows and Ira Sager, "Servers: A PC Money Machine," *Business Week,* March 28, 1994, pp. 166–168.

8. Compare Mark Robichaux, "Need More TV? TCI May Offer 500 Channels," *Wall Street Journal,* December 3, 1992, pp. B1, B3.

9. On the first interactive TV systems, see Ken Auletta's account of Time Warner's "Magic Box," *The New Yorker,* April 11, 1994, pp. 40–45.

10. Bill Carter, "Cable TV Industry Turns Pessimistic as Growth Slows," *New York Times,* May 23, 1994, pp. A1, D9. See also Mark Landler et al., "Cable's Bright Picture Fades to Gray," *Business Week,* May 30, 1994, pp. 130–132.

11. Leslie Cauley, "As Baby Bells Claim New Rivals, Seek Looser Rules, Study Suggests Opposite," *Wall Street Journal,* February 14, 1994, p. B5; Edmund L. Andrews, "A Telephone Role by Time Warner," *New York Times,* May 18, 1994, pp. A1, D2; Gautam Naik, "Southwestern Bell Plans Phone Service for Its Cable Customers in Sibling's Turf," *Wall Street Journal,* May 23, 1994, p. A3.

AMERICA'S ENTERTAINMENT ECONOMY

1. Michael J. Mandel et al., "The Entertainment Economy," *Business Week,* March 14, 1994, pp. 58–64.

2. Ibid. See also Sylvia Nasar, "The American Economy, Back on Top," *New York Times,* February 27, 1994, pp. 3/1, 3/6; Louis Uchitelle, "Job Extinction Evolving Into a Fact of Life in U.S.," *New York Times,* March 22, 1994, pp. A1, D5.

3. Edmund L. Andrews, "Big Risk and Cost Seen in Creating Data Superhighway," *New York Times,* January 3, 1994, p. C17; Mark Berniker, "Big 3 TV networks explore interactivity," *Broadcasting & Cable,* May 23, 1994, pp. 61, 66.

4. Quoted in Geraldine Fabrikant, "$33 Billion Deal by Bell Atlantic Is Presented as a Quantum Leap," *New York Times,* October 14, 1993, p. D11.

5. Harry A. Jessell, "Cable ready: The high appeal of interactive services," *Broadcasting & Cable,* May 23, 1994, pp. 75–78.

6. Barbara Kantrowitz, Joshua Cooper Ramo, and Charles Fleming, "Sex on the Info Highway," *Newsweek,* March 14, 1994, pp. 62–63.

7. "P&G's Artzt: TV advertising in danger," *Advertising Age,* May 23, 1994, pp. 24, 40–42. See also Dan Steinbock, "The Structural Transformation of Global Advertising—How America Lost its Competitive Advantage," keynote address at the annual conference of Finland's Advertising Association, November 30, 1992.

8. John W. Verity, "Truck Lanes for the Info Highway," *Business Week,* April 18, 1994, pp. 112–114.

9. Compare W. Robert Hoye, "Unheeded Warning," *Barron's,* February 7, 1994, pp. 18–19.

10. Quoted in "Barry Diller: TV's Smart Agent," *Broadcasting & Cable,* May 23, 1994, pp. 19–30.

Index

About the Author

DAN STEINBOCK has studied the American media and entertainment industries since arriving in New York City from his native Finland in 1986. He holds a doctorate in clinical psychology, several degrees in the social sciences and humanities, and is currently Adjunct Professor of Communication Studies at the University of Helsinki. He has also been an ASLA-Fulbright visiting postdoctorate scholar, a senior researcher at Finland's prestigious Academy of Sciences, and U.S. correspondent for a variety of major newspapers and magazines in Finland. Author of a dozen previous books, this is his first major work in English.